The Invisible Bones

Sara Lovett

Dear Donna,
thankyou for
going on this journey
with me!
much love, Sara.

This is a work of nonfiction. The events and experiences
detailed herein are true and have been faithfully rendered as
the author has remembered them to the best of her ability.
Some names, identities and circumstances have been changed
in order to protect the privacy and or anonymity of the
various individuals involved, and to facilitate the structure of
the telling of events. I may have changed some identifying
characteristics and details such as physical properties,
occupations and places of residence.

First Edition

@2016 Sara Lovett

The Invisible Bones by Lovett, Sara

Edited by Van Quattro

Cover Illustration Copyright @2016 Sara Lovett

Cover design by Sara Lovett
& L1graphics
Cover painting (photo)
Zuni Lounge, by Kelly Morris
www.kellybmorris.com

Library of Congress Control Number:
2016921185

ISBN
978-0692820179

To the Newspaper Soldier
& Stephen Dunham

Without your lives and passing, the
courage for this journey would never
have been found.
I carried your hearts.

To Joan Thomson Stewart Lovett
You told me never to stop writing.
We begin again.

For Liv & ZZ
You are the loves of my life.
Always embrace love without caution.

TABLE OF CONTENTS

Prologue:
a letter to a first son, once removed

Foreword

Part 1: Conception
The Visitations
Skinning the Face of Friendship

Part 2: Heartbeat
The Blank Beforehand

Part 3: Backbone
Retrieving Lost Direction
Fetal Water
Sifting the Northeast

Part 4: Limbs
Wandering Back Down

Part 5: Extremities
Wandering the Root
The Map Outside

Part 6: The Skull
Sifting West

Part 7: The Marrow
The Feed of Memoriam
Wearing Absence
Descending

Part 8: Bone Spur
A Trail of Song
Flying to Ashes
The Friendship Revolution

After word
Permissions
Connections

This is our meditation practice as women, calling back the dead and dismembered aspects of ourselves, calling back the dead and dismembered aspects of life itself. The one who re-creates from that which has died is always a double-sided archetype. The Creation Mother is always also the Death Mother...the great work before us is to learn to understand what around and about us and what within us must live, and what must die...

You wish psychoanalytic advice?
Go gather bones.

-    Clarissa Pinkola Estes

Prologue to a first son, once removed

These bodies are perishable,
but the Dweller in these bodies is eternal.
- Bhagavad-Gita

This is our history, yours and mine. My story begins in earnest the day I became pregnant with you. It was winter. I doused myself in a perfume called Beautiful in those days. For me now, it is the scent of choice. If I pass it on the street my shadow separates from my body and I can taste you in the air.

I've never truly seen you. There's only one photograph I have of you in my head, and it's the one I was never supposed to see. It slipped out of the file when I went to sign the paperwork. Maybe the lady at the desk did it on purpose; maybe she wanted me to see it so I wouldn't sign our last name to be rid of you. I saw a slight form and shape. You were floating and attached to me. Something in me was able to pretend I hadn't seen it and continue on, to move you from flesh to spirit. I cut our chord. I denied you life. I renounced flesh for bone and spirit.

Out of the almost twenty years I'd lived up until that day, those weeks changed the course of the twenty that followed them. After January 8ᵗʰ there was no more beautiful, no more pretty girl. When my appetite returned I didn't stop eating, and I let a punk cut all my hair off down to the ground so the outside matched the inside - in sync with something at least.

Up until a few years ago, before we left in the car on this journey, I'd been proving to you that I wouldn't break my promise, that this wouldn't be your sacrifice alone, that I would go down with you. I spoke to you every day after. You were my first thought in the morning, and the last before the dreaming started. Our aborted lives would not move into the part of my brain that catalogues memory, they would live in the ongoing file of now, still happening, ongoing, in a never-ending loop.

No matter how I tried to come round and heal in the years to come, what it seemed was being asked of me was to wish you down a well. I suppose they didn't realize we'd both been living down there for years – that I couldn't leave you down there alone in my muddy waters that never broke. We had to come out together, and then let go. That's the part of us that was incomplete until this journey.

You are my family. This is our history, yours and mine. This is our story. Our reason. Our road. We travelled back over this half-lived life of mine again together you and I, although I didn't realize it at the onset. Never at any moment did I feel an empty passenger seat beside me - the airbag sign flashed on so often, seemingly for no reason - except for the weight of you telling me you were with me. Ironic that as the most defining person in my life, you're the one I can never be face to face with.

I write this in the only room we shared, where you were, and you weren't - the womb room. This is my acknowledgment of us. We shouldn't ever want to be free of each other, you and I. Not so long as we've met each other where it counts, not now that we've walked the labyrinth of forgiveness.

Inside a Catholic Mass where I named you, I closed my eyes and I saw you playing in a field with other children. As I whispered your name your blonde hair tussled in the wind, and as you wiped it out of your eyes you grabbed a hold of my leg and looked up at me. I haven't been able to break eye contact to let you go - until today. Today is yours, it is mine, always with what is ours between us.

June 1st, 2016 Plano, Texas

7

Foreword

There's a thread you follow. It goes among
things that change. But it doesn't change.
People wonder about what you are pursuing.
You have to explain about the thread.
But it's hard for others to see.
While you hold it you can't get lost.
Tragedies happen; people get hurt
or die; and you suffer and get old.
Nothing you do can stop time's unfolding.
You don't ever let go of the thread.

William Stafford wrote, "The Way It Is," 26 days before his passing.

A serrated umbilical chord still floats inside of me. Once I had it disconnected from the flesh of him it took on a life of its own, rummaging around searching for fragments of connective tissue left behind in me, rooting itself, eating my bone, finally settling as a fresh creation in the form of a tumor on my left ovary. It went home. That's the way I subconsciously dug for the definition of how he and I could co-exist - a way for me to keep him, having cut our connection. I've never told anyone that, I didn't know myself until they dug it out. None of my friends could possibly see any of this. They may see the workings of some of it going on all around about me but never this, and I have the delusional perception that I can control and contort how they see me by what I reveal about myself to them, that they'll buy into it and go along no questions asked. The way they actually do see me I have no real knowing or control over and without telling them my full story they can't truly understand me. I'm quite sure I haven't been open, that's just the nature of who I am. So are they still friends with me because it's a habit of being in each other's lives, or are we growing and contributing to each other? What have I honestly shared and what have I hidden and coveted for myself, even from myself? This is what I thought I got on the road to answer, but that was only a part of it as it turns out. There's no dipping your toe in an off balanced life, once you've stepped in, it only tells you the truth. Life is always walking home to you. If you begin a search without knowing why, the why will find you. Mine caught me by surprise.

We are a culture of assumptions, I think. It's as simple as

8

someone liking a Rumi quote I put on Facebook. He liked my post = he's paying attention; he accepted my friendship request = he has forgiven me. The machine has all the answers except perhaps one: my friends don't actually see me. They get the picture but not my point. I've certainly never brought my son's invisible bones or what they turned me into, to the pages of the book of faces.

To reconnect with my friends I used Facebook as the matchstick for the journey to light the flame and lead the way. What I was really going after was the wick - presence. The only way I'm going to know how someone else truly perceives me is to be with them; for us to witness each other face to face and acknowledge what it is we do for one another. Bones are able to distinguish these things when they sit down together. I want to know, but at the same time I'm towing this extra tissue that risks exposure alongside me. And so might they.

There was never a moment of second-guessing this walkabout. Once I got started things fell into place and propelled themselves along. I thought the problems along the way would be mechanical ones, but I got that wrong. In the desert I drove, the scent of the past lived along side the present. As the serrated umbilical chord rose to the surface I began connecting the dots to a portrait of a me gone missing, trying to piece it together again. This was my last chance of saying yes to the one thing knocking on my door that I knew would never ask again. It has been extraordinary.

A story isn't just a story - it's a breathing interaction. We're living in a time when faces are grouped together so that one person's actions, or beliefs, or the color of his skin reflects the story of a mass of people, and not the individual. We're losing all sense of individuality by releasing the need to take the time to understand each other's stories. Only in telling the tale of our lives can we come back into community with each other. To know one another is to save one another.

So here is all of mine tucked inside my connection to everyone I've crossed paths with. During the course of one year I listened and exchanged stories with my friends, and gained the strength to face my own. We weave our own story, and in reconnecting I understand how we've wound our individual tales through each other's. Kierkegaard said that although life is lived forwards, to be understood, it must be travelled backwards. So that is where I went.

I've always felt like someone's had her eye on me, from the inside. The blasphemous, lapsed Church of England Anglican

9

in me thinks the Virgin Mary's undisclosed burial place is inside my bones, and that at night she sneaks about on patrol in the marrow, resuscitating herself in my living tissue, practicing the resurrection trick on me. She tunnels through to veer my balance offline. She's sorting me out. She's giving me such a headache. I'm off track. She's here to dismantle my bones.

In my dream of her, Virgin Bone Woman is hiding on the slope of a mountain waiting for me. She sucks me right in with that Angel of the Lord story, sifting my skeletal remains one splinter at a time, while I'm still stuck on, "yeah but was it just a voice or was it like a vision...." She sniffs around my wreckage until the last bone, an extra spur of you, non-child of mine, no doubt, rolls into her hand to be rebuilt. I'm left like that tape the cops use to outline the dead, only mine's skeletal, stripped to the core, to that moment you slide down the birth canal. They say you can hear inception talk in those seconds that tells you you're either lost or one lucky son of a bitch. But she's telling me it's all just propaganda, to sit up with my own spine, do a cartwheel now you dope, strip backwards.

I rattle when she lays the last bone in place - that's the screaming starting, the resuscitation song she's singing through my 206 raw virgin bones. Her soul purpose is to fill this rerouting with the clappity clap don't hold back sound of my bare bones choosing. It's the sort of feeling you take for the flu, but is actually true love.

Whoever she is, she has re-ordered me.

This is how she did it.

10

Part 1 Conception:
The first formation of the embryo;
The act or power of conceiving;
that mental act or combination of acts
by which an absent object or perception
is brought before the mind by the imagination

- The Library of Universal Knowledge

The Visitations

Each of us has a truth as unique as our own fingerprints. Without
knowing that truth, without speaking it aloud, we cannot know who
we are and that we are already whole... our viewpoint has never
existed before... one of the best-kept secrets in this technically
oriented culture is that simply speaking truth heals.
- Rachel Naomi Remen, MD

Morning of Day One.
Twenty years after I disconnected you from the womb, a
dream came for me. It's the mass I feel first, the full weight of
his body crushing on top of mine like a foot stepping down on
an over blown balloon before it bursts. His neck nuzzles into
my breath with the scent of mange, panting a wet heat down
my windpipe. He picks the nerve he came for and bloats me
up with the sadness of empty time.
Tiny, sharp tipped hairs from his cheek impale mine
piercing them open in a pattern from an etch-a-sketch long
since gone from childhood. I have one remaining breath
holding on that his eyes are looking for. I can see through his
face to the clock on the wall. I grab a handful of his orange,
Pirates of Destiny t-shirt, twisting the hair underneath it hoping
that it hurts, but it melts in my hands. He licks through tears
of his own, the ones gushing from the pin prick holes in my
cheeks, and brushes his hand over my eyes to close them like
they do when dead people stare on a minute too long into the
wrong world. His clawed thumbs press through my eyeballs,
forcing them deep inside the frontal lobe of my brain and I'm
forgetting how to hear. Sweat swims from his fingers staining
the hard wood floor that's splintering into my back. A hoarse
invasive pressure grates down my throat. He's trying to
squeeze the final breath out of me like the last bit of blue-black

11

icing from a tube flattened from the bottom up, bulging at the tip and spelling things wrong. His mouth seals mine, drawing my breath into him so hard that his eyes roll back. I bite my tongue. Salt and fur stick in between my teeth. He's hatching the eggs I've been laying for him. From the yolk of a child long since gone he brings you back by simply whispering your name.

Cooper.

I think I say it out loud but I can't be sure and I don't care if I have. Everything else vanishes except for your eyes; they are unique in all the world. I saw them first in my mind's eye passing through me, away, warm, and now you're here moving in what is a still silent and watery absence. I daren't unwrap a moment with you. I could be awake with your voice, alive, you, alive in a way I've always wanted and never felt worthy of, so I see your shadow in the glass reflection of the gold leaf painting my parents brought back from Jerusalem of the Madonna and distorted man child, so merciless, but you're still beautiful, so beautiful in the silence, and I doubt it, God forgive me but I doubt you, so beautiful and mine, all mine to say yes to.

My eyes open, at least I think they're open. I don't want them to be open. I feel like I'm waking up from a coma to the son, the man, there never was a plan for boy. I'm not sure what to do. You're in my eyes and you'll never be mine, and you are mine and you're here. Everything in your eyes in this few seconds here, and I don't know what to do, I don't want to look away, or blink, or fall asleep. Don't be an angel. I stare straight ahead into the concave mirror with the Tibetan flags woven through the tiny holes at the bottom of it that hung in my grandparents dining room. There's blood in my mouth but I can only bear to move my eyelids so I swallow it, some of it dribbling on to the top sheet. The animal is still here as well, in this empty house, the three of us waiting for the alarm clock hand to strike back. I can hear my heart beating - it's sitting inside him in a chair across the room. He's silent. Always silent, but alongside it there's a constant string of words and *it's not a melody*, and I'm trying to pay attention and ignore it at the same time, the I'm alive that always has been and never was, the diamond that belongs to no one that was not mine and mine, an extinct volcano. More blood on the top sheet, *it must be* my tongue. I'm crying in such a way that disturbed people are *locked away* for. You've come for an owed soul. I hear it.

12

Get your breathing under control.
No. You shouldn't be here.
Should I whisper?
Someone might notice and take you from me again. It's best you go. It's better for you.
That's not a decision you can make.
I can't do this. I can't catch my breath. I can't do this now.
Then when?
I stopped this conversation twenty-six years ago.
That's when it started.
Put me to sleep.
I can't do that anymore.
It's just a dream. It's just a dream. I know it's just a dream.
You'll wake up in the morning and see the blood, our blood. A positive.
Is this heaven? Is there a quiz? I'm lousy at tests. You're the only positive I ever got.
Look at you lightening up.
It's a dream.
No. It's us.
Please, let me go back to sleep. Let me go.
One of us has to not let go.
Yes. Wait, you think I let you go? I let you go.
You should go back to sleep.
Can you fall asleep with me?
I always have. Only this time we'll be waking up with each other.
If you think I don't want that, I know you're not real.
My eyes close slowly, like a drowsy chaperone, fluttering.

I wake up in the same position, blood caking my lip to the cotton pillowcase. I'm in that half in half out twilight where the dreaming lives as presently as my state of awakeness. So I panic. I breathe in deeply ripping my lip away, bleeding out again, and scramble from the bed quickly, moving across the room, covers and all, on my knees, to the corner behind the door with my back to nothing, scared to death. I can't breathe out. I feel for my heart.
Just a dream.
Not just a dream.
No, not just a dream.
I'm talking to my brain.
If you like.
I'm scared to see what it has to say.
It's the residue of staying awake with me in the night.

13

Can't you just take my mind and put it in the freezer?
That's where I'm trying to thaw it out from.
I'm awake.
There's a chance you might be, yes.
I can't be dealing with this.
You should try to get up now.
I'm trying.
My left side doubles me over. The pain is piercing and impatient.
Steady. Here we go.
In the shower I drop the soap and I know if I bend down I'll never get back up again. This is no fucking joke. I can hardly move. Why is this happening to me today? I've got to get to work to order the iced tea and muffins for a meeting tomorrow that I'll mess up the PowerPoint for.

At the doctor's office I have a sonogram. I understand your timing - that the wind changing today returning you to the insides of my head is vital for me. It seems your voice has taken over all my thoughts. I'm scared at your hello but not because of it. It's beautiful. It's oddly reassuring to be invaded by the sound of you and to not have to blink without you.
I may sound off key.
Well, that makes us two of a kind then. Keep me talking, chit chatter away in there, won't you? Help put my mind somewhere else.
You're using me as a distraction.
It's an old tune, yes, but would you take me through it a little further? This is not the kind of throw back Thursday I was expecting. The only other sonogram I've had was when I was pregnant with you, Cooper. On that bare bones table I hoped with everything that I was that there was just a hollow inside of me, nothing that could breathe, or wriggle or grow. But a mother knows.
So what do you know now, mummy?
Mummy. That's such a broken sound between you and I, isn't it? It's your first never spoken word.
Yet here it is.
Perhaps let's put it away for now - you're far too old for it anyway. We missed the boat on that word. I'm afraid there's no claiming it back, not anymore. I'm not sure I can bear to hear it. I'm sorry. Not today. All of those words make me uneasy - mummy, mother, mamma. Ma, I don't mind because that would never have been me.
Ma, perhaps if you close your eyes and count to ten, click your bare heals together and promise God anything

14

he wants, whatever this is will breathe back.

Oh, bless your heart, it already has. Of course it's breathing. Just not the way we might want it to be. No, I'll just have to wait and take the hit from your visitation friend, your muscle, the boogieman come to scare your Ma. A twisted turnabout is fair play. I am scared. That's why I'm talking to you. You're the one that understands.

Mummy. Mamma. Mother. One more time, just so you hear me.

Mummy would have been nice, wouldn't it?

Sure, Ma.

My chest heaves you out in muffled breaths. Water clouds my eyes. I can't see unless I blink. The nurse asks me if she's hurting me. I shake my head, suppressing. I blink. This isn't working.

Look at the woman in the painting.

I fixate on a photograph on the wall. It's of some sort of tribeswoman, this girl in the picture. She's covered in a red mud that makes the whites of her eyes and her teeth shine like pearls. She could be a Himba. They're so lucky, those Himba people. They don't have co-pays, weird synthetic drugs, or lubed poles with cameras on the end looking for trouble. They live and they die. I read somewhere that they know their own song before they're even born. It's their sound, and if they're hurt or lose themselves, they sing it. It's handed down to remind them of who they are. We're not conditioned for that anymore - a song of individual purpose, can you imagine? Our societies have been constructed around the forgetting of all that nonsense. I visualize myself on a plane flying off to become a Himba. If I do have a song it woke me up last night in that dream. It's in the final remaining breath I didn't let the animal visitation have.

Ma, you should start listening to yourself.

Why break tradition, son. I hope this nurse doesn't check my heartbeat because I don't think your man's given mine back to me yet. Maybe he's some sort of Himba intuit freak of the night trying to get me to wake up to what I heard in the womb. Bit late now. It's so faint I can barely believe it, let alone hear it.

The nurse is talking and she turns the screen towards me.

"This is your left ovary, and this is, oh, what is that? I wish they'd turn the air conditioning down in here, are you menopausal at all? No, I don't think that should be there. You see the white and how that's covering, see you can see the

15

other ovary clearly over here. I should let the doctor go over all this with you it's not for me to say…" Not for you to say, what? You can't just say something like that and leave it hanging. I scour the screen for the blur. Where's the blur? She flips the switch. Why would you let her do that?

I limp back to the bathroom and I'm fully clothed when I realize I haven't wiped any of the lubricant off my stomach or thighs. It drools down the inside of my right leg towards my knee, winding around my calf, pooling into that round ditch at the top of my ankle. I've always wondered why that was there.

In my doctor's private office my feet press down into carpet instead of hanging in stirrups. No need for a paper top to hide breasts he knows he'll touch, or a paper skirt to slip his hand underneath, not in here. I'm afraid I'm leaving a wet patch on the chair so I rub my thighs together like a boy scout trying to start a fire.

Perhaps you'll spontaneously combust into me, Ma.

Sshh - he has the picture in his hands and he doesn't like the sketch any more than we do. I can tell because he looks at me in that way that gives me about six more seconds of my life standing in a doorway that once it closes, can no longer be used for an exit strategy. He's acting like he doesn't know what he knows. All sorts of diseases race through my mind, from cancer to cancer and then back to cancer again, and his delightful face smiles from across a table adorned with pictures of grandchildren. Diplomas hang on the wall behind him strictly for the purpose of making me feel better. His lips part twice before he speaks. I stare at the scar on his chin and wonder if he rode horses as a child.

He mouths the word, mass, and everything that comes after are words broken and juggling into pieces trying to get my attention. It comes out of his mouth in long, unpunctuated, slow motion speak…

"It's about five centimeters and wrapped around your left ovary but don't panic and certainly don't go home and Google anything we'll schedule the surgery for a month from now when we go in and remove it the cyst and the ovary we'll do a biopsy and if we find that it's spread once we get in there I need to have your permission to do a full hysterectomy do I have your permission we need to agree on that it's best anyway because benign cyst or not these normally come back again and over again it's all sinking in now isn't it here's a tissue perhaps you need some time to take this all in more often that not these things are benign."

I want to take life for granted again. Now I'll have to spend what's left of my sick day crying and unconvincing myself. My first sonogram gave me motherhood, and I've resurrected it in a tumor, a distorted, weird Picasso child. Nothing is in its right place. Perhaps you want to be an only child and curse me into baronhood. Perhaps it's that I have to shed the source of you as well. Perhaps I wanted you back so much that your missing life has been busy growing in my cells, warming to the place you began. There are consequences to you and I, son. I've colored you on my insides. It's more than just bone getting high. You won't remember this, Cooper, because it was before your time but...

It's always been my time.

When I was sixteen I took two buses and a train I wasn't supposed to, to sit in...*the front room of a psychic in Kingston who told you you'd live to be...*ninety-three. Surely she couldn't have been lying. I paid her five quid.

I wanted a mother who believed in psychics. I have always been here, silly.

You have. When I was a child I'd pull back the curtain my own mother had drawn so I could see the moon when I said my prayers. I've become the kind of grown up who's forgotten that voice. It was always very clear to me that I spoke to someone, that someone was out there listening to me, bringing things in for me and taking them away. I visualized them living on that planet, toiling the dust and gravel into my own imaginings. Mary in my bones, watching me.

I've always had a full perception of who you are, as you have of me. You're definition of conception is off, is all.

Then why not tell me you were there?

I thought I just did.

No, back then.

Before you had the capacity to hear or understand it, you mean?

I would have heard you.

You swallowed me.

I wrapped shame around something I won't name. I can't yet. I know the admission is what the visitation man came for last night. I trapped it inside the last breath. I wouldn't let him have it. He'll have to come at me with more than that to get my fine print, because even in my most desperate hour I slam the lid on that.

Which is why you wouldn't have heard me any other way.

You didn't tell him. The only thing now is it just might kill me. It's an off balance conditional consuming love I've offered you, isn't it.

My Ma could have gone to the Royal Academy of Dramatic Arts.

Your Ma didn't take the chance.

The visitation returns to keep me company at the hospital, pushing the post-surgery morphine button. He's alive in a hallucination next to me, throwing my heart in the air and up against the wall like the baseball Steve McQueen used in *The Great Escape*.

He's waiting for you to say thank you.

In my druggie dreams I remember him from long ago, our first meeting. When you and I were both alive for each other he was the only voice that joined mine, the one insisting I keep you with me. He was kinder then, not quite an animal. But then so was I, I suppose – pre-occupied with building up a dam.

I repeat over to him, 'Why did you wait so long to wake me up to all of this?' He walks over to me holding you, so tiny, naked, and places you on my chest. Your nose is flat, ironed sideways, like a broken boxer's. Your eyes are red, fresh, gently swollen, closed - shutting me out so I can't see their color. And you're so quiet. Why are you so quiet? He lies down beside me, his face not quite so prickly now. He turns my head away from you and presses his nose to mine. Pushing the hair out of my eyes the way I would have yours and running his index finger over my lips he slowly melts in to me, taking you with him, kissing his reply, 'Why did you?'

No malignancy. Death holds off for the revolution.

You hesitate. Again.

During the hesitation my brother, Billy rings while I'm stuck in traffic.

"What?" I see Leonard's face almost immediately. He's there at my brother's wedding, standing by the doorway in the candlelight. He's looking right at me.

"You remember him - Leonard?" My brother is saying.

"Leonard… your Leonard?"

"Yes, he died this morning. He had a heart attack." I'm listening to him talk and it's not making any sense. I mean it really doesn't make any fucking sense.

"Leonard?" But he's so tall, and good looking, and athletic and healthy, and open and talented… "But it's his birthday," what a dumb thing to say. But who dies on their birthday, right? This is nuts. He's only a year older than me.

I hang up the phone, turn the radio off and put my head down on the steering wheel looking through one of the holes into a piece of ripped up floor mat. My cheeks are pulsing. That's when I hear a whispering that sounds like a late night drunk.

Goandvisitallyourfriends.

I push the radio button to make sure it's off.

Goandvisitallyourfriends.

There it is again. Leonard? I said your name three times. Does it work like Beetlejuice? I don't understand. This is a voice I can hear on the outside, not like yours, son. My mouth is open in that way my mother would always tell me I'd collect more flies than knowledge. Shit, what if someone's in the back of my car like in that movie where the eighteen wheeler keeps driving up close behind the lone woman on the freeway shining his lights brighter and brighter, and you think this guy's crazy, he's going to ram her and kill her, when he's actually trying to protect her and alert her to some crazy predator that's hiding in the back seat of her car. I turn my head quickly but there's no one there, and the words are still repeating on a loop, goandvisitallyourfriendsgoandvisitallyourfriendsgoandvisitall yourfriends. Shitbuggerwhatdoido? There was this Ted talk I saw where this woman with multiple personalities spoke about how normal and nice the voices in her head are and how you should trust them, so even though I know some of them tell you to go out and kill John Lennon, I'm hanging on to that.

I don't understand.

I roll down the window expecting the Angel of the Lord because that's how out of the blue, outside my head, no one's around, Moses kind of a moment this is. Sacred, in a way that sacred isn't. I need to get home and write.

That's your answer to everything.

Traffic suddenly opens up like the Red Sea. Maybe it is Moses after all.

I open the door to my apartment quietly on the lookout for The Voice. I stand in my living room for a few minutes, bag in hand, eyes darting from one corner to the next, before inking it down. If I don't want another dream visit I'd best pay attention to the one I'm hearing now I'm awake; as weird as it all seems.

Did you send this as well, son?

Look Ma, no hands.

What The Voice says is true – I feel removed from the people in my life. One thing the cells converging around the place you left vacant showed me is how out of touch I am with myself. Goandvisitallyourfriends.

Go and visit.

Go and visit. How silly.

When I get back to work the one thing I do know is that I can't die in this office, doing this job, at this desk. If I need a way to go, a way to get off my ass and out of the uncomfy comfy chair, maybe this is it.

It ruminates. I certainly can't un-hear it.

I take an acting job in Puerto Rico. My friend, Marie's newly choreographed version of the ballet, *Romeo & Juliet* is in need of an actor and she's asked me to step in. This will have me out of the office for three weeks.

Grab it.

On the cab ride to the hotel in San Juan we take the main highway.

"Highway 26," I say, smiling.

"Highway what?"

"26."

"Highway 26? 26, oh, my God, that's so weird. It is following you." The number 26 surrounds me like a cocoon. Another strangeness I only tell a few people because it adds to the deck of my weirdness. I could lose all my friends before seeing any of them. I see 26 abnormally everywhere, in everything. It's the time, it is on billboards, phone numbers, the weight in kg of my suitcase, zip codes, addresses, on license plates, how many seconds are left on the microwave, how many Facebook messages that I have, how many, 'likes' I have. It's in random conversations - *How many seats are left for a play you want to see, it's flashing on speed traps, years your friend has been sober, the year a monument you visit was built* – A birthday, something 26. It's everywhere at all times, in every day, in every moment of my life and it won't go away. I don't have to look for it. I wake up and it's there, the first thing I see.

"I decided that it's some kind of God thing," I say.

"Should I kiss your ring?"

"On your knees, smart ass. Maybe it's God letting me know I'm in the right place, because if my mind gets lost, or upset, or off balance a 26 floats by. It makes no sense." Because she's cool with 26, I talk to Marie about the goandvisitallyourfriends voice. "I think I'm actually supposed to do it."

"How's that?"

"I've got 166 friends on Facebook, right? These are people I know."

"Right, no strangers or people you've never met."

"I feel like my friend list has turned into my own form of natural selection."

"Machine images. Intangible."

"I want friendship like this, here with you. It's engaging, finding out who we are with each other. I haven't seen some of these people for over thirty years, and there are so many of them that had a profound affect on my life. If we move away from face-to-face interactions friendship is a dead man walking."

"How do you get your arms around that though. What do you think it means?" I don't mention the visitation dream. I'm not sure why.

Because then you'd have to bring me in and explain the tumor. She'd understand it. I mean you just told her about a completely irrational voice and she's on board.

Irrational is easy to understand because it's not tied to anything physical.

Even on a road of 26...

I'll stick to Facebook.

You're travelling avoidance.

Well, how do I open up into that?

Isn't that the point of choosing to do this?

"I think I'm supposed to go and see them all. Face to face. In person." I mean what am I supposed to say – I had this dream and this wolf man tried to suffocate me and he whispered my son's name – only I don't have a son, I never did because I aborted him. And I was in so much denial over it I resurrected him as a tumor. Oh, and I had a Catholic mass for him and named him and now he's back... ish.

21

"You mean travel around, just go and visit them one by one?" I breathe on the window and make an outline of a heart with my index finger. I need to understand one thing at a time.

"Yeah, I think so. What would that be like, actually seeing them again, communicating in their space instead of scrolling through it? I don't want us to just have lived our lives in pictures and words. I want to remember it." God knows it was wasted on me the first time.

"I'm always moving. I travel so much that things have a way of staying present."

"And that's what I want. I have friends that live down the road and I can scroll through their Facebook page and see how they are, what the children are up to, all without leaving the house. It feels static. As a species I think we evolved out of the cave only to shut ourselves back up into it again without any reason to leave. We can order whatever we want delivered right to our door sitting on the couch with the glow of the iPad, which is no light at all. There's a new kind of alone growing." I can't stop rattling on. The more I talk, the more my mind moves away from the one thing I need to say that may tie it together, from sharing, from asking for help. "And the dead live in there with us, they've just stopped posting. They don't deactivate, and that's a weird thing to say about a human being. Maybe their account is their restless soul. A kind of built in resurrection. Who knows, we may need that - to keep scrolling back to the last post, their last words. We can be comforted with denial. Next thing you know Facebook will keep posting for them. They have all the stats on past posts; they know what the next move would have been, so here it is. A mechanical heartbeat."

"You need to figure this out and go, Sara. You should give everything up and go. You could do that."

"What exactly is it that I have in my life that's worth keeping at this point?"

"That's the questions then." She looks concerned and eager for me.

On the plane ride home the voices go underground in what I imagine is an attempt to get me to find my own. It's in here somewhere, in how we connect - The Visitation man, Cooper and the goandvisitallyourfriends voice. There's a sort of rumbling happening, a yes reception underneath it. Listen and trust are in a head on collision towards me even though a part of me still wonders if I'm running, and if I am, what from. I hear my baseball heart being thrown up against the wall and

22

the picture of you, child that isn't, in utero that I was never supposed to see, flashes in front of me. Why are you so completely present again now? I'm Eve in the garden looking at the apple. I have to bite down.

Listen to my voice this time.

I call Marie when I land.

"I can't go back to work." Why?

"This is it then." Why is it then?

"I'm a famous ballerina now." Lying to Marie in metaphor.

"Ha! You are, you have the bruises to prove it."

"They're the only kind I want." But not the only kind I have.

"I love what I do every day despite the challenges. Just ask yourself if you can say the same where you are now in what you're doing." I can't. I'm a hamster on a wheel going nowhere. That's the truth.

The day I return to work I turn in my notice - to them, and to myself. I'm not sure what I'm doing. I do it anyway. I feel disconnected from every part of who it is I've ever tried to be. I've never had the strength to just be as I am. I don't know who this voice is, but I want it to be ours, Cooper – maybe just yours for now, and I'll follow along. He whispered your name, like a magic smoke, and despite all the therapy I've had over the past few years to move you into memory, something about us is holding on.

I give up my living space and put all of my belongings into a storage unit. A peculiar numbness falls around the fact that everything I own fits into an 8X10 space. This apartment is also the last place where my ex-boyfriend, Gregory and I will ever live together. He moved out long before, but the place still holds him. Where I am about to go makes me happy and fearful, and the only thing that eased the fear away before was him.

Be careful there. What's in the prism is a little upside down don't you think? Persephone loved Hades, but she never forgot how he took her.

He took the fear away when I needed him to.

This is not the time to tell a version from behind rose tinted glasses.

When something outside of us took me down he was always there for me, and he calmed me and he loved me. It's where we loved each other most.

Yes, that's where your truest love lived.

In this empty apartment windexing the double windows, I can see us out there on the balcony. That day we first moved in we sat on the concrete floor in the heat, hopeful, saying we would leave all that came before us outside and start afresh. I held his left hand - he had a cigarette in the other. He blew the smoke away from me but the wind turned it around tangling it through my hair. The particular end we have come to makes any kind of resurgence impossible. If only we hadn't moved all of our shit in here. The happiest days we had were when we had nothing. That's a playing ground I can work with. This place looks the same now – empty.

Sometimes I think I used him as a replacement for you.

You needed to care for someone, and he needed a lot of caring.

He hadn't had much of that in his life at all; anything to turn love away from myself at any rate. I can't think about all that yet.

I walk away without turning my back and close the door, keyless.

Skinning the Face of Friendship

When a mystery is too overpowering, one dare not disobey.
- Antoine de Saint Exupery

My life, right from its beginning, has been a nomadic one.
My father's work moved us around quite a bit growing up, so
movement is in my blood. By consequence I've never felt
grounded in any one place. There are gaps in my memory
from the roaming, and from the aftermath of your cracked
unevenness passing through my body, Cooper. So much
forgotten because I locked myself away with you - a life for a
life. Having taken yours, to achieve any success or happiness
in my own would have made what I did to you alright, and
that was never going to happen.

The cost for you is a somewhat discarded life.

Plato said that the soul's a circle, so where I'm going, back
tracking into my friends, seems the logical place to fill in the
blanks. Is that why you sent the voice?

I found the house I was born in no longer exists.

You took everything with you when you moved out.

*You wear my grave well. I love what you've done with
the place.*

A homegrown tumor - tres couture.

*But you know you didn't honor me with wasted time
and a benign sibling. Right now your own presence is the
priority. Go back and find it. You'll see who you've
always been, what you're capable of.*

I am withdrawn. Facebook has made it easier for me to
hide - ironic as that may seem. Look, sharing isn't my strong
suit and it's allowed me to mull my thoughts over and over
before I interact. I'm not reacting, I'm constructing - editing
words to reflect a state of mind I think I should have towards
someone, even if it's in conflict with the actual feelings I have
because I don't have to talk to them. It's what I've been asking
for all along, only now I realize it's what's put me off balance.

*You have a gift from Facebook. Its veins reconnect
you to your past. However, by expanding the scope it's
eliminating a piece of the soul –*

Presence. I can't express my feelings if I neglect that.

*Well that's what you've been doing all along. How's
that worked out for you?*

The sound of voice is disappearing.

Yours is faint.

And fading. It's a different world now, Cooper. A tap, tap, taping world that's unraveling into a lonely box that can't sigh. Why am I hesitating to meet the flesh and find out where we all fit?

Don't avoid it like you did with me, like you did years after with pretty much everyone you met. Do you remember sitting on that bench with John when you were in college and he told you how he fell in love with you watching you on stage coming in out of the rain?

No.

Yes, you do.

I looked away.

You looked away. So, go and look at him. Really look at him. He's not in love with you anymore, but he's going to always be in love in that moment. Find it.

I walked through all those years looking over my shoulder for whatever it was I swallowed down that denied life. I was half asleep at the wheel the last time I lived that life. You were there, you saw.

Piece yourself back together. You have a map of friendships.

I'm affected by every one of them.

Use them as a compass to unpack your past.

Like with you.

Retrace it.

Listen to what's invisible, you mean.

Flip it the other way. We'll go down the birth canal together without penance.

No, don't jump ahead – I want to understand the penance. My friends and I have woven a story that connects us one to the other. Even outside of the physical, Cooper, there's a chord to unpick. The Aborigines say the ancestors scatter words and musical notes by the side of their own footprints as a way of communication for those who follow after. A Songline. Maybe mine have done that.

I tried to dust it off for you as you walked it the first time.

A kind of buried compass you might say. It's a breathing map scattered long ago worth retracing. In this place called life no one crosses your path by mistake - like with you and I.

The place to begin must always be you.

Not the one you see in the mirror, the one on the inside that your head stands in that can't see itself - that she, I, me.

Relationship Intuition Number One: **The Knowledge Friendship**. This is the friendship you have with yourself.

Without the honest confrontation of the foundation of that, no one else can be let in. It takes courage to face it and is fearless and forgiving. This friendship is endless.

It's how you and I found our way here.

Part 2 Heartbeat:

A muscular organ which is a propelling agent of
the blood; the mind, the soul, the consciousness;
the thinking faculty; courage, spirit; the seat of the
affections and passions; the moral side of our nature;
the seat of the will; hence disposition of mind;
conscience or sense of good and ill; to have the heart,
to purpose; Heartbreak:
anguish of the mind.

- The Library of Universal Knowledge

The Blank Beforehand

You've got to figure out which end of the needle you're going to be.
The one that's fastened to the thread, or the end that pierces the cloth.
- Sue Monk Kidd

I have absolutely no sense of direction...
Hello.
...which for a person planning on driving all over the
United States and navigating parts of Europe isn't handy. My
father, knowing my lack of direction well enough, gifts me a
navigation system for the car on my birthday. I don't trust it. I
don't have to, not yet. If I'm good at anything, it's deflecting
trust.

Before I leave to drive up to Austin and up the east coast
all I have to do is drive up the road to meet Karen. She's
starting her own mustard business using her mother's secret
recipe. She calls it, Goldrush, and refers to herself as a
Mustard Empress, as you do. She's totally on board with my
goandvisitallyourfriends voice because it makes just as much
sense as the givieupyourteachingcareerto makemustard one
she heard. I meet her at a coffee shop to peel off somewhat
mismatched word doc labels and stick them on trial size
bottles of just out of the saucepan liquid gold.

We've known each other for over fifteen years, but it's
always been inside of a theatre – me on stage while she
directed. She's one of those people who can see the bigger
picture, where as I need help to see my own. We're both in the
same place now - we let go of what we didn't want and
opened up to what we did want and things have showed up,

28

lights came on, movement happened. She understands these new synchronicities because it's happening to her as well. I suggest the idea of packing up a box of the gold stuff and giving out samples of it to my friends as I drive across the country. Get the word out.

"You could do that?"

"We can do anything we want to." She loads as many of them as she can into a boot size shoebox, with a warning.

"Don't leave them in the trunk in this heat or they'll explode or implode, or something."

"I'll make addicts out of all of them," I say. She crowns me, Employee 26, Baroness of Global Sales & Marketing. I am an official mustard mule.

It's good to have her support and encouragement. Knowing someone else is out there doing something seemingly illogical makes me believe in my own possibilities. A rare and beautiful thing if you can find it, Cooper, is someone who shares in a like experience. You need someone to sit up and make you take notice of yourself.

So, *Relationship Intuition Number Two*: **The Mustard Friendship**. She is stirring around in a raw and new circumstance, as you are. She reassures. She doesn't understand how you don't understand yourself, and she keeps you moving. Her path makes you aware of when you veer off your own. She is awareness.

Three jars of mustard in hand I head over to my sister's. She's looking after my dog, Stanley while I go down to Austin for the weekend. He's a nine-year old, 14.6lb toy poodle that sticks to me like glue. We're going to have to get used to being without one another, on and off. Rushing to drop him off, I end up leaving him without his leash, bowl, or any of his food. I just bundle him up like an irritated errand. I'm rushed. I hate being rushed.

So slow down.

My guilt and I head back onto the road only to meet some distracted mother in her mini eighteen-wheeler, texting and driving. (That would never have been us, by the way). She swings into the left lane towards my car and I swerve onto the curb and into someone's garden. I'm sweating so badly I've created my own level of humidity and my hair's falling. I hate being late, I hate being hot and I hate bad hair. My mood doesn't improve much on the road less traveled. It's overcrowded, there are closures, oil spills, construction, and a large barrel of what looks like saran wrap rolls towards me going sixty miles an hour, which I somehow manage to fly over. I am *Chitty Chitty Bang Bang*. My bags fly forward off the seat and my heartbeat's racing. The passenger airbag bell chimes on and makes me jump. It blinks red, only the chair's empty. I have a quick look in the rearview to make sure The Voice isn't back again asking me to do something else, because quite frankly I'm barely keeping up as it is. I roll down the window and squirt the windshield clean. The scent of water mixed with daydreaming splashes my arm and smells *Beautiful*, like your breath might have been, Cooper. There is something more of you in the atmosphere. Our own timeless unity suddenly has weight. Funny, I *expected me to stay as thoughts in your head, controllable* without needing something from me that wouldn't be on my terms - mist. It dings again, light on, and you're the riff chanting in an airbag car signal. Each hair stands up on my arms like a wave around a baseball stadium - if it were just a glitch in the system that wouldn't happen. I didn't foresee the substance of you asking for spirit mothering. There's a chance I may be crap at that.

You have kept a dog alive for nine years.

I'm more your fairy godmother type. I never could quite figure out how to lock a car seat down.

I'd better hold then.

"What is essential is invisible to the eye." I would have read you *The Little Prince*, cover to cover, over and again.

So you see me.

If I look back at the empty chair, yes, I can see into the face I've always seen as yours: adorably awkward, porcelain skin that no one knows which side it comes from, glasses at an early age because you have your mother's eyes – clouded and short sighted. They peak out from behind gold curly hair that frizzes in the rain like your father's.

Keep moving. Glance back without turning your head. We're headed into the evolution of our own fresh eulogy.

Five hours of distracted construction driving later I pull in to see William who is performing in *Harvey*. He's playing Elwood P. Dowd, a guy with an imaginary, tall white rabbit, or Pooka, as a best friend. A Pooka is a spirit that can stop your clock so you can go anywhere you like, stay as long as you want, and when you get back it's as if no time has passed. And no, the irony is not lost on me. In a way it's what we are to each other. You're held up in time, Cooper, suspended. I need you to be. Maybe you need me there too.

Only it won't be as if no time has passed.

That's the way it is with William and I. We lost a lot of time with each other over the past twenty-four years, right after college. Almost as much time as you and I. It's a comfort that we've gravitated back.

William doesn't like to talk on the phone but he picks it up for me. Seeing him is easy company. Certain people just become a part of your blood, like a discarded lizard tail that keeps growing back.

If William has a Pooka, it's his apartment. It's a museum collection of eclectic art that he's gathered together over the past few years. There are paintings of animals doing human things, like eating cake; statues that are part beast, part cutesy animals, part man. He also has his art. Inside large glass jars he's put bits and pieces of his own associations inside. One is filled with multi-colored dry cleaning tags his—

These looks like your insides.

—ex-boyfriend would clip out of his shirts and pants, another one with layers of the different drugs his body is balancing. These are all representations of pieces of his life. He's also filled the remaining wall space with large caricature drawings of strained smiling cartoon faces he's sketched out of brightly colored crayons. They are extraordinary and fantastical and clever and raw. They hover like intense emoticons; faces of his feelings outlined in black, all living in a hundred different kinds of needing expression. The eyes of each one of them say something unquestionably unique and each time I go more of these exposed emotions appear, having slipped under the doorway under cover of night.

All these distorted entities around him are exhalations. Inside his home, you are inside of him. When he opens his front door he walks into himself over and again. The back part of his mind expressing what the conscious part of it isn't willing to face. It has to come out somehow, somewhere, so here it is, waiting in avoidance.

Until the airbag light turns on.

Or the voices come for you. But these crayon colored faces are bringing him closer to the surface, to a crossroads of looking into the eye of himself. Closer because this isn't bought and paid for, this is coming directly out of him. And in the center of it all, and almost hidden away is the reason: a tiny, pale pink almost Egyptian shaped vessel containing his

31

mother's ashes. A porcelain statue of a woman in white dances in front of her, a sailboat held captive inside one of his jars is to the left of her. To her right another holding a stone with the word, 'live' on top of it is trying to sink a dingy dangling by a thread. He's got her surrounded. These guardians hold her in a way she never held him.

It's almost as if he made this for us. Don't stare at it unnaturally.

I built a replica of my own on the inside.

"Do you want another drink?" he asks.

"Why do you keep asking me that?"

"Because I'm one ahead of you. Shut up. You want another drink, I'll make you another drink." When we see each other part of the process is our slow descent into a sloshishness that oh, so merrily floats us into that Pooka time and space where everything slows and gently spins.

"You should look at all of this, William."

"Look at what? You want to see my beautiful body?"

"No, I'll take your word for that."

"No one wants to see my beautiful body."

"Where's my drink, pity boy?"

"Gees, here, not so loud, you'll wake the cat. Woody? It's okay buddy. Ahhh, see you've scared him into taking a shit. I've got to clean that up."

"Now?"

"Trust me. Now. Make me another drink."

"Woody. A gay cat called Woody."

"He's not gay. I don't think he is. Am I raising a gay cat?"

"In your own likeness, as God intended." I toss what appears to be too much vodka for me, but probably a hair shy of what he wants, into a plastic cup and shake it up. I yell over the ice crushing shake noise, mixing it with Fresca.

"No, but hey, have you ever looked at each one of these statues, and paintings, and jars and asked yourself why you bought it or what made you create it, and what it says to you that you can't say out loud to yourself."

"What do you mean? You're speaking to fast. You have to slow down for me." He's got a bag of shit in his hand and I don't want to know where he's going to put it.

"All this. You should take that beautiful body of yours on a tour dude - of all of this. You do know that all of this is you, right? That every hanging, locked up, lit up animal, demon, fairy, emasculated, virile thing in this room is an evasion of your not facing something. You bought it so you won't have to talk about it. You have completely cocooned yourself in. It's like your Pooka play. This space is one big giant white rabbit. You've recreated your mother's wooomb. Wait, womb."

You've recreated your mother's wooomb.

I know, right? That's what you and I are doing - we're traveling womb revivalists.

Hahahahahahahaha.

We're laughing in that silly way where you just need a laugh so much that it overtakes your body and your mind and it comes out your nose and you can't catch your breath and in all of that I hear the laugh that's yours.

Mine?

It's like an out of control violin player who's showing off how he's learnt that part of Summer 1 in Tchaikovsky's *Four Season's* and he's taken off all on his own and strings are breaking but he carries on anyway. Notes across a page I laugh along with. I love that sound of us as we all die down.

I look into my glass and catch the last piece of ice disintegrating.

"Woomb, womb…this is only my second womb, second drink, I mean, right? It's my second one. What's in this?" Make light. Drink up. There's something to the mist of alcohol that slashes guilt down. Your mother's drunk. See, I can even float that word out here in the blur.

"Womb, my mother's womb? She's right over there you know. Hi, mom!" Hi, mom, see how easily he says that. "She's in a tomb." I've no idea where they put you.

Slow down and grab some water.

"It's what we do with unhappiness. It's what I did." I see you squinting. My head's twirling. I change the subject. "You know you're always talking about wanting to escape your job, you talk about that all the time."

"Do I talk about it too much? Do I bug you about that too much, I'm sorry."

"Yes, enough already with your whining. If I have to listen to any more of that."

"Shut up. Really?"

"Seriously? No. I've been you. Now I'm free and broke. What was I talking about? God, don't interrupt my flow." Either of you. "Look you talk about your shit job - about taking acting and making it into something better, but you don't make the choice to change it. You sit in it, just like I did. It's easier to come to a place where you feel safe, and here it is.

I should know, I sat in mine for twenty years." He looks around the room and the ice residue gathered around the bottom of his glass drips onto his t-shirt.

"It's in this too," he says taking a long hard swallow of his vodka and Fresca. "You're right. Why haven't I seen that before?" We know, you and I, don't we?

"Because it's right in front of you. I'll bet if you looked into each piece of art you have you'd find some part of you in it. Then you could just put it away, you know, turn the paintings around, or take them off the walls, turn the statues around, pack them up or something."

"It's overwhelming in here sometimes, but it's comfortable. How do I take it all down? I mean how do I...there's so much of it."

"Just take it one piece at a time. Put it in front of you and write down what you think it means."

"Ah, you with the writing thing. You know we don't all write. I can't write."

"Oh, really, you can't write, Mr. I've got a one man show I need to tell, see I've got reams of yellow notebooks of it – you can't write? Write it down. Jeez, is it so hard to follow my instructions."

"You're not the boss of me."

"Oh, I think I am."

"Yeah, you are. Ok, go on. My stuff. I write about it...."

"Then put it away. You've got a goldmine in here. It's like you've split yourself in half. I wish I had something like this to tell me who I am." Woody jumps on my lap and looks at me with your eyes, Cooper, and I see you so clearly in a pupil's green electrical storm. Pooka magic swirled in vodka, maybe. You're twirling around as fast as you can, as children do, with your arms straight out, your gold curls stuck in sweet sweat - a lucid heartbeat. I was the only voice you had and it was no voice at all. One thing that William understands is that you live in the voice I can't find. How do you have a voice of your own when you've denied someone else's? What do you think? Should I tell him that I'm currently seeing you in the eyes of his cat? I think he has enough to put away already.

Put it away. Turn the statues around.

"Put it away. Where do I put it? How do I put it all away? I love this stuff."

"What? Yes, of course you do, it's makes you comfortable and while it's up there you don't have to face any of it."

"I know. I know. I do know that. Why have I done this to myself?"

"You've given yourself a gift. You've mapped it all out and left yourself clues everywhere. You've told yourself exactly where you need to go, which parts of you to look in. It's very clever actually. As dis-associative as it is, it's impressive. I mean look at this place. It's just wall to wall you. Marvelous." I head for the bathroom.

"Maybe for you, you don't have to face it." Well, it's not hiding in an airbag light.

"It's marvelous for you... it's going to be a brave thing to do." I shout from behind the door, annoyed – why would you put a hand towel rack so far away from the sink.

"And I have the AIDS. I like to call it that, the AIDS. I have the AIDS." He's laughing and saying, 'the AIDS,' in funny deep voices. I emerge alone.

"Of course you do, you're drunk. We're both drunk, toasting the aids. I wish you'd stop saying that. You don't have it. You're positive."

"I know. At least I'm positive about something."

"Everything you feel about the AIDS is out here too. You never talk about it. You handle it in a way I'm not sure I could, but I think there's more in there to deal with or it wouldn't be manifesting itself on the outside as well. If you look at it, I mean really look at it, what being in this health situation has been able to tell you, or help you face, or where it's taken you, how it's affected the decisions you've made, the choices you refused to make, the bravery it may have put on hold, the job you selected to suck the life out of you." Woody jumps onto the back of the sofa and rubs his head on William's.

"I know. I can see how it's all played out to here."

"Ah, what the hell do I know? I'm just talking out my ass as usual. It's all this displaced, unused mother energy. I've got nowhere to put it so I'm pushing it all out onto you. You and a plethrarar...pletharare...plethora? Of friends will all be glad when I finally find a boyfriend – then I can heap all of it onto him, poor guy. I don't even know who he is and I feel sorry for him already."

"Yeah, go and tell him what to do. You're good at telling people what to do. You're so bossy." Yes, me, an unused undirected mother voice. Did I ever tell you, child of the wind, that I used to think you lived where the mismatched lost socks and the fruit flies go?

I do.

35

"Fruit fly heaven, friendly friend. You are right of course. I do that, don't I? How annoying." How annoying.

"No, no you're not. Well you are, but tell me what to do. I need you to tell me what to do. I've told you that."

"Just do what I tell you, it works for me."

"And I will be happy when you're with someone but, not the point. What was the point? I've got to go to sleep. But it's all true, all of this. It's true."

"Ha!"

"No, it is. Can you write this down? This is important and I'm not going to remember any of this. Oh, my God, Sara, this is all me. I'm a cow in a white apron eating birthday cake. I'm an upside down cat's head on a groom's body, a gnome on a porcelain hill. I'm a unicorn with a great pair of legs."

"You'll remember it. It's all around you, for goodness sake. You just got to a point where you didn't notice it. When you get up tomorrow I think you'll feel it looking back at you. You'll walk around in it the way the rest of us do out here."

I don't know where any of that came from, but I know I can say it because that's us - we have an easy trust. We cross each other when we need to.

You should give more vodka Fresca induced advice.

And he does usually do what I tell him, which works for me 'cause I'm so bossy. He's a bit muddled but aren't we all? He's my friend from the lost and found. What's in the air doesn't lie and it finds us – you saw that didn't you - you stared into it with us.

Relationship Intuition Number Three: **The Pooka Friendship.** The friend that is there to stand beside you when you need to stand still, stop and get a better understanding. He is constant, appearing when needed in constant flow, rage, love and courage. Even if you think he can't see you, he can.

The next morning I wake up early with Woody on my head. I look into his eyes, but you, sweet thing, are off somewhere else. I've a busy day on anyway.

Before seeing my former acting professor, Stephen, I'm meeting Elspeth for breakfast. She was in William's acting class.

No, she was in the class behind William's with Cody.

Right. Well, at any rate, they were very close in school, and they don't live far from each other now that's she's moved back to Austin from Los Angeles.

"Hi! It's so great to see you, I'm so glad we're doing this, I want to hear all about what you're doing." She hugs me and we smile at each other for a minute looking each other over. She looks exactly the same. I mean exactly the same. I smile at her as if I do too. "Can I just get this off my chest though, William's not coming. He was supposed to come with us," she says.

"Yes, I know, he's tired…."

"He's hung over." My head is pounding too, not just from the Vodka, but from the truth she's got a hold of. I try to look sober and awake. "I worry about him," she says, in such a way that stops me.

"We did drink a bit too much last night," I begin, not clear on what I should say. "I know what you mean - he's not happy where he is right now with his job… you've talked to him about all this?"

"Yeah, I've talked to him. I know it's hard for him to give up his job needing the health benefits and all because he's sick." The AIDS. I'd be pretty pissed off and drunk a lot of the time if I had it. "I, I don't know what to say anymore. Sorry, I just had to get that off my chest. Look follow me over to Whole Foods, we can grab something over there. This place has an hour long wait."

In the car I think about William. I know he knows he's drinking a bit too much.

But you know why, and you know that he's coming out of it.

Still, it shakes me up a bit to hear Elspeth say it out loud. She's been around a lot more than me, and they have a connection. He admires her so much. I should talk to him about it in a sober conversation, so he knows I've heard him and not just bulldozed through, like I do. I'm writing it down in my notebook waiting for Elspeth—

I'll remind you later.

—when I am distracted by cheese.

I love sitting across from a person that's always in motion, it keeps my mind in redeployment mode. I had no idea what to expect with her but I'm glad we're at the table together. We both moved around with routine regularity growing up and we reek of it. That way of living became instinctive as we got older and it created a restlessness that runs our lives. Elspeth's back in Austin to breathe out a little before she heads back out to New York, or perhaps LA again.

"Do you think that's what draws us to being actors?" I ask her. "It's a life in cycles, isn't it? Rehearsals, intense, brief new bonds with people, performances...it ends abruptly, like when we were kids. We move on because that's what we know."

"Some people see that as us not being capable of ever seeing anything through to the end," she says in a way that suggests someone close to her has put that on her - I don't ask who, "but that's not the point at all, is it? We don't see an end, because it's just the road."

She says she'll be in Austin for a while, but when you lead a life at speed, resting is a place of creation and exploration and it needs executing. Rest as fuel is how she remains steady. "It's all a matter of being grateful, for every last thing I have. I go over what I'm grateful for every day."

"So do I. Do you write yours down? I used to but now I do them in my head every morning when I walk my dog, Stanley." She's focused and doesn't smile.

"I have a book. I write them down every morning. First thing I do."

"Really? Good for you." Every day. I feel lazy so I eat a big mouthful of cheese, 'cause that'll help. I almost joke about it, but I don't know her well enough to know if it's the right time for a laugh. Isn't that odd. I thought I would, but I don't. If this were William I'd be in there all over it, and talk about why I don't write it down, when normally I would because I'm a writer and William would make fun of it because he's not, and he is writing it down, only it's not William it's Elspeth and she's serious and I'm not sure and I hesitate and I've eaten all the cheese.

"I want love," she says a bit out of the blue, or I haven't been paying attention because of the gratitude writing thing. "I see people like Aiden and Jackie. Just friends at school, and then they find each other again after not seeing each other for twenty years and end up together. I wonder if I've already met the person who's going to love me. I think about that so much now because of them." I've wasted love over the years, but I mumble on about how I wish it find's me. Love, sure. I keep thinking about William. I'm glad that Elspeth's here so he has a voice he respects within earshot. I hope she doesn't let go of that.

I shoot out of the Whole Foods underground parking lot onto some street, lost immediately. Lost in all of it. Elspeth's life has been so varied, diversified. She rolled into it and allowed it to happen. I'm glad I'm finally getting my shit together, but I feel behind the eight ball, just now in the game. The hour is a weird tonic for me too. She's going with a flow that's her own – it makes me believe I can.

It's because of how you're letting the game play out that the eight ball's lining up with every pocket on the table.

I'm not sure we'll see each other again. There's something about her that's already moved on.

The car compass leads me to The Blue Dahlia Bistro to meet up with one of my former University acting professors, Stephen. I'm a bit nervous. I don't know if he remembers me that well, what pieces of me come into his mind as he sees me. Hundreds of us passed through his arms, how could we all stand out, right? But that's an underestimation of him. His voice rolls out like the perfect welcome mat - precise, deep, bold, and entwined with a jolliness of laughter without a sense of time gone by. It's mesmerizing from the first bear hug hello. And here we are chatting away again, even before our bottoms hit our seats. I don't even look at the menu. The waitress spouts off a special and I just order that. I'm still a bit bloated with cheese, but I don't care. I just want this. His advice steered my course, which was all over the map at the time.

"William says hello."

"William?"

"The class behind me, or two, I can't remember. You know, William toast of the town, William."

"Ah, yes. William."

"How do you all live in the same town and not know? It's so funny. I'd be dropping by all the time. You're lucky I don't live around the corner, you know." He laughs that sound again, his arms crossed over his still Buddha belly, the whites of his eyes highlighting his grey hair, sparkling next to the darkness of his skin.

"But I do see you, more than I thought I would, with Facebook," he says, "it's opened up the past and so many of my students to come back to me. And so I see you, and where you've all gone. All into so many different venues all over the world. I love it, Sara. It's wonderful to get these notes from all of you after all of these years. Here you are. And I connect people together. You don't know each other of course, so many years of students through many years, so if I see that some of you are in the same place or working on the same kind of projects, I'll put you together. The connections might be useful, it's an enormous pipeline, you follow?"

"How marvelous that you think to do that." I just keep nodding and eating whatever this special of the day is.

"I went to Ghana, with Dr. Brockett. He's like a hero over there, quite a celebrity. They bowed to him. I was along for the ride. I spent some time in Korea, we were doing Shakespearean workshops where we used Shakespeare's language as music."

Wait you have something interesting to say here, but my mouth is full,

"I went to Puerto Rico and did the same sort of thing," I say with quinoa flying and an over eagerness that makes him pick up the camera around his neck and begin to take pictures of me. "I was in a Romeo and Juliet ballet my friend, Marie choreographed. They used me as a narrator and put some of the text into the piece, using the iambic pentameter to feed the music in the movement." Oh, please let him be impressed, it may be the only moment I have something noteworthy to offer.

You could tell him about the voices in your head.
If this doesn't work, I may have to.

"Ah, yes, I can see that... interesting to be in that place, yes." He looks down at his camera screen, "You don't mind me taking pictures of you do you? I like to capture it all." He shows me the screen and flicks through the fast rapid pictures he's just taken. "Ah, maybe we'll delete that one," he says as we come to one of me trying to be impressive with my eyes closed and a green dot of spinach on my lip.

"Do you enjoy living in Dallas?" Of course I don't.

"Umm, most of my family's there, but it's not really... it's not really me. I lived in Los Angeles and San Diego as well for a while."

"Ah, you haven't found your home yet." The saltshaker tips off the window ledge spilling its insides on the table. My sensitive child.

"No, I haven't felt all my self anywhere I've lived yet," I swirl the salt around into the shape of a newborn baby's hair and throw it over my left shoulder. "I'm a bit of a gypsy. I've moved around a lot."

"When I was leaving Ghana I was presented with an African stool by one of the people. 'Take this stool home with you and put it down in your house and sit on it to see how comfortable you feel,' he told me. Did I want to stay seated or

40

get back up? If I felt any sense of discomfort, he said to ask myself if I wanted to go anywhere, to meditate on this question, on those places. If I had no desire to get up - I was home, do you follow? It's called, 'becoming instooled.' I made my wife sit on it for a long time to make sure she was certain." We both crack up at the fact that he'd actually gone home and tried it. I'm making that awful laughing sound that embarrasses me, but so is he, so it's okay.

"I've got to get one of those things. I'll lug it around with me on my travels."

"You will know when you get there."

Something will take you there, and you won't know why.

When we sat together in his office all those years ago he asked me a question. It's staring at me again, hovering. His camera closes in on me and I look in the lens. It was a question for the character to answer that has now come back around for me - Am I brave enough to find my way home to who I am? He takes the saltshaker out of my hand. The way he puts it back on the window ledge is as if he's handing it back to you. And I know why you spilled the salt.

Are you brave enough to accept the entirety of your worth?

Until I do, the three-legged stool will buckle underneath me, won't it?

The unmasked question hangs in what I wonder is my final conversation with Stephen. I watch him walk away before I race to my car and pull out my journal to write down every single word he said. No way that would have happened if I'd just messaged him. That's so much more than I expected. I can't forget any of this. I'm talking to myself out loud. The light for the passenger airbag flares up and dings - your attention seeking technique, Cooper. It sounds like a heartbeat in need of jumpstarting. My pencil's flying across the page in time with it - the both of us, recalling, recording with the silence of his voice. I know what alone together means.

On the drive back to Dallas I keep thinking of more things he said, and I thank God that I35 is a straight road because I'm half in, half out of the ditches trying to find the recording device on my phone, then figuring out how to use it. They say this is the new journal, but I can't wrap my mind around that. Facebook is recording it all for us anyway. It's an open diary we used to have a key for. This is a journal we cannot burn. It's a time capsule. There's no need to sift through years of dust on boxes to find that leather bound book you just had to have back in 1984. I like dust though. I like the smell of it, I like the way my hand swipes over it on the hunt to finding what I'm looking for. Dust is underrated.

Approaching the Dallas skyline at sunset I think of Stephen, and my stool wobbles.

Part 3 Backbone:

Spine; Decision of character; resolution;
to the backbone, to the utmost extent; out and out;
all through or over;
(a soldier to the backbone)

- The Library of Universal Knowledge

Retrieving Lost Direction

We do not go into the desert to escape people but to learn how to find them.
- Thomas Merton

I've a few days left in town until I head down to Destin for a week's vacation with my family. Leaving from there I'll be driving up the East coast sort of solo. For now I've enough time for a cup of tea with Sophia, whose own stool is wavering. She's abandoning our round the corner friendship and moving off into the world that is New York with her husband and two adorable children. I hate this. With my travel schedule the likelihood of us seeing each other again for a good while means a different kind of goodbye than we're used to.

We met doing a play called, *Season's Greetings*. She's from England as well so we reminisce about marmite, crisps, fish paste sandwiches, Savlon, and the irrational need to swim in the freezing cold waters of the English channel.

I hadn't seen her for quite a while until I went into the hospital to have the baby cyst removed.

My creature twin.

Hospitals have an isolating energy that's like walking through lead. Despite the voices, I've never felt more alone lying there at three o'clock in the morning when the happy juice was wearing off.

Sophia, my ex-boyfriend Gregory and my family are the ones who took time out to care for me. I hadn't expected Sophia. I looked up out of my gloom, and there she was. It's when you least expect it that friendship walks right through the door.

43

She comes in as Gregory is helping me out of bed to take a walk and get some standing up time in. My bottom is hanging tits up in the air out the back of my couture hospital gown.

"Hello, chaps...oh, hello!"

"Oh, please don't make me laugh, breathing is hard enough right now."

"We will laugh about this one day."

"We will?"

"Ah, yes. I'm not going to let you forget that I can't forget this."

"Ha! Oh, no, no, please don't make me laugh. It's like they cut the wiring that connects the top half of me from the bottom. I can't seem to stand up straight."

"Well, you've got a good view." I'm leaning on Gregory's arm and his head is over my shoulder.

"He's seen it all before, haven't you dear."

"Yeah, not quite like this. Come on, you've got to be able to do this, they're letting you go home tomorrow."

"Gregory's been here through the wee hours reading to me and watching me hallucinate imaginary morphine vomit into an empty bucket while weeping uncontrollably."

"Now, that I hadn't seen before," he smiles, patiently waiting for me to breathe on my own. The little fake candles he's set up around the room between the potted palms are burning out like little stars.

"The batteries are going," he says.

"Being in here does that to you." I'm being a bit pathetic.

"Listen, I'm going to go and get some things done since Sophia's here." He hands me over. "She needs to walk around a bit." I head back to the bed to sit down.

"Great. When does the sympathy train get here?"

"They're not invited," Gregory says as he heads out to reception to flirt with the nurses before going back to the recording studio.

"I don't know what I'd do without him, you know. This morphine drip is a wormhole. I've got things hooked up my every angle pumping pain meds. I'm so high." I'm making light, but truly, without Gregory there during the nights I'm quite sure my mind would have stayed hidden in a place even further from you, despite your voice offering us one last chance. I have a scar that should be your entry, to remind me that you aren't. Maybe I put myself through it to show you that I could have. I needed to feel something lifted from me. A redemption perhaps. Why were you so quiet? "Cheer me up."

"Well, there's the story of my mother trying to teach my brother, sister and I how to use a condom."

"The one where you abandon James and leave him alone with a banana in one hand while your mother's ripping the prophylactics open?"

"He's never forgiven either one of us."

"Or that time your friend came over and your dad came out of the bathroom brushing his teeth…naked."

"Oh, hello, Maureen, how are you? Mortifying." So much for not laughing. I love the fact that she's here and doesn't care that my backside's dangling out, as if we're having tea on the terrace. She stays and sits with me. What I mean by stays is that she isn't just visiting or stopping by because she feels she should, succulent plant in hand. There's no wandering around the room looking out the window saying, "well, I'll let you rest," so early in the conversation that you wonder if they've left the car running. But that's not Sophia. She wasn't whom I'd expected and now I can't see anyone else standing there. There's a moment in lasting friendship when it shows up for the first time unconditionally complete. Its deliciousness is eating into my skin. Of course it's you. I feel valuable to her. I watch our friendship shift in front of me.

Right before the birth of her first child, when I'd thrown her a baby shower in a pub, as you do, she said she wasn't going to be one of those women that has children and then drops their friends. "I've had that done to me," she said. It made me smile at the time - I'm only responsible for a poodle and I can barely keep up, but she's true to her word. She's an astonishing friend. She's thoughtful, and she listens. I can't stress that enough, Cooper, the listening thing. You know better than anyone how there can be avoidance in that, so to have someone there to listen completely is rare. She allows me to be more open, not that I've been able to be. I could trust her with you because all that I've already shared is safe with her. I hope we end up just around the corner from each other because I wouldn't like to let go of that. As with anything that is rare and true and valuable, I want it to last.

She makes you a better friend.

She does. Thank you for noticing that.

Relationship Intuition Number Four: **The Moment Of Friendship.** This friendship has grown almost behind your back. It's lived a while before you understand the authenticity of it. It shifts from group and sustains on its own. It's revealed through priority. It's an active, moving love that flies through the door and opens your heart.

The week in Destin on vacation with my parents and sister's family goes by quickly – probably because I'm overthinking and anticipating what's coming next. From here I make the first extended trip out - to North Carolina to see Dianah, and from there, all the way along to New York.

The night before I leave, William calls me to tell me he's taken all of his art pieces down. Hidden on the back of one of the abstract paintings he's taken off the wall he's found a hand written note he's never seen from the artist that says, 'mother and child.' My voice breaks a little - he's already moved on.

But it's not about us.
On another painting he turned around he's found a huge black, 'X.'

"I'm shifting with everything in the room. It's making me feel free to move…to leave this womb - right, that's what you called it." Womb, there's that word again, only sober.

He's making his way home.
Like Stephen was saying, you mean.

"I think it's the sanctity of the relationship with your mother - coming to terms with what it was, what you want to take from her and letting her go. Maybe that's the gift. 'X' is the rune that means gift, 'true partnership is only achieved by separate and whole beings who retain their uniqueness even as they unite,' the book says."

"Oh, my God. My story. It's all down. It's so bare. It's just me and my mom."

It's just me and my mom.
"I guess that's how it's been all along. It's the two-year anniversary of her death. I just had a moment with her. She was very comforting and she said, 'don't dwell.' She was here, Sara. I could feel her. You know she was an actor too."

"No, I didn't know that."

"She was so beautiful. I'm looking at this picture of her and she looks so happy and she's got her whole life ahead of her. I feel like she wants me to have the life she never had. She just got lost behind the drinking. She got sucked into the poltergeist TV. I think keeping her up there on the mantle I was holding on to her and not letting her, not allowing her to cross over. Did I do that?"

"No. She has control over her spirit, over the leaving, but her ashes, the physical part of her, that's the part you have control over letting go. Perhaps she was staying for you. Her gift to you is that moment there today when she stayed with you in a room that you were unable to be alone in. She let time stand still for the two of you in a way nothing else can. She was in front of you, protecting you in a way. And now she's behind you. How wonderful. You weren't holding her back - she stayed for you. Maybe the best she could do in all of this life, all she had, came down to this very last minute when you needed her to say, 'what you are doing, I have done; enough now, choose your own life.' This time with her is worth more than the entire physical experience you shared. It's a thank you moment for the relationship, and you both know why." A new silence. Mine not his. Not William's I mean. You, Cooper, are feeding from a womb where the lights gone out, quietly letting me speak from there.

"She's not with me anymore. It feels different in here. It's just me."

"And that's ok. This was always the time." There is a stillness behind him as well.

"Yeah, it is. I mean, I quit drinking and I'm getting up early and I feel like I've got so much energy. What a tremendous time." Yes, it is.

Choose your own life. This time with her is worth more than the entire physical experience... and you both know why.

You put those words there. William's making his way home and it's so clear to him, and I'm so envious because he has a home, he knows what that is, and he knows why.

You know where your home is - but you have to let go of that one thing you're holding on to, to get there.

You're here to take that from me, I suppose.

No, I'm here so you can give it to me.

I am alone except for the consequences of our last twenty-six years. My family has already started their way back to Texas. I'm in my car in a Destin driveway, the ocean behind me barely visible through the rain. It's the same kind of weather as that December when I went to the doctor to find out if I was throwing up because you were alive in me. My peripheral catches the red light flashing reminder of dead weight. The passenger air bag isn't activated, not that you need one anymore. At the very least the goandvisitallyourfriends voice has us looking ourselves in the face.

47

There's a wet chill in the car and I don't know where I am. When I said yes to this it was so far off, I didn't have to think about the consequences of what it actually meant. I find my bravery is more confident somewhere out there in the distance.

Just turn the car on.

I'm on my own, which unnerves me, driving ten hours over seven hundred and twenty-six miles with no sense of trust, which unsettles me. How long will it be until I don't care about that? I reach the first stop sign. "Keep left, and take entrance to freeway...on left," the car compass says. Maybe she's programmed to make me happy. Maybe it's just a matter of acknowledging the fear and sliding sideways. All I have to do is turn left.

I indicate.

Turn.

Dianah and I met sixteen years ago in Dallas during a production of Agatha Christie's, *Death on the Nile*. You remember her; she had that little dog, Bentley.

No, his name was Whittaker.

Whittaker, that stinker, that's right.

She lived through the play, and you got killed off in act one.

Right! She played all kinds of characters - weird souls, abused wives, a mentally challenged confused adolescent man, a classical glamor diva, cranky old southerners, and a Hollywood reporter. She can dance the socks off most people.

And is the most flexible person you know.

I have no illusions coming to see her. No anxieties, or concerns, no feelings of needing to move on quickly. As I pull into the driveway she's waving madly and speaking in an animated silent movie type sign language mimicking how and where to park my car. I can hear her laugh even in its silence. Then comes a hug that wraps all of those yesterdays around us.

Dianah and her mom moved in with her mother's sister and family who have a home with a lower floor apartment built to suit them both. The climate here in North Carolina suits her health, and has made her fibromyalgia almost tolerable. She was told years ago that the stress of her job as a legal secretary was slowly killing her, and the nerve endings in her body agreed.

She looks happy and I'm relieved to see it. She's struggled for a long time with all sundry of health issues that piece by piece have stolen the mobility of her body. The pressure on her knee joints crushing cartilage forces her to walk with a cane. The nerves in her feet feel like someone struck a match and set fire to them. The amount of prescription pills in front of her at lunch is enough for an appetizer.

Dianah's Aunt and Uncle have graciously put me up in their spare room.

"Yur dryvin' all that waaay ba yursayf?" she asks.

Well...

My suitcase is barely pushed under the bed when Dianah 's whisking me off to one of her favorite spots for lunch. Cape Fear. She navigates her city by what she wants to eat. She enjoys food like no one else I have ever met.

Sitting by the water watching the boats go by, eating crab she talks out into the sea. Only the deep can hold how present her past remains. It's a conduit that allows her to speak the words out loud. Listening to her is like throwing a Pollock into the ocean and hearing it melt.

The passing of her brother Dale in a traffic accident in his early twenties and the depth of the loss of her father live in her nerve endings, an unnatural comfort that barely allows her to stand for any length of time anymore.

"Just after Dale died, Daddy was sitting out on our porch and a car pulled up to the house and this woman dressed all in black got out," she says, as the bridge in the distance parts to let a sailboat pass through. "He said that he didn't recognize her at all, but that she looked at him, she looked at him a good while, pointed at him and said, 'Remember, God makes no mistakes.' It was like that finger went straight into his heart, and he grabbed at his chest, and when he looked back up there was no sign of her. She'd just vanished. No sign of the car, no tire tracks, just his hand on his heart. An angel spirit come to let him know that although Dale wasn't here with us anymore, that there was a reason, that there was a time for everything, the right time. That's what he said she was, and even though the nonsensicalness of it never left him, she helped him trust in God's judgment. She was God's messenger." I can see her looking for the same woman in black to walk across the boardwalk to reassure her, now, about her father's death. She's had her own ghost visitations all through her life, warnings to not take this road, ghosts stopping her on the side of the road that as she kept on driving, found it was they who'd been killed in the accident that had slowed the traffic so she might talk to them. Why had the lady in black not come for her? She's come for me. I want to tell her. She's a wolf man.

There's no misconception in who it is.

It connects us.

Listen to her.

It comforts me that someone else has had their heart pressed on and been reminded of divine timing. She holds such a raw depth of emotion on the surface millimeters below joy, and they battle, neither ever winning. When her father died, that divided her against herself.

"At Dad's viewing I got worried about how God would recognize him as he walked in to heaven. So I sat by him and listened. 'Bury all the love you have for him, along side him,' that's what I heard. So I wrote a letter to God telling him all about Daddy, and of all the wonderful things he'd done for me, for my mom, for Dale, the kind of man he was, and what he stood for; how much love he gave, and how much love was given to him; how much love there was swirling around still that was now all God's. I told him what he stood for and what he fought for, and then I folded up the letter and put it in his hand so he could present it to God. Then he would know, really know what kind of man he had been to me, and he'd know why part of him had to stay with me. And someone asked what the note was, asked what the letter was, and a little while later I looked up and everyone was writing notes of their own. When we closed the lid on the coffin it closed down on a man whose life story had buried its self with him. All those people relived the memories they had lived with him, giving it back to him as a gift." She's still looking out at sea, and the bridge that had split in half to allow the sailboat through is closing back in on itself. "This is the best crab in town, aren't these the best crab cakes you've ever eaten? Girl, I could eat these every day. Don't tell mom I had two though, she'll just get mad at me."

How beautiful to care for a father so deeply, that you honor his spirit by releasing it with the physical telling of his life.

There's something ancient about it, isn't there? There's a lightness to her as we make our way home. Sometimes when you say someone's name out loud it's as if they come back for you.

"Can I ask you something?" she says, releasing her dog into the garden. "Do you see Gregory anymore?"

Roll your sleeves up.

"Yeah. I didn't see him for a long time – almost a year, but we've talked quite a bit lately. He's opened up his own theatre and dance company. He's doing really well."

"And you're ok with that? You were together for a long time."

"Yes, I think we are where we're supposed to be. We had a big blow up, and after that neither one of us picked up the phone. It was hard. It was a year of…" *Detoxing* "…detoxing out of each other I suppose you'd say. I had a knot in my stomach for months wondering if I'd done the right thing, not calling, if I'd regret not giving him more." *You loved him.* "Yes, I did, I loved him, but I had to give myself time."

I'm talking so easily about this. And you - I think she understands you without me even saying a word, she can probably see you. Her dog, Poppy is turning in circles sniffing you out.

"Well I'm glad. I worry about you, girl. So, good. You deserve the best of everything. You know that right?" She pauses a minute and simply smiles at me. "So this is exciting - your Facebook journey."

Thank you for saying that to her. She doesn't quite believe it yet.

"Yes, so my journey. Yes. I'm on the road."

Keep going.

"At first I was afraid I'd messed up again, that I wasn't going forwards, that I was still running away from something, but that's not it. I'm confronting myself in a way. Does that make sense? I'm happy, even though I'm unsure about everything." Poppy settles on her lap.

"Yes, I know what you mean. Girl, Facebook's been confronting me with things I'd rather forget. I had the strangest thing happen to me. You know, I was bullied in high school, right?"

"No, I had no idea."

"It's hard for me to remember coming home from school without crying. Those girls caused me so much pain and humiliation and self-doubt, and do you know what two of them had the nerve to do - send me a friend request!"

"What?"

"After all these years. I know. I felt sick. I saw their names and my body went into… I don't know, girl. I felt afraid of

51

them, instantly, just seeing their names took me back to when I was a teenager and it was all I could do not to cry. Those girls I wasn't cool enough to hang out with, that put sick notes in my locker telling me to keep away from them, that made me eat lunch by myself, those bullies now want to be my friends? It's so hypocritical that you can treat someone so cruelly and then come back years later and write it off as just something that kids do."

I'm so glad you didn't have to face any of this.

You did though. I saw those girls throwing spitballs into your hair in geometry class. How many times did you eat by yourself?

"Did you reach back out to them? Tell them how they'd made you feel?"

"You know what? I figured they already knew that. There was no need for any re-hashing or pretending it hadn't hurt, when they had to know it had. I don't owe them anything. I don't even feel they have the right to know that all of that has made me stronger. Going through that gave me courage to refuse that kind of cruelty into my life again. They have no right to the pictures of my life, my blessings. I'm not sharing any of that with them. And I do have that power now to not let them in. So I looked at those requests, and I looked at their faces, and I did what they'd been doing to me for years, I ignored them. I hit that button and do you know I haven't felt as powerful before or since. Like I finally had control over it." And you have to understand these words, what's she's saying, there is no trace of bitterness about it at all. It's closing a wound by saying thank you: thank you for seeking me out and closing this door with me. It's a remarkable moment to watch my phoenix friend's resilience. It is possible, Cooper, to take thoughtless unkindness and use it as a vessel for courage and forgiveness.

Relationship Intuition Number Five: **The Phoenix Friendship**. This friendship sustains and forges ahead with a seaming life of its own. This friendship exists in the air without the pace of time. It pulls you back to something you have continually walked past without thinking. This friend notices you're a diamond in the ruff and wants to make sure you have too. She's bead working your soul.

Before I leave, Dianah zooms me through the park careening our way to the local film studio as the icing from the best cupcakes in town drip down our hands.

52

"Look, can you believe our luck? They're filming out here. Girl, I wish I'd known they needed extras. I should have called and got us in. Look at them all."

"What are they doing?"

"It looks like they've set it up as some sort of barracks. Let's drive up a little closer and see. Wait, what does that sign say?"

"Wait, slow down. Oh, my God, it's a Minimum-security prison."

"That's the set?"

"Ah, no Dianah, I think we took a left when we should have gone right. They're not dressed up as inmates, these people I'm taking irrationally too many pictures of are inmates." We hoof it out of there laughing our asses of, and sail off to eat the fattiest, juiciest donut holes by the beach with the softest sand tickling our feet. Dianah is a swimming pool of the grandest fun you'll ever have.

The next morning before I head out she hands me a necklace she's bought for me – a lemon yellow stone that has a compass wheel on it with the coordinates of her house. "In case you lose your way," she says, "you'll always know how to find your way back to me." As I hug her goodbye, she doesn't let go for a good while. She shared a part of my life that for me was the beginning of a great love, and she was around long enough to see that as much as I wanted it to be everlasting, it would be full of struggle. She would try to talk to me about it, and I'd step behind the everything is fine tree. I'm glad I've given her a little of the truth I couldn't face back then.

People hang on to worry when they don't know your mind; when they're left half in and half out of a story.

Leaning on her cane she waves frantically until our coordinates change again.

Traveling the road from Wilmington, up to Newport, Rhode Island I feel like one of the pilgrims sailing for the new world - it's a long ass drive. I'm going to need a rest point. The problem is, I don't know anyone along that route. Before I left on the trip I called Marie because I knew she's worked with the Richmond Ballet in the past. My thinking is she might be able to hook me up to the kindness of Strangers in Virginialand. I'm right. Within hours she's connected me via e-mail to Jerri, who she works and sometimes stays with. She's agreed to let me crash with her and her family. Now because I come from a long line of British, 'I don't want to overstay my welcome,' minded ancestors–

You start practicing your apology and assurances that they'll never know you're there. But look what waits for you.

I pull up to Jerri's open arms, vodka tonics, and a cheese board that I run at with Goldrush mustard like it's Mecca. Not being the greatest conversationalist in the world and not knowing if my journey's of any interest, and not wanting to go on and on about myself to strangers afraid I'll come off all about me, I babble on about the mustard and about its secret ingredient of magic which all of a sudden strikes me as somewhat wiccan which makes me self-conscious and back track and make comments like, "not that there's a spell in there or anything, it isn't some kind of voodoo mustard powder, it's all totally legal, which is not to say there's anything even borderline illegal in the magic in there."

It's a miracle you don't implode.

But they start laughing, and not *at* me. We all slosh down more vodka and questionable magic mustard on meat and cheese bits and stay up talking about each other's lives until 1:00 o'clock in the morning. Conversation flowed like we'd known each other and been separated for centuries and we're catching up on the miles of road behind us. It's vibrant and delicious. I haven't felt this relaxed in years.

"That's Salvatore Aiello," Jerri's partner, Doug says, "Her soul mate."

"A pure, kind, beautiful, beautiful man," she says, looking at the portrait on the wall. "So much love, dancing with him." Jerri's life is dance. There's a beautiful picture of her on the wall too, arms like a bird preparing to land.

"Her ports de bras, that's what she's known for. Graceful," Doug says. I look over at this man completely in love. God, I hope someone looks at me like that one day. He's not looking at a picture like I am. He's looking at her. I hope she likes me.

I feel held when she speaks to you, ma.

They live with Jerri's mother, Toni. She keeps everything flowing together for them all. Listening to her stories, she bonds you to her by reliving them with you.

I'd mentioned in my e-mail about trying to volunteer in the different states along the way to see how communities gives back, and as synchronicity would have it Doug's just become CEO of Feedmore, a Food Bank, Community Kitchen, and Meals on Wheels organization which he's arranged for me to visit early the next morning.

Doug does what he does because it serves his community, and he does what he does how he does it out of a need to make it better. His strength of business and his desire to give back to his community are the same thing, and that's rare in corporate America. You'll just have to trust my twenty-year screwing in big business on that. Typically there's no foreplay or cuddling afterwards.

Volunteer morning I've got vodka head and my stomach is pretty certain working in the kitchen is going to be a bit of a risk. From the get-go I have the feeling that the head pooba volunteer lady in charge doesn't think much of, "one off" volunteers because she gives me the most menial task in the food servicing line: tray wiper. My sobering up conversation can be quite lucid and charming though and she soon sees how wasted my talents are with just a damp cloth. I'm quickly promoted to black-eyed pea scooper, then to potato salad scooper in rapid succession. I like black-eyed peas, they're easy to control, but these wretched potatoes are all different sizes. I keep serving too much of the stuff. It's all this pressure of being on top as lead carb dispenser, and the head lady who has a hole in her hairnet I didn't mention and could have, reprimands me about waste and proportion so I stand at an angle hoping she can't see my scoops, but the damn thing's on a conveyer belt passing by her beady little eyes. She shakes her head and smiles at me like my mother did when I came in last at the school cross-country running competition.

"Honey, I think I'd best put you back on black-eyed peas," she says, taking the scoop out of my surrendering, failure of a hand. Demoted. I'm just glad I'm removed from the kitchen all together as the red Jello comes out - even the more hardened volunteer went pale.

"That's some sticky, unpredictable stuff," the proficient potato scooper remarked as I slinked out the back door.

After four hours of volunteering, Doug is taking me on a tour of Richmond. We drive down Monument Avenue passed a frozen charge of stone Confederate soldiers, bayonets drawn, lined up one in front of the other. They're all marching, somewhat Twilight Zoney, into a statue of Arthur Ashe, tennis racket in hand.

We end up across from the Tredegar Ironworks, underneath the old railroad at Jerri, Doug and Toni's secret place. Here they climb down to the river to see the Blue

Heron. There aren't any tourists - it's just us, the homeless, and teenage runaways, kissing. It's a steep climb down an iron ladder onto an old, narrow sewage pipeline. We walk side by side the river holding on to an uncertain railing.

As we get about halfway along, without a Heron yet in site, the skies open up. A relentless rain pours down on us in sheets like clean God vomit blinding us - a wind pushing it sideways into our faces.

"Do you want to go back?" I hear Doug's watery shadow dripping.

"Not on your life - we're already wet, aren't we? Keep going?"

"Fine with me. Watch how you walk though." Sweet. I have a rush of needing to stay. I love all there is about rain. I wish you could have known what it feels like to be out in it, Cooper. It's cold, but in a way that brightens your skin when it touches it. When it comes down it's all of the world you want. It's funny because your first instinct is to run from it, but if you stand still, you see that it's really a gift from heaven that's been swirling around waiting for you to come outside. If I lie on my back and stare up into it, trying to make eye contact with each drop and catch them in my mouth, for a minute I almost believe I can breathe it all in, that I could no more drown than...

I could. Yes. How beautiful. Water is the only breath I have ever taken.

I'm taking another one now. I love unpredictable wetness coming out of nowhere to remind you that it can. Right now it's a bit tricky though because I'm trying to do too much at once. I'm balancing on a slippery sewer line trying to keep a hold of my phone in one hand because I'm video taping the downpour, holding an eye out for Heron which I'm determined to see, trying to shield my fashionably useless, paper thin backpack purse from getting soaked and dripping into free falling dollar bills, while wiping the rain out of my eyes so my contact lenses don't fall out. All the while the river roars underneath us whisking off the frantic paddling kayakers. Poor bastards. Two white herons swish down battling with the wind, trying to land in a tree always two inches out of reach. Dammit I'd just panicked and turned off my phone. Doug's gone on ahead and I don't see him until he heads back towards me and we turn around.

Back at the car we're both soaked through.

"Here, you can use this, first. Jeez, sorry, it's the only thing

I have." We both start laughing as he hands me a small white golfing towel. Use it first? It'll be soaked through as soon as I wipe my hands on it. He starts the car and we laugh and drip onto his lovely, but stricken leather interior.

He drops me back at my car before heading home to clean up and change for his meeting. I still want to figure out a way to visit the Valentine Museum looking like this. I'll have to change my clothes, that much is clear. The only extra clothes I have in my car are a *pair of cut off red and white gingham pajama boy shorts* and a neon yellow midriff t-shirt that has, 'Destin,' written on it in huge, black letters. Crap. I grab them from my trunk and walk in.

The two children working the front office look at me. I casually push my hair, which is stylishly stuck to my face like Carrie's, out of my eyes, and stand and drip.

"Are you here to see the exhibit?" One of them asks, as if the answer's no.

"Yes, but clearly I need to use your restroom first. I should change clothes."

A small pool of water is starting to gather at your feet – shift yourself around.

What do you want me to do, a soft shoe? "Down here on the left? Thank you."

In the restroom I strip all the way down and dry myself off with coarse paper towels as best I can. I have no spare bra or underwear so going double commando is my only option. I look at myself in the half mirror.

You look completely ridiculous.

I'm paranoid that the boy shorts are too loose so I'm walking like I have an egg between my legs, and I keep tugging at the neon yellow midriff shirt, painfully aware that the 'i' in Destin is really inappropriately placed, to cover more of my stomach because I've pulled the boy shorts down as low as I can to make sure my "wiffle waffle," as my grandmother used to call it, is adequately shielded.

The girls almost smile at me until they hear the squishy squashing of my canvas shoes splashing across their floor. I think it best to keep moving and seem interested in their History of Richmond exhibit by asking lots of questions, but their eyes keep a sharp watch on my dripping clothes that I'm trying to hide under my arm. I need a bag.

The hundred and ten-year-old lady that works in the gift shop probably goes to sleep at night praying no one like me comes in to purchase things, especially things on sale, but here

57

I am. I find a small velvet pouch 75% off that I can put my Garmin car compass voice in. She deserves it, and at $4, it's perfect.

"Oh deeyah…Ahm naht shoowere ah kin fig rrr out ha to do thayat, to ring thayat uuup. It's a sayell eyetem. Yoooou doooo know yur tryin' to bah a sayell eyetem?" I nod, "Weyell…ahh, layet me staaart ova." Luckily she's speaking slowly because I can barely hang on to what she's saying. All this along side so much sighing it could have filled a hot air balloon. I cannot and will not back down even from the hundredth and one eye roll she's shooting my way. I need the bag she's going to put my cost effective purchase in for my wet clothes.

"Can I have the bigger paper bag that you have? I have these wet clothes you see…I got caught in the rain and I…"

"Wayell, we don't giyave the bigga bayags out fur smal things - fur smal things on sayell."

"I have all these clothes you see dripping wet and I'd hate for them to make a mess of the floor. You'd really be helping me out." She sighs, again, and reluctantly gives in. The longest twenty minutes of my day spent looking for southern hospitality. I head back to the entrance where one of the delicate girls is waiting to give me the tour of Wickham House.

Bless her. She's giving you the full tour as if she were leading a hoard.

Spouting out her memorized Greek history, mispronouncing all the French words, but doing it with such charm and enthusiasm that I can't really be annoyed. To her I'm just this woman pretending not to be homeless, squish squishing across her prized, refurbished wooden floors. I interject moments of intelligent conversation, and walk as slowly and lightly as I can, but the gurgling of water shooting out the sides of my espadrilles is sounding more pained by the minute. At the end of the tour she shows me the back exit and quietly shuts the door on me. I'm not sure how worth it that all was, but the sun's out now.

Homemade lasagna and red wine. Yum. At the end of each day my not so stranger now strangers go around the table and ask each other what good thing has happened to them that day. They don't air their complaints, they focus on the one positive thing, the gem that makes them realize how worthwhile the day has been. I don't know how to pick. I feel

I've known these people all my life. I sit back in my chair and watch them listen to each other.

If I hadn't trusted and reached out into this little piece of unknown, strayed out of my comfort zone, I wouldn't have found the treasure that is Jerri, Doug and Toni. They are a surprise of remarkable giving. I don't feel out of place, or unwelcome at all. If anything, I feel more comfortable here than I have with some folk I've known a good while. There's no word to capture the thanks, love, kindness, support, and hospitality. It's that patch of blue sky you know is above the clouds.

Relationship Intuition Number Six: **The Dubois Friendship.** This is the accidental friendship birthed by the chance of saying yes to the kindness of strangers. Of picking up the puzzle piece and going on the hunt; following your instincts knowing it will lead to new and fresh alliances. It's in this openness and trust that those who are on the same journey will be revealed to you - those with the same kindness in their heart and searching in their soul.

When I get out of the shower early the next morning a piece of paper has been pushed under the doorway – it says, "Safe Trip. Hurry Back!" A long drive looms ahead to Rhode Island, but the memories of this one full day here with new friends lifts me all the way along the New Jersey Turnpike.

Fetal Water

I am not a human being, I am a human becoming
Anonymous

Growing up, whenever my parents went out, I was always afraid they'd die in a fiery crash and my brother and sister and I would be raised via the babycam hooked up to our neighbors in the apartment upstairs. I would watch them drive away from parking space fourteen and lie awake crying until the headlights shone into my bedroom window again. I expect the worst. I don't like this about myself but there you have it. I'm trying to grow out of it.

If there is a worse case scenario out there to be thought of, you're all over it.

When it comes to relationships though, that's something else - I imagine the best. My Rhode Island friends, James and Aiden's was one of the best and always would be, I thought. These two men were my dearest, closest friends fifteen years ago. We were in each other's pockets for years - at the theatre, me on stage with James, alongside Dianah, with Aiden Stage Managing. We lived in the same apartment complex, and they got me a good corporate job working with them that I of course later managed to get fired from. I was the wife they didn't need. I'd call them when I fell apart, to laugh, and when I needed to do laundry. They helped me search for my lost cat, Winifred Hazel who I think ran off with you, Cooper.

Yeah. She was a Russian Blue. When you picked her up for the first time you stepped in a pile of fire ants and got bitten all over your left foot.

Yes, I still have a small, white scar. What a funny thing to remember. I lost her right before they left. They'd asked me to move to Rhode Island with them. I didn't. We'd stay in touch, we'd visit, we'd write. You don't just let go of something like this. We could have written letters, and we did at first. They sent me photos of their new apartment, of "my room," and some of Rhode Island's finest propaganda leaflets. It all looked glorious and I should have bitten. At the very least I could have got on a plane, made an effort at some point - but I didn't. We didn't. In the fifteen years that passed we saw each other once, about a year after they left when they came back for a quick visit and we had dinner. I missed them, but I was distracted by the possibility that the new love I'd found with

Gregory would break the barrier, that I'd get it right. I couldn't see past it into anything else, anyone else, even them. It never crossed my mind that our friendship would disintegrate, that the move would be traumatic, that they would break. I don't want two Birthday cards. I want one with all *our* love and two signatures.

Some people naturally disappear. You just never expected it to be them.

They broke up five years after arriving, which is over twelve years ago now. I know of course, but I haven't seen it. People don't stand still, sometimes they move on while no one's watching. Out here because of the landscape flow, they're separated not only by land, but by water as well. I drive over bridge after bridge wondering which one separates the one from the other.

Probably the one with the toll.

Each of us had pulled out of parking spot fourteen and taken separate cars home.

I'll have to see them one at a time - *spend some time with Aiden and then move to James' for a spell* - a custody battle for my heart.

Once the watery air opens up into meadows and old rock walls, I feel calmer. What looks to be a piece of England leads me up the gravel driveway to Aiden, and his now husband Robert's house. He rushes down the path. The movement of our friendship connects under the rapid scrunching of the gravel beneath our feet.

This kind of hug won't come again, at least not until goodbye.

"We were hoping you would be another hour yet."

"Oh, thanks a lot." He's laughing.

"No, I didn't mean it like... ahh... the thing is the fridge is broken. I was hoping to have it all back together before you got here!" It's standing away from the wall in the middle of the kitchen, "I'm fixing it myself."

"How likely is that?" We keep on laughing in that way you do when you can't quite believe your luck. Childish giggling flashes images of us walking with James through that forest art exhibit...

Connemara.

Watching a theatre filling with dry ice smoke...

...the machine had fallen sideways,

...and half the audience and Dianah under the stage, bless her, were all chocking on it.

61

Packing Aiden's things in newspaper, preparing to move here. He gave you one of his grandmother's bowls.

I still have it. Now here we are fifteen years later standing in a fridgeless kitchen.

Robert takes my bags up to the spare room. It has a small area off of it much like an attic with a peak ceiling and slopping walls. They've set it up as a writing space for me. There's a chair over by the window with a bearskin throw seductively lying on an ottoman. It's perfect. Virginia Woolf would have been very jealous. Time and love has gone in to making this space, their space, into one that supports me.

I unpack and look out into a vast garden that reaches far beyond the thoughts of what I expected at this moment. I'm in half a heart grown whole.

While I hold up upstairs writing and fending off Virginia's ghost jealousy, Aiden works from home downstairs, while Robert's off denture making. For dinner the three of us sit outside in the crisp cool summer air with the bees. Aiden has three beehives at the back of his garden that he pinches about sixty pounds of honey off a year - honey I slather over any kind of bread I can find.

"I have a Johnny Depp story for you," he says.

"A Johnny Depp story?" I say with a little too much lilt to my voice from the bottomless red wine.

"It's more like the tale of the Aiden Taylors," Robert says.

"So I go into work not long after James and I moved here and my boss starts hounding me about how irresponsible I am to get thrown in jail and how disgusting it is that I'm an addict."

"Wait, you on drugs?"

"Right? So hold on - it turns out I have the same name as a local drug supplier, Aiden Taylor, who'd just been arrested. It takes some doing but I'm finally able to prove that it's not me. So fast forward a few years later and this girl calls up saying they're calling on behalf of Johnny Depp's request to find a cannon to shoot Hunter S. Thompson's ashes out of, and they were assured that I would, 'know how to procure one.'"

"What did you say?"

"I told them they needed the other Aiden Taylor." We all fold up into a laughter that breathes together and goes silent until it belts out again. It sinks through my shoes and into the souls of my feet. I love us in this garden.

Aiden does a lot of yoga. He does so much yoga that he's certified to teach it. I like to think I do yoga. I have the right book highlighted in all the right places, but I'm a wanna be Yogi. I don't hold up when faced with serious questions like, which mantras I prefer, what my chanting voice is like. It takes so much energy. If I'm asked I fain avoidance and go home and Google it for the return visit I know deep down I'm never going to make. But Aiden is the real thing - A Kundalini master, a Yogi. So sunrise yoga? Suuure.

Six-thirty am, the air is that perfect breeze you might think of only as being in heaven. The sea crashes gently towards me waking me even though I've been in motion for an hour. My mind is openish and somewhat quiet, and a lovely woman dressed all in white is reminding me that I can "choose the sounds" I want to hear. She sits crossed legged in a way that annoys me because I can't do it. "Remember to breathe," she says, which now because I'm aware of my breath becomes a problem and my mouth dries up. "Focus on that rhythm," she says. Shit. I'd best try allowing it, and stop thinking bad words. I'm so tired but I fake my through it to the second half of the morning which is a lesson in paddle boarding.

Anyone that knows me knows my lack of balance and athleticism, but I suck it up. I push the board into the water, kneel down on it, jump up and by some miracle I don't fall off. I actually paddle - albeit in circles most of the time drifting out to sea, but I'm on the thing. I feel miles from anywhere and I suppose I am miles from myself still, miles from anything that's mine.

Except me.

Going around in circles is so us, isn't it.

Well, it's so you.

I'm not sure I would have raised you to talk back.

Ha! I get to speak my own mind. An aborted perk.

Now that sickish sense of humor you definitely would have gotten from me.

The sea's so calm, the only ripples are happening inside of me. There's a lapping sound against the board and somewhere in the deep is your reflection...

...telling you it's alright to feel happy.

I'm shaken back when I see the husband of the yoga teacher waving his arms, yelling at me. I'm so far away from the shore I can't hear him, but I think that's rather the point of his distress. I panic that I'm in that place where sharks hang out to

pretend they don't know they're eating humans because on
surfboards we look like animals they usually eat. I hasten back
to the beach at top speed in a frenzied circling.

Although I was so far out to sea I probably could have
sailed on from Newport to Providence to see Aiden's lost
other half, James - I drive. James and I connected immediately
when we met during a production of Agatha Christie's,
Murder on the Nile. I played his wife. I got shot in the first act.
The director liked you so much he reincarnated you
in the second act.
Yes! He was wildly unconventional. I came back as my
own ghost, costumed in my wedding dress, a bullet hole
through my temple. I walked in slow motion across stage right
to clandestine music through stage fog reaching to my
murderous guilty husband while Dianah spoke eerily as my
voice from the great beyond. I looked forward to that every
night. Perhaps Agatha's bones turned in jealousy, but she
should have thought of it herself.
It was a production of Odet's, *The Big Knife* that brought
you in with Aiden, James and I, Cooper. The secret of the
character that I played is ours. Towards the end, the wife
confesses to her husband that she's had an abortion. I told
James and Aiden that there was a point on stage where I felt
unprotected. James could see you in my eyes, he said. I
revealed you. I lived what I had done right out in the open
where everyone could see us plain as day.
I held on to every moment of it.
It was a relief to feel the full impact it had on me. I told our
story four shows a week without a soul knowing. It was the
first time you came back to me, exposed. I allowed myself to
feel shame, and anger and frustration and regret and
bitterness.
And love.
And love, yes all the love I have for you.
A naked light.
Some nights I couldn't open my eyes. They were the only
witnesses.
My grandmother came to see almost every
performance.
She did, yes. I'd forgotten about that. Perhaps it was a time
we were both free to be with you.
It was in the next production that I met Gregory - the man
that was to be my circumference for the next sixteen years. It

64

was right before they moved. With all of these thoughts running through my mind I drive up to James' house and garden where he's gathered his closest friends together to meet me. He comes out of the kitchen in his apron, spatula in hand, laughing. I smile with every part of my face, eyes wide, watching him as long as I can before he sees me.

"How come you still look like that after all these years, and I look like this?" he says with a laugh and a never let me go again hug. I feel the gaping hole for the first time. I am completely aware that James & Aiden aren't, not anymore. These two men will never meet in the middle, sit at the same table and laugh about old times - not even for me.

Aiden told me that the break had been his fault.

"It's so long ago now, Sara. Not for you, but there was an unkindness. It became hard to live in the same house." Even Aiden's father had given his son a "what are doing to this man?" look in his eye. They disintegrated in sad isolation and an infidelity that destroyed any hope of them looking each other in the eye again. All these words coming out as he marinates the salmon. I grasp a hold of a glass of wine, trying to keep my composure so as not to spoil the party.

We eat out in their garden, the new and the old, fusing together inside the missing and the buzz, provincially surrounded by flowers, vegetables, compost and bees. An irony that James' new partner has taken up beekeeping. Each is happy with their other, their bees pollenating past each other.

On my first early morning walk at Aiden's I came across a cove by a waveless ocean. You can't hear the sea until you're almost in it. Here in James' spare bedroom loft I dream of our three figures walking hand in hand me in between them, skipping wistfully like they did in *Singing in the Rain*. The grownup part of me understands that I'm the only one this is rational for. It's not that the half is missing, but that the whole is gone.

I hand myself off like a broken latchkey kid, spending time with one and then the other. Kissing one goodbye and one hello, then the other goodbye and the first hello again. I don't want the story to end, but seeing Aiden with Robert, and James with Michael, it's clear that the story is still very much in tact. It's still a love story, one that comes from being in the right place with the right person. They are happy in their new relationships, while I carry on inside myself, but that's the nature of wanting something you can't have, isn't it.

After coming from James' back to Aiden's, I take a walk to my beach cove.

You kissed them both today and somehow that means they kissed each other.

I sit down with my journal, freezing water washing over my legs, and some sort of flying pebble creature crawling over my thighs, which normally I would have swatted away.

But you don't.

I write to them until my hand is sore.

There are times Ma, that love moves away from you. It doesn't mean that love is lost, or broken, *only that for a time you had to be without it -* perhaps to come to an understanding, to find my own way out. It is still, this love, and it waits for you to reclaim it in the awareness of all that it meant - all that it means.

One of those creatures is nibbling at the ink.

I tear the pages out of my journal and let them drift away on top of the sea. I watch the surf quietly washing the ink of our friendship. It bleeds into the water, blending us together. I think the creature went down with the ship.

Relationship Intuition Number Seven: **The Shape Shifter Friendship**. This friendship has moved on while you weren't looking. It is one in which a couple has separated, moved on, and found happiness with another. It catches you by surprise and flings you backwards. It expands your friendships and involves a period of mourning and readjustment. It cradles you in love from the past, into the present.

As I walk back up to the house there are three birds sitting on the lawn in a perfect triangle. We blink together once before they fly off, all in different directions. The sand in my shoes digs miniscule holes into my soles and I cry my eyes out, walking and smiling.

And then you have to go to a party.

I've never been to a tea party before, not a gay tea party at any rate.

It don't take no Kojak to realize that there won't be any actual tea served in Royal Dalton with scones and cream though.

I think it'll be, well, I don't really know. Some friends of Aiden's who live down the road in an affluent area of Portsmouth are having a get together to celebrate the remodeling and now selling of their multi-million-dollar home. Aiden and husband are invited, and by neighborly goodness, so am I.

I'm not in any mood for a party, but in the same light I've never been in such a perfect place to get trashed.

I wish you hadn't drowned the letter.

That was so stupid. I should have kept it. Why didn't I keep it? I'll get messed up, sit in a quiet corner with a champagne flute dangling from my wrist, stare at priceless art and slowly melt into a well-upholstered Italian leather couch covered in silk Parisian cushions. That's my vision of the evening anyhow.

Or read a book. You always go off by yourself and manage to find a book to read.

Walking in, it all looks on the up and up - normally dressed people in their finery – lots of blue and white stripped dresses for some reason – men circulating with drinks on trays – handsome, young, nubile young men with drinks on trays that look so much like a dancing chorus from *Hello Dolly* you expect them to step in time at any minute. I find it so annoying when a man is prettier than I am. It makes me wish I could grow a penis, a really big one, and give him a taste of his own medicine. I'm not in any mood for a pert fucking Dolly Levi in drag, I guess that's what I'm saying.

I hadn't expected to see so many women here either – I'm not sure why. I think the only reason I notice it is because they keep looking at me, and it's making me self-conscious. I look nice. I mean I look nice in my way. A simple long grey dress that falls down passed my feet and gathers like oversized curtains do. I think it's cool. I made sure to put a slip on underneath.

Mostly because when you looked in the mirror you could hear your mother's voice saying, "you know everyone can see right through that, don't you?"

I whipped off my bra though, threw it on the bed, lonely and empty. I told myself it's because I couldn't stand all the different strap marks.

But the truth is you wanted to go against your mother's voice.

I know, get over it. I had to put on my granny underwear to avoid panty lines, but I know these women aren't staring at that. I put boots on because it just looks cooler and I don't want to get mosquito bites – those bastards eat me like they're storing up for some sort of donor program.

I ignore the beards, pick up a glass of something cool, white and crisp, and stroll across the wet grass to the pool house. There aren't many people down here yet. At each corner of the pool they've set up a neon colored glowing sort of box thingamajiggy. On top of each one of them is a twenty-year old ripped young man in a speedo gyrating to guttural dance sounds. In the middle of the pool there's a lone girl clad only in fish net tights and a bra doing synchronized swimming moves. I wish I'm her.

I don't know anybody outside of Aiden, Robert and one of their friends, so as they circulate I cling on like one of those tiny grub fish that won't leave whales alone. I watch the sun get lower and pulse by while the other hundred or so guests migrate down towards me while the music's being set up. For a moment there is quiet as the most gorgeous African American drag singer I have ever seen steps out from the poolroom. She's way more beautiful than me and I don't even care. For the next hour she belts out Aretha, Whitney and every popular classic you can imagine, while the boys do their sultry cube top dances and the mermaid swims.

My ears prick up at "Dancing Queen." There's something about that song that makes me think I can fly. I look over at Aiden, grab his hand and lead him to the top of the pool. Standing at the edge, the empty water glistens like a million tiny mirrors. The Mermaid's gone on break. This is the emptiest open invitation I've ever felt.

"Let's go in," I semi shout to Aiden over the drag singer.

"Are we allowed?"

"It's a pool party, of course we're allowed in." I look into his eyes and he looks back at me with a moment of not knowing, whereas I've already taken off my boots. "You know what? I'll never see any of these people again for the rest of my life. Pretend you're not with me. I'm going in." I pull back the straps on my grey shimmery dress letting it fall to the floor. I feel unattached, isolated from what's going on around me.

You go back into water.

So a tiny piece of white satin and I walk down beautiful, gradated marble steps and into the water.

I summersault under. My ears go cloudy. A muffled sound cuts me off from everyone. I feel like an animal. I don't care where I am or who's watching me breathe something else. I may even need the witnessing. All those years of allowing hits to my psyche, the personal silences, not speaking up when—

I see you, Ma.

—I should have said, fuck you. The tears in lonely apartments, flesh ripped un-naturally, an endless soul mate wait, a fucked up plan B, too late for this, too early for that, no sense, no right place at the right time, no shit – all of this swims with me to the bottom of the pool. I ram it head on into even the smallest crevices. None of this stuff's going back up. If it makes its way in to the drains to find air again, the killing of small patches of perfectly manicured lawn will be its final rest.

I'm holding your hair back with your pruned baby hands *so you can rest your cheek* against the blue green base of the pool. I turn my head up towards the wavy surface, to muted faces and muffled music as *letters float by your right elbow* like a child's plastic toys, spelling something I've already written in salt water. The flying pebble sea creature swims frantically by my right shoulder, the letter I wrote this morning between its teeth. I grab at it, pushing with all my might through water that the heaviness of God's backhand is forcing against me, but it disintegrates in half, and in half again and again and again. The ink words leak off whole and intravenously spread inside my skin like a tattoo, finding their way inside the blue scar on the palm of my left hand where the dirt stayed that I fell in that summer when I was six years old – *that my grandmother never washed away.* My back is to the surface floating up and away from the mirage and the chinks corked with our DNA.

You need to breathe.

My head shakes in a panic trying to find more oxygen inside to feed off. It straightens my body into an arrows firing to the surface, splitting the water open for air. Up above, eyes closed, my ears under the water, I float. And all at once I'm being cradled.

A man's ebony arms scoop you into him and he twirls you around in this new soup.

I'm moving at the same speed as the North Star over my head. When he lets me go I'm still, suspended like a lily pad, and I feel love, perhaps even happiness, certainly the balance of imperfect pleasure.

Aiden takes my picture as I walk back up the steps. There's applause and laughter and smiling faces. As I hug him people behind us begin to fall into the water with all of their clothes on. It's you, me, and the singing drag queen, Cooper, standing on the sideline watching this mass of wet happy people in complete embrace of navy and white horizontal stripes and rented diamond jewels splashing in the soggy disintegrating pages of you and I, of James, and Aiden, of all of us. We both step over the grass through the wet and the electricity.

Aiden's brother-in-law walks in late with a slight out of body "please don't tell me my wife's in that pool with her new diamond earrings on" look on his face.

"I've been swimming," I say, not really knowing how to introduce myself again, tits up in my Bridget Jones' nightmare underwear.

"Yes, I can see that," he says, not taking his eyes off my breasts. *A wet, white satin slip doesn't hide a whole lot.* "How many of these have you had?" A *Hello Dolly* waiter pushes a silver platter of little glasses filled with some sort of green Jello magic in front of us. I've only had my glass of crisp white. I'm completely sober. I look up at all those stars that'll explode one day and I'm so relieved that mine detonated inside a clear head. I swallow a shot of green down whole.

That night I write into the early hours; *pulling the words out of the sea.* There's this giant elephant roaming around no man's land and I'm feeding it. I don't know if it's of value to either of them anymore but I send what I've written to James and Aiden anyway. I have to say what's been waiting for me here.

In the morning after I hit "send" I run away to the store and hide. Later as I pull back into the driveway at Aiden's my phone dings. I stay in the car. It's an e-mail from James:

> It made me sad. I am so happy to see you...
> you really have no idea how much, and just
> like you I miss the time the 3 of us spent
> together and can completely understand how
> you feel. So many things in life don't turn out
> the way we want or expect. But now I can't
> imagine being anywhere else. I am so happy
> and I am glad you are happy that I am happy
> but I also understand the loss you're feeling.

He ends "with love."
Love and loss - one catches up to the other in the end.

As I walk into Aiden's house I see him out the corner of my eye. I can tell he's read what I've written as well. He's sitting quietly, his hands folded in front of him, looking off into the garden. As I head around the corner Robert starts talking about the bees, so I stand in the kitchen looking out at the homegrown lettuce and tomatoes trying not to water myself before making an excuse to go upstairs to wait for the next ding. What if it's upset him? I should go…

A text.

> When you walked in from your grocery trip I was at a loss for spoken words. It is a poignant story for me and I certainly began to feel it even as you drove up last week. It's what was building in my mind. I certainly have relived a lot of moments with James over the past few days and especially so during the last 24 hours. It's a little like that rogue wave I told you about yesterday - you don't see it coming and it hits you - but its impact was bigger than I expected. It knocked me off my balance. You've thrown the lifeline and I am better and joyful knowing that James and I are whole again although living separate lives with different people.

I walk downstairs and over to his desk where he's working. I stand by him so he has to stop typing. He looks up. His breath catches in his throat as he stands up and holds me. "Thank you," he says. His tears drip onto my neck, as mine roll down his, splashing out the discoloration of the past twelve years. It's an evolution of love finding a new way out. All the words between us allow the three of us a moment to be as hand in hand as we'll ever be – the sun setting over bees and honey, in two gardens.

Sifting the Northeast

What may appear as coincidences are not coincidences at all
but simply the working out of the patterns
which you started with your own weaving.
- Claude Bristol

The night before taking myself off to New York for a
Norman Mailer writing workshop I go to see James in a play.
"He's grown so much as an actor… wait until you see him,"
Aiden said. He's never given up on seeing James perform.

On the way to the train station the next morning I mention
this to James, who nods his head quietly inside. He can feel
him out there in the audience. He doesn't mind. There is an
acceptance there between the two of them that as long as it
doesn't cross the curtain, it's a way of allowing what's left to
remain.

"He's right, you know," I say as he kisses me on the cheek
at the station, "you have a gift up there."

As the train rounds to the city, Manhattan appears like
Gotham and Batman isn't real. It's a frenzied, crowded
Stonehenge of a place. Outside the station I stand in honking
traffic clutching my hand luggage like it's my umbilical cord
and wait for Kong to wade out the water and carry me off. It'll
be cheaper than a cab at any rate.

I think your pupils have dilated.

Lenore's coming in a bit later on. She and I had both won
Norman Mailer scholarships and met at his home for the class
in Provincetown. We were thrown together as roommates,
which is typically a bit iffy - you don't know what you're
going to get in those situations, but we fit hand in glove from
the start.

Being awarded our second Mailer scholarship we meet
again here to study at Mailer's brownstone in Brooklyn
Heights. I check into my provided student housing on Clark
Street and go up to our room. There are two single beds, each
not quite the length of my body, with a sheet, a blanket, a
towel and a washcloth folded in a pile at the bottom of it. A bit
minimum-security prisonish. As the door slams behind me,
narrowly missing my suitcase, I check it to make sure it opens
from both sides.

I peer out my ninth floor window into a space outside my comfort zone. Looks safe enough – women and small children are on the street, no one getting shot at the moment. I take the small, shaky, plastic elevator down and ask the texting teenager at the front desk the way to the ocean. She pauses her typing and looks up with a very confused look on her face. The other girl rolls her eyes saying, "She means the East River." The East River, isn't that where mafia types throw the bodies of snitches and such? I'm to take a right outside the building.

Pop some gum in your mouth, it always makes you feel more confident.

Straight down Henry Street I bump into the river.

Even with your lack of direction it's hard to miss, Ma.

All of New York is right there across the water as if out of the movies: the Empire State Building, the new Freedom Tower, the Statue of Liberty; there are pieces of pink sky, children laughing, young film students fussing over the sunset, old men smoking, boatmen waving, and lovers holding hands. The oncoming rain spits on all of us, and we let it stick.

After class the next morning Lenore and I decide to take on the subway and climb the Empire State Building. We're each other's wingman. We should start our own club. There are two ticket tellers working who only seem interested in speaking to each other. I stand in the line and channel DeNiro.

Which for you comes out more like Woody Allen.

We are to take the 2 or the 3 train. How easy is that?

"But my computers down, you'll have to get the tickets from the machine." The machine? What machine? I have to use a machine? I begin to sweat that my dollar bills won't be crisp enough to satisfy it, but as it turns out New York subway machines eat any kind of money you have. Two tickets purchased - derailment of confidence averted.

We take the kind of elevator my mother always told me never to take, down to the tracks. Either train, right? Too easy, my friend – too good to be true. Did these subway tellers see us coming – it has to be some sort of virgin subway rider joke. I ask another friendly New Yorker what to do. "Get on either train the 2 or the 3," she says. Well, they can't all be in on this.

The 3 train rushes by with a lovely well-needed breeze and we get on it without question, like natives. Towards the other end of the carriage I notice a map. As the ride is going smoothly, no sign of any knife wielding gang members or anything, we get up and walk over to see how many stops we have until we get to 34ᵗʰ street.

"It's eight stops... wait, where did we get on?" Lenore asks.

"It's eight stops in the other direction, isn't it? Bastards. 'Take either train, they'll both get you there.'"

"Only if you get on the thing going in the right direction. We'll have to get off at the next stop and figure it out," Lenore says. So off we step, minding the yellow line. I'm really wishing I had some gum at this point.

"Atlantic Ave, does that mean anything to you?" I think I recognize the name from the Monopoly board. How much did it cost to buy that property... was it a cheap one in a bad area, or one of the expensive ones?

No those were the blue ones, Boardwalk and...

No Atlantic was red, wasn't it?

Middle of the road, right?

Yes, the junky ones were the brown ones...

...or light blue?

Were they light blue? Ahhh, shut up, shut up, shut up. Think rationally, this is surely so simple.

"There are only letter trains - D, B, F, N. What does that stand for - Dodge Bullets For Now?" Lenore laughs. A little. We are numbers tourists. What a muddle. "Where do these letter trains go anyway? These street names may as well be written in Sanskrit. Does a ticket on a number train work on a letter train?"

"Wait here's a sign for the 2 and 3 trains."

"Yeah, but they both only go in the wrong direction." I glance back at the Sanskrit and 42ⁿᵈ St/Grand Central Station, pops out at me. Finally somewhere that sounds familiar - I've seen the musical and the flash mob video. As we hop aboard we check the map immediately to make sure we're going in the right direction. As we do the train stops. The voice over the PA system speaking in garbled who knows what says, "Kshckookshhhhh another train hshckkashooshsa."

"Another train, what about another train? You can barely fit one train down here, how could there be another one?" Wing man Lenore shrugs and doesn't seem worried.

No one else is either.

What is wrong with these people?

Twelve stops and fifteen minutes later we disembark at Grand Central Station - alive. We emerge onto the streets of

New York without a clue of where we are – a bit like that moment in *Being John Malkovich* when they're expelled from his body. We walk aimlessly in this giant's maze, eyes peeled for a tall building like the Empire State one. It's hard to see with all the other big buildings in the way.

But there she is.

We take the tiny, ancient elevator to the first level. Having been sardined in with fifteen sweaty people, we take the stairs the rest of the way. I wish people would be honest about their ability to climb stairs. I wonder if I can still figure out how to administer mouth to mouth.

Get ahead of them so you don't have to.

It's raining. Blustery. I lean into the stone and look further up into the sky.

You can fall hopelessly in love now.

How to find our way home?

Let the rain hit your face. Someone out there is waiting to love you.

The following morning a yoga class seems like a good idea. If I'm going to embrace this yoga thing, I actually need to do it. Lenore is really good at it. She finds a class for us while I take a quick shower, drop the shampoo bottle on my little toe, shit, fuck, that hurt, but Om it out, as you do, limp with dripping hair into my "I look like I do yoga" workout clothes, and grab a banana before we head out.

At the beginning of class, the teacher sets an intention for us, "Wisdom." I Om some of that by twisting my body into an infinity sign as far as I can, then eat oatmeal with all the bad stuff in it before we head back to our class.

In Provincetown during that week of intensive writing I was instilled with a new respect and routine for writing, and that's all due to Lenore. We had our own room we could retreat to in our apartment. Lenore didn't surface as much as I did. She stayed chained to the thread of writing with more commitment and consistency. I could see the sea from the living room window, and were it not for Lenore I might have allowed more than a toe of my time to be swallowed up there. When I'm around her I syphon the energy she writes with and my work becomes clearer - without knowing, she makes me better at what I love to do most. It's a fortunate thing, Cooper, to find someone that sees the same value in the same passion, and whose opinion you respect and willingly listen to. She is a wife, mother, and a full-time teacher. The writer fragment piece of herself she fits in the cracks, getting up at dawn every day to write. If we did have a club I'd just take the minutes.

Relationship Intuition Number Eight: **The Totem Friendship.** They say each of us has a Totem or Spirit that guides us, to draw our purpose and meaning from. This is she. This friendship is the door that opens you to your quiet mind. It steps inside your reason with verve and intensity and becomes an example to follow. She just might be the muse in the room, the genius inside the wall that makes you sit up and take note of yourself, to consciously listen to what you have to say and make your voice clearer. The Totem jumps inside your own skin with a sharper sense of understanding.

The Mailer class ends as quickly as it began and Lenore takes a cab to the airport leaving me on my own to figure things out. I've pre-arranged to stay with Trudy, a friend of The Mustard Empress who lives on the Upper East Side, wherever that is. I know it's on the other side of the bridge, inside the Manhattan I've been staring into every night at the edge of the water. The taxi driver, who has what appears to be thirty years worth of used air fresheners that I first take to be rattraps in the back of his cab, asks me the quickest way there. This does not instill confidence.

Two almost accidents and three altercations with fellow drivers later, we pull up outside Trudy's apartment. She's put a blow-up mattress in her office area for me, turned down the bed and put a mint on my pillow as my smartass e-mail response to hers jokingly suggested. I like her. We talk of 9/11. She was in the building behind the World Trade that, although badly damaged, didn't fall. Every day, over the years she watched as ground zero went from the silent removal of remains, to a space clear of debris, to a new building that once again blocked her view of the water. It was nice, she says, to have been able to see the river, but it came at such a price. It was difficult to look out into it at all. I tell her that I plan on going to the memorial, and ask if she would like to come. "I'm not ready to see what's not there," she says. Not ready to see what's *not* there.

Not able to stand on what's gone.

I'm going for Aiden. I promised him I would find his cousin, Richard Rescorla's name and whisper a quiet prayer for him. He died in the south tower when it collapsed. I head down to the site the next morning. Marie, the roaming choreographer has now arrived coincidently in New York at the same time. We decide to meet there, so I order a cab that says it can get me there for $20. A bargain.

"The 9/11 memorial, please."

"Where?"

"The 9/11 memorial. Freedom Tower." Blank stare back. "Where the World Trade Center used to be." More blank stares. "Ground Zero?"

"No, I don't know. You have address?"

Does Ground Zero have an address?

Luckily Marie and I had made arrangements to meet at the corner of Liberty & Greenwich so I tell him that's where I want to go.

"You've never heard of the memorial for 9/11?" I ask again.

"No. I need address." He hands me his GPS and asks me to enter in a location. Seriously dude? Put a GPS in your car and you're a cab driver these days.

We pull up by the sign that clearly says, "9/11 Memorial." I hand him a twenty and point to the sign for his future reference. He looks confused. I tip myself.

You've only been to New York three times and each time this site's transformed. It was intact in 1985, wire mesh surrounded the rubble in 2005, and today names lie down in DNA water. *I see why Trudy can't be in this place.* I feel like I'm trespassing. The spire on the Freedom Tower strains, a crystal tear sparkles as it balances on its head like an unblinkable open eye.

Aiden never met his cousin, Richard, did he?

No. When he was back in England in 2002 he decided to try to look him up.

He started at his grandmother's old house.

As he was taking a picture of it his camera battery died. He went into one of the local shops to get a new one, and while he was in there he asked the shopkeeper if he knew his cousin, to see if they still lived in the area.

The man looked perplexed and pointed to the guy standing at the counter smoking.

"You need to talk to him," he said. The man turned out to be Rick's best friend.

"Do you know where I can find him?"

"You'd best come with me," he said and led him to a graveyard and to a memorial erected in Rick's name. He'd moved to New York years before, and was working as the security director for Morgan Stanley at the time of 9/11.

He'd told everyone from the company to get out of the building after the first plane hit the north tower.

Two thousand six hundred and eighty-seven Morgan Stanley employees were successfully evacuated because of his actions.

He was still going from floor to floor to other companies when the tower collapsed.

He survived the atrocities of Vietnam to meet the enemy on his own land and save 2,687 people. Aiden was a year too late. He came to know his cousin's life through his death. So there's the magic, Cooper - if his camera battery hadn't died he wouldn't have gone into that shop where Rick's friend waited for him, and he would never have known him at all. Sometimes these momentary chance happenings, of looking over your shoulder at the last minute to catch someone's eye, of no rush hour traffic on a Friday afternoon on your way to the airport that gives you the extra five minutes to bump into someone whose plane's been delayed just that many - it alters the course of your heart, and the direction of your path. Down here it's the way I trust. I don't take the car to the mechanic's to get the airbag light fixed because I know there's nothing wrong with it - that you'll fix it when this journey's over. I'm as sure of that as I am that the battery was put in Aiden's camera at the right point in time so it would fail in front of his grandmother's house, giving me a reason to take this journey and stand at ground zero for him because of it.

I type Rick's name into the machine and a piece of paper pops out. I wasn't expecting to see his picture – but here we are face to face: Rick Rescorla, S46. His name is etched into the Southern well. I run my fingers across it to trace the way it feels, thick and hollow around a negative space that bounces water back up at you.

I hear it before I see it.

Yes, it's the weight that's alive, isn't it. Any peace that exists here is not without a price. It's an unrecoverable burial site carved out of crashing smoke, dark sorrow, falling cries and flames and terror and fear. None of it can ever truly wash away. *Each one of the Wells is completely different from the other.* The South Well has a still calm about it - the water rushes down and you can see a sort of secret entryway where the water catches on a jagged corner and rolls off. The North Well is noise and confusion where the wind moves the water into an expressive mass. It sweeps sideways, aggressively rotating itself into the pool with the sound of shattering glass streaming *down into something sacred with no seeming end*. Wells in a cathedral - the source of holy water. For all the efforts to cleanse it and move on - it stands still.

The taxi ride with Marie up to Washington Heights is a quiet one. I don't suppose it's something you can talk about - being there. Not initially. My mind's busy inside itself and so is hers. We simply look at each other processing the same thoughts. My eyes focus on trees, and the color green.

With me in between.

It's perfect timing to see Luke and Cindy Jackie today. They've offered to have a reunion party at their house and invited some other folks from our class who relocated to New York that we haven't seen for the last twenty-four years. Sweet. I went to UT Austin with them. Cindy Jackie and I were in the same acting core classes, *and Luke was the year behind you with Pooka William.*

Yes, yes, I know that. And Cindy Jackie isn't her real name. *Obviously, that would be ridiculous.* When we met her name was Cindy. She changed it to Jackie when she joined Actor's Equity.

Cindy never felt right to her anyway, she said.

I have to put the two together to make it easier to keep track of her. No longer Cindy and I share an erect secret from an acting assignment. We did a scene with a dead man who was supposed to be on stage with us so we created a dummy, as you do. The scene itself must have revolved around his "bits and pieces, as my grandma would say, so we made those too. Penis construction was a serious business for us. For the skin we used stockings – I had a pair with one…

Oh, so embarrassing.

No, no, listen. I had a pair with one fuchsia pink leg, and one pale pink leg so we cut those up. Once we came to an agreement on size we shoved some toilet paper in it, then made one pale pink hangy bit and one fuchsia one, separated them through the middle with twine and yanked them up to attach them. Glorious. At the end of the scene we dismembered the body and split our creation between us: she took the penis and I guarded the hangy bits.

"I can't find my penis. I lost it in all the moving around."

"What? Well that sorta kinda pisses me off a bit. How do you misplace a penis? I don't understand that, I don't. I really don't."

"I have to say, you look exactly the same, and it's freakin' me out, man," Cindy Jackie says shaking her head and opening a bottle of red wine. I suck in my stomach.

"Me? You've stopped time. Look at that outfit." She worked retail all the way through college. When she checked people out her catch phrase was, "would you like some socks to go with that?" She said it in a sort of valley girl lilt that almost always landed her a sale.

You bought a hat from her once and still ended up with a pair.

She doesn't need a fake fuchsia penis though. Surviving in New York with her company, Manhattan Theatre Source, she's grown one of her own. She was always strong, with the kind of strength I drift off to sleep wishing I had.

She and Luke are the couple that Elspeth was talking about in Austin.

They found each other again a few years ago and fell madly in love. Like in the movies. It takes a minute to balance out seeing them together, quietly snuggling on their opium sofa together. It seems silly that it wasn't there all along.

Someone's reaching to look at you that way. True love doesn't break eye contact.

There's no negative space between them.

Luke's very cool.

We didn't make genitalia together - our glue was poetry and writing. We wrote letters to each other about love and all the mixed up feelings that struggled inside us, and the characters we played. Never any hesitancy between us, hearts in ink. They weren't love letters, but a kind of love nonetheless. We had the sort of friendship that let us exist in whatever silly state we were in; one that didn't judge or twist us up into something we didn't recognize anymore. We supported each other. Being with him I felt safe when I looked into that place where becoming an adult loomed and lured me away into unsureness. I was never an easy nut to crack, so when he stepped in front of me accepting my shadow and all the rest, I looked back. Shifting became easier. I wish I'd been aware enough to say, thank you.

For my party a plan is hatched. We receive our guests between 6:30pm and 9:00pm, serve nibbles and alcohol, and after they've left we'll retire to a steak dinner of our own.

"Do you think they'll bring the baby?" Luke says as a child's cry comes from behind the doorbell.

They brought the baby.

In walks Tania, with her husband, baby son and a brash exuberant energy that hasn't changed a bit.

She tried to teach you to sing at school, bless her.

When Amanda McBroom came to UT to teach a singing class we had to prepare a song and I hadn't a clue. I can't sing my way out of a paper bag. She brought in her big book of songs for me and we sat down at the piano. There must have been a couple hundred songs in there, and the only one it turns out I can sing a little better than half ass is "Tip Toe Through the Tulips."

Now that is embarrassing.

Hour after hour she banged away on the keys as I tried as hard as I could to put a little Bernadette Peters into the tulip song.

Ma, I have to say it was hard to watch. The look that washed over your face when you realized that not only did you have to sell your voice, but that silly song on top of it all.

The horror. I should have done what my friend, Jim did and gone for comedy. When you don't do something well, make them laugh.

Fran arrives midway through the laughter with the same hyper nonstop energy. She's uber interesting. She learned Chinese, made movies over there, traveled to the deserts in India and works as an actor in New York. What have I done? I mean what have I really done so far? All these people are so vibrant. Where have I been hiding?

Let it stay simple - enjoy the people around you.

Luke and I sit outside. He wants to escape the energy - I want to understand it. It's after 1:00am when the bubble of company flies off to catch the A train.

"Well, damn it, I want my steak, and I'm going to have it!" Luke opens the fridge and another bottle of red seems to uncork itself. The three of us talk and eat until we fade off to bed at 5:00am savoring the most out of every word, and every bite.

When we wake up later in the day, Cindy Jackie and I walk the streets of Washington Heights to the park and around the monastery. I'm tired and mopey.

You're turning in on yourself.

Well, everyone had so many interesting things to say about their careers and babies and exotic experiences. My life is a list of almosts. I just sat there listening.

Isn't that what you're here for?

I know, but...

What?

I let the fear win. Last night I saw exactly how empty I'd made myself without you. I mean, felt it in such a way that I understood it. And do you want to know what the worst part of it all was? I felt a sick validation - mission accomplished. I achieved exactly what I set out to do. My voice vanished with you.

Well, you can't have a voice if you don't take responsibility for not using it. And you are, Ma. Look, you're standing here in one state looking across the river into the eyes of another one. It's only water that separates them. You created a sense of urgency in you that brought you here. Be thankful.

Yes at least for that.

This is more than just the first note.

I should step outside of myself for a minute.

If that's what it takes to hear it, yes.

That afternoon Luke and I leave Cindy Jackie waving on the curb as we split a cab into town. I've arranged to meet our old classmate Ethan downtown. In the car I'm bloated with so many preoccupations. So much to say but I'm a mute. I want to tell Luke that the supportive love we had for one another all those years ago meant more than he could imagine. That in a time of so much self-doubt he filled a space I never thought light would go into again.

He already knows.

That I remember him playing the piano for me.

Walking in the rain with him.

Listening to him on stage under the maze of a set for *Measure for Measure* in those shaky parts he thought our voice teacher was sure to notice.

And then reassuring him. What makes you think he's not had those thoughts grazing as well?

All I end up doing is looking into his face and smiling while he tells me stories of the haunted hospital across the river, and the garden on top of the freeway. There's a moment when he stops talking and we look at each other for just a minute, and I see we haven't vanished after all. As I take a breath to speak the car pulls over to let me out.

Standing on 53ʳᵈ I can see Ethan over Luke's right shoulder as I hug him goodbye. I take a hold of his arms in my hands and I see happiness in his eyes. I hope he sees my happiness for him in mine. He waves at Ethan, but he's looking away. When the car pulls out I'm waving goodbye to one, as I am hello to the other. How odd to be standing in the middle of Manhattan in a triangle with two people that used to be tightly threaded together - almost back in the same corner again.

Initially there's something unrecognizable about Ethan. "I hope this is okay. Would you like to perhaps get a slice of pizza?" Would I perhaps like... what? Who are you?
He is the suit of corporate America.
This is no good.
"So, I rode up here with Luke and he and I were waving away at you, but your eyes looked everywhere except at us!"
"Oh, no I hate that. Luke. Man I wish... man. You know, he's the reason I had the courage to move to New York City."
Finally, that splendid boyish grin on his face.
"Really? How did he do that?"
"Well, you know I was supposed to move to LA to live with Mickey, and about a month before I was supposed to move, he disappeared. I couldn't reach him."
"That doesn't sound like him. You two were joined at the hip."
"I know, I know. The only thing I could think of is that not long after that, he came out. I wondered if he hadn't known how to tell me. You know, he had a new life there, new friends... and then of course I started second guessing myself – had I made any homophobic jokes unintentionally - given off some bad vibe? We used to joke all the time, you know. But I've talked to him since then and it's all good."
"Good, I'm glad. You were so close."
"Yeah, and I ended up in New York and somehow got a hold of Luke and he showed me around. It was so nice of him, showing me all the places to go, what to do and what not to do. And you know, I thought, dammit if he can do this, so can I. So this is where I met my wife, had my kids and it's all due to Luke. I've found so much here. God, I wish I'd looked up and seen him."
"Well I have his contact information, and you two do live in the same city. It's not like you need me to share a cab to get together!"
"Yeah, it's strange isn't it how we've lived in this city for so long, not too far apart... opposite ends of Manhattan, but still... so, yes, I need to do that. I will do that."

We grin our way through the fact that we're sitting across the table from one another.

It's like you've suddenly been transported from twenty years ago into the future.

Yes, it feels like it's happened that fast. As if we're glimpsing from the past into where we might be.

Time is a strange partner.

"So how can you do this? I mean quit your job, and just... do this."

"I got to a point where I couldn't continue on as I was."

"Yes, I know that feeling. I do. This job, it just isn't what I want. I'm where you were in a sense, but I have a wife and a family that are accustomed to certain things - so am I. There is that."

"Well, yeah, you have more to consider. I don't have anyone else in my life that relies on me. You don't have to let go of everything though, just the part that's not fulfilling you. I don't think what gratifies you can come in until you've let go of what isn't. And let go isn't the right way to say it. It's more about listening. Listening to yourself. We don't listen enough, not to ourselves, anyway. When

Lost in static.

something feels off – it is."

"I want to have a creative link. There must be a way that I can use the skills I have and contribute. I'm not doing that. We live in a great neighborhood - my kids have access to the best theatre in the country. It's me, my 9-5 living."

"You know what you don't want. That's bigger than you think. Plus you know what you do want. You feel that urgency in you. That's what's already creating the life you want. It'll find you."

"Yeah, yes, it will. You're doing it. I can do it. This is good. This is good. I'm so glad you're here."

Do you still feel hollow?

A little boy's toy rolls by our table. I catch it in my palm and as I put it back in his hand he keeps his eyes on me. His footing is unsure and he sways a little before teetering back to his mother's clapping hands.

"We had a son who died," Ethan says, watching the child run off. He says it so quickly that I

Please don't make this about us.

thought he said, "you had a son who died."

"He was born with a heart defect. He passed away during the surgery to correct it."

84

"I'm so sorry." His love for him smiles in his eyes.

"I just wanted you to know him as well. He's a part of my family. He's buried upstate. We go every year, my four girls and I. We lay flowers. His name is Austin."

"Austin. That's beautiful."

"Thank you. Yes, it's perfect, actually. That place was so special to me, so I gave it to my son." As we get up to leave I notice a mural half painted behind us. It's a string of purple people reaching out to each other surrounded by large green hands - one larger figure above them hovers like an umbrella connecting them all together. We hug together underneath it and head to the door. Ethan walks back down 53rd with his son on his mind, as I walk up Lexington with mine.

The next morning after saying my fond farewell to Trudy for letting me crash, I take a cab over to the nightmare that is Penn Station. Providence James is waiting for me on the other side of it.

"Honey, you're home!" I hug him and his happy face with every New York emotion and eye I've looked into, and wonder if he can tell. We stay up late, talk and drink and rinse repeat until the next morning when we say goodbye. The hangover makes it foggy with a potential that it's not what it is. I've just got used to his face looking at mine the way he used to. I hold it in my hands, soft with a small patch of red where he cut himself shaving, and I tell him that I love him; that I'll come again. I'm not far away. I can come again.

I drive back to Aiden's for the next goodbye. I'm not far away. I'll come again.

It's up to you to feed it with phone calls and flesh.

"Did you tell her you almost died while she was away? Did you tell her about the bees?" Robert says as I pour our first glass of red.

"What?? What about the bees?"

"They went after Aiden."

"Yeah, I got cocky." Aiden is deliberately not looking at Robert who is deliberately looking at him. "I didn't suit up, didn't zip my hat down. I didn't even bother to wear the pants. It was my fault. I could tell that the one hive was edgy and being aggressive, but I went in anyway... and they came at me - hundreds of them chasing me. They got in my suit, up my trousers, in my shirt, stinging me all over. I ran inside the house as fast as I could and stood in that entryway and locked myself in to get rid of the ones on me. I could hardly breath - I'd been stung so many times my body was filling up with poison. I keep an EpiPen in the cupboard so I grabbed it and stabbed myself."

"If it wasn't for that he'd be dead. Married a few weeks and almost a widow."

"Why did they turn on you like that?"

"They didn't turn on me. I knew better. I didn't take precautions."

"You know, one bee sting can kill him now."

"No - well yes it could, I mean... my immunity is down now. I have to be careful."

"I'm not sure how much longer I feel safe having those bees here." Eye roll from Aiden, eyes to the ground, more wine is poured.

"They gave him a Benadryl shot at the hospital, that's all they could do."

"When we came back I got into bed and didn't wake up until the following morning!"

"You were lucky." Robert's final stamp of opinion.

"I guess the bees didn't care if you were trying to give them room to make more honey. You're just a thief in the night with your britches down." He sorta smiles.

"It was frightening. You have to respect them, and I do. I will."

Aiden and I stay up late to watch the predicted mass of shooting stars. He's looking for something else though. I can see it in his eyes when he's not speaking. The job he has, that sucks the life out of him, is in the best place it'll ever be: working from home in a room with a view of his marvelous garden and attack bees. There is no improving on it. This is the end of the road for making ice into water.

Look up - underneath the bathroom window.
There's a small patch of white paint about two feet wide in the middle of all the yellow on the side of the house.

"Why did you leave that part of your house unpainted?"

"Oh, it hasn't been treated yet. I can't paint it."

"But it's so small. Why did you stop there? That would drive me crazy."

"Huh. I don't know. The snow got here too fast, I guess."

"It's a kind of a metaphor, don't you think?"

"For what?"

"For you in this casa paradiso. It's funny, isn't it? You keep improving it, but you've kept this tiny little blemish up there. You added this paved patio, the outside shower, the gardens keep growing, the vegetable patches, the bees are harvesting... You've basically remodeled the whole thing. I don't know, maybe you're using this house to find that part of you that you don't have inside of yourself; putting something that's not in you, out here, but you don't know what it is so you keep adding on, only you're putting it in the wrong place. Like you're using it as a way to avoid looking at what's not building inside of you, maybe. Because all that you've achieved, all of this, it's so incredibly gorgeous, and it should be enough for you. But it isn't, is it?"

"No." The quiet sits for a minute. Then two.

It's all so immaculate.

"You have almost everything just the way you want it."

Who wouldn't want this?

"It's nine out of the ten things you need, but it doesn't give you the one thing you really want. That's still missing. I've felt that."

"I feel that, yes. And it's not here." He pauses for a while.

"It doesn't matter how much you keep pruning away out here you're not going to find it this way. I did all of this in a different way. That patch up there, that white space that's so easy to paint, that won't take a couple of hours to wash over - that's your one thing, waiting for you. I mean, why else wouldn't you paint it? It's keeping all of this from being perfect. I think if you find what that is, you'll paint over that empty space."

He's hesitating to tell you something.

"I have this guilt around my mom. Her not being able to have the life she deserved. She got pregnant, married my father. No choice back then. The three of us came along. She had such a great future ahead of her, so much that she wanted to do and she couldn't have it. She gave it all up - all of her dreams gone to become a wife and a mother. Nothing for herself." The wind blows in my face making me defensive in the head. Neither did I. I gave up anything good for myself as well. Cooper makes my napkin fly off the table into the garden.

Hold.

I know, but it's making my own past life uncertain.
A little wine spills as I get up to chase the napkin down. The parallel between his mother's life and mine are a cracked

mirror image. We chose different paths in pregnancy and walked into a denial of ourselves. Hers by convention, mine by choice and construction. But she has three sons, that isn't nothing. I jump as Aiden's black cat, Flo, springs past me across the garden. She pounces on a field mouse that squeals, tiring into oncoming death. Aiden jumps up from his chair screaming after her to put it down. She looks surprised at what he's asking, but drops it and runs into the trees. The mouse is on all fours in the wet grass. It darts from left to right with no sense of direction. Moving, not wanting to move, not knowing where. I can't take my eyes off of it. The white of the napkin next to it is bright, blinding, disintegrating in wet. I pick it up and smash it in my hand. Aiden looks at me shaking his head. We turn towards the house and look up at his patch of white.

"So you've done all this for her? All this is for your mom. And you've done it with money from a job that doesn't make you happy, and you've done it for over twenty years. That probably eases the guilt that you feel."

"I think I thought it would." We smile at each other and don't move a minute.

"It's not your responsibility to take that on. You know that. She wouldn't want you to be responsible for that. The best way to honor your mother is by living what you truly need." See, I am calm. I have learned from us.

I walk through you and sit in the chair you wanted. I choose it anyway.

"I know, you're right. I do know that. And my mom never regretted it at all. She always says that having us is the best thing she's ever done." I wish I knew what that felt like.

"Well, there you are. Whatever that one thing is that you've been pushing down, that's hesitating in you, that's what will allow you to move away from those feelings to what's positive. It's hard. It feels like you're being disloyal because you've held on to the old thoughts for such a long time. What it came down to for me was figuring out how to go from sacrificing something in myself that was never asked for, to honoring the person I thought wanted me to be less than I am. No one wants you to be less of who you are, and neither should you. It takes some unwiring. But you re-wire systems, though - that's your job. Ha! How ironic that your job is rewiring things outside of yourself. What happens if you turn it inside to rewire yourself? Maybe there's a thank you in this job after all."

"Yeah, more than a little irony there. Sometimes the answer's glaring at us." Flo jumps on to his lap licking missing mouse scent. "She is proud of me, my mom. She tells me that all the time."

"You being happy and successful can only make your mom proud of you. And when you find that one thing you will be proud of yourself. It's knocking away. You can choose to ignore it, but it's not going to get clearer than this. It's up to you. Either way you have a beautiful life." His face is glowing in the embers of the fire he's building. We slump down in our chairs, heads bent backwards by an open fire scanning the skies. "I've never seen a shooting star before. I'm always looking the other way, spilling something when all the magic is about to happen," I say.

"Well, you're going to see a thousand of them tonight," he says, "and all I have to see is one." He smiles and we wait. And they do shower down - my first shooting star, my second, my third, my first floating satellite masquerading as a star, my tenth on to uncountable. All that light from trillions of years ago made it's way here at the same time as I did. I stare down into the embers asking them to last. No matter how much I poke them to stay alive I know the next morning he and James will go and live inside my rear view mirror.

Cooper, we are fortunate in our friendship with Aiden. He knows our story and takes it inside just as much as his own. He and I are on the same threshold - questioning answers. We find our way to ourselves through each other.

Relationship Intuition Number Nine: **The Yogi Friendship.** The friend that sits patiently and waits for the explosion to pass and in the same breath validates it and makes sense from it. The Yogi is the emotional center of your path because when the fall comes he snaps you awake. He is fear's antidote and courage's champion.

The gravel crunches loudly underneath the wheels of my suitcase - two deep grooves mark a blue unwilling exit. Aiden lifts it into the car and I slam the door shut. I'm paranoid about trunk doors—

A piece of us will stay here.

—screaming open when I'm on the freeway. God knows where that comes from. Aiden and I stand face to face for a minute looking sulkily at one another until I reach for him, kiss him on the cheek and pretend I'll see him later. I'm better at hello. As I pull away from the lemon yellow house with its little white patch I watch Aiden in the rear view mirror walk into his vegetables. That sticker's right - things are a lot closer than they appear.

A few weeks after I left, Aiden went to see James in a play. Afterwards he stuck around, and they spoke to each other, face to face, with actual words, in front of each other, in the same space for the first time. In some small way I felt that I was there - it's not just a written reconciliation, not anymore.

Emptiness refills itself.

Part 4 Limbs:

the, b is added as in crumb.
one of the jointed members of the human body or of
any animal; Having limbs: mostly in composition; an
arm or leg; more especially the latter; a pretty large or
main branch of a tree; to supply with limbs;
to dismember; to tear limb from limb.

- The Library of Universal Knowledge

Wandering Back Down

All the cells of my skin that you loved to touch
have flaked away and been renewed
I am an epidermal stranger
- Ruth Stone

Last night I watched a flame in a candleholder try to fight
its way above the rim to stay alive as it ran out of wax. The last
puff of thick smoke twisted eagerly with everything it had left
trying to spell something out that I missed. That's how I feel
driving from Rhode Island back to Richmond. There's always
so much I think of to say and I'm back on a road of green and
rain and hours. The passenger airbag sound lights you up in
red. I've been up and down here, in and out of who I was – a
part of me still hanging on to the belief I worked so hard to
convince myself of: that of a discarded life having value for
your names sake. Also, though, for the first time I feel a
forward momentum of understanding for us. I am often still
silent, but I feel full leaving here. At least I've been able to
share how I feel about both of them, how their absence
affected me. I'm pleased that we could be open about what all
of that means to each of us - giving without expectation. I felt
rounded with you there as well because they know you in
terms of who I am, Cooper. They know a part of me
understands myself through the hollow sockets where your
eyes should be. The bridge between us was you.

I feel ambushed by goodbyes.
There is an abruptness to this loving and leaving.

91

I'm moving through a breathing photograph album - the pages flip by at blink speed. And one early morning, another one comes back in Richmond as Jeri, Doug and Toni and I all go our different directions again. They leave a note by the coffee urging me back soon and wishing me a safe journey. I wheel my bag down the stairs, passed the dining table where we shared our thank yous for the most important time of our day. All I have to do is close the door behind me and I'll be locked out. But this house, whose existence I hadn't even heard of four months ago, won't ever be a place I'm shut out of. The knob may not turn now, but all I ever have to do is knock.

I'm oblivious to the road to North Carolina. I stop off with my sister-in-law's sister's sister-in-law and family, if you follow. I met Becca at my sister-in-law's sister's wedding. Her children are young, rambunctious and her homemade beef stew warms and sends me on. It's heart warming to be invited in to someone's cluttered beautiful life. They open up the door to the rawness of family life, and their couch is comfiest because it's offered without pretense.

I have another reason to stop off there as well. Before I left Richmond on the way up, Jerri gave me a bookmark she'd made. It has a quote she took from a blog called "Pathwriter." Choreographer Marie had shared the blog with me a few months before. I ask who wrote it.

"Viki. She used to work with us at Richmond Ballet. That's how Marie met her too. She lives in North Carolina now." So we know her. North Carolina is a large state though she could be anywhere, right? I send her an e-mail anyway to check out where she lives, to see if we could meet up. As it turns out she lives a fifteen-minute drive away from Becca, in Raleigh. Somehow I knew she'd be in reach.

It's those footsteps in the songlines we've already written.

As illusive and metaphorical as you might make it, I'm walking on them.

Viki and I wander around through the roses in the park by her house and talk about writing, about making a new start towards something that for both of us still seems uncertain. There are moments I feel out of my depth, and it's reassuring to talk to someone who feels the same buzz in the potential of the unknown. We are perhaps pushed together for this moment alone, there isn't anything else we need from one another.

You are each other's affirmation.

On the road to Aiken, South Carolina, in amongst the straight green parameter of trees that pass on and on, the strangest site drifts by me. It's a large kidney shaped pond decorated with bright colored—

Pull to the side a little. Slow down.

—flowers and life size unicorns. All around it and dotted throughout the garden there are winged horses, flamingos, and distorted body parts in pinks and pale marble whites. A giant centaur of a man, muscles powering up in the rain, is cutting the grass around them with one of those old fashioned mowers. If Lewis Carroll had a garden, this is the one he'd mow. I roll down my window to smell the wet grass and make sure that what I'm seeing is real. I wave at him, but he doesn't notice me.

It's apropos that I'm seeing this distortion now, on this road, considering the space I'm about to put myself in. I'm driving towards the doorstep of my ex-boyfriend Gregory's parent's house. I've known them for seventeen years. The relationship between the three of them is strained - it has been since the day he was born. They go head to head, that's the way they communicate, and now the way they don't. They've always liked me though.

I don't know why I'm going.

Well, yes you do. That's why you want to veer off the track and bunk off with the unicorns.

Yes, I do, that's the problem. Gregory says he doesn't care if he ever talks to his father again, but I don't know if that's true. His father's validation has always been withheld from him, so it's what he's craved most of his life. I want to tell his dad, "you'll have to be the grown-up, you'll have to make the first move, pick up the phone and fix it, because Gregory won't. He can't anymore." Somehow I want to find a nicer way to tell his father not to ration out his love. He told him he was worthless and wouldn't ever amount to anything. What effect did he think that would have? Then enter me to fill it up, which I couldn't. And I know they were always nice to me but his mother used to come into our house and throw away all my towels and buy new ones she liked, and tablecloths and tablemats and my house would be rearranged and I didn't like it at all if you must know. I liked my towels and the Buddha mats. I mean - they were mine.

Have a little pent up frustration there?

I'm going to tell them this. I will, even if it's out of some still twisted sense of attachment to a man I've mostly let go of because he's my friend. Something along those lines.

But maybe the attitude thing may not be the best approach.

Let's face it - it's not like me to do it anyway. Seventeen years pent up and one too many glasses of wine might see it flying though.

Gregory faced you with aspects of yourself you never thought you'd have to face.

My skin has been turned inside out knowing him. I found out how brave I can be inside of love, anger, frustration and passion. We loved deeply and without reservation, but after sixteen years of on and off, of yes, no, maybe, no, maybe, yes, it exploded in a silent noise only our dogs could hear. In that silence we finally understood that we could only grow without each other.

Flashes of this time swim around in my brain driving past the bent lawn ornaments and shirtless white rabbit mowing. Simple joys, glassy eyed young promises are all romanticized in my backward memory of it all. It's leaking out the exhaust as I pull into their driveway. Cooper's airbag sign goes off before I put the hand brake on. I wonder if it's my place to go after this. I'm always trying to fix things I should leave alone. There are repercussions on other people I want to say to them, but I'm not sure I can. In fact I'm pretty sure I can't, but I certainly can't say it unless I knock on the door and knock back a few shots of vodka. So here we go.

I don't know what I expect to find here. I know they'll be welcoming.

You know there'll be love for you.

I knew there'd be him. But I didn't expect to find a piece of me in here with them. I don't even recognize myself in the photo album.

"This picture must have been taken almost twenty years ago," I say, looking at Gregory's face, his brother's, mother's, father's, without noticing my own.

"That is you, no, Sehrah?" my coulda been Polish mother-in-law says, mispronouncing my name as she's always done so beautifully.

"Yes, yes that was me." I can't remember feeling that fresh. Look how in love I am. I'd saved him. I stare into my eyes. It's true, this love - no matter the years.

Tucked up in bed later, I feel alone, and I know this is how I've always felt with it. We are both strong, stubborn people. At some point the switch went off and in that dark room we turned away from each other. We can all justify the why for ourselves in one-way or another. I realize that towards the end I didn't support him fully – not the way the irreplaceable replacement of me does now. I'd been exhausted by all that came before it, so my ability to believe in him disintegrated completely.

I remember the moment that picture was taken - all huddled together in the snow.

I feel a kind of twisted joy in an absent love.
I fall asleep staring at pictures of him as he was, as he is; at pictures of his brothers surrounded by children – which is what he sees for himself now. The girl in that picture wanted that with him, but I'm one ovary short of a conception now. My womb has a clock even the best of intentions can't halt... and with that she crept in - framed and on display in his parents house - embraceable, replaceable me.

His parents and I wander through Hopeland Gardens. I want to walk my life with him in the Labyrinth. And I do. I feel all those promises of safety and trust as soon as my left foot crosses in. I've been lost in here before, and I've walked back I don't know how many times. Each time, at the same point, he was there waiting for me. That's what we did. So I sit alone in the center, a frantic bee laden down in yellow. His parents sit on a bench waiting on the outside of the perimeter wondering why I'm doing something so silly. They should walk this for themselves. There are many demons in here. And it's so ironic to me that I'm the one who doesn't mind facing them.

Perhaps you should say what you have to say to them now. There are no dead ends in here.

I turn my back on them instead like a pissed off cat in a dirty litter box. You clean it up.

Our evening is Polish – wine, platters of olives, humus, bread, tomatoes and onions, and conversation that naturally flows into their son.

"I don't know how to talk to him anymore. I don't know how to start," Polish daddy says. I'm almost biting my tongue straight through.

This is a good moment. Say something.

For God's sake.

I go the bathroom. I sit on the cold tile floor with my back to the wall staring into the eyes of a porcelain doll avoiding my attention. I can't do it. How do I tell him constructively - all your son has ever wanted is the one thing you'll never give him. He wants love. He wants the one thing he'll never have – your approval. You really don't see that? That with every negative word you said he's had to move so far away from you he'll grab a hold of any emotion in the air. You don't see it as a disease, but I do. "Why is this plate dirty," smash against the wall. "You think you're a super star because you fought in the war," smash, smash. How did you think he'd treat other people? Did you really think he'd love me unconditionally, that he wouldn't dish out love to me in bite sized pieces like you? Do you know what I lost in loving him? I'll bet it never even crosses your mind. I love in spite of it, and so is he. But what chance did he have at the beginning feeding off of this? You think it's all his fault, that all this disconnection is his choice. All he wants is for your love for him to not be conditional on his being successful. When he's lying in the dirt grasping a hold of his last thirty-seven cents, that's when he needs you to show up, not the limo rides and ribbon cuttings – that's so fucking easy.

The painted doll's eyes are making me self-conscious. I flush. I flush again and turn on the taps. I don't wash my hands. My absence hasn't been too long. I don't think so. I walk into the living room in slow motion and swill all this around in swallows of Pinot Noir and marinated tomatoes. I offer up some bait in as non-threatening and open way as I can, but I fall short. I go in again.

"Let's call him." His mother's eyes light up and his father starts uncorking another bottle of wine.

"This is a good one, Sehrah. We giving you all the good wine here. Nothing but the best," he says. I pick up the phone. Facetime. We're all in now.

"Hey, they treating you well?"

"Gregory, oh, you look so gooood. You hair is nice. You do something. What you do?" His mom takes the phone over to the table. His father fidgets. He pours a glass of wine. He goes into the bedroom. He wanders back out. I turn the phone around so he can see him, making sure he's aware that he's giving his own son avoidance, a peripheral second glance. I'm nothing if not passive aggressive today.

We hang up.

He didn't make any attempt to talk to him at all. Was he waiting for me to wave him in to the conversation? It was on the tip of my tongue a few times. I should have said something. Why didn't I say something? What the hell is wrong with me?

You were afraid of what you were always frightened of – that it would turn into a fight, that the yelling would start, that one of them would start it and you'd had such a lovely day and you just want it to fix itself calmly, only their version of calm is paralytic.

Why don't I just say, hey do you two ever look at the relationships he's had, how he's tried to destroy himself. I had him committed. You stood in my kitchen and he told you about it, and you said, "Gregory, you should be nicer to that girl." Surely you must have wondered why he did it, why he thought of suicide. He locked himself in a bathroom with a knife, for Christ's sake. When the police arrived and they took him away to the institution, he was screaming that I didn't love him, that no one who loved him would ever do this to him; but it got him some therapy and some pills. You released him into the world like a pack mule. I tried to care for him, I did. Why couldn't you just love him, then I would have someone to love. Then he would have loved me.

As much clarity you are getting, you still want the answer to whatever it is you don't think you're asking anymore.

Fuck it. It's not me framed on the mantle anymore. Let her tell it like it is. She loves him. She sees it. I walk to the window with the intention of smashing my hand through it in my own frustration, but the only thing I manage is, "You have a really nice patio." Polish daddy doesn't lift an eye.

"The fucking squirrels keep destroying my bird feeder."

This next morning my no longer mother-in-law makes me some green tea. I think about that pink flamingo and the half-naked centaur man I saw mowing in the rain. At the moment that scene makes more sense than my being in this kitchen. Sometimes you have to sit with the devil to see how much you're like him. I walked away from Gregory too, didn't

I? I gave up on him just like they did, just like he expected me to.

You wanted happiness with someone who without ever having known love before hadn't a clue how to give it back.

If I'm honest I know I'm not here for him, or for them. I'm here for what I allowed it to do to me. A part of him is still in me. I haven't let go at all.

The next morning I hug them both knowing I will never see them again. Why can't you be as nice to him as you are to me? Why can't you just say, sorry and begin again and earn his love back? As they wave goodbye to me they get smaller and smaller in the mirror behind me, but keep growing.

Three hours until I get to Cody in Alpharetta. My head is pounding. Twenty sixs whizz by – phone numbers, flashing MPH signs, license plates, so many I lose count. The rain starts as soon as I hit the freeway. My hands are clammy and my heart rate is running away with me. I don't have see-through tears.

Pull over.

I pull over to a rest area. In the mirror I see something red smeared across my temple. Blood trickles from a hole that's not there - a Braxton Hicks stigmata. It's my right hand. I've been pushing it so deeply into the steering wheel that the nail on my little finger has dug into my palm, drawing blood. I put my hand into a cold cup of tea and watch the caffeine swirl into the sour red pattern of my life. The windshield wipers are frantic and I try to follow them with my eyes without moving my head. I turn the car off. This rest stop is so isolating.

All that time that went by with Gregory - I lost another chance at having you.

There was never another chance at having me.

Did you help me pick him out? Did you tell him to wear those funny yellow pants and flatter me silly? Did you facilitate it so you'd be my only child?

There is nothing in this world I wouldn't do to take away the noise in your head.

Tell me that you love me.

I love you, Ma.

I can't hear you. You steered me clear of that baby smell that was never yours.

You've been your own dearest recruit in that.

Cars slide past me in the rain.

What if my car won't start?

It will.

I think it would start with no engine inside it. I merge back in with other people.

Think about where you're headed.

To Cody.

Your newest distraction from something you still don't want to think about.

I think about his cheeky grin. How he was always hanging with our theatre class at UT when he was a year behind us.

Two years.

Always so many people around me all the time back then. I'm not sure what going to stay with him will be like. This could be awkward.

Boys leave their dirty dishes five inches to the left of the dishwasher and sweaty piles of clothes on the floor. So I've heard.

Cody 's waiting for me as I pull into his driveway. He lives in the suburbs - I hadn't expected that. I roll my right sleeve down over the dried red holy stain and walk towards his smile. It's as if a few minutes have passed and I'd just popped out to pick up some more beer. How stupid to think this would be uncomfortable. He's my friend. And he smells delicious. He takes my bag upstairs to a lovely white, clean crisp room.

"Look at you all organized with the clean towels on the bed."

"You were all prepared to sleep on a couch, weren't you?"

"With questionable stains and a bottom sheet on top." He smiles. He looks the same with only a hue of gray that's crept in to overtake the boy. It hasn't succeeded.

"So whose class were you in, Elspeth's?" I ask.

"No, I was in the class behind the class behind you. Two years."

Told you.

"That makes no sense."

"I know. I was always hanging around you guys, just wanted to be a part of whatever was going on, you know. And your class was so freakin' good, so many talented people. I looked up to you so much. I'll never forget watching you in, *Good.*

When she came in from the rain and started braiding her hair.

God, you were great in that.

99

She was, wasn't she?

I just wanted to be around all that, all the time. I'd audition for anything, anything I could get my hands on. I wanted to get my face in front of Stephen, or Lee."

"Such a whore."

"Yeah! But you know, it's hard to get noticed when you're a jock like me. They boxed me in. It was hard to get out of that. I just wanted to work. To do good work." I wish I remembered being that focused. "So you went to LA after graduation?"

"Yes, I went out to San Diego first then we moved out to LA a year or so after that. Then I went back years later, lived in Burbank, North Hollywood. My brother lived in Santa Monica, then Glendale."

"I was in Santa Monica. We were there at the same time. How did we not hook up?" He shakes his head.

There was that moment on the pier - you got off that ride that made you sick - he was rinsing sand off in the shower by the stairs. You walked by. The water splashed your sandal.

"How did any of us stay in touch, really, you know. If I didn't have your address, it was hard to keep track. I know I moved around a lot. It's interesting who we did keep in contact with initially."

"How did we not run in to each other, Sara? It's just so odd."

"I got swallowed up in other things. I didn't really hit the scene out there, not like you did I'm sure." Over lapping.

You zigzagged all around each other. Your world's not all it seems.

"It would have been so much easier if we'd had Facebook," he says.

"Sometimes I feel like we're the last gang of people to know what being anonymous is like. You know what I mean – we still have a perception of what it's like to not be able to be found. We could actually disappear from each other, or withdraw if we wanted - there's no escape now."

"And I'm glad we have come back into each other's lives, in person, it's..."

"I can see your face light up, or not... I can feel your emotion even when you don't say anything. Sorry, I interrupted you."

"No, no, it's okay."

100

"I do that - my mind works ten miles ahead. But, it's just – there's no faking it, being with you. What we talk about flows out of what we're feeling, right, *because* there's no distance."

"Yeah. Yes. That's it." We look at each other for a few seconds and smile looking each other up and down. "Man, let's have a drink. I'm taking you to The Punchline Comedy Club tonight. I used to be a bouncer there. I lived a lot of my life out there. They're like family to me. I want you to meet my family."

When we pull up we park next to two license plates with 26's in them. "See. You thought I'd lost the plot didn't you."

"Fuck, no way." He circles back around to the cars on either side of us, but it doesn't hold his attention long. A gang of people converges out onto us and surrounds him in the parking lot. He's heralded into the building like the head of a dynasty. We sit at the bar and I order bad red wine while he jokes around on Instagram telling his friends we're "going on in five." He shows me the comedians secret hideouts, pictures of all the people he's met, nooks where comedians hung out and left notes on the wall. It's his history I'm seeing though - he has that sense of knowing his way around that says this is home.

His stool doesn't wobble here.

When we sit down to eat afterwards, talk goes to love - the ending of it.

"How long were you with Gregory?"

"Sixteen years, on and off." The number sounds absurd, almost embarrassing. I want to suck it back down but it's out loud now so I fixate on the pink lipstick tattooed on the rim of my glass.

"Sixteen years! Shit." Water words of beer spill down his chin.

"I'm supposed to choke on that, not you," I say trying to veer the conversation off, but he's still looking at me. "On and off," I repeat, as if that makes the fact that I never married a man I loved for a third of my life only to produce a phenomenal failure of a relationship sound any less of a fuck up. "I don't know why I say that, 'on and off.' I say it whenever I talk about him, whenever anyone asks. I always say that. The truth is that even off we were on, and on we were off. That makes perfect sense and no sense, doesn't it? It was always going to be complicated, and anything that hard to balance is never going to end well, is it?"

101

"No, and I do know what you mean."

"Do you know where I was before I got here? At his parent's house. I hadn't seen them in years."

"Why did you go there?"

"Oh, I don't know, Cody, a lot of reasons. Gregory had a pretty messed up childhood and a lot of people stuck in that cycle pass that shit on whether they want to or not. When I met him he was, well he still is a little bit locked inside all of that abuse. It had to come out and grab a hold of something, and at the time it fell to me. I wanted to go in there and stir all that up, tell them how it affected me, tear into it." My fist bangs on the table making my wine wobble red over the edge of my glass.

It pools down at the bottom trying to hide underneath. Apropos.

"When it came to it I clammed up. Isn't that ridiculous? I should've just knocked on the door, screamed nonsensically and got back on the road. Ha! That would have been easier. Band Aid cure. But I realized when I was there that it's all too late."

You didn't say anything at the time, so what's the point in saying anything now, is what you thought. You've got to figure this one out.

I pick up his empty beer and start pealing the label off of it. "On my way there all I could think about was how a part of me blames them for the time that was stolen away from me by being with him. But that's not even true. I made a choice to love. But that's not the point."

"That's what's still going on, whatever the point of it all is. For you, I mean."

"Yeah, and no matter how irrational it might seem to work this out now after all these years, I feel like I'm a little bit closer to knowing what it is."

"Yeah, I think so too." I look up at him, look him in the eye. He grabs his beer back and starts scraping off the glued down remnants of label. "For me it was the long distance thing. I knew deep down it was never going to work, but you love, and it, it just creeps out of your control. I don't know. I hung on to it as long as I could. This one was really hard for me. It broke my heart." He's looking away into nothing specific. It's all too abstract to talk about - that feeling of loving too long and wanting so very much to be very wrong about a love that you have to let go of. We're the same kind of people -

we hang on to the bitter end, leaving no stone unturned, no mistake unmade, before we let go of someone.

"It's that slap around the face, the one that kind of wakes you up and tells you who loves you and who doesn't. Sometimes you have to let your heart break, I guess," he says. The beauty in him though, is that instead of letting it cover over with an impenetrable mesh of self-pity, like I do, like I'm doing - he's leaving it exposed. How much mesh does someone have to plough through to get to me now?

He might want another beer and then you'll have to talk about that.

I reach for our check - $25.99.

A penny shy.

If we lived closer to one another I'd reach out to him - answer the next question. Because I know he'll listen, and I know he'll share. I don't know why I hadn't expected him to reveal a part of his heart to me, but here it is, and it made it easier to expose a part of mine. I wish the world was smaller.

Funny, I thought you were realizing just how small it really is.

There is uneasiness driving towards New Orleans the next morning. This isn't a place I'm drawn to. It makes me edgy - like I'm driving into that part of a Disney movie when the spell floats over the forest in a green haze turning the trees the kind of black the devil won't wear, and twisting the branches so I'll be locked in forever. And I've just driven away from such a beautiful piece of openness.

Cody's heart is so open. I feel an infection around mine. Do I put the blame for that on you, child who never came? I didn't love you so no one will love me – not for long anyway. Is that the flesh of the mesh?

Aren't you tired of misconceiving?

You have no idea what that word does to me.

You did love me. Begin there. Just because it hurt doesn't mean you didn't feel it.

I can't seem to allow anyone to love me without thinking there's some awful consequence to it on the other side. Katrina tree remnants stretch up out of water like stick people - their bare roots are just holding on. This town is the raucous unexplainable. I feel stripped of what little balance I'm managing. What if this rickety bridge fails and I fall into the marshes below?

Your left wrist's dangling over the steering wheel.

103

My wrist.

The hair on my arm crinkles up like burning skin does - voodoo magic reminding me of his picture in the paper, the moment I first saw the soldier who died in a war in Afghanistan.

He was the first visitation to come.

I don't know him. I'd never seen his face until a year ago. I'm not the smartest person to understand this. I don't know what he is, I don't. Even in the recollection of it...

It's the kind of thing I can hear your mother saying you should keep to yourself, to not tell anyone. Deny it three times, Ma.

But I just can't say it didn't happen. I saw his picture. I saw him.

I roll down my window and breathe with the sticks.

Last September a lady I worked with brought in the obituary page. She had it folded into quarters, open to his picture. She knew his family - they lived in the same neighborhood. He'd been killed in action. The war, she said, was now on her doorstep. I picked up the paper. The way your right wrist drooped over your left arm - that simple, beautiful hand. I recognize you, only I've never seen you before but I know you. It's in that gesture. I feel dizzy and irrationally upset that you've been killed. My heart rate goes up like it used to when I had anxiety attacks all those years ago. I'm not sure what to do. How do I know who you are?

I felt his hands on my shoulders as I drove home that day, and a whispering all around that frustrates me because I can't understand it. It' not clear, not like the goandvisitallyourfriends voice that came after it. I keep clapping my hands together trying to kill it like I would a mosquito. Something about him I know but don't know. I feel who he is and who he's always been and I don't know what to do with this information. I still don't. It makes no logical sense.

Does any of it? Should we not just give over to it - one inward world to another?

I can't tell anyone about this. Maybe one or two people will accept it, but most people will just think they've finally got an answer to why I am who I am; why I've flipped to the point to risk all I have to drive around aimlessly meeting people I once knew. I should just shut up about it. If I keep it to myself it will all go away.

I hope that's a joke. And none of this is aimless.

I have to actively not think about him. I write to him in my journal, talk to him. I even start running, which if you know me well is something that I just don't do. I need Jesus to spare a few minutes to explain how maybe in one of his conversations with the Buddha when this topic came up of lives coming back to correct and reconnect, to tell me the Newspaper Soldier is valid. What do I do about this man that I know I don't know, that I know? I start to whisper around other people because a part of me thinks they can read it in my face - these radical types can, you know – I've seen it on reality TV. A limp wrist, like mine here now, that was all it took to turn the connection switch back on for us, like in a dream. To everyone else it might only make sense if it was a dream, but it isn't. And no matter what I do, or how much time passes, it never gives up in me. No matter what I do. Like 26.

I parallel park outside of Harper's house. I need some alchemy and she can dig it out. If I'm going to make sense of the nonsensical, this is the place I'll find it, I think.

A cartoon version of Harper is one of those pinwheel fireworks spinning a hundred miles an hour showering sparkles all around you - except it's all balanced with Zen calm. A woman that moves at this speed has a life to catch me up on. She sits across the table from me, glass of wine in hand, and bares it out.

Having suffered abuse at the hands of her second husband, she divorced. That wasn't the worst of it though. Her grown daughter chose not to believe that her torment could be real at the hands of, "such a nice man." Now the relationship with her only child has all but vanished. What is remarkable is her calm about the situation, a quiet that maintains a sense that things are as they should be, without any animosity. She will come back to her in her own time.

We met nine years ago at work in Dallas. She's been a single mom most of her daughter's life.

Whenever she visited the office she was all she talked about.

She was so proud of her. Is proud of her.

"We all have to grow up though," she says. "She has to find it all out for herself. I'll wait for that day." She trusts in the love she gave as a mother and she survives in a tight knit group of friends she's had forever. They keep her strong, they keep her moving, and they keep her engaged in herself.

105

On my first full day in New Orleans, Harper's got to work so she heads me off in the direction of Metairie Cemetery, an above ground graveyard minutes from her house.

"You should try and find that statue, the weeping angel one," she says, "She's in one of the tombs. I've always wanted to see her." Perfect. A cemetery. She hasn't a clue about the Newspaper Soldier; she's still sending me where I need to go. I'll go and touch this weeping cold marble skin.

Look for her and maybe that piece of him that you're never going to feel anywhere will answer a question you're forgetting to ask.

I've no idea what I'm doing.

The cemetery is huge. It's built on an old racetrack – one big oval. I know that the name on the tomb the angel's camped out in is "Hyams," but that's all. Harper's Google information says it's at the top left... of an oval... with multiple entry points. I pick a direction and start walking into stone.

It's way too hot. I walk for hours peering in every single tomb. They're all so beautiful, but they aren't it and it's starting to piss me off and hallucinate. I keep thinking about a dream I had the night before. I'm in the back of this old fashioned, old world kind of horse carriage, except that it's a pick up truck as well, and I'm loading a huge electric sculpture of a woman into the back. She must be at least twelve feet tall and she's standing straight up, lit up in pink neon and multi-colored Christmassy lights. Her head and shoulders are above the back of the cart I'm strapping her into. I pick up the reins and charge a white and a grey horse down a long stretch of lawn, and we're going so fast my hair is blowing into the wind and I feel like some sort of Clockwork Orange/Laurie Andersonesque vision warrior. It's the same feeling I got when I stood at the Newspaper Soldier's grave - knowing he's down there, still and hungry and there's no trap door to sneak whiskey through.

You're mumbling this dream out loud.

Am I? I feel drool on my lower lip. Why didn't I bring a bottle of water with me? It's so hot. My feet feel like they're weighted down - like magnets sucking up the last breath from all these poor cracked bodies through my soles. I should go back to the car. I have to sit down. I crash on the edge of some tomb. I look up and this angel's staring back at me. The sun is blazing while I'm staring her down and she's giving me that look I give myself when I catch myself daydreaming, only she's caught in it forever.

If you make a face and the wind blows, it'll stay like that - one of the scary fairytales Grandma used to tell you as a child.

And, you know, even though I'd always laugh at it, there was a huge part of me that secretly believed it might be true. I've always stared back into the past, like Lot's wife, grounded in a Salten sea. Maybe that's what I'm doing here. I've turned completely into the wind of the past and it's taken me even further back than I intended to go; beyond any past I recognize.

Except that you do recognize it.

I'm getting really dizzy now, my head is pounding and all my makeup's melting off my face and into my breasts and I'm way too vain for all this. I've looked in hundreds of tombs and I can't find the weeping angel. Some part of me thought I'd walk right to her. This is bullshit. I sludge back to my car for an air conditioning break.

I turn the air up full blast and lift the edges of my bra to let soft, sweaty flesh turn hard and cold. I rest my head back in the seat and catch a glance of myself in the rearview mirror. I look like I have malaria. The sweat under my eyes has washed my eyeliner down my cheek. I pull off what's left of the mascara. I don't like myself like this, it's the way I wake up. Just me.

Holy raw.

My hands grip the steering wheel and I flip the mirror up the way you do when someone's headlights are blinding you. I can see myself the way I want to. Why should I find this angel anyway? It's a Wednesday. I should be at work. I should be organizing and complaining. I'll just go to the quarter and get a nice cold glass of white wine. How stupid is this anyway, sitting in a parking lot with my face melting off. But I want to find her for you, Newspaper Soldier boy. I don't know why. This stands out of the way of my son, who's wandered off already. It's our story to tell, and if it is, then I'm going to need proof. I'm going to start my car up and I want you to drive me straight to her. Just show me where she is and I promise to believe in you, that there was or is an us to us despite the nonsensicalness of it. Finding her through your eyes will affirm the provenance of our friendship.

I'm sitting in a cemetery parking lot, talking to a dead soldier, bargaining for a stone's proof of life, confident in one thing – that through word or action, the dead never stop talking.

107

My right eye itches. A clump of mascara is caught on the inside where tears hibernate. I push it out and wipe the black on the seat as I start the car. I drive I've no idea where, it isn't in my head. I reach a fork in the road where I can go forwards, or turn left down a side road. I turn the air slowly down. I close my eyes. "Take the dirt road."

Maybe it's because I'm getting used to the voices that I don't hesitate, that the car makes the turn without me, and then stops at foot of the Hyams tomb.

He's smelt her out. He's driven me right to her, to him, to me, to where angels process like rain quietly shaping beliefs. I turn the engine off. I can't move. I stare straight ahead because I can't believe what's to my left, is to my left, that he's done it, that he's in the car with me. I look in the mirror. I look at myself. I want to see me see it in my eyes. I look at the tomb. I wonder why she's crying.

I see the chains before I reach the door. It's padlocked. I knock my forehead into the glass. There's got to be a key, all this can't be happening to leave me five feet away. I can just about make her out through the window. The sunlight streams in through three blue stained glass windows. She's glowing.

I should leave something of us here for her. I have a pink petal I found at your grave in the car so I go back and get it and stuff it inside the padlock. That's when I see the reflection in the window. I see a man standing on the lawn a little way behind me. I can only see his outline because there's a glare bouncing around and he's shrouded in a hue that seems to lift him off the ground and for a minute I think it might be you. I turn around, and he's reaching his hand out to mine. It isn't sweaty like I thought it would be, it's cool, and dry and I can smell baby powder. I don't look at him at first. Will I have to go? I don't want to share her with anyone else. I want to get in there.

"I saw you driving. I thought you were looking for her." He says this with a tenderness that I hadn't anticipated and it makes me feel a bit guilty for thinking that he's come to ruin my moment. He's fumbling with a large set of keys that look like they belong to a hundred year old haunted house. "My name is Richard. I'm the funeral director at Metairie Cemetery," he says, as he pushes a key into the lock on the door. My pink petal falls onto the tip of my right shoe. I want to pick it up, but I don't. He pushes the gate open and smiles at me. His hand is so very still and strong on the glass. "Go on," he says. "Go in and see her."

108

My eyes fix on the angel bent over a pedestal, a scroll of names inches just out of reach from her dropped hand. Her wrist is limp, dangling down, just like yours. There is a release in this marble that is unnatural. It's how I felt when I saw your picture in the newspaper. I half expect her to turn her head with that look in her eye that's mine, and that she'll walk towards me in a gait that's yours and embrace the other part of us standing here. I want to hold her hand, to pick up the scroll and give it back to her so her arms will raise back up and she'll look less like you, and feel less like me. I reach over and touch the top of her hair and slide my hands past her cheeks, and cup her head inside of them. Cold. Alone I'd kiss her, but I feel him looking at me, only it can't be him because he walked back to his car to wait for me.

The sun is streaming through the doorway distorting shape.

It's not him. It's you, not newspaper him, but a hue of you, Cooper. You.

The heat waves catch your silent form. And I can see you. I see you – light, warm, guarded from harm, and I can see into your eyes. I can see your eyes, and they are green like mine, just as I knew they would be, and your hand with newspaper wrist reaches out to me in the light and it's warm in mine for a second, maybe two, maybe a half hour, I have no sense of time, and just as cloud cover takes you away you lift my eyes to the name of the woman interned here.

Sara.

The name on the tomb is mine, and she died in September, like Leonard, like Newspaper you, and on the 26ᵗʰ. Here is the recipe of all of us. The gatekeeper walks back towards me and pushes the door aside. He watches me push my fingers inside the grooves of each letter of myself, tracing a me on the other side. I tell him, this is my name too. He nods as if he expected it to be. He smiles a little, and I smile back. I look at the angel in blue light, and when I turn around the door is closed ever so slightly and he is sitting on the steps, swinging the padlock around his index finger.

Here is my safety, here is the space of a truth I don't have to understand, a marble pillow of sacred clarity full of Grace with one answer resting on it – here is the place where I feel all the love I've ever held for both of you, and all the love you've ever felt for me. Here is the place you have traced us back to – here is where we begin. You have brought me to a moment of

instinctive trust, and shown me a small piece of what my
entire existence is for.
There is great love here for you.
I don't want to leave this space because I know it's the only
moment that will ever be ours - who we were, who we'll
always be, all of us inside this tomb. It's a treasure trail of
recollections in my blood that I have an understanding of. You
came back for me to show me we're all connected; that every
soul's the circle. A woman I don't know well brings a
newspaper to work with your picture in it, I cry myself to
sleep because I feel your absence from a life I had no part of,
and your voice almost a year to the day later, whispers me
down a dirt road leading me to an angel guarding a tomb with
my name on it who shows me my son in the sunlight.
No story is ever over.

Clearly I need to drink - you'll have to trust me there. I
need to reach for a blur that makes things clear, that lets me
hang on to this feeling. I need to sit somewhere and describe
you in my journal. And to get to that place I need something
running through me that equals your face.
*The Carousel bar at the Hotel Monteleone rotates in
circles.*
Anti-clockwise I go, mind inside a tomb. I'm scrambling to
  write it all down. My pen is moving so
quickly the waiter raises his voice to ask me what I want to
drink. I want so much for it to all be true, and I'm glad it is
true. I want to live it again.
It will never stop living.
  I want to go back, but I know it will never leave me. I
don't want it to fade.
You will always see it.
I want your heart to beat.
It beats in yours.
I look out of the window and strain to see you. Again.
Greedy.
I am out there.
Across the street, outside a shop - I don't see you.
There's a woman on the ground.
Homeless. She's on her knees, bending forwards with her
head bent over her arms, which are crossed in front of her.
She's weeping, and not through any stained glass blue light.
This marble is warm. She reaches her hand out to a bearded

man walking by. He stops and he does something I don't expect. He takes a hold of her hand and he kisses it.

Acknowledging her.

He hugs her and he kisses her on the head, he whispers something in her ear and kisses her on the forehead again. Then he kneels down, still hugging her, and she wraps her arms around his neck. They don't let go.

She's not invisible anymore.

He lights a cigarette for her and one for himself. They're sitting side by side. People continue walking by with their mutterings, stepping around them in their designer shoes with their designer judgments. They don't bother to wonder what her story is, not like him. And then there's me of course. Sitting behind a glass screen, like I'm watching a reality show.

You see her.

Witnessing, you mean? Is there much in that, I wonder. In here people are busy splitting their bills 50/50 including tax and tip. Out there he's crossed over into a neutral territory that seems invisible to unlock the padlock of this woman shunned inside her own mausoleum. He's giving a hundred percent of himself. He's etched his name with hers. There are people who don't ignore, who sit down to give kindness. Not because they feel they should, but because it's who they are instinctively. He woke up this morning seemingly to walk right to her.

Relationship Intuition Number Ten: **The Gift Of Friendship**. This friendship extends without question to someone friendless and alone. It gives of itself, for all but itself. It drops wherever it's going and stops where it's needed. It sees within; it recognizes a story and listens. It's tender, giving the pure love of human acceptance. It doesn't walk home to pray, it engages. It transforms action into the only thing that matters: love. This friend doesn't ask, "What would Jesus do?" This friend is what he would do.

Harper picks me up at the bar and asks how my day has gone.

Make our world bigger.

Maybe it's because the sensation is still sweating out of my skin, I don't know, but I open up and tell her. I answer her as completely as I've ever answered that question in my life. I don't stop to think, it just pours out of me. The hair goes up on both of our arms and I see you in that sunlight as clearly now as if you've just walked through me, and she's smiling with me in the unlikeliness of it all, that this beautiful moment has happened. That she's the one who told me about the angel, that she's woven into this. So many things to see and do in this town and that piece of marble is the first thing she mentions. We exist to give each other company and love, and sometimes guidance, and at times more precisely, perhaps for one moment only, for a tracing of direction. This has grounded me and anchored both of you in my waking life. Someone else knows.

I would never have imagined that someone I don't know well would factor in to such a life shifting moment. She was on this road to get me home, and I almost sidestepped her because the prospect of New Orleans left me edgy and uncomfortable. Perhaps subconsciously I felt what it held. Now she's a piece of the newest most confusing part of me.

We head down to the Quarter. It's a crowd drunk on jazz hidden in dark corners. We drink Mint Juleps because we should, and listen to local "Whodat" talk. The people here are survivors, and the feeling running through the streets where the water used to be, is one of closeness.

Then it's no surprise that here is where we all converge.

That even though it's staggering and untenable, it is true. It's late, but we head to City Park for Beignets. I feel fat and more out of my depth than ever before. I cover my hands and mouth in powdered sugar and lick all the deep fried magic off my fingertips.

The next day I volunteer with the St. Bernard Project to help in the rebuilding of those still stuck in shop doorways. The irony of the timing isn't lost on me as I drive to an address into Gretna.

The onsite project managers, and the six AmeriCorps volunteers partnering with St. Bernard's look over my clean shorts and pristine tennis shoes.

Like an action figure fresh out of the packaging.

I take notice of their spackled uniforms and sturdy boots.

"How much sheet rock experience do you have?" My "what is sheet rock?" response clues them into my cluelessness. They walk me passed several ladders all strewn about the place.

You should probably mention your fear of heights.

I don't want to seem overly inadequate all at once.

It's Thursday, August 29ᵗʰ - the eighth anniversary of
Hurricane Katrina. We don't start work right away - we sit
down on crates and up ended paint cans to acknowledge it
and introduce ourselves. These kids have so much unselfish
passion. The kind of person I imagine you would have been,
Cooper.

Tell them why you're here.

That feels so self-involved.

When it comes to my turn in the circle my paint can wobbles. I
hesitatingly tell them that I'm travelling around revisiting all
of my friends to regain connection.

"We don't interact anymore. That's why I'm here." Ken
starts kicking the plastic mixing can he's sitting on, "People
post, they don't get out and live in things. Not much anyway.
Not anymore. I mean, why aren't more people helping? There
are avenues here for healing, re-building, replanting. We come
back, and come back, and come back. It's like continuously
trying to untangle the biggest ball of Christmas lights you've
ever seen, but at least we're here trying."

This tribe is together for a year of community work that
today they have made me feel a part of. All day talking - about
books, travel, politics, music and dreams. They are full of
questions about the world, where I've lived, how the politics
are in other countries. For them it's about sharing their space,
and already having been together for eight months out of a
year, they aren't in a groove that's at each other's throats –
they're a family. By lunch I am just as covered in plaster as
they are, skim coating with the best of them.

There is no paradox to smoothing out the walls, to
searching out the holes and filling them with something
new.

This house is no different from me, from any of us. I see
the many chinks in me. I should give my own mind the
delicate time and detail I'm giving to this home.

Relationship Intuition Number Eleven: **The Healing
Friendship**. This tribal friendship grows out of a drive to serve
others. He comes into the community, takes your hand, picks
up a hammer and restores. He's not just rebuilding a structure
of wood, brick or stone, but one of home and safety, of respect
and dignity. It's in the execution of giving out to others that
they retrieve pieces of each other as one.

Leaving Louisiana, one bridge at a time, the tall, thin,
immovable sticks reach out of the water bowing me out as

113

they bowed me in. The roots stretch one into the other as they have for hundreds of years - just like the people of New Orleans do, like the homeless lady in her shop doorway, like the Jesus man's love kissing her flesh, like you in the sunlight, like the Newspaper Soldier in the marble bone of the Weeping Angel. There is a root even in what can't be understood. The clearest thing to me now is that I've been hiding away, dishing myself out into the world in pieces I think it will approve of. In the blue sky I smell rain.

Friendship smells like rain.

The return to Dallas holds me over only briefly. My parent's 50ᵗʰ wedding anniversary is September 14ᵗʰ and they're having a reenactment. I've been asked to be the old maid of honor, standing side by side with my sister, and my brother who is flying in from Portland to read a passage from a bible he's not quite sure he believes in. My mother is slightly worried about what I'm going to wear. My sense of style is something she puts up with, not something she wants anywhere near her wedding.

"You're not going to wear one of your negligee type dresses, are you?" she says with as much humor and lack of concern as she can. I see the fear, so for the first time in forty years I tell my mother that as long as she buys it, she can dress me up any way she wants to for her special day.

My God, you're brave.

Sarcasm aside, I can hear the panty hose being unwrapped and my legs itch. Then when my mother invites my sister along to shop with us for matching outfits I know I'm in real trouble. I've never matched anyone in my life.

My sister, Joanne and I are polar opposites in many ways and our lives have gone in decidedly different directions - she found her soul mate, married young, and has a beautiful daughter.

She's always so delicately coordinated.

She lives a life in balance, where as I seem to live to challenge it. She communicates openly with common sense.

She confronts. She has no fear of noticing the elephant in the room, and reminding you that it's there. Not now.

Usually because I've invited him in. You know, I honestly didn't realize the effect all of it had on her.

Of me you mean, Ma.

114

That there would be repercussions - that she would feel less loved because of the over compensation, the attention people gave me to try to erase, well not erase...

Forget, to forget the fact that I could have happened to you.

Forget, yes. Unachievable from the start. My choice...

Our choice.

That my choice shifted her life. Something I did put her life in a completely different place. She made different choices, she felt less supported. I was so involved in what it was doing to me I didn't look around to anyone else. It didn't even occur to me, that's what so disappointing. When we talked years later about how she felt, and the outcome of you not being here - it through me so off balance. I have a hard time digesting the dislike I have of that part of me - that I put her in that position.

She doesn't hold any blame towards you.

I hate that word.

That's the word you need to look at.

She handled it all. She makes me want to hold my head up higher. And look how beautiful she is.

Ah, avoidance. We will come back to this you know.

And I do – I do hold my head higher because I want to make her proud of me. My tendency is to leap through security – she makes me take off my shoes, take everything out of my pockets, and look at what's there before I cross the checkpoint. She is my heart, and my treasure. She encourages me to take chances because she knows that the road to my happiness is in the opposite direction from hers. She always wants the best for me – even if it means parting from things and people that I love for a while.

My palms still sweat opening the door to Nordstrom's though. It's a place I used to drop my coulda been Polish mother-in-law when she visited. Mum, Joanne and I have a laugh in the dressing room as I pick inappropriate things out to try on and give us a giggle. But of course I eventually leave the shop with a not so me dress. It has a belt that hits me in the wrong place and a white panel that highlights a stomach that's eaten too much chocolate and beignet powder. Super. On the day of the reenactment I'm stitched into it and decorated in my mother's jewelry.

You look so beautiful, Ma. You can't help it. I wish you felt it more often.

It's hard when your knickers are in a twist.

That's funny. Grandma looks lovely in her cream suit. Look at her with the turquoise heals.

115

A pop of color - that's your Aunt Joanne's eye. And dad's coordinating tie.

I love that they race down the aisle in seconds.

The fugue didn't stand a chance.

And we all sway and pretend not to notice. I see you all smiling.

Happy giggling. I can't remember the last time my brother and sister and I sat together like this. Maybe it's because we're away from everyone else, on the altar, that I feel a deeper sense of us like I used to. A link I haven't felt for such a long time. It's just the three of us, like when we were children. Only we've come through childish things; we've been away from one other, so far away at times. So many things having happened both spoken and unspoken. Although we sit individually in all of this, those weaknesses and strengths belong to us collectively. Those moments, no matter who else comes into our lives, no matter how intimately, they belong to the three of us alone. You can feel it, can't you?

I can see it, yes. I wish I could feel it.

I hope *they* can. I wish I could have given this feeling to you.

All of my parent's best friends are here - other British families we've grown up with. One of the best things about the reception is watching them. These ex-pats have formed a collective friendship. We smoke each other out in any culture as if we've all been chipped. I'm not sure why we feel the need to talk about Branston Pickle, Salad Cream, Blancmange, real football, and a good cup of tea – but we do.

And those cheese & pineapple on-a-stick thingys. You never liked those.

But I'd still have served them at your every birthday with twiglets and fishpaste sandwiches. It's just something we do! Now every week about fifteen of these English get together for an Indian meal where the Gin & Tonics, wine, and Rum & Cokes flow. They're family – what happens to one, happens to them all. If you invite one, they all come along. It's a friendship that's been true to itself for over thirty years. By all appearances they've always been with each other.

Relationship Intuition Number Twelve: **The Comfort Friendship**. A group by definition, this friendship strikes out of a need for the familiar to seek those that come from the same homeland or upbringing. It grows into a life long sustaining bond. It's the fire never allowed to die out. It is the comfort of home.

At the reception Allen, one of the comfort group, asks my brother when he'll be giving his toast. Billy, who likes to prepare to prepare and then prepare, pales.

"No one told me I'd have to do this," he says retreating to a quiet corner. I watch him with his pen and cocktail napkin writing an ode to my parents.

He's muttering to himself.

You wait - it'll be a great speech.

"It's nice to be at my parents wedding," he begins as Champagne bubbles, "and to have a front row seat. As many of you are aware we were hidden shamefully at the back of the church for the last one…" Murmuring and uncomfortable shifting which turns into laughter follows, which I think is terrific.

His delivery is so on - so deadpan. I love that for a second or two they don't quite know if it's a joke or not.

And the rest of the speech is just what I felt in the church. Only about our unit - the five of us moving around the world, exploring, laughing, fighting, loving, all those things you do without stopping to think how they've affected you.

Unless you're you and you've been overanalyzing it since you were three.

It's very rare that we're all in the same room anymore. I crave it. It's a lit fire I don't want to go to ash.

Part 5 Extremities:

a limb or organ of locomotion; the verge; the point or border that terminates a thing; extreme or utmost distress. **Appendage,** what is attached to a greater thing. **Finger**, a digit; *to have a finger in*, to be concerned in; to touch, to handle or meddle with; **Toe**, having toes: often used in composition. **Nail**, the horny scale growing at the end of the human finger and toe; a small pointed piece of metal with some sort of a head used for driving through material for the purpose of holding separate pieces together.

- The Library of Universal Knowledge.

Wandering the Root

Immediate self-observation is not enough, by a long way,
to enable us to learn how to know ourselves.
We need history, for the past continues to flow through us in a
hundred channels.
-Fredrick Nietzsche

My flight leaves for England the day after the wedding. Sitting at the gate, where I did not get an upgrade to business class, I drain a glass of white wine. I abhor white wine but I drank a glass years ago for luck and survival and it worked, so now it's a superstition. I have to keep on drinking it when I fly.

And on top of that you write your will out every time you get on a plane.

Because I know this time the ocean will swallow me up as the plane plummets down to a fiery and shark ridden end. I've seen enough movies to know that's possible.

Unbelievable. As if you have any control of it. Your own family won't fly with you anymore because of that panic attack you had on a flight from Florida to Dallas.

Sixteen years ago, and they still bring that up. We were flying through a severe thunderstorm and the plane was shaking every which way so I had my eyes closed. I felt a shower of water all over me I thought part of the roof had opened up and I was being rained on.

118

When it was turbulence spilling your drink all over you.

And I may or may not have screamed, "We're all gonna die." Ridiculous. I mean, sure there might have been a little screaming involved and perhaps a lot of praying out loud that could have been misconstrued as shrieking. I know I made a panicked phone call to Gregory who wasn't home. I know that's a metaphor for something, and I know I've never been so scared in my life. Besides, everyone else was doing it.

Traumatizing.

I know, right?

Not for you, them. I can't be traumatized.

Well, you're welcome.

That ride is not in my head as we take off though. My mind goes back thirty-one years to the plane that took off from Gatwick airport in 1982 carrying me away from England, albeit towards you. Moving from one culture to another isn't a happy New Year gift for a girl of sixteen. It's the great disrupter. That last New Year's Eve before we left, my grandparents had a fancy dress party. My grandfather had a bar in the living room – not just for the party - it was always there. The drinks flowed all night – although my granddad's, Special Martini was most popular - Gin and a slice of lemon rind in a cold glass glancing sideways at a bottle of vermouth.

Eight days after the party we would all leave England for the land of JR's shooting. I had bad feelings about it – I was a teenager. I was losing all of my friends, some of my immediate family, and I acted out. I'd sneak cigarettes and take the dog for "walks." I just took her down the side path to the back end of the woods behind our house, by the tree where that boy whose name I can't remember hung himself that my friend Edith found. I'd sit there and try to smoke. I hated smoking but I knew they'd hate it even more even if I didn't tell them about it.

So bloody passive aggressive.

Language. Point taken though. The reason that party sticks out in my mind is because it's where I broke my father's heart open. Everyone at the party was being so supportive, wishing us all well, and my dad's best friend, my Uncle Toby came up and said something to the affect of, wasn't I excited about going to America, and I said, no, that I hated the idea and I didn't want to go, that I'd never wanted to go, I wished I didn't have to go.

Your dad's eyes shut.

119

To un-hear it. His face fell, and his shoulder's drooped and he downed the last of his drink.

You walked away.

I sat by the fire in my rented, pink and gold oversized Anne Boleyn costume that came because they gave away my Tinkerbell one by mistake. For the first time in my life I knew my own enormous selfishness. I can still see the look on my father's face thirty-four years later. I stopped sneaking the cigarettes they didn't know about anyway and tried to just accept it. It wasn't worth seeing that.

This is the Darwinian origin of your people pleasing.

At the time I didn't realize that life as I knew it was about to end. The close connection to the country I grew up in had begun its evaporation. My London family seemed to just disappear as if they'd lived at the bottom of the garden with the fairies and the hedgehogs I'd buried.

I'd say you are being overly dramatic, but I don't think you are.

No. For all that I gained, there was a price behind me. Our relatives are slipping away, so we're reaching back. Over thirty years later, I'm taking you home.

It's like a symphony hovering in the air waiting for paper to land on.

That's lovely. Yes, and it's not enough for me to just watch it up there floating around anymore. If I'm going to know it, to understand it, then I'm going to need to experience it all, every note of it however I can find it, whether that's on my knees digging through graveyards or listening to relations still alive and reminiscing.

So nineteen hours after takeoff, via Heathrow Express into London, tube to Euston station, and a connection on through Chester, I arrive in Bangor, Wales at 3:00pm local time to catch a taxi to a small remote village called, Llanystumdwy, to David Lloyd George's house, Tŷ Newydd. Well, you have to start somewhere. I've come to Wales first because of the author, Jan Morris, born 1926. I read her book, *A Writer's House in Wales*. I researched where she lived and found that in this remote corner of Wales they have a literary festival, so I signed up for a travel-writing course.

I glance at my reflection in the taxi window. I look like the scarecrow from *The Wizard of Oz*. God knows I'd probably drunk the equivalent of a bottle of wine on the plane, I've had no sleep, nor have I brushed my hair.

120

But here you are in the middle of nowhere, just as you intended.

It's cold and raining, and I never want to leave here. Others have already arrived and are milling in the lobby waiting for room assignments. "Your room is at the top of the windy staircase on the right," Awen, the administrator, tells me. Of course it is. It doesn't take Macgyver to recognize that my suitcase is wider than the actual stairway. I have one of those slow motion, wavy moments like they have in the movies where the stairs fall up in front of me like a beanstalk I'll never climb. I haven't been to sleep for twenty-six hours at this point, so this should be interesting. Eyes down, firm grip I hike one step at a time. I muddle at the entryway when I get to the top. I'm having a thing with doors lately - I can't seem to get them open and I slam them shut without meaning to.

I'm sure Freud would have something to say about that.

The room is sweet, and at five feet nine I have to duck under the doorway to get in. I find this out the hard way. There is a small desk at the window overlooking the side of the house, a single bed and bathroom that is so white it looks like the smile of well brushed teeth. I hurriedly unpack and run downstairs to check absolutely everything out.

Our first night's dinner is a gathering: Jean, a Scot.

She reminds me of Great-Grandma Joan.

Yes, she does. That's how I'll remember her name. I'm useless with names. Unless I say them three times out loud I'm lost. So there's also Lora, Emily, Otis and Louise from Carmel, CA; Jane, Rachel, Audrey, Jessica, Portia, Gordon and Stewart, best friends taking the course after not seeing each other in quite some time; Crissa, Russell, Sam, a Snowdonian from Australia, and our teachers, Jay Griffiths and Rory Maclean. It's all too confusing but I'll manage, I'm sure.

We're all seated around a large wooden table covered in candles and wine. The door is open to a garden, pitch black and invisible, noiseless except for the wind pushing leaves through the entrance. All the different dialects sparkle in the candlelight.

I wonder how much of a factor this country where I was born has been on who I am.

What effect could it have had if you'd stayed here?
Why didn't I move back?

You've had several missed opportunities to return along the way.

121

This gnaws at me. I feel surpassed and cheated out of a chance to know exactly who we could've been one to the other. All these other people at the table have their country inside already. It's alive with familiarity when they talk about it.

You come home to England every year. That's what you call it, how you tell it. Just because you don't stay, doesn't mean that it isn't alive in you.

You know that photo of earth that was taken in space, with all of the whirling white clouds, that's my country. I am removed and adrift.

It's a little after ten when I get back to my room. I sit on the bed and look out of the window into a bright white light somewhere off in the distance. I fall asleep with all my clothes on.

When the Welsh 6:00am arrives it's light already. I hop in the shower, throw some clothes on and walk down the lane to where old Lloyd George is buried. His bones are by the River Dwyfer, tucked under a circular altar stone covered in moss that seeps in to protect him. The dust to dust of him returned to the dirt he came out of. The river he walked, flows through him. I wonder if I'll return to a womb foundation like he has. My stomach rumbles.

After our first day of class I ask Awen, the administrator, for directions to Jan Morris' house. I'm determined to find her while I'm here. She and her book are the reason I found this place. I can't come all this way because of her and not try to find her.

"Two pastures up, past the white house you will see a farm track - turn left. There's a natural turn to the right, follow as the road goes along. Go all the way down and you'll see Trefan Morys. I hope you find her, she's always open to visitors." She smiles encouragingly and lets the door swing closed.

Two pastures to the left, and a clear turning - can't be that hard to find, right.

Ah, bless your heart, Ma - but you don't suddenly have a sense of direction.

Skeptic. This is my country. How do you count a pasture though, is it where a hedge dissects them?

I find a pathway right around where she said I would, but the sign on the gate says, "No Trespassing," and I'm pretty sure it's not cool for some British woman to randomly wander through Welsh land.

Plus your Welsh accent's rubbish. No fooling anyone there.

I only know four Welsh words and those are the names of houses. If someone's welcoming you in, the sign wouldn't say, don't come in, right?

Go on, I dare you. Climb over and go down there.

I don't think that's it.

You know it's it.

I'll walk on.

A lorry slows. I tuck my body over to the side, into the mud with the berries. He waves and honks at me. The path goes in a windy line; even I shouldn't be able to get lost. I see the sea, and a castle and it'll rain again in a minute and I look down at my feet and I watch them walking. As turned around as I can get, even I know that I'm about fourteen pastures too far from Jan Morris' house, and if I don't turn back now I'll be late for Rory's talk on publishing. A beep catches me off guard. It's the same lorry driver that passed me a half an hour ago.

"We've got to stop meeting like this!" he says in that Welsh way that makes me want to marry him. I want to ask him where Jan Morris lives, everyone knows everyone in a village like this, but my blushing face is laughing and he's on his way again. I suppose it's enough to just be walking where she does.

Who are you kidding?

How could I have missed it?

My head hangs low as I pass the office.

"Did you find her?" Stewart is standing at the bottom of the steps looking for a hopeful story.

"No, I think I went too far. I missed the turn off."

"Oh, I'm so sorry, that's too bad. Well, next time. Don't give up hope. You get out there and look again. She's right here."

"My problem is I have no sense of direction, even in a straight line." Stewart laughs as if I've made a joke. Awen rounds the corner.

"I saw a turning sort of where you said it would be, but it had a, "No Trespassing" sign on it, so I didn't think it was the right one and kept on going. That was it, wasn't it - I missed it?"

"Oh, yes, that was it. Oh, you should just have ignored that and walked up there. There's a turning right passed that."

123

Awen seems disappointed in my inability to follow her simple directions.

I can't believe you'd would come all this way and let thirteen painted letters keep you from a once in a lifetime meeting with the writer that made it possible for you to find this heaven.

I sit in the dining room brooding and listen to what percentage agents take, and how much money publishers abscond with of your work and my attitude rounds out the day. Aren't quests supposed to yield a golden fleece? Shit, bugger, crap. It's so much easier to find the dead.

Our time together in class culminates on the last day in the writing and sharing of a moment that has defined the way we live our lives, a time where certainty disappeared. Each of us moves into a different corner to write. I head out into the garden. I know what I have to say, and I can say none of it. The roots of the tree I'm sitting under have made their way to the surface, and they want me to do the same. I can't.

Me.

I should tell these people about you. But then I'd have to read you out loud. It's not that I'm ashamed of you or being the anti-mother. A part of me is afraid of being seen as heartless. Maybe there's someone in there that's been where I've been, but perhaps there's someone in that room who's lost a child, and she might look at me the same way I look at myself sometimes, and think the way I do about what a part of me was capable of doing, of what lives inside me, that I'm a selfish, coldblooded animal with no regard for human life; that what they'll see me feasting on is my own ego needing to survive away from the fear of being responsive to anything outside of myself. But that's not it, not who I am, and that's not why I did it. It isn't.

Calm down. I know and that's what's important.

I can't take you in there with me. You'll have to stay out here. I'm sorry. There's a larger part of me that thought perhaps I could. That's worth something, isn't it?

Yes, it is. It's enough for now that you know I'm winding through the grass, without having to dig me up and paper trail me back to the table. Write about him.

Yes, something of an equal ridiculousness that no one will believe anyway. I don't understand the presence of the Newspaper Soldier any more than they will. But I can't go in there and say I know a man I don't know and his spirit took control of my car and drove me around a cemetery to find a weeping statue to prove his existence; plus, oh, I cry for no knowing reason because he's dead. There is also that.

Just tell them how it feels in your heart.

I'm going to have to masquerade that as well.

There's no chitchat around the table as we gather back. One by one we raise our hands, and in a parted red silence begin speaking. It comes to my turn. I've used a distance exercise. I read a fictional letter to me from the Newspaper Soldier's point of view. The safest place I know to go is to have him explain it. This waltz for me is a lonely one.

"I knocked a bottle of water off your desk and into your lap the moment I left

my body and you looked right up at me. This is not déjà vu. I found you."

The bottle did fall that September day - inside my keyboard, disabling the letter b and making a huge wet moon shape on my skirt. I didn't see you.

If you listen to your heart, the pieces of what you remember fall into place.

I wonder if it really was him.

Before dinner I wander back to the tree to get the cardigan I'd left propped up on one of the lower branches, and I tuck you into bed, Cooper, safe again for a while. Back inside I pop my pound coins in the kitty and grab a bottle of red wine.

As I'm pouring Russell a glass, Sam sits down with us. Sam grew up in Australia and Britain. He spent time bouncing back and forth from one to the other. He spent a lot of time with the Aborigines learning their culture and traditions – walking in The Dreaming - the story of how the world came into being - handed down the generations through storytelling. Songlines. I could chat with him for hours.

The story of you and I is laid down in the earth and it's come for us.

Until the last few months our dreaming has been voiceless.

"I've been asked to play Prospero in a new version of *The Tempest*," he says, as if he's not impressive enough. I wished I'd been paying closer attention. "I haven't been on the stage for thirty odd years, so it should be interesting. A friend of mine is directing it. We're performing outside in a forest at Penpont. They have the largest Green Man Maze there."

"I can't miss this. When is it?"

"October 29ᵗʰ to November 2ⁿᵈ not far from Hereford, just across the border. When do you go back?"

"October 18ᵗʰ." But I have to stay. "I wonder if there's a way I can extend my stay..."

Why wouldn't there be?

Why wouldn't there be?

Later that night, Sam, Emily, Lora, Rachel, Jane and I all walk down to the seashore to build a fire and howl at the moon. All I really want is to get a good look at the shoreline. By the time we get down to the sea though, it's almost pitch black.

"I wonder if we're getting close to the water?" Rachel says right before she steps in it. "Oh, oh, I think I've found it." Sam reaches out his hand and brings her back - a bit soggy, shoes soaked through. Sam starts scouting out for branches, and Rachel, wet already, follows him. Both of them seem to know what to look for. I haven't a clue. We build a camp. Well, they did. I just said things like, "we need some more of these stick things," and, "did anyone else hear that?" Luckily the moon's giving us a bit more light and Sam, with his he-man powers and Australian voodoo techniques, is able to light a fire. We stare into it and watch our breaths hover in front of us for a while. We tell stories and Sam recites some of the Prosperonian monologues he's been rehearsing. The reflection of the flames is in his eyes and his voice lilts and booms. I bite out a few bars of the Queen Mab speech.

God, I loved watching you in Romeo and Juliet.

I can't believe I remember as much as I do.

When the flames begin to dwindle down, Lora has us all on our feet for a song of the sisterhood. She initiates all of us, which pleases Sam who says he's never been an honorary sister of anything before. We dance and sing like the only ones on a desert island with no thought of rescue.

Look.

And then for only the second time in my life a shooting star crosses the sky, waving across this collective burning out with the fire, never to gather again. Not like this.

Back at the house we settle into the plush red cushions one last time to read our work. We've lost the self-consciousness of sharing now. I can still feel the doorway full of the lot of us, all huddled in out of the open rainy Welsh sky, cases overflowing, laughing with the excitement and relief of making it here.

Relationship Intuition Number Thirteen: **The Collective Friendship**. This friendship is intense and temporary. A group formed by time and circumstance; people drawn to the same place, far from home, gathering to share a like interest. These people are the exception in that if one is absent from the mix the collective would not birth. Once you step through that door and the first kettle is boiled everything drifts off and the compass needle freezes. The remembrance of this union is for the rest of their lives, but rarely, if ever, gathers again.

The next morning I try to slow down the leaving as much as I can. I watch Jessica fiddling with her coat, and Louise and Otis trying to maneuver their many wheelie bags out the door. I go out into the garden one last time, back to my tree overlooking the sea. Our tree.

I think you might have buried a part of me here that day you couldn't take me inside.

Maybe I've brought your missing bones home to rest. I have nothing other than my inability to birth you to lay here. Nothing more than thankfulness that we knew each other as one person for a few short weeks, and, for the last twenty-six years, as two. You outside of me hasn't worked out so well, has it?

I think it's working itself out as it should.

You've given me so much time for introspection. I see that as a gift from you. I hope you know that.

The weight of me is still at the bottom of your handbag.

Reverend Jay.

Years ago, in the sermon he spoke shortly before he died, he told you that for the one thing you carried around, that lay heaviest on your heart, to pick up a large stone.

Hold on to it, he said. Only put it down when you're ready to walk without it.

I reach around into the bottom of my bag. The stone sways into my hand. Sticky. I close my eyes and run my fingers over the smooth crevice on the top, the lump on the side. How cold it feels. This is the only physical representation I have for you. I urge it into the wet mud with the palm of my hand. Deep down you go, passed the root trying to push it's way through to the air. I leave your invisible bones here, in this country that would have been yours, and continue rebuilding my own.

Pulling away from the train station I strain my neck looking back with Lot's disease. It's up to me to make the life at the end of this lane my own.

The train bumbles on and Welsh mix with British as the border gets closer. England arrives and the rain drifts off. The conductor stops to clip my ticket.

"I reckon you're older than you look," he says, looking me square in the eye in such a way that he knows he's said the right thing the wrong way. My hesitance at wondering if this is a compliment or not barrels him on. "There was this woman, see, I saw her on the trip up here. You remind me of her. Blonde, very pretty." He pauses and sits down next to me putting his feet up on the chair opposite. "Sorry, I meant it well. You are both pretty ladies." I give him a smile to match his wink. "I was a soldier you know, in the war. When I got out I went into the Fire Brigade, and now I'm doing this. I'm 63years old you know. I have a pension... but the ex-wife gets half of that, so here I am. I'm not bitter or anything. No, not bitter, not me. I get paid to do this – talk to pretty girls." As I pull into enemy England, he's off to clip the wings of other pretty things.

Home's quite welcoming, then.

My step-cousin Irene lives just across the border in Hereford so I'm here to see her and to meet up with my mother's brother, John, and his wife Susan who've driven down to see me there.

After a divorce we don't talk about, my Uncle got remarried to a woman that's perfect for him. Kind of like the Prince Charles and Camilla story without any of the cheating stuff and with prettier people.

As I get off the train, there's Irene waving at me in the parking lot. I haven't seen her since my brother's wedding ten years ago.

She was only eighteen then.

She's twenty-eight now, married to an army man and has two sons; sweet little hellions aged four and two. She's left them with their grandparents to come out and meet me.

Coming into Irene's back garden, two small faces from behind a bicycle and a plastic lawn mower look up at me. George, a four-year-old whose green sweater hangs over his hands, wipes his nose leaving a streak of dirt across his face.

"This is Auntie Sara. Remember, I told you she was coming. Why don't you give her a hug? George is my hugger," she says. The poor child doesn't look like he wants to put his arms around me any more than I want the remains of his day on my jacket. I quickly hug my Uncle. Mathew, her two-year-

128

old looks at me sideways as he runs to his mother and jumps into her arms. His cheeks are red from the cold and he twists his right hand in his sweater and pulls it over his head.

So this is what it's like to be a little boy in England.

My aunt comes out of the house and for the first time I see the toll of the cancer in her life. She's not wearing a scarf or a hat on her head, and she hasn't shaved her scalp clean of what the chemotherapy has left of her hair. It's the only sign that something has gone horribly wrong. It takes me back for a minute and I have to consciously try to look her only in the eye. She doesn't even think about it now, nor does anyone else, it's become a part of their everyday lives with no shock punch left to it. Susan always manages to look on the bright side though.

"You've just got to get on with it, haven't you, Sara," she says. And she's true to her word. She never ever uses it as an excuse - as if the sickness doesn't exist. Recovery is her only endgame, and it becomes the smile that heals so much faster. It may have taken away some physical strength and 90 percent of her hair, but it hasn't diminished her courage, her outlook on life, her demeanor, her laugh or her love for what she has. She doesn't complain about it. She doesn't give it that power. She doesn't give her illness any power at all.

"That's disgusting, George. Aw, you never hit him with that, did you?" Two smudged faces press themselves into the pane glass door that separates us. They are early risers.

"Sorry Sara!" Irene's apology comes as two pairs of lips are yanked off the door by my uncle. "What *are* you two doing?"

"I'm awake. No worries. No worries." I carefully open the door. George is climbing over the couch and onto the window ledge while Mathew's standing by the door naked eating fruit from a bowl.

"Sorry, Sara. Cup of tea? Oh, ah, Sara, be careful sitting there," my Uncle fusses as I go towards the sofa. "There's a board missing on that end so you might sink down." Sure enough with every second my sizable bottom drops. I look like I'm sitting in a giant's chair, knees to elbows, a cup of tea at my lips.

"No, it's alright, perfectly fine here," I say as only the English do to avoid any discomfort for others. George, in his sweet way, jumps down beside me and pulls me up so he can give me an immediate, gratifying, for no reason unconditional love hug.

"Just push him off if he bothers you, Sara," my Uncle says, taking my tea. "We're leaving for Tintern Abbey in an hour."

"That's the place I was telling you about. There's a poet, I forget which one…" Irene says.

"Wordsworth."

"Lines written a few miles above Tintern Abbey," your favorite.

"Yes, that's him. I love it there. I can't believe you've never been. It's a great place for the boys too. They can run wild and it doesn't matter if they climb up the walls because they can't break anything. You can't say that about many places," she says, wiping sticky fruit hand stains off the windows.

As we pull into the parking area at the old Tintern Abbey station the guide asks us if we're just here for the park, or for the WWII re-enactment.

"Wow, we lucked out," I say, knowing this will annoy John, "A re-enactment, how great is that?"

"Oh, crikey, you don't want to see that as well do you?"

"Soldiers on the battle field, people in costumes and tea and cakes on the lawn with Vera Lynn in the background, oh, yes, we're not missing that." John rolls his eyes.

Blighty overload - fantastic.

May as well have the whole tour.

We walk to Tintern along the River Wye after a rainstorm. The boys skid up and down in the mud chasing their dog, Layla, who's frantically jumping in out of the river trying to avoid them. They've all seen the Abby before so they hang around there while I wander it with you.

So many faces staring out of the stone.

As if the monks are inside the walls.

The monks are the walls.

It smells like rain soaked mud in here - the same as it did eight hundred years ago I shouldn't wonder.

Time may move on, but we all walk the same earth. The air is constant.

Breathing in the generations you mean.

Generations still breathing.

Walking back across the field George runs up to me.

"The proof is in the question. The proof is come from the water, bare water. That's the question. That's what I'm saying." George drifts into a way of speaking that makes no logical sense to anyone but himself. He's excited about what

130

he's saying and he repeats it without losing eye contact with me.

"The proof is in the question, yes, that's where the proof comes from, George, in questioning something. That's where the truth lives."

"That's what I'm saying!" he screams with his arms wide open jumping back on to the monkey bars. I wonder what put that into his head.

Asking is proof something's happening. He's right about that, Ma.

Back to the car park at The Old Station, World War II is in full blast, but we've missed the battle re-enactment. I'm sorry not to have been able to make Uncle John sit through that.

Why you want to keep reliving a time when so many people died is beyond me.

It was a time that brought the country together.

You can't sustain it so you relive it.

In a way. It's the simplicity of it that latches on to me. Who doesn't want Scotty dogs in tartan outfits urinating on the remains of summer flowers, Vera Lynn blasting from speakers on an old train carriage, soldiers resurrected from the battlefield packing up their tents in what is forever England? We can't go back to that part of history so we step back into it as best we can.

Without realizing it's always here.

Grandma Joan used to say, "even though there's a war on...

...we didn't have much money, but we had a lot of fun."

I wish you two were here, drinking cups of tea and having a singsong with me.

I know you do.

I can see you here running around, one sock up, one down, waving your flag, picking buttercups, asking me to shine them under your chin to tell you how much you love butter.

Again, I'd say, now your turn.

So much love waiting for you. It's a warm wish with a sparkle of sadness around the edges. Everyone's smiling, children running, chasing after the train.

Vera Lynn promised we'd all meet again.

When John, Susan and I head out for the journey to their house in Weymouth the next morning it's more of a see you later to Irene than a goodbye. Since Sam's fiery Prospero play is across the border from Hereford, I ask her if she wants to go

131

with me. If I'm able to change my return ticket and stay longer I'll come back and we can go. She's all in. After a few sticky hugs we're on the road.

"What do you want to see while you're with us, Sara?" My aunt asks. "There's Clouds Hill – that's Lawrence of Arabia's house, his grave and St. Nicholas Church. Then there's Thomas Hardy's house, Max Gate just up the road, you know." I stop dithering - hadn't Virginia Woolf been there?

You're like a crack addict with Virginia Woolf. By the way she says, hello.

Really?

No.

I've read all of her books twice. I own a rare copy of a novel called "*Flush*," which she wrote about Elizabeth Barrett Browning's dog. And, yes, it is a page-turner.

"Yes," I say.

"What, yes? Which, yes? You don't want to see them all, do you?" John has a devilish grin on his face that must have driven my mother a bit do-lally when they were little. Susan rolls her eyes and swings into action with inspiring verve and marks out our plan.

At Max Gate I touch everything I can because I just know that Virginia must have touched it at some point. A fruitless obsession, come to find out. The house, well lived in after Thomas Hardy moved out, was reconstructed according to existing photographs.

You should ask for your five quid back. Start touching the walls instead, the paneling, the staircase, that's all original, she must have touched that.

Good thinking.

You are so ridiculous.

On to St. Nicholas' Church, Moreton where T.E Lawrence had his funeral. His casket was wheeled in on a small wooden carriage that's now used in the café across the road as a cake stand. I touch that too. We bundle in the car after tea at the coffin holding cake café and head to Clouds Hill, T.E Lawrence's house. It's isolated and tiny, no windows, like a sort of white concrete shed. I look out the window to see what he and E.M Forster had seen.

To cap off the day Susan and I drag John off to the village hall to listen to some good old-fashioned folk music he'll hate.

It is truly mortifying. They've got some Canadian in with a ukulele. Not what I was hoping for at all. But when the guy that runs the place gets up and says he has one last song, the lights are dimmed. As he strikes the first chord on his guitar the entire room breathes in together to reach for the words of, "The Streets of London."

Your eyes well up immediately.

I've sung this song a thousand times with Grandma Joan. It's a part of our family and it brings the dead back to life. All the people around me have their heads bowed, holy. They remember the war, the way the city was ravaged - when it was damaged so was the collective soul of this country. It is in each one of us. I'm as conscious of it as I am of myself. I've never sung these words with a sense of meaning for myself.

"Yesterday's paper, telling yesterday's news... well let me take you by the hand, and lead you through the streets of London."

It's a meditative whisper but I can just about hear you. I read yesterday's paper every day.

You did. Now you're down to just the help wanted section.

I am. I love a good metaphor. London's streets inside me.

Even John sings along and wipes away a tear. It's the perfect affirmation of our family. I wonder what it means to him.

This next morning my blood cousin's supposed to drive down to pick me up here at her dad's, hang out and then drive me to my Great Auntie Alice and Uncle Cyril's house in Crawley. She calls to let me know that she can't come down as she has her son that night, as she does every Wednesday night, and couldn't imagine why she would have said she'd be able to come down and get me. Could she pick me up at Gatwick when I got back from Cyprus and I could spend the night at her house and we could hang out then? We'll reconvene. A train is the best way to travel anyway.

Before I leave, John gives me a spin in my dad's red Porsche that he's left here.

"Better you than me, Sara," my Aunt says as the engine revs up. "See you later… I hope." Now, I don't like rides as a rule – the ones at fairs and on piers – anything that pops you up and down, around and around or at great height or speed. So it's probably not the best decision to go willingly into this good morning in a red Porsche with my Uncle driving at 100mph.

I'll puff up your pillows on my end just in case you come up earlier than expected.

It'll be fine. It's kind of a rush to feel this much English wind in my hair, leaning back and looking up at the trees reaching together towards each other over the lane.

Let's have that left-brain kick in a little bit shall we, mother?

You mean the part that tells me that we can't actually see if there's a car coming towards us around the bend until we're speeding towards it, unable to stop and most likely to plow into a fiery mess.

That's the one.

Still, done, off my bucket list - if it was ever on it.

We've been apart for so many years, John and I. There's only a twelve-year age gap between us, and we'd been close growing up. Moving to the United States diluted that. Getting to discover each other as adults now is precious time. This world, although people remark how small it really is, is far too wide for me. I've lived in so many places, the seeds of my friendships are scattered wide. Constant motion is the only way to keep my arms around it. I wave goodbye with a great sense of missing.

At Crawley station my Auntie Alice is waiting to collect me.

"Oh, allo, love!" she says, holding my cheeks in her hands and then hugging me while wiping her nose from the English rain.

Remember how Auntie Rose used to squeeze your cheeks.

I know, so tightly. The price I had to pay to get my chocolate Easter eggs. Alice is lovely though. I love her so much. She's my Godmother.

"Alright, Sara? You've an 'alf got a big case, haven't you, love?" She may have moved out of London in her late twenties, but London has never moved out of her. She's walking so quickly and doesn't seem to notice my strained attempts to keep up, heaving my enormous case.

"Oh, yes, no worries."

"What you got in there anyway?"

"Well I am staying for almost seven weeks, you know."

"As I was saying though, Cyril's not doing so well. It's his leg you see, there's this pain he's had since the accident. Did we tell you we were in a car crash, Sara?"

"A..."

"Well, you know I never tell Cyril how to drive, but you know I thought we were a bit close to this truck thing, but I didn't say anything. And you know, Sara, I should have. But his foot must have slipped or something, and there we were. Your cousin Jessica was so good, came to the hospital and everything. Now, Sara, here we are, love. Home again. You remember our little house, don't you? Now you'll have to carry that suitcase upstairs yourself, love, Cyril's in no fit state these days." More bloody stairs. The thing about most English houses is that the staircases are like the ones you see on ships - vertical.

You're not kidding. I'd have taken it up for you.
"No, no leave it to me. No worries," he says.
No worries. You say that all the time too.
If you're born in England, those are the first words they teach you.
The sitting room is full of loved ones long since gone. We're back at the end of the garden where the fairies and the hedgehogs lie, where the Londoners went. Those we lost contact with when we left here thirty-two years ago sit here on the mantelpiece.

"I give my mum a dust and a kiss every morning, Sara. That's your great-grandmother, you know."
My great-great-grandmother. Uncle Billy looks a bit like her.
I've always thought so too.
"Good morning, David. There's not a day goes by that I don't miss him." She picks up her brother's picture. The last time I saw him was my fortieth birthday. I wanted a family reunion for my party. All our same blood, what's left of it, in the same room.

You went up to him and said, "you look like my granddad."
He was all smiles, wasn't he, and said, "did you hear what she said, I look like her granddad." His only brother, dad's dad, your great-grandfather.

You and Alice both have the same sense of nostalgia.
She misses, like I miss – living without accepting what's passed on, as if there's some island somewhere they've all drifted off to we'll someday get the coordinates to. When she and Cyril pass on she said she wants their ashes, "scattered into the four winds" in the churchyard where they got married.

"Not many of us Lovett's left now, darlin'," she says. "Six children, only two of us now. I'm eighty-three, you know." And you know I didn't know.

She looks the same as always. I thought she was sixty something, but of course she can't be, can she?

My own mother is seventy now. Alice still moves like a gazelle, especially when something's rotten on the streets of Crawley. Her chair faces the street and she's on patrol for her neighborhood. "Drug addicts next door there were, Sara. People going in at all hours. I called the police, didn't I, Cyril? You wouldn't believe, would you?" Cyril's pretending to read his paper, peering up occasionally over the top. "What are those you're taking, Sara?" Alice hands me a glass of water.

"Vitamin C. It's time release, it helps ward off colds and flu."

"Oh, there's nothing you can do to ward off a cold. It's a bug, if you get it you get it. Nothing you can do. Those vitamin things don't do nothing, Sara. But you take them if it makes you happy. Some American thing, no doubt."

"No, really it does help a lot. Your body can only…"

"Well, you take them, dear, but mark my words, if you're going to get sick, it'll knock you down." I start that birth breathing, taking in oxygen too quickly at high speeds. I'm right. Why do I have to always be right? AHHH. I know I'm right.

Then why let it upset you? You'll only make yourself sick.

Oh, ha, ha. But AHHHHHH.

Saturday night my friend Davey and his mate, Sig, are playing with their band, Los Bastardos, at a pub not too far from my Aunt's. Sig's picking me up on the way.

"What have you got on now? Why did you change? You looked so much nicer in what you had on before. And why did you take your hair down, it suits you up, Sara. You should wear it up more often."

She sounds like Grandma. Look at your phone.

"Sig's outside!" I give them both a big hug and a kiss goodnight, knowing I'll see them the next morning. In the same outfit. Without makeup. Or my hair up. And hung over. That'll go down well.

Thank God you're taking Vitamin C time release.

That's enough lip from you, Sonny Jim. She says that as well.

136

Hugs slice off like butter with Sig, Davey and his wife Lee. With gin and tonics in hand, all's well in our world. When they step on stage they take on Los Bastardos personas - Maverick Lee Beauregard (Davey), "Mighty" Quentin, (Sig's son) and Bobby Lee Lewis (Sig). They're armed with guitars, attitude, and a mounted confederate flag. You can hear the tumbleweeds blowing through Bookham on this Surrey, Texas rainy night in Blighty. Maverick takes the microphone.

"I'm doin' mighty fine tonight! How are you bastards out there? I can't hear you!" And this 666% Punktry & Western Band (not for sissies) opens up its lungs. Three hours later they're still screaming out to a dancing crowd.

I grew up with Davey. He and Sig play in this band and their original one, The Witchdokters, with our other childhood friend, Matt. Davey is Abby's brother. She and I were best friends growing up. We spent every New Year's Eve together as kids – his mate would stop the night with him, like I did with Abby. I loved vertical stairs in those days - perfect for a scheming child.

Remember sliding down them on New Year's Eve?

At their parent's party we'd get out the silky, blue sleeping bag and slide down.

Crashing into oncoming dolled up alarmed adults walking through the front door.

Brilliant. I'm not sure how pleased their parents were, but you don't care when you're ten do you.

I don't know.

You see a banister – you slide down it, full stop.

There might be casualties.

What I love about Sig and Davey, and Matt, the original three Witchdokter's, is that they've remained close in a kind of friendship I've never had. They've always lived in the same town or nearby, and gone to the same schools. My family moved around from country to country which made sustaining a long lasting group friendship ridiculous. I'm sure they go through patches where things aren't as snuggly as they sometimes were, but they've known each other all their lives, they come together for each other more often than not. I envy that. I wish that I had that kind of kinship circle of friends close by. I had them when I lived here – that same kind of group. When you move around, never knowing when the next move will be, investing in friendships is an emotional risk. I suppose that's why the relationships I've sustained over

137

time have been the ones I formed as a young child, when I didn't know any better.

And why you closed yourself off at an early age. It didn't begin with me. It nested.

Yes, I suppose it did. The unfelt needs its own foundation. I hope these three realize what they have. I wonder if they assume everyone has it because they do. I hope they know it's rare. Friendships are sweaty, and the ones that endure deserve to be untidy, chaotic, jubilant, fragmented and recharged by growing in the direction it wants to move - they are elastic.

Their friendship syncs up. In the music they write their own peace together, compose their own song – it's enticing, it grew out of something already established in childhood. I'm just grateful that I can snatch a piece of them here and there as I go; be a part of the posse, of this gang of Bastardos as I drift through town.

I crash at Sig's and we stay up for what's left of the night chatting and drinking wine. I drift off in my clothes with only my boots off and fade into a sofa sleep.

The next morning he brings me back to Cyril and Alice's, but on the way he does something lovely for me - he drives me around to where I used to live, my old house, and my old school.

You haven't been back here since you were nine.

The cafeteria had the best butterscotch pie in the world.

You'd sit next to Brett and give him your mysterious meat thing, and you'd get to eat two butterscotch pies.

Funny what you remember. Abby and I met on this playground forty-one years ago. We'd walk to school together, play together; we kissed our first boy together, and skipped away from nosy neighbors.

A part of you still lives here. It stayed.

I've swung around to pick her up. I want her sense of play back.

I get home with just enough time to shower, cover up the sagging dark circles under my eyes, and shake off the kinks before meeting Zaina for brunch later on in the morning. I reached out to her not knowing where she lived in England. As it turns out, and with synchronicity conspiring with us, she lives on the other side of the village from my Aunt and Uncle. "This is wonderful. I am literally right across the park from you." She's here in minutes.

So the big wide world is not so big for you when it needs to be.

I know, it's funny, isn't it?

No. It's perfect.

Zaina's part of the UT, *Midsummer Night's Dream* crew. We used to meet at Zaina's high-rise apartment, sneak up to the roof and read poetry aloud.

Carpe Diem – that was your slogan.

Our code, you mean - Seize the day.

The flash of time you shared was intense. The heart of who you are is the same.

But time has moved on and claimed something of her. Her mother has Alzheimer's disease and her stepson has Autism, and it's through these two people that she finds most to gain and learn from life.

"I was watching my mom the other day, she was trying to peel an apple in one go, without it breaking. The look on her face as she held it up to me was like she'd conquered Everest. It's the little moments now. I took her up to bonny Banff in Scotland where she grew up. Mum stood there looking out at the sea with the wind on her face. She had all she needed." She sees the beauty in it.

The situation is always present – she's just not allowing it any control. You should see her again.

We plan to meet up again when I get back from Cyprus.

So I'm up in the air again with white wine and my newly re-written will and as the plane bounds through what feels like bullet filled clouds shooting at us on descent, my Hail Mary's praying in the background, Cyprus is where I'm up, up and away to. I'm flying on faith that the pilot is sober, and that I'll live to see Arina again in this physical life. She's one of the acting core 16 that made up the class I was in at UT. She has this long, black hair, all one length, that she used to flip out of her face with the back of her right palm in what is probably *the* sexiest move any women ever made ever. All the boys waited for it, even the gay ones. I tried it in the mirror once but I just looked like I was trying to get a bee out of my face. At parties she was the one quietly smoking in the corner, looking at the scene with her one exposed eye under all that hair, mysterious, before she exploded into the part of the party that engaged her.

In contrast to you, in the middle of the room dancing around in circles in your lime green pantsuit with hippie flowers all over it.

139

Ah, well, we're all remembered for something.

On the doors at the arrivals area as you come up the tunnel at Larnaca Airport it says, "Open Up To New Experiences."

You might just be on the verge of something wonderful.

On the other side of this provoking message there's a man with white hair whose eyes are darting around lifting up a sign to any woman making eye contact with him that has "Sara Lovett" written on it. I wave, and not knowing if he speaks English, start miming out, "that's me, this name here, this is me."

As if you're losing a game of charades.

As this comes to a painful close, he speaks to me in perfect English,

"I'm Vasilis, Arina's husband. I have come to fetch you. She is held up at work."

On the drive out of the airport to Nicosia, a long stretch of road reaches out ahead of us with a strange picture imprinted in the hills. It is always facing us.

"What's that sign in the hills over there? It's fantastic."

"That is the Turkish flag flying in my country," he says, reaching for a cigarette, and putting it back in his pocket again. "Not even the UN recognizes it. It is a self-declared state."

So, not so fantastic then.

I obviously know nothing about the politics of this country, past, or present, which seems at this moment to be tied very closely together. I change the subject quickly to nature. Can't go wrong there.

"What kind of trees are those? They look exactly how I imagined the landscape - like in the pictures."

"It's a Cypress tree," he says without looking me in the eye.

Out of kindness I shouldn't wonder. Try not to speak.

I'm off to a roaring first impression. I don't know where to begin, what to say. After a few moments though, he begins to speak. I've rustled something with my flag comment. He was a soldier in the mid- 1970's and he's seen his country torn apart. His life went from sipping coffee in his home in Famagusta, to never being allowed beyond the barbed wire to collect anything that rightfully belongs to him. He doesn't take his eyes off the road, off that flag always north of us.

"We will take you there, if you want. Into the occupied side. I haven't been over there for years. We will go. We will

140

take you there." Occupied territory? Do I like the sound of that? Occupied means that an army is there, and they'll have guns and whistles, right?

People live there though, go on holiday. Where's your sense of adventure?

I look over at his face and at the spears pumping the blood through his heart. Occupied or not, I want to know who fired them, and what caused this man's shield to bruise.

Arina isn't home from work when we arrive so I settle my things in. I'm staying in her youngest daughter's room and so now I'm overly preoccupied with where she's going to sleep. It's that British thing – I don't want to put someone out.

Sleep on top of the sheets so you don't dirty anything.

I know. Ridiculous. Just say thank you and get over it. I am secretly glad not to have to sleep on the couch, if I'm honest.

When Arina returned here after graduation she was on TV for a while, as well as on the stage. It occurs to me that she might be a celebrity - her sister, mother, father and her husband are known as well.

I'll look for paparazzi.

When Arina walks through the door we stand face to face about ten feet apart and look at each other for about twenty seconds - the amount of time to take in that it's all real. With the sunlight behind her in the doorway she might just be a vision. We say each other's names and dash towards each other reaching through all the missing years. There are hugs that fade into the background of time, and there are hugs you can still feel because they became a part of your body. We can't stop looking at each other, laughing at the idea that we are physically in the same space again. It is breathtaking and feels remarkable.

One by one her children, Maarit, Sabella and Antreas arrive home. We sit on the patio chatting at a pace. What takes me off guard is the kind of conversation that I'm having with three teenagers. They're not sunken with their heads in a machine; they are lively, talkative, curious, intelligent. They show me a dance they've learnt, and our discussions aren't mundane or slight – they are about music, politics, how it relates to them, their country, and their future. They are rooted in culture, so they are intrigued by other peoples - the United States, England, Europe, by every border that crosses them. We sit and paint stories of our related experiences.

Her eldest daughter, Sabella, is strong feisty and restless. She's that sound a match makes right as it comes in contact with the flame. Her son, Andreas is in his last year of high school and what that means for him is quite different from a seventeen-year-old boy where I'm from. There are no college applications being filled out, no scholarships being applied for. After his High School graduation, for twenty-four months, he will automatically be drafted into the Cypriot army. This boy is full of energy, passion and intensity. He's so full of everything I hoped you would be, Cooper - untamed, explosive and clever. It's so beautiful, looking at him, and saddening at the same time. I see what I could have had with you. I hope once he's paid back the state with part of his childhood that he'll have found a way of safekeeping all that drive and goodness for who he really is.

Tell him that. It's what you would have told me.

"You know, when these pauses come into our lives it feels invasive, doesn't it. This one especially, for you. I've never had to deal with something like this. It's a kind of ownership that's being lorded over you in a way. But it's the uncontrollable for you, right now. In those situations, the one's beyond our capacity to alter, I find they force me inside. They have a way of grounding us in who we are, but they also challenge us, to see how much we want what is being forced into a kind of holding pattern. It's asking us what we can withstand, what we will compromise, how true to ourselves we will truly be. It's a place where, as difficult as it is, by walking it, and believing with our whole heart that at the end of it, because of it, if we make use of it, there is a gift of this waiting. At the other side anything will be possible." For a split second or two he believes me. Such a sweet face, so innocent and ready to dive into all he wants to be, and I'm droning on about patience and challenges. "And if that fails, I'll put you in my suitcase and sneak you out of this country." He laughs and he and his sister, Maarit, dance around some more. I'd forgotten that "watch me, watch what I can do" childhood feeling. I watch every moment of theirs.

Maarit, the youngest, is the peacekeeper, the social connection, the rational, wise one with the open heart on the table. She is kind and caring and tosses her hair the same way as her mother did. She is her mother. She gave up her bedroom for me; she made her space into my own space to live in without grudge. For a teenager that seems extraordinary to me. She's a string that connects the siblings together.

I will leave with a piece of each one of them in your

heart.

The school schedule here has them all home at 2:00pm - all at the lunch table together, always at the table. A wild freedom of discussion, food, laughter all carries on under the watchful eye of a beagle.

"Where's Orestes?" Arina asks, laying the table. It's at this moment he bounds through the back door and makes a b-line for the chicken lying in surrender on the table by my left arm. It's so fast, I don't see him coming. The chicken flies off the table as if the Holy Spirit has resurrected it and Orestes swallows half of it down whole before being jeered and chased outside. He looks very confused about the whole situation – "what an overreaction." This is the pace of the whole family though.

After each child is settled, Arina and Vasilis take me for a ride around Nicosia. Initially, I feel uneasy. It's so unlike anything I have ever seen. The shops have closed down in droves - the walls and metal doors are padlocked and covered with graffiti. It's not bored teenagers or gangs that have done this though – this abandoned graffiti is a sign of a frustrated, disappointed people. It's a testimony.

You should put your phone away.

We drive on to where The Green Line splits the border of their country in two - right through the center of Nicosia. It's patrolled by the UN. Vasilis says something to Arina in Greek.

"Sara, put your phone down. No pictures here. I don't want them to take it away. It wouldn't be good for them to see that." It's no wonder that the population explodes creatively when they're so restricted by the confines of their own land.

We pull over to a restaurant and drink red wine served in bronzed Elizabethan style goblets, which I find marvelous and odd. Arina wants me to sample all the local dishes so they bring out a sampler or, Mezedes.

You're not all that good at trying new food things.

I've always been an annoyingly picky eater.

You just need to buck your ideas up, lie back and think of England.

Yes, that's what Grandma Joan used to say anyway. At the sight of some of these things coming out of the kitchen though, I might find it better to lie back and think of Liam Neeson. All things have to taste better with Liam Neeson, don't they?

143

Halloumi cheese arrives. All's well. I love cheese. Cheese is also remarkably in love with attaching its fat molecules to my stomach, but I devour hundreds of creamy bites of the stuff anyway. Next, some sort of animal arrives in pieces in a bowl mixed with vegetables and the like.

You're all in with Liam now.

I pick up a handful of olives to help my taste buds out just in case. The spices and the texture are a combination of lusciously interesting, mixed with a bit of don't tell me what this is. Rob Roy and I take our first bite. It is surprisingly good. I would never have ordered it myself, but I'm glad I tried it.

"So, what is happening with everybody?" Arina wants to know about our entire class and where they are now. Who I've seen, how they are, what they're doing. I visualize my journey step by step and one by one I tell their stories from where we left off to where they are now.

"Are you getting tired of repeating all of this?"

"No, not at all. It's all just happened. It hasn't sorted itself away yet. I'm not sure it ever will. It's all so fresh. I love talking about everyone, are you kidding?"

"Well good. You were going to have to tell it all anyway! How's Stephen? You know we Skype every once in a while." Our instooled teacher, Dr. Gerald.

"I had breakfast with him a few months ago. I wonder if he could Skype while I'm here? I'll send him a message."

It's only 2:00pm there, I think.

Sitting on the porch an hour later, Stephen pops up on the screen.

"Before you say anything, I've been ill. I took a semester off, but I'm alright now," he says urgently after hellos have been exchanged. The Stephen I see is not the man I saw a few months ago. He looks thinner, but healthy. I look over at Arina. Did he say that right away so we don't worry, or because he truly is well? In school there was never any bull with him. In his voice today, for the first time, I hear the tremor of a heard of them. It fades away quickly though. Our words only bleed the happiness of being together - the three of us connected in a way that we were, in a way we have never been.

My throat wakes me up the next morning. I'm swallowing sandpaper.

This after all your boasting about how much Vitamin C you take and how you haven't been sick in years.

My God, I've proved Auntie Alice right, "It's a bug, if you're going to get sick, Sara, you're going to get sick. Nothing you can do about it." AHHHHHHH.

It sucks to be wrong.

Arina gives me a numbing spray and her mother hands me hot tea with honey and a cinnamon stick.

"This is what makes difference good," she says. I believe every broken word. I have to have something to believe in now that my Vitamin C theory seems a bust.

I cough and spray my way through the archaeological sites of Kourion, and Akrotiri, where the nasal drip arrives. I drown my throat in local honey in the Troodos mountains where British radar looks like huge golf balls.

Still hacking it up the next morning, our plan is to cross into the occupied area. Vasilis and I travel into the center of Nicosia to wait for Arina and he walks me around a little towards the border crossing where you can pass on foot. We've driven over the other border. The Lidra Street crossing has a sign above it that says, "Nothing is Gained Without Sacrifice, And Freedom, Without Blood." A slogan in broken English - a mission statement of a country with a zipper holding it together.

Much like yourself. Curious isn't it, that out of all the countries in this big wide world, this broken one is where you find yourself.

I could have that slogan written on my tombstone.

Not anymore.

A man sits on the ground playing his guitar, a hat flipped upside down.

"Such pretty music. Lovely."

"It's embarrassing." Vasilis lights his cigarette, blowing the smoke into the music. "You would never have seen that here five years ago. Beggars. Unemployment was at 1%. Now look." It's funny - I don't think twice about this sort of thing, it's just a musician. Not here. To him it's a physical representation of the decline of his country.

So many without work singing for their supper. Their blood is in the soil here.

More than anywhere I've been.

After we meet up with Arina, we drive on to the border. Vasilis takes all three passports to the window. It seems odd to me that we don't have to show our faces at the window, that the passports are accepted without the physical proof that who sits in the car, is who is on paper - especially me, a real

outsider. It doesn't take very long. A piece of paper is issued
with a stamp. It's a hard pill to swallow for the Cypriots - to
have to show their passports in order to go home, but they do
it.

They have to.

This stretch of land, once you're on the "other" side,
clearly isn't theirs anymore. Signposts have been changed,
removed, reworded, and towns renamed. It makes it difficult
for those that used to live here to find the towns they grew up
in. That fake flag I saw flying the day I landed now flies,
gigantic and static, in the Pentadactylos Mountains to the left
of us. There's no forgetting where you are.

The Varosha section of Famagusta where we're going was
fenced off by the Turkish army immediately after being
captured in 1974. The Greek Cypriots who fled were never
allowed back to their homes. It's a city frozen in time - as if
someone's hit the pause button on a T.V. Boiling kettles were
abandoned, half eaten dinners still on the table and children's
toys left at play. Department stores and hotels stand empty,
looted right down to the tiles on the bathroom walls. All
displaced into camps to begin again.

Famagusta is where Arina's husband is from. When The
Green Line was drawn on this no man's land it was drawn
right at the doorstep of his house. Twenty feet further back
and his home would have been spared to freedom. It's so close
you can stick your hand through the wire and touch the tree in
the front garden. All Vasilis' family history and traditions live
in a place to which there is no return. What they can't take
away from the evicted is their sense memory. Closer to the
town, memories flood in.

"There is a model train up here, yes up just there I think…
yes, there! It was the first locomotive, a replica…" As we
round another corner, closer and closer in, "Our church I think
is up the street… yes, there… oh, there is my elementary
school! Our house, this is the street – number 37. Oh, my
goodness… oh, my goodness." You can hardly make it out as
a structure anymore. There's an overgrown tree stretched out
across his front door making the archway barely visible
anymore. His bedroom window clings on to the last wooden
slat of a light blue shutter. His parents' bedroom wall is open,
grass pouring over the side like a still green waterfall, trying to
make it breathe.

*An entire life washed away; a theft that will never be
returned to any of them.*

I watch Vasilis walking up and down in this sandy, reddish soil where, "nothing is gained without sacrifices, and freedom, without blood." There is a strange happiness to be home washed over with the sadness and frustration of not being able to touch any sentiment of it at all. The most he can do is peer in as far as he can, from every angle that he can stretch around, then close his eyes and see it as it was when he looked over his shoulder that last day running for the hills. He was a soldier, a man of strength, born inside the original entrance to the city, in Othello's castle. His family's blood ran here for generations and now he has to show a passport to come in– disregarded, with no direction. It is this that moves a man of great success and a happy life to sadness. Here is the spear that pierces his heart.

The barbed green line goes on for miles with naziesque red and black "Forbidden Area" signs attached to it and a cartoonish picture of a soldier holding a gun telling me that "No pictures" are allowed. That's a laugh in this day and age.

There's no carpet big enough to sweep this under. The road home is paved in the rear view mirror.

"Which side do you think is nicer, Sara?" The question coming as if from a child asking which parent is loved more.

"It feels desolate on this side. Most of what they've taken is barren. It feels dead. It feels like nothing is growing. They have a beautiful piece of your coast, but they've gutted it. It's held up like a warning, you know - with the guards and their whistles that came after us when I was taking a photo."

"They don't want you to get Famagusta in the picture."

"Then why have it? It's like Wonderland, you know? It's all upside down and nothing stands for what it looks like it should. What you have on your side is vibrant, it's alive. I mean, sure there are areas where you can feel the loss and the poverty with all the shops closed, but that's just being open with the past. People are out in the streets; they're having coffee and talking. It's still breathing."

"Yes, it is. Yes, I think so."

"You can't take sides in your own country just because an enemy's living there, can you?"

That is exactly what you did.

"No. It was our home. It is our home."

I took your side.

No, you divided yourself. Your body housed the repercussions of a soul you sliced in half. You exorcised all the love you had for yourself out of your body with

147

so much intention that your soul had to grab it in to itself and wait.

I pushed it out.

Your soul is always home.

I could still smell it. I thought it was my love for you.

It's your own inward love, for yourself.

Waiting to be remembered.

This country is both sides of you.

We are a Cypriotic metaphor.

That, Ma, you carry on your own.

To have passed over going to see Arina was a possibility. I thought it might be too far to go, too expensive. I'm glad I didn't let that stand in my way. I had no idea what to expect, or how long to stay. And from the moment I arrived the conversation was, why are you not staying longer? A three-year friendship during college paused for a twenty-year intermission. The likelihood of what's actually come out of this is extraordinary. I have clear memories of her specifically, but none of who we really were to each other back then.

You connected because you were both from far away.

Yes, we talked didn't we, about that. About being from somewhere so outside of what America represented to us.

And she returned home after graduation.

And I didn't.

Because it had become your home. Without asking.

She came home to the richness of this family of fascinating people. When we talked years ago I had no idea what was out here for her. What she'd left, or why she'd left, or why she came back. Of course she'd come back.

She already knew what home was.

I didn't.

Until you arrived here.

When you have no expectations it allows for the heart of what is to appear, to happen. To be what it is without conditions. So we are. We're in tune with each other in something so bright. In this world where I have no sense of direction, only here have I known at all times where I am. I have my bearings.

Flying out of Cyprus this evening full of a goodbye I'm not ready to say, my mind attaches to that first moment when we saw each other in the doorway. It seemed like a dream to get together again, and there we were. We kissed each other's cheeks, hugged without want of letting go, and looked each other in the eye as if only a day or two had passed between us. I'm still there now, locked in that moment of the door opening, and walking in.

I am so much better at hello.

I arrive back at Gatwick airport in the early morning, around 1:30am. The cheaper flight that makes logical sense at the time of purchase never makes sense at the execution. My cousin is a no show to pick me up.

You didn't remind her. Just get in the Taxi line.

I'm so tired. I finally catch one at 2:30am and arrive at my poor relations around 3:00am. My Aunt said she'd wait up but has changed her mind, and my incessant tapping on the door has woken her up. She greets me with a hug and the usual, "Alright, Sara?" I've never been so relieved to get into a bed.

True to form she's knocking on my bedroom door at 7:30am with a cup of strong tea and a biscuit. She hasn't been able to get back to sleep, and I had just about drifted into a deep coma to escape my cold. She pulls the curtains sharply, letting the light in. I'm not sure if it's the shock on my face from being startled back awake or the post nasal drip stuck to my face that gives me away first.

"Now, Sara, do you need any Paracetamol?" she asks. This is England's answer to any ailment, along with a cream called, Savlon that you can put on almost any wound to heal it. It always works. I call it miracle cream.

Before you head down, you'd best do something with that un-drunk cup of tea.

The reprimands of a week before hang in the air so I tiptoe to the bathroom and pour it down the sink.

Why are you tiptoeing? You've got to go to the bathroom anyway.

Guilt most likely. Only when we do something sneaky do we act irrationally. It's how criminals are caught. I try to spritz my throat as loudly as I can to cover for the flaw in my plan. It needs numbing anyway, so I can swallow down the remainder of the physical evidence: the crisp Rich Tea biscuit and the Paracetamol.

And, oh, who in the world is that 105-year-old woman looking at me through the mirror? Saggy dark eyes. And my face. I slept wrong and the creases from my pillow have chiseled themselves into my right cheek into the shape of a badly carved rune sign.

149

Branded! Pretty funny. It looks like your face is pealing off as well.

Thanks a lot. It's the postnasal drip crust from the restless sleep. I look like crap, and this afternoon I'm leaving to go to Los Bastardos Davey's sister, Abby's. She was the prettiest girl in school. She always looks lovely. I don't want to look aged and decrepit, which I do, which I hate.

Blow your nose again. Plus you may make them sick.

They'll be so glad to see me, won't they? The bulbous, dripping nose and scratchy voice are too much. This is going to take some work - a steaming hot bath and two weeks of sleep I don't have. Ah well, onwards.

I go downstairs for a last meal and goodbyes. They've been extraordinarily kind to me, my Aunt and Uncle, putting up with my comings and goings at all hours and popping off here and there.

Despite your aching on.

This part of our family dropped off the map when we moved to the other side of the world... easy to lose track - even of family. It shouldn't be, but it happens. It happened.

They have a closeness, don't they, our London relatives. Tight knit.

There is a whole supportive swing to them I wish I could have been a part of. But it's hard to jump on a train already barreling thirty years down the track.

I take a last look around the living room, at all my framed relatives and wave so long as my Aunt kisses them all good morning.

The Map Outside

Once you know the truth, you can't ever go back and pick up your suitcase of lies.
Heavier or not, the truth is yours now.
- Sue Monk Kidd

My friendship with Abby is a stark contrast to the way my relatives faded. With me moving around, Abby lived on the same foundation in the same house. Still, you wouldn't think the friendship stood a chance, but we managed to stay close. We met at school at the age of seven. We walked to school together, pierced our ears, and -

Had your first kiss with the same boy.

Scott, ha! I'd forgotten about him. Less than two years later I moved to France. We wrote letters and hung out whenever I came home. When I moved back a few years later we'd crossed over the teenage threshold with bras on and without each other. She was the most popular girl at school; I was the weird thing in the corner with the sensible Clarks shoes on.

We came in and out of each other's lives with just enough regularity to rejuvenate overlaps. We stayed in touch. She's a constant in my life, regardless of how different we are from each other. She's another sister to me in many ways, the one that rolls her eyes from a distance at things I do; shakes her head and has a laugh at me, being me. Maybe our friendship endures in part because it's the only way we know how - with distance between us. Because of that space though, even though we know a lot about each other, we know so little of each other's inner heart.

My taxi pulls up outside and she's right at the door. She looks fantastic, and has obviously lost weight. The last time I saw her I'd dumped a lot of my own. Now in my crawl across the globe part of it's found me again, and twelve of the twenty pounds I've lost have reattached themselves to my stomach.

Suck it in, old girl.

I'd secretly been wishing we'd be sitting down to two jam filled donuts like we did last time I was here. That's not going to happen, now. I hoist my enormous suitcase up to the attic room. More windy stairs.

On the bright side, you'll shed a few pounds going up and down these.

151

This glass half full attitude can be really annoying at times, my lovely.

If I had a self, I'd make a note to it.

I need sugar.

Abby's husband has been renovating their house for the past twelve years, all by himself. Since I was last here stairs have appeared up to a second floor. I'm in the new bedroom with en-suite bathroom. She's blown up a single mattress for me with cuddly covers and pillows. Cozy.

"It's only just finished. You have arrived as the paint and grout are drying. I'd love to have a bath in there, but you're here now." I feel guilty, even though I know she's only joking. They have been working tirelessly to ready the house for my arrival, and it all looks so perfect. I put my case under the sloping attic wall and graze the top of my head on the newly painted wall. I back the rest of me out slowly, aware of myself. "You'll have to be careful with that," she says. I'll walk with a permanent slant from now on just in case I take more paint off the wall.

After the delicious obligatory English cup of tea we're off to pick her daughter, Maya, up from school. When she comes bounding into the car I can't believe my eyes. She's grown from an adorable little girl into a towering, teenage, take your breath away, runway model. So much happens in two years at that age.

Abby is careful with her, encouraging, supportive, mindful and loving. She gives everything she wished her upbringing had been to her. The relationship she had with her own mother was often a battle, and she's not passing that forward. Her daughter is curious, calm, interesting and vital.

She told me she liked the idea of being a horror movie makeup artist - knife wounds, burns, you name it she can create it. So earlier this year I sent her a package of fake blood, skin and scars. She's showing me pictures of what she's done with it all. I am proud and repelled at the same time. It's all so convincing.

Later on in the evening in the lounge, all the family take their usual seats on the two couches. Abby and her husband are on one sofa, and Maya and their dog Cleo are on the other. One slight problem - there are only enough seats for three and a dog.

"Oh, you'll have to take Cleo's seat by Maya," Abby says calling the dog over to sit by her, where the remote controls usually go. The dog looks at me sideways.

Duck Dynasty is on the TV. They have it on as a kind of joke in all its absolute ridiculousness in the background. Here I am thinking it'd be all *Downton Abbey*, or informative, creative, imaginative television and I've got men in beards stripped down to their nipples pretending to be ducks. I try not to watch but am sucked in. No one else seems to be watching. They have their own iPads, and while mother and daughter scour the day's Facebook events, her husband is playing a word match game. Together. I pick up a book called, *The Journey, a practical guide to healing yourself,* by Brandon Bay. I readjust my now tight-waisted fat pants and curl myself up like Cleo and have a read. If the woman in the book intentioned away a basketball sized tumor, surely I can wish away a dynasty of duck men.

The next morning, my cousin and I are due to go to the cemetery together to see our grandparents. She sends me a message to say she isn't feeling well. I'm beginning to doubt if we'll ever hook up. Uncle John says she's secluded herself off a bit. I'm just not going to give up. I've come all this way and she's minutes up the road. I pick up my phone.

Why don't you just ask her?

I want her to want to see me. I don't want to have to bend myself sideways.

What's the point in being here if all you do is hide away and pretend everything's fine?

I'm in England. The belly of the beast.

Ha, yes, truer words...

Ask why she's pulled away, and try to understand that, you mean. Yes. We moved to America before she was even born.

So maybe it's time to get to know her. This is the timing. There's no such thing as bad timing.

She has to meet me half way though.

I walk to the crematorium alone after Maya kindly shows me the way to the woods. I'm holding the map she's drawn me.

"It goes this way up," she says, becoming aware of my non-sensical lack of direction. I tell her not to worry and bustle on.

The path through the woods comes to an impasse. I don't want to, but we have to turn off. One road leads to my grandparents old house, and the other to what's left of them. I wish I could take you where the joy lived.

It's not our path anymore.

No. The crematorium. That's where our ancestors live.

Grandma Joan used to bring you here once a year to lay flowers for Granddad Bill.

She did, yes. We'd go into the chapel and I'd sit behind her while she prayed and missed him.

She lived with you your entire life, didn't she?

Well, your great-grandfather passed away when he was only forty-three, a few months before my parents got married.

She moved in when you were about two.

And now we're all buried here by the lake. It drifts past the marker where your great-grandparents ashes were poured in. No names, just a three letter identifying marker on each one. I don't want them to be here, under foot. Ashen ears.

A spider weaves around the left arm of the wooden bench where I'm sitting eating marmite sandwiches and stolen weight watcher crisps. There's little use to my being here other than the irrational comfort of sitting by what's left of the body.

I was never in presence.

Perhaps that's why I brought you here. I thought it might help explain that to me. We bury all of our dead here on this meadow by the water where the swans glide on by. Not you though.

No, not me.

There is no place to love you. No headstone, no three letter marker. I dread to think of where your cells washed away. Your mass grave is a place I cannot go.

You've been in presence with them, not with me. You shared lives. The place to love me has never changed. It's always been all around you.

Now you're only trying to make me feel better.

That's the problem. You still think you need to feel better about it. All life is, is a series of choices strung together. God told Adam and Eve not to eat the apple; he didn't take away their right to make the choice for themselves. Life is choice. Singular to us all. It's how we define ourselves.

I ate the apple anyway.

And there are some of us who serve to allow that path to happen. What you don't see is the knowledge, the outcome of the action. You've haven't had the courage to look for it.

I can't see that yet.

So we'll just sit here a while.

How can I miss something I never had?

That's precisely why you miss me.

It begins to rain. I sit still and munch on a salt and vinegar communion wafer when what I really want to hear is the clink of gin and tonics - *for Granddad George to make you your Snowball drink,* and to watch the sun streaming in through the silhouette of the dove that crashed into the window that year whose outline you can still see even after a good washing. The only thing I want is the one thing I can not have, which is to be with all of you who've disappeared. I want Christmas back.

Remember when you got a new James Galway tape for Christmas.

I was about twelve, wasn't I? I put it in my Walkman and turned it up as loudly as it would go. It was so peaceful, and I watched my family laughing and talking. I couldn't hear a word they said, but they were happy. I remember thinking at the time that one day I'd wish I'd kept the music lower so I could hear and remember the sounds of their voices.

Then I suppose that moment would be like any other.

I can still see the picture in my head.

The geese want my crisps. I don't share.

I walk into the village past the old wool shop where my friend, Jayne's scary mum worked, and into the teashop where Grandma Vera and I used to go. It's a small room with only four tables. I sit at the back. Bugger it. I'm going to eat cake. A woman from the blind school up the road is sitting by the window with her head against it, feeling the cool of outside. I wonder what she sees. The door drifts open and no one comes in. The breeze blows a menu off the shelf in front of me that's stacked with all kinds of teapots shaped like houses. There's a sign tucked at the back that says "Vera's Scones."

When a search is in motion, something will always, always be found.

I wander up the hill to the house I grew up in on Highlands Avenue. It's now a pale yellow color, no more 1980's white. The front bedroom windows are open and there's a red car in the driveway. I want to walk up to the door and see if they'll let me walk around in my memories.

That might be strange.

You never know with people these days do you - I could end up chained to the wall as some sort of sex slave.

Seriously.

I'll stalk around the outside of the house instead and take

as many pictures as I can, because that isn't weird. They've put up a much higher fence which is annoying, so I hold my camera up as far as it goes hoping to catch something of the back garden where I skateboarded down the old air raid shelter and waited for fairies under apple trees. I walk to the side where my old bedroom window is.

You used to look out of that window every night and tell the moon everything you thought.

I'd watch her slowly become whole.

Dear God, thank you for this day –

Thank you for mum and dad, and Billy and Joanne.

And Grandma Joan and Granddad Bill.

And Grandma Vera and Granddad George.

And on and on you'd go saying all the names, thankful for every one you've ever loved.

Even Elvis. Remember when he died, I thought the world had ended.

You had your "Elvis Lives" badge!

Yes. He made the list for years. Why don't I do that anymore? I should start doing that again. When did I stop?

When you moved in with Dad. You felt silly. You thought he'd hear you.

I said them in my head though, didn't I? For a while.

Until they eventually drifted off.

That was after you'd come and gone.

I made the list, yes.

I let it go with you then.

I've been saying it for you, don't worry.

Thank you. I've got to start saying what I'm thankful for every night again.

Out loud.

Yes, out loud.

From the age of thirteen, for three years, I walked to school every day with the same four girls. I reached out to each of them before I left for England and by a miracle of timing three of them are available to meet for dinner. I'm really looking forward to this. Four out of the five of us together is a good starting point.

Back then Grace would make her way past the blind school every morning to my house, where I'd wait just outside the gate. We'd wind around the corner to Cora's house. Her beautiful black dog, Heidi kept a lookout for us. We'd all walk up the hill to the Horse Chestnut tree and catch leaves in the wind and wait for Emelia and Claire to meet us. It is, of

156

course, all romanticized in my head, I know, but thinking of it makes me happy in childhood. When I moved, and my plane took off for Dallas I closed my eyes and wished we'd land down there by that tree thirty thousand feet below. Today it's thirty-three and a half years later. A flash and a blink since these misplaced pieces of childhood friendship faded into invisible ink.

Grace offered to host the dinner at her gallery - dinner by the fire within reach of Teazle Wood and the trees which held us as children across the bridge.

And other than you going to meet Grace, you all arrive in the same flow of your childhood walk to school.

At first we stand in a circle staring at each other in a sort of trance. It's one of the strangest, happiest feelings I have ever felt – like that breath you finally take in after you've been tickled with out of control laughing for a long time. Our childhood hangs in the air because we're stepping over the threshold of how we last knew each other. We adjust to time - to find what was, and compare it to what is. We've grown up, but I can see the child's face that I left so clearly in the grown one smiling back.

We talk non-stop for hours about wedding days, and children and all the messiness our lives fell into, and all the unbelievable joy. The unexpected things we struggled for, what we eventually found and didn't want or hadn't expected or couldn't believe was ours. And it's all love, it's all about love in the end. We've all been forsaken by one thing or another, at one time or another, to end up at this table digging inside a kind of communal thought mine. And that makes me look across the table to Grace.

You were both pregnant at the same time.

I didn't know it then. I found out later.

Abby told you when you told her what you'd done.

Grace kept her son. He's just bought a car.

I don't need a car.

I'm inches from putting you on the table of conversation. I feel self-conscious and envious that her voice spoke up for life, where mine put you on the other side of the door. I have come all this way to say nothing.

You have come all this way to realize you have something to say.

Enough that you are here as the chatter flies around us. I take you back inside.

What's happening in this room feels like the culmination of a social experiment - as if as children we'd all been sent away from each other to come back years later and report in: this is what life has done to me... what has it done to you? Did you expect that? We're telling the collective story of us and I don't want it to end. I want it to go on and on. I don't feel time moving at all, but of course it is.

"We need to get a picture of all of us. We need to get at least one picture," I say, getting my phone out, as you do.

"I'll go and get my husband to take it." Grace is almost out the door.

"Ah, won't he be asleep? It's long past midnight, you know." Emelia says finishing off her wine.

"What?" Grace, Claire and I laugh out at the same time. "It can't be."

"Ok, we'll have to do one of those selfy things," I say, "A collective one."

"No, I don't want my face on Facebook." Grace is spinning her face into my chest as I'm clicking away trying to hold the phone steady while shaking about laughing.

"Don't worry, I'm not going to put it on Facebook. Well I will do if you don't look up for one of these." I'm trying to get us all in the frame of my tiny phone. We're all laughing so hard, still talking, still spitting life out in forgotten things, one thing sparking another until the car doors shut.

Emelia gives me a lift back to Abby's and I get the last of the hugs.

"We will keep in touch now, won't we?" I ask Emilia.

"Of course. We will now that we know where we are."

"I'll be back next year. This is great. It's weird, isn't it? I can't explain it."

"I know. It is, but it isn't. It's so wonderful to see everyone. Thank you for this." I watch her drive away up the road, the last one to go.

I wish I'd never left here, I wish I could have kept on knowing you, been at your weddings, seen your children born, kept it moving at a steady pace. I wonder what we could have been to each other. We could have been the cowgirls of Surrey. On this dark street at 2:00am I feel what it's like to miss out on a collective friendship.

Your collective is just wider, Ma.

And for you – these are the kinds of friends I would have wished for you, Cooper. But one's that stuck around with you.

158

Ones you find at the beginning of life and laugh with until you can't stop. I wonder what kind of friend you would have been.

Like you. A friend like you - kind, reliable. I'm sure there would have been times when I'd have pushed someone for calling me names, or been pushed, and grazed my knee.

I'd have been there for you.

I know you would.

But all these friends of mine, are yours too. You may not have known them in the flesh of beginning, but as a part of me you do. And you can see, can't you, that I did well with childhood friendships.

How could there be so much laughter and ease, if you didn't, Ma.

"We're just off, Dora." Abby calls me Dora, the explorer. I guess I should get myself a monkey sidekick.

Maybe she's referring to the Dora of Freud's first major case history.

Abby has her husband all bundled up, high on the miracle Paracetamol drug. "We're going for a drive in the country. He needs some air since he's been cooped up for three days."

"Yes, sorry about that. I tried my best not to get any of you sick. One out of three isn't bad though, is it?" Sneezing after I say this doesn't back my case up.

Why don't you ask if you can go?

They need their space back. When I first reached out to her to let her know I was coming she asked if I could separate my visit up to give them a bit of a break, let them roll with their own routine. Understandable - she'd just had surgery on her elbow and needed some down time to herself, and in I march with all my needy glory. Maybe I've withdrawn too much here.

Maybe you're reading into the situation.

I wonder why I can't open up more to her. I used to. She's the only one I told about you as it was happening.

No, not as it was happening. You told her when it was all over.

That I'd been pregnant and we'd decided not to have you.

"What a whalley," she said.

That's what she said, yes. I felt better. It made me smile and not feel so rotten. I was glad I called her.

159

That's when she told you about Lucy, that she'd just had her baby.

I don't want to think about that.

I take my break and go to London.

I'm in London to visit with my dad's cousin and his wife, Geoff and Nancy. They live in Fulham where this side of our family has lived over the generations, where I now walk over their footsteps up Novello Street, towards this row of houses where at one time we were born and died. I can feel Grandma Joan nagging at my lack of attention in not coming back sooner. Why have I waited so long? Her spirit nuzzles into mine. Like Alice and Cyril, these bank holiday relatives faded so much into the background it was as if they had only ever been talked about in stories. On holiday returns there was no time to spare to London and all the DNA that went with it. Even as a grown woman I didn't choose to come home. That's the rub she's been inside me waiting for.

Well, you have finally begun a return.

The last time I saw dad's mum, Grandma Joan, she'd come along for the ride to drop me off at the airport on one of my trips to San Diego to see Gibson – to see your father. It was March. What I remember most is the softness of her hands. I can't remember what I bought her for her birthday that year, or any year for that matter. But I remember that. She was ill and about to go back to England to live with Alice's sister, Rita.

Back to the Londoners.

Yes, she came back to her husband's people. Her people, after all those years after leaving Edinburgh. She held my hand and her thumb rubbed my palm, soothing me because she knew I didn't want to leave her. When I let go of her hand in that car, I let go of her physically, forever physically. I can still see that fragile smile driving away from me. She died that May, the day before my 22ⁿᵈ birthday.

She sent a greeting card on ahead to you.

So strange to open a message from the other side. I didn't even think to go back to see her, did I? Even knowing she was so ill, it wasn't a thought in my head. I went to San Diego to see your father.

She never knew about me.

Best not, my mother said. You wouldn't have even been two when she died. She'd have loved you.

160

She said the same thing about Granddad Bill missing out on loving you, Billy and Joanne.

Yes. "He'd have loved you," that's what she said. She's very present at this house a stone's throw from Parson's Green tube station because it's where she lived her life after she married Granddad Bill, moving here from Edinburgh as a young bride. I've seen the black and white photographs of this street a thousand times over because she kept a large box of pictures of all things past. Those images walk ahead of me, under foot, pour out onto the rainy pavement. I can hear my three year old father's laughter, see him wheeling his tricycle along in the street, socks fallen down to his ankles, face dirty; his cousin Geoff, clean and pristine with long blonde curls, behind him. I know I'm close to number 48 when I see my great-grandmother glancing away behind the rose bush next door at number 49, staring at her eldest son Bill, in uniform doing his part in WWII. The wool of his green tunic itches my hand as it scrapes by me and for a split second I hear the clicking of four feet marching past. I see a soldier's arm draped over my Grandfather's shoulder. That hand hangs in the same way it does some seventy years' worth of sunsets later in the newspaper photograph that starts me on this journey back to this clip clock cobbled road where his shadow stands alongside my own bloodline. Soldiers marching alongside each other toward the war that will always be the war, as war is only one and goes on and on and on and on. I can hear the sirens in the air raid that frightened my great-grandmother into screaming down this road in panic from the bombs and the terror and desperation knowing her son is tangled in it all somewhere out there in the blazing fire of the pitch blackness. I smell her pass through me - her talcum powder, pale pink lipstick, and sweating honeysuckle perfume, all this and the breeze from her lace nightdress tickling my leg as it rushes by me. We're all rooted at this gate.

And you began the physical movement of this journey, reaching the first friend on the road to North Carolina fifty years to the day Granddad Bill died. Both of you crossing into something new.

At the dinner table I sit down with only a wall dividing me from the same space where my great-grandfather and great-grandmother's bodies were laid out after they died. Grandma Joan told me the story of how they washed them clean, delicately honoring the body, waiting for the undertaker to come.

They died so young. My great-great-grandmother was only 47.

Yes. She ran out into the streets that November night, panicked by Hitler's on coming bombs, barefoot in her nightdress. She caught pneumonia. Her husband was walking home from a long shift and it was people on the street that told him he was a widower.

At the same time, up in Scotland, Granddad Bill was proposing...

...to Grandma Joan and as she'd said yes, staring at him with such love. He blinked away from her, she said, and asked her not to look at him with his mother's eyes. When he got back to the barracks he had the telegram telling him that his mother had died of the Fuhrer's flu. Seven years later, at 54 on my great-grandfather went himself, with Bill by his side.

No telegram this time.

And twenty years on at 43, Granddad Bill followed them, his heart weakened by the war after all. We're all gone from here now except Geoff and Nancy; just these strands of us hanging on now, breathing alongside the pulse of the train. The railroad track bleeds off the end of their garden feeding the trains past – a kind of ancestral heartbeat. Time converges in on itself overlapping then and now so that they're indistinguishable.

All their voices are speaking at the same time as ours.

We are all still very much alive in here.

Leaving their house for the train into central London I'm in a crowd, knocking elbows to Blackfriars Bridge, on my way to meet Jayne. She and I'd walk home from school together once a week so she could go and see her Nan, as she called her.

Her mum scared the life out of me. She's a small woman with pointy features, and always had half a cigarette hanging from the corner of her mouth – a sort of modern day Fagin without the dancing skills. Her older sister was the biggest bully on the playground. She scared the crap out of everyone. I remember her coming up to me once when I was about thirteen and telling me about an operation she'd just had. They thought it was a cyst, but it turned out to be her twin whose head had been growing inside her stomach for the past fifteen years. When they took it out it was all covered in matted black hair with no eyes or ears - the mass of a double neither she or her mum knew she was carrying. Part of me wanted to believe that this was the evil twin and that now they'd carved it out of her and burnt it, that the good twin would win over. But she was still an asshole. I guess you really can't judge a book by the horror inside. That head may have been the only power encouraging her towards any kindnesses, and now it was gone... She told this story a lot and it made her harder and cooler than she already was. I always wondered if they'd let her keep it, you know, pickled, or something. Knowing her she'd have kept it by her bed and lit candles for it.

You pushed in on your stomach for weeks after she told you that story wondering if there were any rogue twin parts floating around inside you.

Because Jayne lives further north now we decide to meet in central London outside The Old Globe Theatre across from the Wobbly Bridge. Even after an absence of over thirty years I pick her out of the crowd immediately. I wave frantically and we collapse into hello rapture.

Touring The Globe, chatter is incessant. When I bring up her sister I realize I had no idea how much of a demon she really was. You always imagine the bully to be out there waiting for you on the playground. For Jayne though, the persecution came from the reverse. She lingered on the playing field and found alternate, longer routes home because the aggressor after her waited quietly at home.

"You remember walking home with me to my nan's, don't you, Sara? I looked forward to that day of the week, you have no idea." Her grandparents were a haven of normality, support, of quiet conversation and a laugh with the tele. Walking along the South Bank she stops and look over the water.

"I had no idea," is the only thing I can get out at first. I didn't.

Her bullies were well hidden.

"She held us all captive really, Sara. We all had to have a lock box in our bedrooms with a padlock on it so she couldn't steal any of our things. She'd picked the pocket of one of my coat's open so it went through to the lining, and on the way home from school she'd force me into the local shop to pinch sweets so that she could sell them for cigarette money. If I didn't she'd threaten to beat up one of my friends." One of whom could have been me, I'm thinking. "I left home at eighteen, as soon as I could, really. I had to get away from my family. She was mum's favorite. Nothing she could do I

163

suppose. But I could leave." We stop under the London eye and watch life go around in a circle. Love. She'd never had much of it, and that's a place of need that some people will take advantage of. And they did.

She left wanting to find love, someone to love her. She found two consecutive marriages to men that affirmed only the parts of herself that'd been conditioned in childhood: to be used, mistreated, oppressed and abandoned. She's talking so openly and willingly about her life to me, as if we've known each other all our lives, which I suppose we have.

You both went out looking for an affirmation of the part of you that you loved the least - your heart.

Yes, perhaps that's why I tell her about you. You flow out as naturally as sharing should because I'm in the hands of someone caring. She listens and she hears you. And she understands - even without seeing her for so long I knew she would. I could have hidden you, but I introduce you.

Sharing me is unearthing how each of you has built up - like one of those wooden Russian doll sets, where one smaller doll is hidden inside another on top of it, and another and another.

For her the tyranny of the larger dolls peel off to the smallest one, the one that has endured the long years of darkness, until she finally stepped out. That's what Jayne's done. She surfaced to the top knowing she's not made of glass, that she can't be shattered after all. I need to begin unloading like that.

You just did.

Jayne studied to become a midwife while raising three children on a pittance of an allowance from her second husband, with no child support from her Houdini of a first. She saved herself. After one final attack, she made a phone call, packed up her children and began a life for herself in earnest. She's done it on her own, knowing she doesn't have to be defined by it. Her resilience comes from the courage to bare her heart on the outside. She looks exactly as she did the day I last said goodbye to her, but she is completely transformed. Layers of skin have been shed, so many tears and torments and an aloneness no one should know.

She was the life and laughter of my school days. The girl I paled around with and shared jokes with. I remember us dancing in leg warmers and headbands crazily to Olivia Newton John's, "Let's Get Physical," in her bedroom one day when I spent the night, unaware of the lock box and the devil inside. And this sunny day in London she takes the time to ask about me, to listen to the ink that's gone into my story. From the onset of our friendship she always treated me with a kind heart. That part of her hasn't changed at all. This internally cracked piece of glass escaped with her self. There is a great love inside of her that shares with the rarest of care. This is the beauty of who she is. It would never occur to her to become the thing that held her captive. She's escaped to the peak above, and I envy what waits at the top for her.

Jayne's going back my way which is nice so we're able to just wander about London, have a drink and head home together. We make the train with time to spare, but as it lurches forward it stops with a pop and all the lights go out on every platform. There's a lot of eye rolling and tuttings of, "typical, just typical." Eventually, a railway man who looks like he remembers the days of shoveling coal on steam trains gets on and tells us what happened.
"Some woman dropped 'er compact on the rails and the
stewpid woman jumped down onto the
railway loin to ge' i' back. The sensor on the rails triggers an automatic shu' off don't it. All the lines are down now. We're resettin' 'em all."
"She jumped in front of a train to get her make-up back?"
"Naught so queer as folk," he says. Naught indeed. We finally speed away about an hour later and take a taxi on in to the village. She pays the driver for my journey as well.
"Take care of her, won't you," she says, "she's my most important friend." We look at each other a few seconds and hug before she disappears into the night that used to belong to her sister.

The following day I change my plane ticket and extend my stay so I can see Snowdonia Sam as Prospero in, *The Tempest on Fire* later in October. I spring up from the dog's chair at Abby's one final time to move up the road to her brother's (Davey of *Los Bastardos*) for a few nights before heading up to the Lake District.
"Would you like a Gin & Tonic, m'dear?" Coming from the welcome, sober, healthy eating at Abby's, my eyes light up at the prospect of Indian food and a good, stiff drink. A nip here and there is known to not be beyond me. I settle upstairs, put on my big trousers and get ready to feast. Whatever

weight I've been able to lose at Abby's eating sensibly and by example, I'm about to jiggle back on again. Hurrah!

The flow chez Davey is totally different because it's a house full of boys. These two teenage sons and a rock star are woven together by Lee, Davey's wife. It's a well-balanced household. It's a moment-to-moment game of who's doing what next. While one child does homework the other is making desert. While Davey's out picking up sides for dinner, Lee is sewing on Boy Scout badges. I sit on a couch in the kitchen and sip gin. These two parents both work full-time and their bullshit meter is very low. One boy is reprimanded for this, the other laughs, bringing attention to what he's got himself into. It's like living in a controlled mosh pit. I love it here. They have a Standing Stone in the back garden, a birthday gift for Lee. I want to go and touch it. They say they make women fertile –

You'd certainly give it a run for its money.

I walk to the train station the next morning, about two miles, to make my way down to Seaford, where my Auntie Doll lives – she's my Auntie Alice's older sister. She's eighty-five, never been married and lives off her pension in a one bedroom flat by the sea. Doll always seems to get past over on visits because she's down the coast, and I want to make a special effort to see her. She's got a wealth of information in her head about Grandma Joan, about my father as a young man, about the war and how this family of six children coped in the blitz. I intend to blitz her with a thousand questions of my own so I have the knowledge, so that it keeps living.

You learned the hard way on this one a few years when Grandma Vera's sister called you from Canada asking for help putting her memories down on paper.

Her daughter and grandchildren said they had no time to help her, she said. I told her I'd write them for her. She had bad rheumatism in her fingers and her sight was fading so she couldn't write herself.

You told her you'd send her a cassette tape recorder, a hand held one with instructions on how to use it so she could talk into it; then she could send it back to you to write it up.

A month later I finally got around to it, because, you know, ninety-something-old relatives live according to my schedule. I sent it off with color-coded instructions. She was excited about getting started. She had it for about a month

166

before she passed away. I asked my mother's cousin for the tape and the recorder back but she said she couldn't find them. I lost whatever beautiful memories were to be had about my grandmother and her vivacious sister to a past that drifted right in front of me, that I wafted aside one moment too often. My insides turn just thinking about it. This will not happen again.

Doll's waiting for me at the train station, right on the platform, tightly clutching her shopping trolley.

"Hello, Sara. Fancy some fish and chips?"

"It's lovely to see you, too, Auntie Doris." She's already off down the road to the restaurant. We're back at her flat in under an hour.

"Can you believe my view, Sara? There's the sea right there. And I've got my bus pass, and I can travel on the trains as well. All free, Sara. And I've got a good pension coming in. Nice, isn't it? I'm so lucky, ain't I?"

"You are, Auntie Doll. You're happy here. What's not to love - it perfect for you." Her flat has a small kitchen, bathroom and one room she has divided with a curtain that separates the bed from behind the couch. I've no idea where I'm going to sleep.

The phone rings and it's Auntie Alice checking up to make sure Doll's remembered me at the station.

"Yeah, no, no, she's 'ere. I took 'er to the fish and chips just like you told me. We're just going to watch the tele a bit. Yeah, yeah, alright. Sara, she wants a word."

"You alrigh', Sara? Now where you going to sleep? There's not much room in that little flat of hers you know, and all that stuff she's got. Have you seen it all, she's even framed a newspaper picture of little Prince George. It's strange, Sara, isn't it? And her pound coin, I'll bet she's already got that laying on the table for the morning paper. Have a look. It's there, isn't it? Now, where are you going to sleep, Sara?"

"I'll just pull the cushions off the sofa and put them on the floor, Alice. I'll be fine."

Going into the bathroom to take a shower I pull back the curtain to find it full of boxes and nick-nacks. How on earth does she wash? How will I? I remember Grandma Joan saying when she didn't have time for a full bath she'd have "a lick and a promise," which meant you only had time to wash all the tricky private bits.

She also used to say, "it's a bit cold up your wiffle, waffle out here" when the wind blew up her skirt.

167

A lick and a promise up the old wiffle waffle it is then.

The night passes with a series of loud wind pops from an elderly bottom, and stifled giggles from a middle-aged woman perched on two pillows by the buzzing of a TV not quite turned off. It's the best night of no sleep I've ever had.

The next morning as she makes tea I look at her old photo album. Her brother, Granddad Bill, died while the whole family was on holiday in Italy. Out one evening, the men walked ahead. My grandmother said all she saw was Bill falling down. She thought he'd tripped - only he didn't get up.

"Died right then he did, Sara, just like that. And him a man that was never in a rush," Doll says. "Plenty of time for this and that, he used to say... and then he was gone." She's looking off over the cliffs. "Your dad wanted to cancel the wedding. I can still see him in the kitchen, drying the same dish over again, keeping busy, trying to forget it..."

It catches me off guard.

I can feel it from here.

I've thought about it quite a bit over the years -

Your father's grief.

What it must have been like for him to lose his so young. He's my father. I don't like to think of him in pain - that hurt. He's the strong presence in the living room, the one who sustains, the football player, the man in prayer, the one that's provided for us time and again.

He was down here at the root; in the vanishing; a scream no one could have heard, least of all himself, I suppose; *a repressed silence.* Perhaps it came out over the dishes, *into the water falling down the drain.*

Perhaps it's been leaking out all along, moving forward into a family of his own. Maybe that's why we moved around so much - if we stayed in the same place too long something might catch up to him - *so he kept moving on to safety.* It stayed with him.

I wonder if he's figured out how to let him leave.

To make sense out of why it broke?

Or if he's just mastered faking it like the rest of us.

Why don't you ask him?

Doris wheels her trolley into the café by the side of the station and buys us a cup of tea before I leave. It is a difficult time, saying goodbye to my Auntie Doll. It's the age-old problem - I don't know if I'll see her again.

She chats on to everyone there and they chuckle back. She's a true innocent, always smiling. I've never heard her say a cross word about anything. She's so thankful and grateful for everything she has. I used to be like that. Why am I so grumpy? She's well into her eighties and content - a woman that came through the war with scars somewhere. I wonder what they are as the train pulls away from her waving madly, drifting out of sight, perhaps forever.

On the way back to Davey's I spin off for a day trip to Monk's House in Lewes to see a woman I wish was my friend, but she's dead. I want to breathe in some of Virginia Woolf's overhanging Argon. The B&B I've found notes itself as being "close" to Monk's House. The landlady advises me to get off the train at Southease turn left out of the station, cross the bridge over the river, through a gate, over a meadow, and follow that along passed the church until I get to a pub called, The Abergavenny Arms, then turn right and the house is a little ways up on the right.

You can barely deal with actual roads.

I am foiled from the beginning. Southease has no station, not a proper one. It's just a platform. I don't see a bridge on the left, but to the right I do, but it goes over a road, not a river. I don't see any kind of

Maybe if you slowed down and looked a little closer.

village at all, just a large hill. Maybe that's the meadow she talked about? I plod on anyway. The sun's out and I'm itching from heat even before I set off across the bridge and up the embankment. I find a gate, check – but there are a rather eager looking bunch of cows on the other side. I know cows are vegetarian and all that but they've no idea of their body weight do they. They could conceivably trample me to death, and I'm not dying before I see Virginia Woolf.

Yeah, cow-trampling deaths are up this year.

You know what, smarty-pants –

What's cow tipping?

I'm backing away slowly anyway.

Watch out, there are a few more behind you behaving a bit too much like the Velociraptors in Jurassic Park.

As I close the gate again I look back down the hill. Ohhh, there's the other bridge.

And it crosses the River Ouse, just like she said.

I crossed the wrong one.

Should we sit with that metaphor for a minute?

169

I collapse into the grass with it, into the smell of yesterday's rain. The sky is that perfect azure, cloudless. I wonder what horror in your head makes you want to take your own life when you have all of this within arms' length.

I make my way, slowly, across the water where Virginia washed up, tangled to the surface weeks after she drowned. I look for her on the path with no name, on up past the empty church, through the gate to another winding meadow. I wish I wasn't burning up, it's so freakin' hot, all the magic and poetry of the moment is running out the back of my mind in sweat. I hate that this is happening. I'm supposed to be enjoying the walk, like she did. My bag weighs a ton, my shoulders ache and all I can think is, please God just get me there.

So just sit down for a minute. Why are you rushing?

I'm always rushing. If only I had a servant to carry my bags.

Finally, the Abergafuckingvenny Arms. I turn right and see a sign for Monk's House. My B&B is almost next door to it. I pick up the key, strip naked and stand in a shower of cold water, scarf down a croissant and walk six houses down. I've wanted to be here for years, and here I am, at the gate of my dead mentor. I'm going to sit, stand, stare, and touch every piece of furniture, grass, wood, ornament, book, wall, window, brick, flower, apple, grave, I can. Every time that National Trust lady turns her back I'm going to touch something else I'm not supposed to. I want to lie in her bed and take a nap and look at the ceiling like she did. I want to see what thoughts come to me; sit in her chair with her shawl around my shoulders and put ink to paper until I run out of space or my hand falls off.

The little room in the garden, where she went to do most of her writing – that's the place I want to get into and pissshitfuck, if it isn't closed off. The breath that was her creativity is in that vacuum and I want an inhale of it. My nose is pressed against the glass staring at the table where Virginia sat, closed her eyes, and wrote away the need to walk into the River Ouse for as long as she could. I dig my nails into the wood frame and keep trying the door handle. I approach the elderly volunteer.

"Excuse me the door to the summer house is locked."

"Yes."

"It's locked," I say, as if he's misheard, or I'd said it in French by mistake.

"It's being cleaned out. It's not open today."

"But today is the day I'm here!" I want to say, "so can't you just open it up for me!" Now _I_ want to walk into the river Ouse.

And I do. I wander by the gift shop and ask the man the way to Virginia's walk to the river. He points me in the right direction. He doesn't understand why people want to go, but they all do, he says. I tell him the summerhouse is closed and I've been driven to it by the National Trust. He just looks confused and tries to sell me a book I've read twelve times.

I head down to the water along a path bordered by rocks. Reeds tangle up the bank. The river must have been higher in those days. I wonder what keeps any of us from lifting the latch off the gate for the walk towards the river. There are times we must all dig down to find that one thing that fills the space where the stones want to go. She just couldn't anymore.

I pick up one of the stones she missed and wander back to the B&B at nightfall. I've been hiking a small bottle of red wine in my bag with me and I intend to consume every drop off it with the remainder of the croissant-baguettey thing and cheese. The night is warm too so I sit outside on the patio, entirely and wholly alone in the middle of England far from anyone I know. I am in no way lonely.

I get up early to re-walk the path I took to get here in a calmer place. I hop a fence and stand in the mist of the color yellow.

My Uncle John is a few train stops up renovating a house he and Susan bought, so he picks me up at the station and I go off with him to see the house, have a cup of tea and a chat. Before he drops me back off at Davey's house I ask him to stop off at the house I grew up in on Elm Way. Granddad George and Grandma Vera's old house is on the way so we drive by there first.

"It's all flats now. I was really upset when I found out they'd knocked it down," John says. He pulls off onto the side, but I can't bring myself to take a picture. There is nothing recognizable about this space. Even the iron-gate is gone.

"I wonder how much of Granddad's garden is left. I always thought I'd get to go in there again. Whenever we drove passed it I could see Grandma Vera up there where the bedroom window used to be, waving like mad until we were out of sight. You know, how she used to."

You could still see part of who you were in there.

171

More proof that our life here has turned to ashes. It's the same feeling I had after she died. I knew I'd never be allowed in to the house again, never pull the curtains to shut the day out, never make the beds or wake up in them. The doors I pass on the road where I used to live are locked with a key that no longer matches the one swinging around my heart.

We roll on to Elm Way, the house my dad's parents owned. At least it's still there. My parents and I moved into it a few years after they got married so Grandma Joan wouldn't be alone after Granddad Bill died. This is the house where my brother was born, and that is my earliest memory - Grandma Joan holding my hand as we walk down the stairs leaving my mother and father upstairs with the midwife.

You had on a pink, orange and white stripe dress with a bow and white collar.

"Let's go downstairs and make your mummy a nice cup of tea," she said, "she's going to need one." I can feel my hand in hers, like a pearl as it slid through my fingers. I wish people wouldn't die before you have a chance to reach the age where you're brave enough to know what to ask them about their lives. I mean, how did she survive the death of her husband at 43 years old? She had to learn how to drive; she got a job up in London when the IRA bombs were coming down like lightning. She always said she spent half her civil service career under her desk quivering as they went off down the road.

She got ill while I was in college so I drove home every weekend to see her. Each time I bent down to kiss her goodbye on a Sunday evening she'd say, "don't go... don't go," and I'd think the same thing silently to myself, please don't go. And then one day on the way to the airport she sat in the back of the car holding me with her silken hands of pearl and we spoke the same words and smiled and her hand slipped out of mine as she chose to go.

I want her back.

You want us all back.

Uncle John's getting uneasy, "You can't take all those photos, someone will think you're a terrorist or something." I'm snapped out of my moment.

Before heading up the road to Davey's, John stops off at Abby's so I can drop her a card thanking her for letting me stay. She's not home so I pop it through the letterbox.

172

I wish I'd been able to be more open, that we'd talked more, that I hadn't felt so awkward. Abby's opinion matters to me and I get the feeling that what I'm doing seems illogical to her. As if I'm stealing time from real life. She calls it my gap year, and I know that this gap is the portal to the rest of my life. I want her to understand why.

And how exactly will that happen if you don't tell her.

I've been able to be somewhat free along the way and here I am with someone I thought the same thing would happen with as well because we've known each other the longest. And that simply isn't true.

And that simply is only true because you are quiet.

Something's rattling on inside ourselves that's not joining up – that neither one of us is allowing to join up at this moment.

Well there's the place to start.

Because it's one without assumptions.

It's an assumption, but neither of you are coming to the table first. You've been apart during the most significant parts of each other's lives.

I was there for her wedding, but not for her pregnancy or her daughter's birth, or her dad and then her mum's death. And she's had so many challenges with her health. As a teenager she kept telling her parents she didn't feel right. The specialists she went to a few years ago couldn't believe her heart defect hadn't been detected sooner. They said it was a miracle she'd given birth without complications. Then she got the pacemaker.

I'm not sure you've ever acknowledged any of that.

Not the way I should have, no. I imagined a sort of connection that would stitch up all of the years that had been lost - make up for us not being there for each other.

You can't do that though. Share the space that segregates you.

Explore that.

You're different people, you've reached apart from one another, and that connection is brewing into something of its own.

I'm still detoxing out of that corporate American sense of being inadequate and the smallest nod away from my direction sends me back inside. I should have slowed down to her pace more often to see more of what lives inside her but I got defensive about myself instead. I flew around her like a panicked butterfly. She let me be who I am.

You're a bit like jazz – her steady notes shift alongside my scattered dissonant ones.

Relationship Intuition Number Fourteen: **The Woven Friendship**. This friendship began at your beginning. While you've been apart, sometimes for years on end, you've still felt their footprints marching beside your own. It is the delicate violet on the windowsill that grows best when it's next to another – often under watered on its vigil, it needs revisiting. It is ever present on a path leading to two different capitals.

Staying in England two weeks longer in order to see Snowdonia Sam from Wales in *Tempest on Fire,* means I've a few more weeks to rummage around England. Sophia's parents, who've turned their home into a Bed & Breakfast in their retirement, offer me a room at no charge to come and write and explore the North with them. I can't believe my luck. I hop on the train from London to a small village called Gamblesby, after a lift to the station from Davey. With a car hug and a kiss on the cheek he says, "This is quite extraordinary, isn't it, Sara, what you're doing." I nod into his profile and kiss his other cheek.

"I think it's putting me back together." He smiles.

He understands.

Sophia's dad, Edward, is at the other end of the line to meet me. Her mother, Ellen has hurt her ankle.

"I was on a stool and a bee came at me," she says. Taken down by an insect in Autumn. "Now Sara, we've given you this wing of the house so we won't disturb you. I'll just knock on your door at meal times and you can take those with us," Ellen says, showing me around. It's hard to describe this amount of kindness.

While I'm here, Joe is driving up to see me. He was a graduate actor going for his MFA at UT when I was an undergrad. He's also a displaced pat like me, only on the reverse. "I fell in love," he said.

I'm glad of the sun because I have a mile and half walk into the next village to meet him. I slip between the peat and the stones. It'd be a lovely walk even in the rain. I told him I'd take the train down to him, but he wouldn't hear of it and is driving the 2 hours up from Yorkshire to have lunch and reconnect to me. "You've come a long way already," he said, "it's the least I can do." I hadn't expected that. I don't know why.

You have a deep seeded feeling of being an inconvenience.

I don't expect people to meet me on a journey I took off on, you know.

You don't want to place any expectations around them.

And when you do that, more often than not, *people do rise to meet you.*

I didn't know Joe well outside of school. We did share the stage together though. I played the imprisoned, heavily pregnant, Juliet to his Angelo in Shakespeare's, *Measure for Measure.* Luke played my husband. Every night I pulled on a nine-month-old pregnancy pad. No one knew about you back then. There we were, concealed under period costuming.

"I want to ask you if I can feel it kick."
Luke said that to me.

"The way you're moving it's like there's a real baby in there."

Of course there was a baby in there - a masquerade of one, of you, anyway.

Who else were they going to cast in this role except the girl who'd been living her life in the denial of the thing she was made to attach to her body - for a month of rehearsals, and four shows a week. It was my secret, my knowing, and the first time I could be exposed with you without anyone realizing. I could hold you inside my burgeoning stomach, sing you lullabies and anticipate birth.

And all under the guise of research for performance.

I hated hanging you up in the dressing room at the end of each show. It's the last image I left the theatre with when we closed - a dangling bulge of cloth on a wire hanger. I even conceived the idea of taking it with me. Playing that role was a gift and a curse to me.

Joe hadn't a clue of what I had in my head then. He and I had one scene together. I only had seven lines, but I stretched every iambic syllable out of them. When Joe's on stage there is this quiet, steady evolution inhabiting his character right down to his skin on the inside. I wonder if he's kept at it. The last I heard was that he was switching majors to become a doctor. What a waste, that's what I thought – all those roles that were going to go un-played; good for the patients he'd save… but, really, what a waste of talent.

Waiting in a small tea room full of old ladies using the right spoon, a six foot Texan walks in.

175

"Well hey there, Sara, you look a lot less pregnant than you did the last time I saw ya!"

We're all in from the get go.

He leans across the table to hug me, spilling my tea. Every elderly eye is upon us.

"Well, I should hope so!"

"This place is gorgeous. The drive was great. I've never been up here. I'm just sorry I only have a few hours. Anyway – tell me about this, these travels. What are you working on?" We talk about how he met his wife at an AA meeting in New York, and how he relocated to the UK to be with her; about the one man show he's working on, his theatre company, my writing, the fulfillment of how we can connect on stage. We stream each other's projects, pick apart one moment and feed into others. He looks at life for every moment. He swallows them down hard. Perhaps that comes from being a part of a twelve-step program where you focus on one moment into the next in a very conscious place. You remain on the path as long as you filter out the demon.

Identify the demon.

Or who. I was my own.

And invite yourself back.

"Thank-you for finding me again," he says.

"Thank-you for allowing yourself to be found. And for sharing, for listening, for allowing parts of me to come out. It feels good to be able to be so open and think all these things through with you."

"We could have spent the entire day talking, couldn't we? But I have to get back to my son," he says. In two hours we connected in a way I've sometimes spent years trying to grumble out. He's got my mind ticking over and filling up. He met you today too in an odd way, like he did twenty-five years ago, without even knowing. Thank you for finding me.

Relationship Intuition Number Fifteen: **The Pathwriting Friendship**. This friendship is the mirrored perception of what we give of ourselves as a friend. It's the person that comes in respect, in awareness, and with a willingness to share. He is the form of ourselves that we honor most: open, attentive, allowing, captivating, encouraging. He doesn't just jump down the walls of the story, he climbs back through it with you. He leaves you the better for the knowing, and provoked to keep on moving, because only when you learn the responsibility of taking the call are you equipped to answer it.

Every morning here I've been able to write, and eat, and allow any thought into my head. The morning before I leave I walk up to the top of the hill, through the mud in the rain listening to Annie Lennox's, "No More I Love You's." It's magnificent. The road is canopied with trees - leaves are falling by the hundreds in every shade of yellow, red and orange you can imagine, and some you can't. I twirl around in them like some mad Jerry Garcia spinner girl. Grandma Joan said to catch a falling leaf was to catch a wish, so I'm leaping about in them trying to catch a few when a car comes by and has to stop because I'm in the middle of the road high on leaf wishing. The lady driving doesn't honk or get impatient - and when I turn to finally notice her, it's not startling. She's not bothered with me - she's looking up at the fall as well. She smiles and carefully drives by me, so slowly. In the back seat there's a little boy with his face smashed against the window, grinning and waving at me madly. As she passes me the rain starts up again at a blustering pace. I wander back looking in puddles so I can see what's above me and around me all at the same time. I've never felt more myself than in this shower.

I needed a place to empty the bag and plug back in, and Sophia's parents, Ellen and Edward have given me that – given me all this – all these colors. It's the un-repayable gift to people who are allowing me to just be who I am. They are a journey kind of people who understand wandering, so they share their story with as much warmth and attention as they do when they listen to mine. They have allowed me a space to retrace. There is nothing I can adequately say that fulfills all I have felt here, other than this has saved a piece of me from escaping without my notice. I see myself in the soil. Do you feel that? Do you feel her singing over your bones as well?

Rattling under the root of the tree.
A forceful invisible sound.
Do you hear your song?
I hear the beginning of it. Do you hear yours?
Oh, yes. It's the sound of Grace in a raindrop falling.
For me it's the sound of a stool not wobbling.
Whatever waited for me, I have found.

Relationship Intuition Number Sixteen: **The Foundation Friendship**. If I had been able to talk to you about the country that we come from, and the relationship that is ours inside of it, Cooper, I would say that this friendship is the pride you feel in citizenship. The joy and heartbreak you feel in the country that you fight to protect, protest to keep free, walk in every crevice to discover, and pause to breathe yourself in. There is always an unrelenting pull to her over your shoulder even if you've moved passed her. You are in-stooled here in the cobwebs, and in the footsteps of all those who have paved the way and walked on ahead. You exist with her past, present and future, and no matter how far away you walk, the never-ending story is your inseparability.

As the train pulls out from Penrith I make sure I'm sitting face front, back towards the future, so I can catalogue every disappearing tree.

Back in Hereford my step cousin, Irene and I are going to see Snowdonia Sam from Wales as Prospero in, *The Tempest on Fire*. Irene's husband is babysitting the boys. Bless him. James is in the army, an Action Man in all respects. The question on this night is - can he safely guard two toddlers... The first call comes after only fifteen minutes on the road.
"Where are the band aids?"
"Band aids? Why?"
"Ah, no, nothing really. We were making lemonade and George's cut his finger trying to slice the lemon." He's on speaker. There's an eye roll on my end and soothing words for George before hanging up.
"That didn't take long did it? How long have I been out the door? They'll be fine. They'll be fine." She repeats.
"They'll be fine," I say to make it three times, and therefore true.
After parking, we're bused out to Penpont House in Beacons National Park on the River Usk. As the coach rounds into the property in the pitch black Irene grabs my arm tightly. Fire shoots up through the forest inside a labyrinth.
"Thank you so much for asking me to come to this! I've never seen anything like this. I mean I've only ever seen one play and never any Shakespeare. I may not understand any of it."
"You'll be surprised at how much you will, trust me." As we get out of the coach it's absolutely pissing down with rain. Soggy Jugglers and circus performers surround us, weaving into the light of the Green Man Maze as the shipwrecked Miranda and Prospero appear through the mist with fire breathers, iambic pentameter and drumming. It's mesmerizing. We don't even notice the rain soaked hay bales seeping into our clothes when we eventually sit down.

178

It's as great, but the complete reverse of you in A Midsummer Night's Dream. I loved watching you in that play.

Outside, in June, in Waco, TX. So freakin' hot. A ladder - that was our entire set.

Irene would have loved it.

Irene wasn't born yet. God, I'm so old.

Standing with Sam you're back where you started, in Wales - talking to him after the show, about writing – only it's better because we're revisiting, like Irene and I. It's the spiral space, slightly shifted.

Irene's all smiles on the road home. She doesn't mind standing in a field in the pouring rain watching fire-eaters thrown around in Shakespeare. She smiles at possibility. She's a grabber of the sky when it's too dark to see; of your left arm in the excitement of trying something new that tastes so delicious she can't imagine not having tried it before. If I could fit her in my suitcase she'd be with me along this entire journey. And she would, except for her two spitfire boys. As boisterous as these precious terrors are, they are equally loving and kindhearted, and that's where you see their mother most of all.

She's supportive of her husband out fueling his own aspirations, while hers lie dormant for now. When Action Man gets home he stands at the doorway and his sons, now two and four, tug his legs tightly as they each take off one of his shoes. In this battleground he turns instantaneously back into daddy. The boys, who think they can run circles around their mother, run almost calm when their father enters the room. And here he is lying on a couch covered in boys giggling madly.

He's a quiet man. When he looks at you, he's trying to find what you are - like he's trained to do, I guess. It's not a look of judgment; it's a gentle look from behind kind eyes that love his wife and family deeply. It's the kind of family I would have wished for you.

We can't sing that.

They are the kind of happy that when you're in a room with them and they look at each other, you disappear. I hope someone looks at me that way one day.

Relationship Intuition Number Seventeen: **The Matrimonial Friendship**. This friendship envelops itself on the inside and acts on behalf of the whole. It rotates and stands to protect itself. It feeds on encouragement, support, and mutual respect.

There is adventure in them, at the door and on the horizon. It's never out of sight. The endurance is refreshed from within. It's the breathing heart of the happiness puzzle.

The next morning I board the coach from Hereford back to Heathrow Airport. As we wind our way around Coventry Cathedral a face waits for me up in the sky. His nose, smashed sideways, is the first thing I notice. His hair covers the edge of his left eye, but it's still in motion, like a lion shaking his mane. He's looking straight at me - a boxer I can't take my eyes off of. I wonder how no one else is looking at him. I strain to keep him in view.

You've seen him. Let go.
And all the while the clouds sit still in his face
Until he comes down to meet you.
until we round a bend that puts him at my back.
He's on his way.

I don't know where I am when I wake up the first morning in Dallas. I roll over to the right side of the bed, straight into the wall giving myself a near concussion. My dog Stanley is so overwhelmed to see me I thought he was going to have a coronary when I burst through the door. He won't leave my side.

At home I meet Tess for a coffee and talk about her baby girl. I meet Milly at the Harikrishna Temple for lunch to find eager inspiration that I wrap myself in. I spend time with my sister, my parents and my nine-year-old niece, Cate.

She is your heart, that child.
From the moment I saw her, only minutes old, looking around smiling, she was as she's always meant to be.

Here with all of us.
When my sister went back to work for a few months to finish out the teaching year I got to be at home to care for her during the day. She never cried, or made any sound of being unhappy. I'd peer in her bedroom to see if she was awake for the next feeding -

And there she was smiling, looking around, happy.
Happy to be alive and with all of us.

You wore you sister's t-shirt. Remember?
So I'd smell like her.

So she wouldn't miss her mother.
She's fortunate to have the parents she has in my sister and her husband. They are supportive, open, forthright and fill her

180

life with so much laughter, just as much discipline, and exciting possibilities. And while she still wants to hang out with her old Aunt talking about dreams until we fall asleep –

Lap it up.

Finally, although I've never been a big fan of high school or college reunions, I go to one I've organized for my junior college acting class. I haven't been to any others because I'm put off by the inevitable, "Oh, you've never married, and you've no children?" questioning.

Oh, you could come up with an answer to that.

I wish I had the nerve to say I've been too busy on location with Keanu Reeves.

Or the newspaper you work for has had you on such long foreign assignments you couldn't possibly bring others into your life right now...

But it's wrong to lie –

Even though you're really quite good at it.

But these people I like. We met around the age of nineteen or so, in theatre studies. Some of them I stayed in contact with, some dropped off – so what the heck–

Open the karma can and see what jumps out.

And it's a string of memories that does. What had been disjointed pours out again in our stories and turns us to full color. We're parts of the same puzzle - a picture we formed long ago, and here we are sliding into our old spots, a piece of sky, an edge or corner piece, all roll into place.

This is where you met Dad, isn't it?

Yes, this leads us into the face of your father. Gibson did make me smile.

Gibson. I love that you gave me his name. That's really cool.

Your middle name, yes, well, it's what we would have done. He can't be here today, he's teaching in Washington and there's no time to get away. It's a shame. Everyone wants to see him.

But you have a plan.

I come up with the idea to Skype him in.

That gives you just enough distance, doesn't it?

Well, with a lot of people at the party we'll be able to hide. I can put away all thoughts of the three of us for now. I know I'll see him when I go to Tacoma, so no questions tonight, not tonight.

Perch him up on the table by the hors d'oeuvres.

We toast remotely, clinking the glasses to my computer monitor.

He looks happy, doesn't he? He's a good-looking guy.
As each one of us arrives we hold the laptop next to our faces for a "cheese" moment.

I love his laugh too, Ma. It's funny isn't it, the way he kind of breathes backwards.
We pass him around the room like that pass the parcel game I used to play as a child - that we would have played at your birthday parties.

I love how long his hair is. It's thick hair. Is it thick?
And we laugh.

You can kind of make out his office. Do you think he still has that old wardrobe you left behind?
Maybe it's because as actors we shared the diversity of the human experience with each other in what were often intense circumstances, that we fuse together. We had our moments don't get me wrong, but we came back together for one another.

The one Grandma gave you with the newspaper from the '60s that lined the drawers.
I haven't found this kind of bond in any other type of friendship that I have.

I can't stop looking at him for now. I'm sorry.
When you stand in front of an audience, Cooper, you stand on a precipice risking all you are. These friends have been a cushion of support in the wings and in the heavens; they stood with me in the light.

Even Dad.
Even though there is the occasional ego "I" in theatre, at its best there's an "us" that intertwines.

Relationship Intuition Number Eighteen: **The Unit Friendship**. This friendship comes with the artist connection. It finds its foundation in trust. Support surrounds the performer like a cocoon. If you fall backwards you will be caught. Another human presence has leapt into you. It allows you to stand complete in yourself in front of a crowd of strangers, confidently fueling the first breath to speak. It's part of an agreed whole – each knowing their role in the picture's collective. This is a portrait no one can infiltrate or destroy; only each piece can shift the unit.

I meant to reach out to Mary Jo, who I hooked up with through an online writing course. She reached out to me because we live close by. I'll have to pick her back up in the

New Year when I get back from the West Coast. I have to get to Austin to see D'Ann. I should have gone down almost two years ago for her baby shower, but my niece ended up in the hospital with pneumonia so I didn't go. Time clicked by and her daughter, Lila, is twenty-one months old now.

D'Ann's always been your favorite person on the planet.

My friendship with her is incredibly important to me. I feel like myself around her, more than anyone. She's the one who helped me step into my own skin.

Over the past ten years I've moved around a lot. During a particularly difficult passage of her life, and for the birth of her daughter, where she nearly lost her own life, my only contribution was a gap. Even though we may not have seen each other for a time we've always been constant. I wonder why it was we went through these particularly difficult times without one another.

Now I'm here in the driveway, there's no door to knock on, no need to take a breath... she's simply there, standing in the doorway, her child in her arms, waiting.

Don't even stop to get your stuff out of the car.

We first met in 9th grade in an after school advanced chemistry study group. We were the only two in the class.

Really I think you met in a small library somewhere up in heaven, writing out your story, chapter by chapter.

With her I'm able to infuse creatively with anything and face myself.

She always points you back on course.

She is the most versatile, talented, flexible, morphing person I know. She is no statistic to be averaged out. She is that moment that hangs in the air when you've heard something wonderful and you pause to take it in. She assures me that whatever I think, whatever I believe, whatever I act on is okay. Perhaps we did as Leon Botha describes and left an artistic footprint behind for one another to someday find and understand. We all walk on stage through different curtains - she and I just made sure we had the same call time.

Her husband Lucius is in his element as a father. He is an amazing improv artist. His mind is working at warp speed all the time, so keeping up with a toddler is easy measure for him. He swoops Lila up into his arms, wooshes her around the sky, then lays on his back as she stands on his chest first on the left foot, right one sky high like a ballerina, then the right. Then he lifts her up into the air and drops her like a log as she giggles into a fit of unrecoverable joy. She is the tornado toddler that commands a room with soulful laughter. The way he looks at this baby will be the same today as it is on her wedding day. Parenthood has been a long time coming.

But these things arrive at the right time for each of us.

I sit next to D'Ann, her child on my knee, leaning back into my chest falling into a light sleep, and I relax and close my eyes. I think of you and the flesh that never had an opportunity to nuzzle like this, and I choose to feel you anyway. This silence of brief sleep and T.V glow holds the simplicity of us again.

It holds the unity of all of us.

Part 6 Skull:

So called from forming a kind of vessel.
Allied to *scule* (of a balance).
The cranium or bony case that forms the
framework of the head and encloses the brain;
the brain as the seat of intelligence.

- The Library of Universal Knowledge.

Sifting West

Before I set out I thought the problems would be practical...
but the problems were odd, perplexing knots of disorder within
myself
- Jennifer Lash

Well, Stanley, angel dog of my heart, off we go. First stop
San Angelo, Texas. From there El Paso, Tempe, San Diego, Los
Angeles, Santa Barbara, Oakland, Portland, Tacoma, Seattle,
Chicago, Milwaukee and over to Minnesota.

Bless him, he has no idea what's about to happen.

Ah well, it'll be nice to have a navigator. The car is packed
to the gills and I've carved out a nest for Stanley in the back
seat. His dog bed is tucked back behind the passenger seat
with cushions and his favorite blanket. It's so cozy I want to sit
back there. I have his little backpack with his food, medicines
for his allergies, water bowl and treats tucked by my large
overflowing suitcase, which I'll have to trundle out at each
stop. I can't think about it - if I do it'll bring on another hot
flash and those are coming on too often as it is.

The drive time from Dallas to San Angelo to see
choreographer Marie is a little over four hours so we start off
easy. At first Stanley sits straight up and leans over the
armrest trying to come up and sit on my lap, which of course
won't work.

*Your arms thrashing about with panic in your voice
hurtling seventy miles an hour on an open freeway isn't
helping matters either.*

Stanley, remaining calm, gives me that sideways look from
underneath the hair I've forgotten to cut away from his eyes,

hops back into his bed, jumps his front paws up to the back window and presses his nose against the pane. He's so human, what with his irrational allergies, sorrowful eyes, stubbornness and selective hearing.

A Buddhist more than likely.

I keep peaking back at him, then to the road ahead, then back at him, then back to the road until he's tucked up into a spiral of himself and asleep. I wonder if I'm being selfish, bringing him with me. He would have preferred his three square meals a day of chicken cut into perfect squares and the last four spoonful's of Greek yogurt that mother feeds him.

He'll be fine. It's the adventure of a lifetime. Charley did it.

Texas is larger than an entire European country. Crossing it out west takes a day of solid travel I find hard to endure. There is nothing spiritually awakening or remotely interesting about this drive. Either side is flat endlessness. My car compass barely speaks to me at all for three and a half hours. "Drive 137 miles on Highway I-20," is all she's said before going into snooze mode. I don't blame her.

My expectations of San Angelo are low – somewhere with a Dairy Queen and a post to tie my dog to. But out of the darkness and over the bridge there are Christmas lights - like a sort of Disneyland, only free. I feel irrationally happy.

When we pull up Stanley leaps from the car like Mandela from captivity, running in circles in the front garden, tinkling as if he'll never see a patch of green again.

Marie has arranged for us to stay at her friend's house next door in their spare room. I put Stanley's blanket on the end of the bed and get him some water, which he gulps down as if he's just crossed the Sahara.

Such a drama queen.

Marie and I first met when she dated my brother about a quarter of a century ago. We got along pretty well, but we never had the kind of conversations that connect people together. I was fascinated by her though. Her life has always been dance and choreography. After performing I remember she'd stand with each foot in a trashcan full of ice to soothe her feet. I've never seen anyone walk around a room in two trashcans while eating a red pepper before. I wanted to do that.

After they broke up we lost touch, and ten years washed past.

And something seemingly insignificant pulled you back together...

A jewelry box. Almost three years ago I was out in the garage and I found a small, slightly damaged box full of earrings, bracelets and a ballet slipper charm. I knew at once they belonged to Marie. If these things were mine I'd want them back so I Facebooked her, as you do - hello out of the blue... remember me... I found these bits, would you like me to mail them to you. So that's how our conversation began again. We started texting, then calling. We weren't just catching up, but opening up to mutual thoughts and experiences that wouldn't have made sense to each other all those years ago. These are words to give and receive now. We committed to seeing each other by the end of the year. I made it down to Austin on December 19ᵗʰ that year.

She's beautifully unrelenting creatively. She's in constant motion - an hourglass patiently sifting through ideas like poisonous darts until one infects her. The only antidote to herself is fruition, and that's when something special happens. To experience her vision in movement, you feel your own heart opening.

She moves and I understand what true love might feel like, where chaos and loss come from, why joy and gratitude run in.

You were there in Austin that summer before we went to Puerto Rico - when I performed the words I'd written for her ancestral dance piece.

At the last minute she decided to dance with the words, to dance with you.

She hadn't performed for a long time – and there she was, moving all around me.

What felt like through me.

Tucking me inside of each emotion her body shaped itself into.

The room hushed when she moved, I felt that too.

It held its breath collectively because everyone knew we were witness to a swan that would not die, flying as high as she ever had, holding on to her reflection. She gave that gift to all of us.

Relationship Intuition Number Nineteen: **The Crossroads Friendship.** The friend that exists as much in the silence. The one whose voice is as strong as your own, and hears your calling as loudly as you do – who has already gone out ahead and at the crossroads, is there to stand with you and encourage you to believe in your instincts. There is someone like this for each of us. Her face, as unlikely as it is, just flashed in front of you.

Although my stay is short, it's full of casual cups of tea and little excursions around town. There is a sculpture outside the visitor center called "The Angela's" by Luke Noelke. They remind me of the two of us. One Angela looks forwards, arms in mid-gait; the second one's eyes are intensely focused on the first and walks into her path, arms outstretched, into the other. They are intertwined and the same, floating in their roles. That's how we leave each other, floating. We talk and text most days - we deal with the same line of credit in our heads. I don't know how long this will last – but I'm thankful to have it now.

On the road from San Angelo to Tempe we're stopping off half way in El Paso.

You've taken into account the time zone change, right?

Time zone? We're still in Texas. Twelve minutes, Stanley, and we'll be there.

How can you drive sixty-seven miles in twelve minutes?

Sixty-seven? It's not a four-hour drive? I have an hour that's not accounted for. I've defied time, cool.

Desperation can convince you of the most outlandish thoughts.

But I'm in the desert and I'm almost out of gas. Why didn't the idiot car compass clue me in on this? I've driven through a time zone, and inherited its problem. I have one more hour to go, a dog whose tongue is dry from lack of water and needs to tinkle, and a gas level below the red line. Okay, no problem, no problem, we'll just stop at this gas station.

It looks like the set of CSI over there. Is that a third fire truck pulling up?

And three Sheriff cars. Great. And.... yep, big yellow bags over the pumps with "Outta gas" written on them. Well, that's just great. And now I've wasted gas getting off of the freeway circling back to get to the closed gas station and then more to get back on track again. And the sun's going down... crap. I'm not normally a sweater but I'm leaking buckets of the stuff, even Stanley stays in downward dog prayer until we somehow make it to the lights that are El Paso with only fumes to spare.

I don't stick around. I don't even see daylight. There are few things more beautiful than a desert sunrise in your rearview mirror as you ease yourself west so we get up and out with that. I'm filled with positive isolation - infinite. The faces of all the Indian spirits wake up in profile along the desert mountains in the distance - sucking me along.

It's great to be able to see Lenore again after NY, and to meet her family. She has a dog named Honey so it's going to be interesting to see how the friendship game will play out with Stanley. The first of many get to know yous with other dogs, cats, chickens and goodness knows what along the way. Today Honey is on the menu.

Riley, Lenore's adopted fifteen-year-old son, answers the door. Lenore isn't home from work yet. Honey and Stanley run after each other's bottoms while Riley shows me around the house into the back garden. We chat and I'm boring him with how marvelous I think bamboo is - how it takes its time below the surface rooting down so when it hits its fullest height it can't be easily broken. He's nodding and smiling, his hands in his pockets, looking down, his hair a little long over his right eye, and he tells me he's going to be an entrepreneur. He's a well-spoken, thoughtful, athletic child, and so beautiful. I can still see the child in there, a still little sparkle I hope never goes out. There's clarity and an openness about who he is which for some reason surprises me. Both his parents are teachers. Genetically he may have nothing from either side, but from their example, from their energy, he has made these two parts a whole inside of himself.

I only stay a day and a half because initially I didn't want to intrude too long on a family life unfamiliar to me. When I arrive though I find us quite familiar to one another. We know each other as I step through the door because Lenore has already shared her husband and son with me, and me with them. I love sitting in their fourth chair, laughing, chatting, smiling at each other's stories. It's all so comfortable and engaging - time inside a light bulb. It's one of the most valuable evenings I've had, and it's that I drive away from.

There's good news about going up a mountain though, you have to come back down again.

"Come back over a weekend, we'll take you into the canyons," her husband, says.

"We just didn't have enough time. Come back over a weekend. We'll make a plan. You'll love it, it's sacred up

189

there," Lenore's packing Riley's lunch. We're all in the kitchen, and they're smiling at me. I ink them down.

You're collecting families - not just friends.

It's the unit, the extensions of their lives that weave us all together. Lenore's right too - driving alongside these canyons it does feel hallowed out here.

Desert riding onto San Diego, six hours feels like twelve. I'm in the sand's custody and it's carrying me into a 6,000 feet climb through the mountains. As the sun goes down the road becomes crowded and isolation builds in my head. Stanley sleeps, the car frustrates and coughs, I mount, and every car slows. The moon somewhere shadows its light across the "turn off the air conditioner" signs. I'm wired to panic, lonely, driving in an echo.

Ancient faces inside the rocks form themselves out of the dying light, alive, surrounding me like fallen angels, and they're looking right at me. I spray wiper fluid onto the windshield smearing body pieces of dead moths in a white rainbow arc, wings caught in the blade. I watch these mountain eyes through a watery slush as the reflection of the life I used to have here begins to wake up. All those remembrances of what could have been when I lived here at the age of twenty-six; somehow the watery mountain eyes have it. I spray more fluid trying to distort the shape of the memories I'm seeing into a Picasso shape logic - the way I understand them. They make even more sense this way, especially on the inside. On the inside that swirl is how what happened to me here has always felt to me.

I followed your father, Gibson, out here after I graduated from University. He was still studying at San Diego State. All my belongings fit inside the back of his Subaru truck. We drove this same drive across barren land and through these mountains. I thought love would live here forever. I'm miles away from that house now where I used to sleep under his arm.

All these doors you walked through that aren't yours anymore - here's one more.

This is where your father and I lived. We'd said goodbye to you a few years before. We never spoke of you to each other again.

Why?

I need the radio, music, something to out sing the smiling rock people, stoic, knowing more than I do. Knowing more than I let on. This is a kaleidoscopic return where everything has kept growing despite the fact I'd cut it down.

None of the radio stations work. There's static or Spanish, neither of which I speak. The last hour stands still. The car compass keeps bumping my arrival time to later and later. I can't keep up with her time estimations. We are sloth.

I slam the *Abba* tunes out of my head and sing happy me sounds with Stanley's howling backup vocals. I get through my repertoire so quickly I have to move on to *The Carpenters*. "Mr. Postman" gets me to the doorstep.

Sitting at the table with Sky, her husband ZsaZsa, and their daughter Erika, I melt in like I've woken up from a nap. Pancho, their chihauhua, sniffs and yells at Stanley sitting on my knee. The last time Stanley was here Erika was only ten and used to fancy dressing him up. His knowing look telepathically lets me know that this will not be happening again. Anyway, she's got Pancho to dress up now.

We brake naan bread dipped in Indian spices, wash it down with a glass or two of red wine and the mountain eye shadows back off.

For a little while.

Sky's like the older sister I never had. She's always giving me clothes and jewelry, beautiful bits and pieces that look like they came with me, my batteries included. She dresses like a gypsy goddess. Any sense of style I have she helped to define. All through my childhood I wondered where my older sister was. Who knew she was in a town a few miles to the north of me in England all along; that we'd both have to move to San Diego to find one another.

In my "sweep it under the carpet" mentality here's someone who wears everything out in the open. She met me in my darkest happy time with Gibson.

She's the first person you had a conversation with that eased a kind of directness out of you. Things you hadn't expressed to anyone.

I was constantly trying to pretend I was happy, when really all I'd done was push everything that was ruining me down as deeply as it would go. When we met I was working for her boss as a nanny. She'd moved here from Edinburgh as an art conservationist and my boss had said something like, "she's from England so I thought you should help her." So I stepped in.

191

As like a cultural interpreter.

Ha, yes. She didn't have a car so I took her grocery shopping, leant her my vacuum cleaner, helped her move -

And to make her first batch of margaritas from scratch - for a housewarming party. I was so envious of her lifestyle. Her apartment seemed so grownup to me, maybe because it had more than one room. Her spare room wasn't just a space with a futon in it either, she had a piano in hers, and it wasn't just for show, she could actually play it. She could do all the things I wanted to do. And she fixes old paintings. She knows art so well that she can clean, retouch and fix any picture out of sync with itself. I didn't even know that was a job. I can't imagine what it feels like to be face to face with art work from hundreds of years ago, to touch the past and make it part of your present life. Her handprint comes alive in paint. She's embedded in the history of their artistic vision with them, instinctively knowing how to blend inside of it.

I don't know much about art but if you juiced Judith Leyster's tulip florals, O'Keefe's fire, sensuality and stroke with Frieda Kahlo's internal mind, what would flush out are Sky's paintings. There's an emotional complexity to her work that reveals her. Cleanly.

Remember that painting she did for you -

"Cosmic Roses," which somehow got lost in all the moving on. Pink, purple and pastel roses against the darkest navy blue night sky. Those flowers knew they'd reached their pinnacle. I miss those roses.

For the past eight years though our relationship has had its definition through Facebook and so much has moved into something new. The tantric theatre, where she and her husband both write and perform, has become a significant part of their world. Provocative pictures have popped up, and she looks gorgeous. She's never seemed to have any inhibitions about her body at all. Her husband has taken some absolutely beautiful naked pictures of her, and of them together. He captures her as nature, in a stream, almost a part of a tree in the simplicity of her spirit.

Then there's this one other teensy little thing in terms of lifestyle shift. They appear to be dabbling on the edges of the polyamorous movement. Now if you know your Latin, you're way ahead of me. Photos appear of people, male and female all smiling and somewhat scantily clad, laughing with their hands weaving into each other's. Looks happy enough. From what I can gather it's polygamy minus the religious stuff and the marriage license. The view is that the human animal was not created to be monogamous. They don't believe in marriage, but in multiple partnerships. For a while most of the pictures she posted were of the two of them with another woman. I don't talk to her about it over the phone.

Of course. But now you're sitting at the table with her.

She's always been a free spirit, although I'm not sure if she sees herself the same way. I want to ask her how she found herself in this place with so much openness and transformation, but I'm not sure how to bring it up. How do you casually blend this into the conversation as potatoes are being peeled, or dogs fed? I don't see any sign of the woman I saw in the pictures on Facebook.

Maybe the movement isn't all it's cracked up to be.

The first night the polyamorous thing preoccupies me - how it works, I mean. I love my friends dearly but I don't want to love all of them. I'm not sure if they're still active, in pursuit of multiplicity, still go to meetings - I wonder what their twelve steps gatherings are like - lots of liquor, dancing horizontally, drumming and chanting at vision boards presumably. Which in and of itself is a party I'd totally go to. Should I lock my bedroom door?

That would be ridiculous.

Ha! I'm totally kidding. I always feel comfortable here. Talk of Burning Man allows it to slide into our conversation. They go and hang on the playa as often as they can. It looks like a sexy sort of Thunderdome to me. They drive out there in their camper they've christened, Karma. Sky takes her tricycle with her. I'm entranced when she talks about Burning Man. Her entire being lights up - you can smell the air and see the dust creep back onto her body. I can feel it on my own face. She's talking about the closeness it brings to her and her husband. They'd tiptoed around in a polyamorous relationship, she says.

"But it takes so much work. Another person comes into your life and then feelings come up that you don't necessarily want to come up but they do, and it's exhausting. It takes a lot of work. It's just not for me." She gets up and checks to see if the sheets on the clothesline are dry. The wind blows them into her face and she breathes in as she catches them. "I do think what they say is true though. I'm not sure we're meant to be monogamous. Premkala and her husband are getting a divorce. They love each other, they have a young son, but they

193

believe in the principles so… Erika calls her our Guru. I'm not sure she like her very much." There's something in her face that warrants a question, but she doesn't ask it. She begins unclipping the dry clothes and laying them in a basket instead.

So not so polyamorous after all.

And that takes courage, to not judge a new space, just go there and know it.

A few days later, on Christmas Eve, we stop by the Guru's house after a day at the beach. I stay in the car with their daughter, while they go in. We watch through the window, Erika and I.

"Do you know how to become a fake guru?" she asks me. "You look a person in the eyes without ever losing eye contact with them, and you tell them something you know they want to hear, over and over again. You can rule the world like that." She's smoothing her hands over the curly hair she works so hard to straighten. I wonder if she realizes that it constantly fights against her because her insides are so open and untamed. I watch the lingering hugs at the front door while she looks out the other car window, away. There's a certainness to her voice, and for a minute she looks much older before a strand of curly hair falls over her left eye grazing her cheek. I push it aside before she has time to break it.

I know something about breaking things, and as Sky and I drive into Hillcrest I can feel all the pieces of it swarming in a giant pressure around my hand trying to dangle out the window in the wind. I'm back on a planet I discovered years ago and haven't walked the surface of since.

I walked us around Balboa Park obsessively, Cooper. It's a short walk from the apartment your father and I shared and it couldn't have been better placed for the emotional knot my brain was training me into. Some people need a place to walk and untangle themselves; some of us need one to twist ourselves deeper down.

Yours was the lily pond.

It feels odd to be here now. A performance artist is dancing at the bottom of it and I can't stand where I want to. He's trespassing in my moment. You'd think the stench of the breath I left here would be enough to ward him off, but it seems I have to fight to walk through the actual space where I left it.

194

Old silences chronicle away in my head. The deeper into the crowd I get, the louder the laughter, the children screaming to be picked up, the pitch of the music, and the elbows of people resisting me getting by. I want the crowd to go away, for this man to stop selling whatever it is he's selling, take the coins they're throwing at him and move on. My blood is in this pond - they should be letting me through. I don't want to go to the top end. This was my view, the one looking up to the cage house where all the exotic flowers live. I'm not being allowed to hear myself think.

That's the purpose it always had for you though, to stop thoughts.

I shuffle over to one side to get a better view of the pond and walk up towards the cage house. That's when I notice that all the water lilies have gone. There's not one left. Sky is talking to me about the renovation of it, or something that's happening but I'm not paying attention. Were people getting in the water, contaminating it? The left part of my brain is nodding ahas, and yeahs, and protests with hers, but all I'm really doing is imagining the water lilies back.

You'd sit on that far edge corner and stare at them like lost pets.

In my life they were the things that calmed me. Maybe all the thoughts I unloaded on them all those years ago took them down, maybe I killed them, maybe it was the Sara virus that got them.

And not a word of this do you speak aloud to Sky.

Sharing this is non-existent for me. I can't remember how much she knows about you. I was young, surface wounds couldn't help but talk about themselves then. But I've been so very closed into myself for so many years now, that no matter what I feel, I can only give it over to professionals by the hour - the same way I spilled the truth into my own blood hoping it would turn against me. As it did.

We drive back across the bridge to my old apartment on Anderson Place. It's a traffic cut through so I hop out of the car while she pulls over to the side as best she can, out of the way.

You're always rushing.

I can't rush this.

Top left living room window, that one was your father and I's first, Cooper. The curtains look the same as they did all those years ago, a faded yellowy lace. I never washed them. It's funny the things you remember. There's a silky shadow of myself peering out from behind them, full of inadequacies, misused guilt, and an elastic guidance that snapped me inches away from where I could have been alive. This is the apartment we lived in when your Great Grandma Joan died. I can feel her silky smooth left hand on my cheek at our goodbye at the airport. I knew that it would be the last time I saw her, otherwise why would I remember that moment out of all the others so well? Your father answered the phone that morning to my mother telling him that she'd passed away. I could hear the conversation, barely awake, pretending to not know the knowing.

Your birthday was the next day.

Top right bedroom window – that's the next apartment we lived in, slightly bigger than the first. We moved there after I graduated from college, when I came out here permanently to be with him. The chest of drawers that had been my parents when they were newly married was in the back left corner with a linen runner your great grandmother embroidered across the top of it. When we finally broke apart I couldn't take that chest with me. I hate that it's gone. Each drawer was still lined with newspaper clippings from 1967. I want it back.

You're all around this building like a cloned shadow.

I feel the aching of that. That girl up there is so pretty, so desperately sad, and in the middle of a life she hasn't a clue how to direct at all.

She breathes in rapid spurts like a fish at the surface as if she can replace it with something stronger.

When I moved in with Gibson I believed it would be the end of the chaotic blank pages, that somehow this doorstep would be different. I'd found him, the one. I crossed over holding the hand of a man I adored, and it would be love, it would hold fast where no one could tear in and rip me away.

You would make your home here and water down the plants in a life expectancy that paralleled your own.

Remember that winter we drove through Arizona and stopped off to see the Grand Canyon.

The gate lady let you in for free because she said visibility was zero.

I didn't believe her so I made your father drive on. We stood there hanging over the rails of those canyons and the only things in front of us were clouds. Gibson started to take pictures thinking maybe we would see something more in them later. When he held the camera up a black crow flew out of the mist right by the lens. There we were, at the edge of the world it seemed like - that I could walk right out into it and somehow all that invisibility would hold me. All that depth and vastness and we couldn't see into any of it, no matter how hard we tried. As vacuous as we were to each other.

Time stays constant when you shelter DNA.

How could it have left me alone here all these years later? I've cycled through other men with no more happiness or acceptance than the time before. What if I've got it all wrong? Should I be rolling around in piles of polyamorous people, scantily clad, sucking in my stomach with too much makeup on and a push up bra? I feel so lonely standing here –

– and Sky is waving at you to hurry along.

I stare up at the her that was me until she lets the curtains swing back. I have so many more questions to ask her and they rattle around in my head. We roll forward down the road.

You're still trying to save her.

I think about her on my way to connect back with one of Gibson's best friends and his wife. They only know her. I haven't seen them since your father and I split up. Gibson's stayed in contact with them over the years; they were really more his friends than mine. They were people he confided in, people he turned to instead of me. At the time I saw myself as a problem he had. Whatever strength I'd built up in myself in college quickly vanished after moving here. I lost my friends, my creative output turned to zero, and I'd committed to being with someone that I could no longer connect to in a loving or physical way. There had been you; we shared you – we had to stay together otherwise, what was it for? Maturity I did not learn early. If trauma freezes your growth, mine was done at twenty.

I meet them at a local bar, Richard and his wife Lisa, and one of Gibson's other good friend's, Jeffrey. I'm nervous, at first, waiting outside for them. Twenty years is a long time, children have been born.

And not.

Life has piled on.

Only smiling faces walk towards me, and hugs of disbelief that we've come back into these lives with each other. At this moment does it matter who I was back then? I'm not sure. It mattered at the time because it shifted us all into the directions that we took. I'd expected to live out my life with your father in California. From San Diego this group had all moved off to Los Angeles together.

Dad said that he was going whether you wanted to go or not.

Yes. I'm afraid I'd pushed him to his limit by then. Of course I would go - we're us. I couldn't stand on my own there. What did I have without him?

You knew, didn't you, that he was trying to...

It was a good enough place to end things, yes. You can't un-hear the first bit of snapping out loud. My ears heard it, but my body couldn't. As soon as the boxes were unpacked I began to suffer from anxiety disease. I went on Prozac until my heart rate settled back to its normal hidden beat. Synthetics rock.

Lisa's last words on the phone to me when I told her Gibson and I were ending things, that I was going back to Texas were, "I'm so sorry, how awful to have to start over again. I'm glad it's not me." With those words I knew I was on my own.

I walk into the bar with all of this.

But it doesn't hang around.

"What you're doing has had quite an influence on Lisa, she's been wondering how to leave her job." Richard edges a glance at her as he speaks.

"You just sort of do it." I'm not sure what else to say. I mean, wait until dreams attack you and you realize you have to take back your life by acknowledging voices you hear in your head –

– is a little much.

"Seeing you do it makes me realize it's possible. People do actually do it - someone I know is doing it. It's so exciting. My girls think it's very cool." Lisa has this beautiful way of always smiling when she talks. She looks over at the door.

"Here's Laura, she got a camera for Christmas so don't be surprised if she takes your picture," Richard says as she waves and heads over to us. "Laura, this is Sara."

"Wow, you're so cool lookin'."

"Can I take you home with me?" She laughs and holds up her camera.

"I hope some of my coolness comes off in the photo." She snaps a few shots as I try to act natural drinking a glass of wine, being as nifty and stylish as possible. I have all of her attention for about forty-five seconds. A lovely focused, noticeable attention - then she whispers in her dad's ear, is given twenty bucks, grabs a hold of her friend's hand and slips away. If she only knew how those few seconds lift me.

She only knows you as you are, and you are intriguing enough.

"Both our girls sit and write for hours, or play music, all creative interests. You should see them, they get home from school and they go right into it. It always surprises me. I don't know why."

"We're in the machine age. It doesn't seem like that kind of creativity should be what we're drawn to first now, you know. Maybe as creatures we truly are creatively instinctive. Maybe they have a piece of your evolution in them. You're not exactly inside the box kind of people."

"Maybe that's why I'm feeling blocked in with what I'm doing. It's counter intuitive," Lisa says. Richard's looking at her, holding her at the same time.

Lisa and I never really connected years ago.

You didn't reach out much.

No, I know. Now with time behind us, we have the same sense of movement needing balance. We've arrived from opposite directions.

She's got one of the most beautiful faces.

I wonder why I haven't noticed that before.

On the way home in the car, stuck at a light, I check Facebook, as you do. Not always a good idea. Condolences. Mary Jo, the Facebook friend that I met in an online writing course and should have hooked up with when I was home from England, has passed away. At the age of forty-six, in her sleep, she just hasn't woken up. I should have put more thought into who she was so that she and I would have met… but I didn't. I chose to delay reaching back even though we would have had so much to share. Her heart just stopped. Time has complete disregard - it has two hands and they'll both always and forever be waving goodbye. I scroll to the top of her page. The last thing she did was to like a page called "Peaceful Life."

In a few days Facebook will remind you that it's her 47ᵗʰ birthday.

Someone should tell them that she won't be 47, or 48, and that we won't be buying her any virtual gifts. Someone should really tell them. It sits in quiet ignorance - maybe I like it that way. There are limits to what I need an app to know, even though we may be beyond the point of choosing.

There is someone long since gone whose posts I would love to have read but she died before the machine days. She taught dramaturgy at UT Austin. Flynn was magnificent, like a gazelle.

From the moment she walked into class you wanted to reinvent your life into what she was -
- beautiful, expressive, smart, she had everything. Her hair was always sensuously disheveled the way every woman wishes hers was. She always crossed her legs over when she sat on her desk, never in the chair. Everyone would wait for her to do it, even the girls. She made research a living being; she made me a better actor because of the in-depth way she looked at each part of a play. She was gone at 38 years old, gone before the Facebook chip could be implanted in her. Now I have nothing, no way back to her, not like I do to Mary Jo. No site with her past posts will pop up on my news feed when someone comments on how grateful they were to know her. She is the other extreme to outpouring – vacuousness.

Not so much. Look at all you have living in your head about her. You rely too much on records today, and not enough on memory.
After the sun explodes, and we're all a part of some other world's fairytale story or myth, I think Facebook will be our proof of life to other lands. You know that superman movie where the bad guys were locked into a pane of glass doomed to spin in space for eternity for their crimes? I don't think that's too far off from us, you know. When the world is wiped out and things float off into zero gravity – there we'll all be – all of us trapped inside the glass of our phones, locked in our machines, floating through space, destined to loop through our past status updates with our friends, our likes, our photos, our entire lives recorded for no one to see. I wonder if at that point we'll have evolved into a being that sustains life inside a machine– swimming about in our photos – walking around in what we've recorded -never allowed to go forwards, stuck in reminiscences.

I guess you should be more careful what you post.

Packing my bags to leave and head down to Hermosa, I have one last wander around Sky's house. There are a few of her paintings on the wall - of flowers, foxgloves and sunflowers, all with their petals open, waving at the world. It's how I think of her. She looks outside of herself as much as she does inside. She paints out who she is, like I write, I think. If I need an answer to who she is, it's hanging here in watercolor. Look how much more life she's received by fearing with her arms wide open, than I have, guardedly with my arms folded up. Sky says she's still waiting for her moment of epiphany. I think that's the way she lives already.

Her polyamorous experience caught me off guard, but perhaps the lesson for the moment is that love is open. It's not always a two-character dance. Intimacies are shared and a part of your heart is gone forever, but that doesn't mean that the best part of it doesn't keep beating for the rapture - which is coming - it's out there somewhere, walking towards me.

Just make sure that everything in you walks openly towards it.

Yes. Like she would.

Funny, how you don't tell her about your own epiphany moment in Rhode Island where you swam free and found your own open doorway.

Ironic that it's the one moment where I feel the most like that piece of her that I've coveted all these years, and I don't mention it. I want to. I suppose I'm still not sure how to explain it, even to the one person who would understand it for what it truly is. But then perhaps I do know how, but I'd have to say what's behind it.

Me.

Even though she knows about you, perhaps the person I go to with those thoughts isn't her. Perhaps I wait to talk to your father about you first. To tell him your name, that I had a mass for you. Keep it in the family.

That's poetic, but maybe it's an excuse and you're hiding.

Anyway, the moment passes on. And there's poor Stanley as well. I do feel for him here. He's had two dogs, two black cats, and two chickens to maneuver. On top of which he's fallen off the bed twisting some canine bits, and as if this isn't enough Erika accidentally sat on his leg, and his allergies are flaring up. He has not adjusted well and it's the tip of the iceberg on our trail. Now he's limping. I've made a mistake in removing this ageing old man from his safe routine. Just because I'm reclaiming myself doesn't mean he should. Even if Stanley has a hitch in his giddy up, Sky has taken care of us. That's what she does. It's how she breathes. She battles on because it's inside the fight that she finds her own colors. When those colors are released out into the air you have a rainbow, and the gold at the end of it is her heart wide open. I'll miss every hue of her.

201

I wonder if on my way back through here I'll be able to tell her something that means something to me - the way I think I used to.

I'm stuck in traffic and there are no voices. I'm trying to get to Jill in Hermosa Beach. The drive is a short one - just under two hours of coastal driving with one checkpoint near the border to make sure I'm not hiding any illegals in the back seat or the trunk. Stanley barely has a spot for himself, they'd have to be awfully small aliens to fit in this car.

We arrive to find the spare key to the downstairs apartment that Jill's letting me stay in while I'm here. The space is glorious. A gorgeous white bed full of fluffy pillows, a lamp that looks like blown glass but is actually feathery, a private garden space for Stanley and no black death ray cats for Stanley to side step - and it's quiet. Stanley is just heaving a sigh of relief when I see his head shift and his ears lift up – a chicken is standing in front of him.

Jill was a barrel of energy back in college - so full of everything around her. She's pretty, petite, athletic, can talk to anyone and her way out of anything. I envied that in college. I was a ball of immature neurosis and she was all in, in whatever it was, good and bad. We supported each other's success - and cried over the Callboard when your names didn't show up as cast - again.

We didn't hang out that much outside of class, she had a separate group of friends outside the theatre with her boyfriend, Mac. She married him. He must be upstairs somewhere.

I knew that after graduation she'd gone back to California somewhere when I'd moved to San Diego, but I didn't know where.

Remember when you and dad were out having lunch at a restaurant and you saw her walk by the window.

She and Mac stopped outside and were laughing about something.

You hesitated.

All I could think about was how fat I was. When I moved in with Gibson it was the first experience I had living with a man. I ate as much as a guy six feet four, and a hundred and eighty pounds. I was only twenty pounds off his weight.

Your body image wasn't something you struggled with until that point.

Well, who could afford food in college - staying fashion model svelte was never an issue. Now, with love in my heart, guilt in my bones, and food on the table, I struggled to control something I'd never had to think about before. On top of which Grandma Joan had just passed away and I cut all of my hair off. She had always told me, "don't cut your hair, it's so long and beautiful," so when she died I went straight to the local Punk hair studio and had them sheer it all off.

Grief takes all shapes.

Mine went straight to my head… So I hesitated. I wanted to run out into the street and say Jill's name. I could see us hugging and screaming and laughing outside the window.

But you didn't move.

I was too embarrassed. I couldn't let her see me that way, so transformed. I just couldn't. So I sat there and she and her friends moved on down the road.

And an opportunity to connect to someone you thought you might never see again was gone.

It was a chance to reach out to a friend and because of my own insecurity that option took off down the road. I thought I'd never have that chance again. And you want to know the crazier thing - I don't even tell her that story now I'm face to face with her. I'm still embarrassed. It doesn't seem a good meet and greet opener somehow. I'll get to it later.

No you won't.

She on the other hand hasn't changed an inch. She bursts through the door embracing my dog as heartily as me, with a screech.

"I can't believe you're here. Get settled, and…"

"This is so nice of you to let me stay down here. It's just beautiful. So peaceful."

"Thank you. I did all the refurbishing and design myself."

"Did you really? It's a perfect little planet down here."

"Ha! You're so sweet. My God, it is so good to see you. Oh, and I see you've met our chicken, Molly. Yeah, we'll keep her out of the way for you guys. She gives us a few awesome tasting eggs. But the yard is nice for her – but it's Stanley's while he's here. So get settled, you'll come up, we'll have a glass of wine and you'll eat with us. Is that ok? I don't want to cramp your style while you're here."

"No, I'm here to see you. I've got lunch with Carol tomorrow, which I told you about. So do please come if you're free. If you want to."

"Yes, no, totally would not miss that. I've made arrangements for that. No, that's great. You don't think she'll mind if I come, do you?"

"Why would she mind? This is all about us getting back together."

"Yeah, but she's there to see you."

"Jill, you guys live a half hour apart from each other... well, an hour and forty-five minutes with LA traffic, but sill – if it takes me to get you to have lunch let's go. Why not? I'm sure she'd love to see you." Besides I want her to have the same experience that I'm having; it's a happiness high and I want to see what it looks like, to see it cross over someone else's face. I want to watch her face see Carol's, see it so I know what mine looks like.

"I just think she might just be expecting you."

"There are no expectations here. Done deal. It'll be great."

"Ok, I'll go. Anyhow, get settled and come up when you want. Bring Stanley. Our dog, Daisy is pretty territorial so we'll have to see how it goes, but he's here to visit too."

Not five minutes upstairs and poor Stanley has met his match in dainty Daisy hiding under foot. I carry him around like a wriggling, oversized purse for the rest of the evening, except for when poor Daisy's banished from her home onto the balcony for bad behavior.

As we drink our red wine I catch Jill up on everyone I've seen so far from our class, and I notice a smile behind her eyes.

"I've got a surprise for you. Come over to the computer. I'm going to take you back." Back where?

When you were at school do you remember Jill videotaping some of your goings on during your last college moments on one of those huge old 1980's video machines?

Oh, my, no.

Oh, my, yes.

Jill recorded our final movement class, our graduation send off, a show we did, and the after party. As she started playing the tape my eyes dart to the younger faces of all the people I've just seen again. Then the camera paned...

But who is that pretty girl?

It takes me a few seconds. Me?

It's you.

I thought I knew what I looked like, in my head I mean, but that's not her. I couldn't have changed that much. And so

204

it is, along my way up the California coast, I meet someone I hadn't expected.

"That's never me." I say it out loud trying to make it true.

As the evening wears on her two daughters need putting to bed so she lets me take the DVD downstairs to watch again.

"No, I mean, take it with you, so you can show everyone else that we know. See if you can make copies of it and I can send them out to our class."

Back downstairs I stop and start it in slow motion. I pause it on my face. This girl is already trapped, her mind is unraveling already. She was pretty.

She is pretty.

Bless your heart, the mirror shows a strangely contorted twin. I thought I was so grown up. I'd played Queen Margaret in *Henry VI part III* for goodness sake. I look like I need a chaperone. It shocks me how doll like I am. How could that face have been strong enough to leash itself into the world?

She wasn't.

It's funny - I've always felt so old inside my head.

This video was shot right before you went to live with Dad.

At the springboard to the high bar my palms got sweaty and I walked underneath it instead. I was a girl with a permanent ear infection, so swimming towards a calling was off the menu. I'd already let the fear win by defining it wrong. Fear is stopping to feel the comfort of one place and ceasing to reach forwards into possibility – that was our new planet's mission statement, Cooper.

You wouldn't be where you are now if it wasn't for that child's blind wanderings though. Without her holding on to certain feelings and people, without her sightless walking and seemingly impulsive choices...

She's brought me here. Turned the hourglass upside down. I'm thankful for that.

You're a dot-to-dot puzzle hanging on the wall.

She laid the foundation for all of this, I didn't.

She carried a lot, that little face with the forsaken mind.

Jill and I arrive in central Los Angeles to meet Carol. It'll be the first time we've been together since May of 1990. Although they've been living in the same city they haven't met back up with each other yet.

Waiting outside Urban Outfitters I see a girl with that unmistakable gorgeous red curly hair a few feet away.

"Jill, there's Carol!" We start waving our hands wildly and speed walk into smiles pealing around the sides of our faces.

"I can't believe this! I cannot believe we're all here. Together. That I'm seeing you guys! I don't know why I'm crying." Carol's crying. We're all crying. It's marvelous.

"I know, I'm so, so happy, I just can't tell you." We sit down at our table and look across at each other, laughing and letting this be.

Although the three of us have all veered slightly to the side of our artistry over the years, we've kept it zipped up and humming with us. Now we're activating into it again, at the same time.

"I chased after Jeff Corey when I came out here," Jill says.

"I remember him. His acting workshop changed all of us I think."

"Well, it changed me, I followed him out here." Of course, why would you not follow a guru? "Then I went to work for a casting director. I learned exactly what I'm capable of with her. She taught me so much about this business. Then Mac said, you know, I want to have kids, and I thought - do I want to have kids? I didn't know if I was ready, or what to let go of, or if to let go. But I love him, and yes, of course I wanted to have children with him, so I sort of let all of this go."

"It's been really hard for me. When I met my husband he was clear that he didn't want kids, and I thought, ya know, well, I guess I can deal with that. But it's hard. It's been really hard." Carol's eyes well up a little. That decision came upon her. I don't think she's actually made it for herself yet.

"I didn't make a decision at all about kids, it just sort of played itself out." *You made a decision about one.* "Like when a record gets to the end and the needle keeps going around. I feel like that, you know. It's the end of the song and I didn't notice, and now, well..." *You scratched one record. This is the table to talk about this. To talk about me. This is the table. Now. You can bring me up.* "But I have my two nieces."

"Yes, I have my new little niece too. She's so beautiful."

"I pour all of my affections into them. Just love."

Why are you falling around my words?
Maybe it's helping me to repair a boned womb is what I'm thinking. But I don't say that out loud. No one wants to hear

the words, boned and womb at lunch, do they? Especially not strung together in a sentence.

The sound of your voice is the wrong color.
In the time that Jill spent with her children she was never really away from what she was building artistically; she had a clear direction that kept growing. She's producing theatre now, but in a way that involves everything that she is - through her community that's become a huge part of her life. And Carol's throwing herself back onto the stage - keying up to audition more. I've always admired Carol's drive. On the last day of school, she was set to move to New York City. She had a job kinda lined up and a roommate situation set. She just went out there and took it for herself.

What did she say on the tape you watched last night?
"I'm never going to be ready. You're never ready to do it. There's never going to be enough money, so why not just do it." All kinds of fear ripped through me and she just hopped in the car and headed north.

Why don't you tell them that?
Over the past eight years now, she's kept her creativity moving by working at the Inner-City Arts Center in central Los Angeles. She followed her instincts like Jill did. And me, whatever's going on with us, Cooper, this table is alive with us.

Not with me, it isn't. It could be. You withdrew back to Dad. Say that. You secluded yourself off and stayed with a man who tried to love you but you wouldn't let him in. That's what you did.
He didn't let me in either.

You weighed yourself down with me.
I did.

And that's all as it should be. It's brought you here when nothing else would. It's okay to say it out loud. They are giving you an open door to share because they are.
Can't I just have a nice lunch? I'm having such a lovely time here.

Who you are right now is my obstacle.
I don't have to tell everybody everything you know. Look, however we went, we'd all gone about our lives - shot out of the college cannon in all different directions. Now we're in resurgence, without a curtain, re-loading. We've come full circle on different rides - now is the time. We have a clearer understanding of what we don't want and that's not only the power of the thing, it's the fuse.

207

"Can we come and tour your work? The Arts Center?" I ask Carol as we push towards leaving and I want a way to hang on.

"I'd love that. Yes, just let me know." So the hugs goodbye are long, and we're smiling and it's not an end, and it's not a beginning - it's us and we're all in, and I thought we would be. What we had was electric then, and it contaminated us for now.

A few days later Jill and I do visit Carol at the Inner-City Arts Center. From the moment we get there I can see how proud she is. She devotes so much of who she is into it. She's taken all that she's learned as an actor over the years and she's giving it away to children of all ages - offering each one of them an opportunity to grow and expand their creative life. Who she's become since the years we've seen each other in college is inspiring. There might be a piece of herself that she struggles to find the placement of, but this part of her is fulfilled.

Driving home, Jill and I know this kind of passion and reward is what we want.

"I know what Carol means when she says that she wants to get back into her creative self, but doesn't it seem to you that everything she's done has been preparing her for what she's doing with those kids. She thinks she's not being creative, but she's creative all the time here. She's already in it."

"I'm bringing my kids here," Jill says as we wind our way out of downtown. Yes. It's not cold water Carol will jump into when she gets back into acting. This steady drip has warmed the path, and when the next phase of her life takes off I want to be around.

My dad's oldest friend, who I've called, Uncle Toby since the day I could speak, lives practically around the corner from Jill so it's a good chance for me to catch up with him. He's always been a bit of an eccentric. With him, what you see is what you get, no veiled topics, no hidden agendas.

My dad's known Toby since his school days. Back in England when I was growing up, he and his wife and her two daughters would come to our house for dinner on a Sunday. Or we'd go to theirs and watch The Muppet Show.

What I remember most is that at some point during the day he'd invariably make you cry.

Yes, and who knows over what. I was a crybaby of most predictable fashion. I remember my blossoming bosom arriving at quite an early age. When I got my first bra I was terrified he'd notice and say something. I sat on the couch all evening covering my Jayne Mansfield sized boobs, crossing both arms in front of me to flatten them as best I could. Looking back on it, there really wasn't much flesh at all, just a ripple in the water, but at the time putting a bra over the top of that made it feel like Rushmore. I was mortified... and of course the story of "guess where we went today..." was bounded about. With each syllable of it that came galloping out I felt like my breasts swelled an inch bigger. Mortified. To cap it all off all those extra hormones that had escaped breast duty raced straight to my tear ducts and cascaded out in over emotional distress. I can believe how unstable I must have looked, and to a comedian like my Uncle Toby, that was food for fodder.

Today I've evolved from a gangly, top heavy, weeping wreck, into a moderately pretty girl capable of handling her feelings.

For the most part.

Besides, this is a great opportunity to hear about my father when he was young. I want to hear the old stories.

I barely recognize him with his white head of hair and full white beard limping towards me from a leg injury.

"Hello, darling girl." He scoops me up into a big hug and a kiss. It's funny when you see someone that was so much a part of your everyday life for so, so many years, so many years later. The scent of him brings the past whispering back and I start humming *The Muppet Show* theme song, remembering when a large black spider walked across my hand as I lay on their carpet the day Elvis died, weeping over pages of my diary, the smashing of a brush against a mirror, swimming in Spain, camping in the rain on the Isle of Wight.

You're in a time travel hug.

The things that walk through you...

As soon as we sit, the booze and stories start flowing. His thrilling adventures with Ken, a mutual friend of his and my father's and their run in with the infamous East End Kray twin gangsters back in the '60s. Apparently Ken told Toby they were just going to run a quick errand, but before he knew it they were way out in the middle of the countryside and Ken had the boot of the car up getting out something he never should have had in the first place.

"And as I turned around there was Ronnie Kray walking towards us. I almost shit myself. 'That's Ronnie fucking Kray,' I thought. I can tell you I was never so bloody keen to get out of a place."

He smiles while he remembers my Grandma Joan.

"She was like my second mum. There was always kids over at your dad's house. We'd all go over there. She was a beauty that woman, your Grandma. A star." It's nice to be able to sit with someone and talk about her. I hadn't expected her today. She's a big influence on who I am, she encouraged me to keep writing, and for the first time in a long time, I'm doing it. It's wonderful just how quickly the entirety of a person can come back to you at the quickest mention of their name.

Smell her walking by.

Toby has a new family now out here, one that parallels the one he had in England with a woman and her two daughters.

"I'm a bit worse for wear this morning, darling girl," he says. "Lil, my stepdaughter, you know she's been ill, we had to rush her to the hospital last night. We were afraid we'd lose her. Somehow she always manages to come back, you know. She's a fighter that one." He glances out the window and mellows into a subject change and talks of his peacocks in the garden and his grandson's beautiful eyes and how irritating he can be, making fun of him the way he used to make fun of me. I see it for what it is now - it's a love that he doesn't know how to express, and so he puts it in a different place.

A piece of you is cleared up in here somewhere.

Yes, some people need to carve themselves into a sense of humor and laugh about things that pull them completely out from their comfort zones, and I think that's where he lives.

You were cellmates for a time.

Walking back to Jill's house I detour off to the end of the pier and walk out into the water, to the edge of the world where I shouldn't be able to stand. What a silly, over emotional teenager I was - what a pain I must have been.

On my final evening with Jill, I want one last look out from this pier so we drink and walk to the end of her.

"I can't remember the last time I came out here," she says.

"You're kidding. I'd be out here every day. It's like an inkpot this time of night. You can stare into all this gorgeous blackness, and you don't remember the last time? You're nuts."

"I know, right? Thank you."

"You're welcome." Sarcasm and laughter.

"No, really, thanks for making me do this. You forget all the things you have around you that you take for granted. I don't come out here. I just don't. I will now though." We huddle there at the edge as the wind picks up a little and watch out to nowhere, to someone's somewhere which is not a part of our own. We look over the edge and fall into that moment together, watching all the tiny shinning mirrors floating on the ink of the story we're writing.

I leave for Silver Lake mid-afternoon the next day to hook up with Elliot, my brother's writing partner who I've known since I was sixteen. He's offered to throw a party for me at his house for all my LA friends so I'll see Jill this evening. She's coming up to the party so she can see Carol again, amongst a few others in our UT acting class.

The street in Silver Lake is your typical busy, no parking space in sight, LA street. I grab the nearest spot I can find. *While pissing off ten cars behind you as you try to remember how to parallel park - inching your way back into to LA life.*

I'm in. I'm not sure how I'll get out, or when, but I let that go, retreat to Elliot's house and get Stanley's heart rate down... or is it mine? Who can tell in all this smog?

Not wanting to leave Stanley alone in the car with all the traffic going by, or take him upstairs and leave him with whatever fresh hell awaits him there, I do the decidedly stupid thing and try to take everything up at once: my purse with laptop and other heavy plug type things, my suitcase, Stanley's overnight bag, and himself on a leash wrapped around my wrist. *You're determined for this to go well, aren't you. Bless.*

There's a gate, and the lock is just about two inches higher than my right hand can reach without strangling Stanley on his leash. I'll have to put something down, but it's all so well balanced - putting one thing down will whack me out of kilter. I drop the hand luggage. Good decision. I get the gate open lead Stanley in, pull my wheelie bag through, let him off the leash and drag our luggage around the corner.

Oh, good, lots of stairs. Well, at least Stanley can fend for himself now. I pick up the hand luggage again and drag the wheelie bag up the first step.

"Come on Stanley man, come on, up you come." I can see this almost seventy-year-old animal trying to judge the large steps that must look like Everest to him with his one good eye. The sun is setting and the light has cast a shadow that from his angle makes one step appear like two. He's trying to be brave and figure it out, but he finally sits down and starts meditating. Crap. I drop the hand luggage again, pick Stanley up, balance him against me on top of the wheelie bag, throw his back pack over my shoulder, throw my bag over same achy limb and proceed up inch by inch. At the top we all drop to the floor. I look like the sweaty, exhausted Ethan Frome from the opening sequence.

When Elliot opens the door he's on the phone wheeling and dealing, as you do when you live in this city of famous people – it's a required course to be able to live here. They don't allow you a CA driver's license without it. Two large, friendly dogs make a run at Stanley's ass. I scoop him up after a respectable sniffing time and try to figure out how Elliot, his girlfriend, his assistant, me and three dogs will be able to sustain in a one-bedroom apartment.

It's just two nights. It'll be cozy.

Elliot's girlfriend was born five years after I graduated from high school, and his assistant, probably five years after I graduated from college. I feel as old as Eve. Luckily Elliot is hobbling around from a skateboarding accident he had a few years ago and its subsequent surgeries. Not that I want him to feel badly, I'm just glad while I'm with these young, nimble, pert beautiful people there's someone who at least looks as if their body has broken down as much as mine. Here's the cool thing about the young though, they just flow - it's all good, it's all, like, relaxed. They also use that word "like" when you shouldn't – like after almost, like every like word. It's got a music to it so to fit in I join the "like" club with them.

You're so passive aggressive at times.

"So, like, how many people do you have invited to the party?" I ask, all young like.

"Oh, no one we called could like, come. So I don't know. How many people do you have, 'cause, like, I need to get some food, but I'm like really sick so I'll get it later."

"Ok, like that works. As far as I know, I have like, six people that will be here. Like, is that ok?"

"Yeah, I like, gotta nap though."

"Dude, you totally should," I say, panicking that when people get here she'll just be rousing from her like, bed to get things together. I am a planner, I like to have everything done and dusted a week before, all confirmed, ordered, picked up.

You're a control freak. You want to do it all yourself, like a total, control freak.

I blame Mercury for being in retrograde, even if she isn't. I need to chill, but even Stanley's picked up a pen to make a list of things we need.

And you said the word, dude.

Cool people still say that, you know.

Go for a walk.

"There's a dog park up the road on the left – just around the corner. You'll love it!" Elliot says, dialing his next deal.

"Great. I just want him to stretch his legs and pee himself out before people get here." We trail off up the road towards the dog park that I know Stanley won't cross the threshold of because all he'll want to do is sit on my lap. We wander on passed the park ending up in a sort of jogging circle – like the one that Dustin Hoffman was running on in *Marathon Man*, at least I think it was him – but somehow I can't imagine Dustin Hoffman jogging. At any rate – it looks like that. We wind our way around a barbed wire shielded lake sort of area. I'm not sure if the wire's there to keep us out or whatever's in there, in. Regardless, it's beautiful.

On the way back I see a Bronco parked in Elliot's spot. Not quite his style. I lean on the bumper to pull up my sock and instantly I know where I've seen it before.

This is Leonard's car.

"Yeah, I'm trying to renew the registration, get it a little fixed up. I didn't want his wife to worry about it. She couldn't you know. I've had it over a year now and I still haven't done it. I keep meaning to. I am now though. We're going to sell it." Elliot says looking into the floorboards. It's a large physical piece of their friendship. The last piece. If the car is still there it stands to reason that Leonard will one day come back and drive it away, smiling in the rear view mirror.

All this, where I am, is due as much to him as the Newspaper Soldier. They died fourteen days apart. They both lived their lives in pursuit of that one thing, and trusted in it. I wasn't and now they can't. I want to exchange my car for Leonard's, have him help me climb the mountains to Oregon. But I think Elliot needs it in his driveway.

The stress of what people would eat, and who would show up slips off me. I already know why I've made this stop. I needn't have stressed for even a second anyway, the young

213

have it all under control without even thinking they needed to. Platters of delicious bits and pieces appear with wine of every color. They slide into the room as I run in and out with a poodle slung over my shoulder to let everyone in at the gate after they all knock at a mysterious back door I can't believe they found. I'm drenched in sweat and Stanley looks confused, glued to my lap for the evening.

Slow down and look around and what you've done.

Here we are, all of us together. There is so much thankfulness, surprise, a smidge of relief, and laughter as we all come into each other's faces again. It's a tub of love, you know. There's no tension, or anyone bringing in anything from the outside. It's all from the inside. We are changed and yet not changed.

We talk about art, the return to art, to that piece of passion we felt from the beginning that we're tracing back. Our re-launch. There's a momentum that's been building up, pushing behind us. I can feel it releasing in this room.

Before heading off to the airport to drop off one of the lovely like girls and pick up my friend Iris to drive out to Carpinteria, I take Stanley out for a final stretch. As we round the final turn back into the neighborhood on a smog induced high, a man looks our way and says, "Oh, soooo beautiful, so beauuuutiful." I flush a little red, my insides feeling all lovely. Just as I'm about to nod back, all Grace Kelly like, he adds, "Your little dog is soooo beautiful, beautiful. He should have his own TV show. His own show, you know – so beautiful."

Hahahahahahahahaha! Now that is funny.

Not so much. My flush washes pale along with any remaining sense I have of youth and beauty, and my order amongst the Los Angeles crowd is restored to the expected "average." With great jealousy I squash Mr. Hollywood a little more deeply into the back seat with like girl's luggage.

As her flight leaves a few hours before Iris' gets in, I take a detour back to a film studio to see my friend Penelope who I used to work with there. She wants to meet Stanley. We stand in the parking lot and chat just inside the security lines and watch Mr. Hollywood pee all over the lot. I'm staying with Penelope on my way back down the mountain, for now we've time for a quick laugh at ourselves.

Turning into the studio makes my blood run cold. This job in particular makes my palms sweat at the thought of ascending those stairs and turning on the computer to see what I'd already messed up, or was already behind on. This job was no walk in the park, this was a forest of despair littered with ROUS, and those rodents of unusual sizes came in every day only after having their teeth sharpened. Under them, my boss, and then me.

In this particular business everything rolls down from the top the old fashioned way - at tsunami speed. With my poor boss being two away from the big, head honcho boss lady, the demands hit hard. I think her upstairs had a peephole under her desk to spy down into our offices. I can see her curly, tangled mess of crazy hair being held out of her face by one of her minioning man servants as she crouched on the floor, eye to the ground, viewing our quiet calm before pushing down the mess of requests so she could watch us scramble. I'd stare down into my e-mail and wait for my inbox to flip to the "1 new" that contained the world's un-rectifiable problem needing to be solved by yesterday lunch.

When did she forget civility?

Or how to drive a car and blow-dry her own hair for that matter.

With a chauffeur and three hairdressers on standby, who'd have to worry? Remember that time you got called up there to put her contact lenses in for her.

When I hung up the phone I knew I was a dead man walking. Can you imagine prying a high-powered corporate executives' eyes open and nervously shaking your finger into her eyeball as you prayed not to drop the probably gold lined, one of kind Prada lenses? Thankfully for me, before I picked my fainting body up from the floor, her assistant's assistant called to say she'd managed. You'll be glad to hear that it didn't go to her head - she still had someone in to blow-dry her hair for her.

But you had an ally in your own hundred-year war.

Penelope, yes, and we waged it together. In war you keep your friends close and your enemies closer, so they say, but more importantly you know what team you play on, accept that position, and never, ever defect. Our team was clear, and the side we picked was each other's.

You waged on with each other, for each other, and at times in spite of each other.

To say we had each other's backs would be minimizing us completely. We operated as a unit – a living, breathing machine of organization. While one lay on the floor scraping blood stained sweat out of the hard wood floors, the other

215

tapped away the daily dictate, poured coffee, laid out the day and covered the footsteps needing to be walked. We acted on pure instinct for the other. We backed each other up in time, coverage, health and with courage.

Without her at the table to your right you would have gone the way of the loony bin right after the first day or two.

Sectioned, no doubt about it. With each other we could laugh the stressed tears of madness to the back of our minds until the comfort of our cars could conceal the primal scream on our two hour, ten mile drive home on the 10 and 405 freeways respectively.

From nine in the morning until six at night, five days a week, we were each other's best friend, confidant and supporter - the one that stepped in when the other needed a moment of quiet readjustment. She gave me warmth of heart while I lived with the tap tapping of the keyboard. When I struggled, she gave me perspective. I arrived prepared, because of her. Some nights all that was left were the burn marks on our hands, and we'd smile at the kill having warded of failure, inadequacy and self-deprecation once again.

We're both free now, unchained from those cubes and rodents of unusual sizes, to walk on for ourselves. When you fight that hard for someone else, achieve almost impossible goals for someone else, imagine how much you can do when you turn all that energy around and make it work just for you. That's what you've helped me to see too, Cooper.

That's the crux of who we are.

Turn the negative in on itself and take the rest, finally, for ourselves.

Flip the coin and bet on the side face down.

Penelope resurrected my spirit on a daily basis, and I hope that I contributed the same for her. She was an injection of strength for me. Although she'd step up to help me put my contact lenses in if I needed it, if I ever forget how to blow-dry my own hair she'd call me out.

Relationship Intuition Number Twenty: **The Survival Friendship.** This friendship is found in the workplace in a time of peril. It lifts your head above water and enables you to breathe in the day with all her awkwardness and challenge. She does it with joy, focus, and longevity. She makes life in a cubed world bearable and sustainable. It's a gift of the rarest companion. It is a mirror dance for two, where giving is without question. This friendship, due to its eggshell birth, is

216

based in mutual trust, honor, respect and fortitude. In the challenge of the day you are compassion to the other. You are clear perspective. You are the answer.

Pulling out of the studio I can see their rainbow in my rear view mirror - I smile that I am finally at the end of that. Thank heaven to have met Penelope, and thank heaven I never have to deal with a movie head's needy eyeballs.

I pull back into LAX and find Iris waiting for us at the curb. Stanley's once small area of freed up space is now cramped with different smelling luggage. He propels himself into the front seat to have a quick, excited hello with the new human that's come to break up the monotony before he pops back into his hole.

On then to Carpinteria, just outside of Santa Barbara, where Iris is pursuing her masters and Ph.D. in Mythology at The Pacifica Institute. I'm so jealous. I want to know everything she knows, for some of it to sparkle over to me.

So you inundate her with questions all the way up the mountain.

She is open to my talk, and I am open to hers - the best kind of newsfeed. It's a tennis rally with a few great lobs that you have time to watch sail through the air before you smash them back with insight, or if you're me, more confusion; as long as it keeps flowing though, the journey's on.

I haven't known her for very long, a year to date. I just happened to sit down next to her at a writing course. We click in that as many thoughts are running out of our heads, there are just as many seeds piling up without solutions. We like it better that way. We leave the table with new ways to approach things. Our exchanges are always face-to-face, full of hand gestures, facial reactions, live laughter and compassion.

I love watching you guys talking. It's one uninterrupted sentence.

The power behind a conversation is what you see in the other person's eyes.

I don't know her well, in that I don't know a lot of her life history, yet. What I do know is that our foundations are alike and the time I spend with her is valuable.

The last time you saw her, you sat in your car, turned the air conditioner on and wrote down as quickly as you could everything you'd just talked about.

Like I did with Stephen Gerald, yes. I couldn't get the words down fast enough. We talk about myth in terms of friendship. I know that we have to learn to live a human lifetime under any circumstances, especially now that the machine is inhaling itself into this new myth. But who would have guessed we'd have to fight for the right to be forgotten.

This is our ultimate irony.

That I tried to forget you, only to realize I hadn't allowed you a voice.

Why don't you allow your heart to think in terms of who I am, regardless of that.

As if your hand's been holding mine.

I'm born that way.

We meet in the middle, *to know each other. I can't disappear unless I'm acknowledged first.*

I can't let go of something I've never held in some way.

Yes.

Even in metaphor.

Metaphor is poetry, and poetry is the word of communion and understanding.

I am in the right space *with the right person.*

She's linking me. This is the same track she and I would play. Iris helps me to trust that I'm meeting the right people at the right time in my life. We walk the same path to completely different destinations.

Relationship Intuition Number Twenty-One: **The Depth Friendship.** This relationship lives only out in the open. It's unstoppable. The chitchat chatters on long after the venue's closed down. It's the foundation sharing friendship that aligns you with yourself – the one that is too precious to let slip into a world without presence.

It's a straight drive up the 101 with a few twists and mountain bits here and there. All's going on swimmingly when the car lets out a croaking grown as I put on the brakes veering onto the highway.

"Was that us? Was that my car?" I say in the most non-alarmist way I can.

"Ah, I don't know." Iris doesn't seem concerned.

"What do you think that was?"

"I've no idea." We approach an incline and I put the brakes on. Yep, that's us.

"Not to worry, I'll get it looked at once we get there. There aren't too many hills, it's pretty straight forward. I had the car checked before I left so we'll be fine - probably just needs a little oiling or something like that. Nothing to worry about."

"Yes, I'm sure you're right." Iris nods, probably wishing she'd taken the bus now instead of driving up with me and the brakeless car.

Inside your head the story is going a little differently though, isn't it – it runs a bit more like this: "fuck, you've got to be fucking kidding me. I mean, come on – I've got the worst part of driving ahead of me and it's all mountains from here to San Francisco. San Francisco! It's all vertical streets isn't it – crap, crap, bugger, fuck, crap, shit. There goes the money right out the window." Am I close?

Perhaps but with a lot less rude words.

Noooooot really, no.

"Yeah, it's nothing. Nothing. So… tell me what I get to do up there with you guys at the Ashram." Notice how I change the subject, add a little humor, and dismiss all worry even though my palms are so sweaty they're slipping off the steering wheel while my heart rate elevates.

"Well, we'll have tonight to explore and have dinner – then you'll come up to campus with me tomorrow and have a tour and lunch with my class. You can wander around a bit until after my session and we'll all have dinner. It's nice that they're doing this for you – they don't normally let anyone in. I wish they'd have let you sit in on one of the classes though. You'd enjoy that more than anything else."

"I would, yes. I wish there was some sort of chip they'd invent that you could put to someone's temple to extract all the good bits and feed it back into yourself."

Eyes on the road, Ma.

The hotel is right off the freeway and Iris checks us in while Stanley and I wander in the grass. When I look down I notice that we're walking in a sort of Monarch Butterfly graveyard. Wings are scattered around the trees in dirt ashes. I can't bear that they're going to be tinkled on by dogs and picked at by birds. I pick them up and their black ink, alive, stains my hands.

We set off to the campus the next day. It's a beautifully calm place in this sea air and it smells of lavender. Lemon groves line up for miles and waterfalls run in hidden groves. You feel as if you've crossed over a magical mist, what a cult must feel like once you've been hypnotized into it – only this one you can leave any time, once the bus arrives at any rate.

219

The TV screen in the lobby flashes quotes from Rumi, the Dalai Lama and Joseph Campbell. There's a free Carl Jung bookmark tucked behind the frustratingly unpurchasable Carl Jung Action figure. I wonder if they throw one of those in with registration. It's just a little guy in a grey suit - as far as I can tell he doesn't do anything special. He has leg and arm joints, but he doesn't talk or beam anywhere or anything. He just stands, or sits, that's about it.

It's Carl Jung - his superpower is his little plastic brain.

Maybe he starts speaking to you on an unconscious level.

He's telling you to walk the labyrinth.

Iris hasn't walked it yet, so after lunch we head into the lemon groves where it's hidden away. I step around the old ragged stones, eyes closed, letters jumbling out of words towards silence in still images. It's a strange walk with a Newspaper Soldier, a child without feet, and a man without a truck.

You should seriously think about seeing someone on staff here.

You should seriously think about seeing someone on staff here.

Imitating me - that's so childish.

That's so childish.

Who's the child here again?

Neither one of us actually.

Ouch.

The opportunity to hook up with my old professor, Peter Whit is a surprise to me. Honestly, I didn't think he'd remember who I was. He taught directing, and as an actor I'd been a puppet for his students. On Facebook a dialogue opened up though, and we found that we walk a similar ground - so I reached out and asked him right from the beginning if he would be open to meeting.

"Sure, but I don't know how much help I'll be." Really? This is one of the most gifted theatre minds I know. The fact that he remembers who I am is more than I could have wished for. So early this night while the myth folks are probing into things I plan to quiz them on later, I drive to a pier in Santa Barbara to meet up with him. I admire him so much and I want to know more about him. At school he was the mysterious one in baggy pants with shaggy hair in love with the dramaturgy professor, Flynn - that's the story I made up anyway. She took an accidental overdose a few years after my graduation. She's the one I wish had a Facebook page because I'd like everything she posted, and comment obsessively hoping she'd like it back. I wish she was here too.

She'd been your mentor without knowing it.

You never really know what demons hide inside that much intellect. I want to ask Peter what happened, but I'm not sure I'll have the courage to bring her up, to invite those particular torments out. I don't have the least idea how I'd go about it either, but this is what this face-to-face contact is all about?

Especially for you who finds it hard enough to bring up the fact that you have toilet paper on your shoe, or something hanging out your nose.

I'm nervous too at wanting to be able to contribute to a conversation. Would he recognize me? He is instantly recognizable. If you visualize Einstein mixed in with Tom Stoppard, this is who walks through the door.

"I thought that was you. I saw you in the parking lot," he says. He recognized me before I saw him. Wow. I order a glass of red wine as soon as possible because alcohol makes me instantly smarter.

"I have about an hour and a half, then I have to get to my rehearsal."

"Ok, great, that gives us plenty of time to catch up," I sort of blur out, wondering what on earth I have to say for ninety minutes.

"What are you working on now?"

Good thinking. Put it all on him.

"*The Fairytale Lives of Russian Girls*, have you heard of it?"

"I have!" I spew with a little too much enthusiasm that I know it. Relief.

"So you know the story - Post-Soviet Moscow Annie comes home with high heels, designer this and that and basically finds herself inside a kind of enchanted motherland with evil stepmothers, wicked witches, and bears. It's about being brave enough to tell your own story really, isn't it?"

No shit.

I love synchronicity. "But tell me what you're doing. I'm intrigued, we can get back to all that later."

"But, no that's it exactly – wicked witches and bears for me too. It's about all that, the story of telling your own - so serendipitous isn't it all this, my being out here, leaving everything behind, you know - without the designer heals and furs of course. It doesn't make a lot of sense when it first happens, but the more it goes on, it's just as much about me as it is about anything I think, maybe more so, even from the start. I hope that doesn't sound selfish."

"No. Why would it? It's your story." It's my story. Yes. Talking about myself here, it's different - I'm usually talking about everyone else, catching someone up all the "others." And we do that too, but not quite yet. Eventually I bowl all the names at him and some he remembers and some not. It's the production names that link him back in to the people.

"Luther, do you remember Luther?"

"Luther... He was in a scene from, *Betrayal*, with you?" He remembers my work. I can die now.

"Yes, that it's, Alfred directed it, Alfred Smith."

"How is he?"

"I'm not sure, I haven't heard from him for over fifteen years. He used to send me postcards from Paris. He'd go back to Houston, save up some money, then go to Paris for six months and play his trumpet. But we lost touch. I moved around quite a bit and we didn't have email back then so, we just drifted off." He smiles with a slight glaze over his eyes, like he's catching up on a picture show. He sees memory in the vision of the work, and when he speaks it's with all the right words carefully placed – a balancing act like walking on water. I want to ask him about Fynn but as soon as the question gets to my lips it falters.

We talk for an hour until we realize that our food hasn't arrived. We aren't focused on it. It's one of those conversations that's as delightful as it is intense because you're talking about an aspect of both of your lives that connect you so immediately. I don't want it to end, and as we gobble down the food and the rest of the cabernet he pushes all the old fairytale myths out on my plate that he's in bed with for his play. I pipe up with my Pacifica visit and the myth-crazed people I'm in bed with and he confesses all the old school politics.

"...well, you're old enough to hear this now..." and my mouth is agape at all the oddities of the professors I held my education with. It's friendly this talk. I'm conversing on a level of intellect with a man that I'd gladly just toss a question at and press play. He makes me realize just how much I've learned and the depths of what I still feel to be living back on stage. He makes me miss it.

What? Not staying up there instead of jumping down here.

I want to get back up so I can learn more, have a deeper perspective. I want to read all the plays ever written and remember them all word for word like he does.

You have made him late.

"I've never been late in my life – these people are going to be so alarmed. I've never been late for a rehearsal, ever!"

"I'm so sorry. At least I've made it a memorable day on one account then."

"This has been wonderful. So intriguing what you are doing. You have my full support. I can't wait to read and hear about more. I'm so sorry I've got to go."

"Mustard. Your mustard, I left it in the car."

"I'm sorry?" I'd forgotten the Goldrush Mustard story in my updates so I give him a quick low down as we walk to the parking lot. I run to my car as he wanders over to his own and I rush back and hand him his jar.

"I hope you enjoy it, it's really yummy."

"This thing of yours gets more interesting by the minute. I'm sure I will. Take care, Sara. Safe journey." He tussles back his cool shaggy hair and sets off for his home at the theatre. I wish I was going with him. I should have asked to sit in on it. Damn. Oh, well, I guess I have to get back to the myth people anyway.

I didn't expect to miss him as he drove away, but I feel really bummed. It was only when I turned on my car that I realized that I hadn't asked about Flynn. Maybe things are best unknown. One day I'll ask him, ask him for a complete story of her. She deserves her own conversation in entire anyway. I'll find her - just not tonight.

Tonight you found him.

The next morning I take the car for her brake inspection so we can head into the treacherous streets of San Francisco without worry. They tell me that something I can't remember the name of is cracked but the brakes are fine; that I'll have to get it fixed eventually, that it will make a frightening noise that will drive me crazy, but the brakes are fine; that they will have to be replaced completely as this cracked thingy is not reachable without a complete overhaul. Of course. It makes me feel good to know I won't be in brake peril, but the thought of a grinding noise leaves me in a cold sweat.

You'll have to drive in the pooh a while longer.

223

I check out of room 126 and leave Iris in Carpinteria, to her studies. She lives not far from me in Texas so I know I'll see her again very soon. I force her into having lunch with me often so I can siphon off her knowledge.

I make my way back to the 101 freeway headed to Catherine's house, who I keep saying lives in San Francisco, when she does in point of fact, live in Oakland. I'm not sure why I think they are the same place, but I do. In my head it's just one big lump of crowded ocean with a bridge connection. I met Catherine when I lived in Los Angeles eleven years ago. Other than one brief weekend in to celebrate her birthday four years ago, we haven't spent any real quality time together since I moved back to Texas.

I'm not too worried about the beginning of the journey as it's pretty flat highway driving and it's by the sea, and the prettiest of pretty. I relax a bit. Then the car compass interjects with, "Take next exit onto 154. Then stay right." Exit? Why am I exiting? I just got on. No I'm sure we stay on the 101 until it runs into something else much further on. Stanley sits straight up in his backseat bed. He knows when I start speaking back to the car compass something is going wrong.

She is silent for a while – then, "Take exit on right to 154…" Damn it, I hope you know what you're doing. Shit. The exit curves off and away from the freeway and starts going up, and when I say up, I mean it's climbing - into mountains. We can't be up here, we have a non-brake brake issue. If we go up here how in the world are we going to get down? The thing about mountain driving is that you can't make a U-turn, there's never a chance to pull over and go back where you came from.

It just keeps on winding up and up and up and up and up and up.

Yes, thank you for that. I'm so far up I may as well stay up because the thing I was trying to avoid is the coming down bit and I'm going to be stuck with that whichever way I look at it. Stanley is standing erect like one of those meerkat's you see at a zoo. I reach my hand back and tell him it's all fine, just fine.

Signs are starting to appear.

The yellowy orange ones with trucks on them on top of a large black triangle that say, "Steep Decline next 3 Miles," yes, I see them. Crap. I'm breathing as if I'm about to give birth to the fattest baby ever born out of a stitched up vagina. When they say decline, they're not kidding.

What would Liam Neeson do? He's brave, what would he do?

Hire a stuntman that's what he'd do.

In between the stream of consciousness that tries to drown out the cracking noise of the thingy that is of no concern to my brakes, I notice these sand pits to crash into if your brakes fail. But they're only for eighteen wheelers – what about the rest of us? It does make me feel a bit better that there's an option if I'm out of control, but it alarms me that it's a real possibility.

Three miles at the bottomish, sweat is retreating a bit from the palms of my hands, heart rate is stabilizing and breathing is almost normal again. This is doable.

It has to be because this carries on for thirty miles until you rejoin the 101. When we finally come out of the mountains it'll be like a rebirth.

Finally, to see those mountains in the rear view mirror and be on flat as a pancake ground – I kiss it. I pull over and walk in a rest area and sweat everything out while Stanley pees like it's a fountain with no off switch.

As I exit the freeway in Oakland I drive through the two giraffes painted on the under pass as instructed by Catherine, and climb – again. I hadn't considered whether the car would be capable of parking on a steep angle, and Catherine's street is all incline. There is one spot open.

It's an incline and parallel parking.

Great. I've got to improve my attitude. I'm so high that the last six hours are over though that I parallel park beautifully. We will not roll back down this hill, I tell her.

The car?

Yes.

Ok.

Catherine is minutes behind me in traffic. I get everything out of the car like an expert, taking all I've learnt from the last scenario in Los Angeles. It's a quiet street so Stanley isn't stressed and I don't feel the need to rush everything in. I take my enormous wheelie bag and him.

Funny, all the houses seem to be above you.

As we reach her house Stanley and I find ourselves at the bottom of a staircase with the most enormous stairs I've ever seen. Stanley's looking at me for a harness, pick axe and rescue kit. I tug the bag up one step and look to the wee dog man below.

"Come on Angel, try one – you can do it." He eyes the stairs, crouches into a prep down-dog position, sways back and forward eyeing the jump, looks back at me and sits down. Fair enough. Up he comes into my arms and the drop and drag heave-ho begins. Catherine arrives as we reach the summit. We meet up in one sweaty, well-earned hug. It's a relief to see her, to be surrounded by the marvelous and always inspirational Catherine.

Her animal family is waiting inside - her dog, Wolfgang Birch von Bowsen, a blind cat named Simone de Beauvchat, and a mad cat named Ava Kaminsky. Wolfie is the first one up Stanley's butt. He's all in and Stanley true to form is holding his head a little bit upwards in discomfort, energy back on his hind legs ready to bolt at any minute. Ava runs out to see what all the fuss is about and hiss arches her body into a curve I'm not sure she'll recover from. Stanley looks at me sideways, but I refuse to engage – what he does in his acts of desperation I don't know, maybe he's channeling Liam Neeson as well.

Time to climb off his Mr. Hollywood pedestal and drop the barking in a fake French accent and adjust.

I've arrived to be on time for Catherine's birthday so she's arranged a reservation for us to dine at Bouchon, in the Napa Valley. We take off in search of a crisp Sauvignon Blanc. The chef's name at Bouchon is TK something or another – he keeps a clean kitchen they say and if his chef's apron is anything to go by, it's crystal.

Isn't that the chef?
As we drive up, he's right there making sure every pea's in place, and each frite's pointed towards its true north.

"Isn't that the chef?" As I'm pointing at him Catherine goes quite pale with excitement, as if she's seen a holy incarnation.

"Oh, my God, that's Chef TK – that's him. Oh, my goodness – what do I say to him? I have to say something. I've always wanted to meet him. What do I say? What should I say? I love you? Should I tell him I love him?"

"Of anything you can think of to say, you probably shouldn't say that."

"Yes, of course, yes. I'll tell him I keep a dirty kitchen."

"Or that."

"Yes, that's what I'll say. Oh, Sara, can you believe he's here. Come on we've got to get over there so I can tell him I love him." We race across traffic and loop around to the garden area where we can catch him before we check in for our table. "I can go up to him, right? I should. I mean, Sara he's like rock star famous to me." TK is standing a few feet away from us and Catherine plucks up all of her courage and launches in. "Hi, I'm Catherine and I have a dirty kitchen I'm afraid, but I am trying, and I just want to say that I love you." TK smiles back at her and shakes her hand.

"Well, we must keep on trying – you'll get there." Catherine can't seem to set his hand free, like she's looking for his Pope's ring to kiss. I nod and say something like, "how lovely to meet you," and wander away with a shaking Catherine who's smiling like she's won a million dollars, a starring role in a movie and has just been kissed by Liam Neeson. But I might just be projecting.

"We should have taken a picture with him. Why didn't I think of that?"

"So you can light candles under it and work yourself into a stalking frenzy, I think it's all best left just inside of your head."

The drive home, she's on a high. Catherine is one of those people that gets out there and explores what fuels her up. She travels straight at it. She's saved and flown all over Europe taking all kinds of classes - baking, writing, collage, painting, and she does it all on her own. I envy the courage it takes to get up and do that. She has an acute awareness of what she's drawn to and allows it to play inside her. It's how she traces herself, to reveal some other hidden aspect of herself.

This is important work for her to do because her beginning, her bloodline is a mystery to her.

I wonder why I'm drawn to certain people, to certain cultures, certain interests, who I inherit my lack of, or enthusiasm for something from. What side of the family does my artistic talent come from, my mad, joyful behavior? What country was all of that bred out of? Catherine comes from two families – her ancestry is split between a DNA family that gave her up into a "better life," and an adopted family that waited with the promise of giving that to her - those that loved her before she was, and those that loved her into becoming.

Her adopted mother was the mother that needed her closest, that made the sky so blue, who dreamt of her arrival, whose body couldn't carry her conception. She felt the pulse of her daughter's life in the promise of her

227

- until the moment she walked into that room and laid eyes on the red-headed beauty she always knew was hers.

Her husband told her to get another boy, but she picked up the child she recognized as her own, and brought her daughter home.

The mother whose womb held her couldn't keep her, not in those days. Catherine knows her story and she understands the choice without bitterness. She's already walked down that road looking for answers. For Catherine the question has always been one of abandonment – if there is no love greater than that of a mother to her child, why did she leave me in the hands of someone else?

And when you get on this train it turns your skin inside out to the place where self-doubt bleeds in, "what is it about me that turned love away? What could I have done differently for my mother to have loved me, chosen me and stayed with me?" It's a dangerous place to go.

You both have the same question.

You have to sift through it to get to your own understanding. It will take her towards the real answers – to the border of rational explanations. A baby can take no conscious action to be loved more; the choice had already been made.

And to get there we have to deal with the ticker tape of garbage – you've heard mine often enough.

The negative newsfeed fat in your head that keeps on asking, "what is wrong with me?"

We have to get a handle on the selves of someone else's making, to go into the fuse box and reset the switches to a place of believing in ourselves again. That's what Catherine's done, what she still goes to battle with from time to time. She sought her birth mother out, she found the records, she opened the pages, and as an adult, as a woman, she looked with clear eyes to the place her mother had been in her life, and to what at the time she thought had been a better choice.

She spoke to Catherine every day when she carried her about inside her, spoke to her of this woman that waited for her, the one that would run and swoop her up into the arms of happiness for the rest of her life.

She released a tide of necessity that changed all three of their lives.

The faces of the parents that fed, clothed and chose to shape her, Catherine tracks with a love rooted in an honest awareness of just how far their love was capable of reaching. There is the constant, delicate, beauty of it in her mother, trying to win out over the eye-to-eye challenges of a father who expected a second son. This is no joke of a shadow - it looms large, even after his passing.

But having made peace with her father just before he died there is a window of escape that allows her to finally make peace with herself.

The journeys she goes on are a confirmation, proof that she is all that she originally thought she was, despite the father's voice still rattling on inside her head. Inside of her is that seed of something quite extraordinary pushing up. Those instinctive behaviors she feels drawn to might seem untraceable, but she's found a way in – a back door left ajar.

She can slip sideways back into the womb again.

And she listens. She follows. She trusts her blood past, that they are all in it with her, that they are her adventurous spirit. No matter what Daddy said couldn't be done, shouldn't be done or would never be done, at least not by her – it's on the list to conquer because that is what her people do, she can feel that. And she's doing it. For most of us it's a thought in our heads that we'll someday get to, but she trusts in the discovery of what lives in the unknown. She considers what she was and is capable of now, and she goes with it.

What she's actually doing is reconstructing her foundation. She doesn't wait for the echo because the reverberation comes from her bloodline.

She's chartered a course going backwards to her beginning, and it's given her a forward momentum, as strange as it sounds.

Yes, to the root.

To carve it out like the blood of the bamboo.

Bamboo takes a long time before it pierces the dirt to breathe the air. It waits, not quite yet, rooting. The bamboo is wise. It grounds itself. There is certainty in that. The deeper the root, the stronger and steadier the sway as it grows. This is Catherine. She is the bamboo. There are questions to answer, and she prepares with patience to hear the answers.

Relationship Intuition Number Twenty-Two: **The Explorer friendship**. She encourages you to not only think outside the box, but to take the walls of your comfort zone down so that you can see that they really are made of air; that around the corner there aren't lions and tigers and bears – there are adventures in waterfalls, open fields, and in the depth of other people's eyes.

It's 6:00am when Stanley and I leave the next morning. It's over ten hours to get to where I want to be in Oregon and frankly I just want to get there. Catherine has taken the day off to spend with Wolfie, who is losing his new stay at home buddy. I lumber down with all of our stuff and come back up for a barking and impatient dog, who has, once again, mistakenly assumed that we are going "home."

It's a different kind of sadness I feel as we drive away from her in the darkness of the morning. It's not a sadness of our time coming to an end, because I know that I will see her again in three months – it's a sadness that I've just renewed something very special with someone who is no longer in my day to day, pop over and have a cup of tea, life. She is gone from that. It's unlikely that I will ever choose to live in the California area again, and her heart is here. I don't know where mine is, where it's physically grounded yet. I really see that in her though, that sense of home, of this coast being where she breathes most completely. Pulling down her street and back on to the vastly open freeway I look ahead and wonder where that word will finally stop for me.

This is the longest drive I will have to do - this section from San Francisco –

Oakland.

Sorry, Oakland, up to Portland, Oregon. Hours through mountains, over mountains, down mountains, all with those crazy steep decline signs with trucks on them with the black triangle, and my brakes are still making a noise that sounds like the final piece of the Titanic going down. I hold my breath again at every decline and pump and pump with prayer aloud with Stanley rolling his eyes blissfully unaware of the unknown terror.

After an hour or two I reach a clear stretch of hilly green and yellow and the sky is crystalized in a clear blue.

Look right.

Curving around the bend, outside my passenger side window, a white Heron is flying close beside me. If I were sitting in that chair I could reach out and touch the tip of her wing. She flies along at the same angle of turn, keeping pace by the side of my car at eye level. Her wingspan waves like water in slow motion. She turns her head, looks over at me, and holds her eyes with mine. It's surrealistic, like how I imagine God will see me. Time slows. I roll down the window to see what the wind feels like with her waving in it. I breathe

230

out and she veers off on her own course to the east. I watch every last piece of her, trying not to blink, until she's out of view.

The Heron appears to those unsure of their place in the world.

I know.

They tell us the way to truth is through intuition.

To trust it, yes. I didn't. I learned that the hard way.

Well, you are now. Reflections change. She was flying with you.

Not across me.

On the same path. An Affirmation.

I wish I'd taken a picture. I couldn't take my eyes off of her.

It wouldn't capture the moment of you together. A lens snaps the connection in half.

It was the silence of us that connected us on the same road.

For a moment you're in her sense of instinctive direction, travelling without a map.

So that's what that feels like.

As I come through the mist of the mountains and start to make my decent past the snow that had been in the far distance, high above, but now close to me, I meet rainfall again and there is a rainbow. It's reaching from behind one mountain and down in front of me across the curving highway and I have no need to search the end of it, I'm driving in it.

In Oregon with my brother and his family I expect lots of chats.

You like chatting.

And lots of writing. Then we'll all have dinner outside, because you can. We'll drink red wine, Pinot Noir, play some ping pong, load up some old LP's and dance the night away with Abba after spinning the soundtrack to *Oliver* for my niece, and screaming out to my brother's favorite, *Part of the Union*, by Strawbs.

Talk about controlling your expectations.

As I pull into the driveway, Billy is walking out to the curb with my sister-in-law, Mary who is carrying my seven-year-old niece, Madeleine, on her back. She's been calling every few minutes over the last few hours to see when I'll be arriving. It's a relief to be hugged by them all.

There's nothing like coming back to the blood of your own tribe.

231

For the first time in the journey I unload the entire car, inclusive of my "main" suitcase, which is half the size of the trunk. I'm a slight clothes fanatic with an irrational need to have all different types of clothing with me because, well, you never know when you might need a lace petticoat, or what length and color, so it's prudent to pack them all.

And there is a slim chance you might fit back into those skinny jeans, you think, so you've thrown those in as well.

Ridiculous, I know.

Stanley rejoins his two cousins, Hansel, a Havanese, and Abby, a Lassapoo. Hansel has a territorial growl that channels the Tasmanian devil, plus he's on diet medicine, so he's after your food, any food, at all times. Abby just prefers you not to get in the way of her snuggles with family members. If you do she'll go after your bones. I can see all these remembrances going through Stanley's brain as he jumps up at me to be held and removed from sharing floor space with these maniacs.

We settle in.

I'm camping out here for ten weeks, on and off, using it as a base for travel up to Seattle, Chicago, Milwaukee and Minneapolis. I'm grateful for how long I'll be here. I'm not sure if this opportunity will ever come again so I plan to enjoy and annoy my brother as much as I possibly can. He's a screenwriter working on his first novel series. He works from home. I love that all that creativity is here.

My brother and I are close now, as adults. As I kid I was a pain in the ass to him and each time he's nice to me now I wonder why. We're only three years apart in age so we've always been in each other's pockets I suppose. He's the only one in our family who lives outside of Texas and so we only see each other for a few weeks a year.

Life moves so fast and before you know it half a year has passed and all without any physical interaction.

So I'm glad I'm here to spend a good amount of time inside his life - their lives.

My sister-in-law and I have never had much of an opportunity to deeply connect. We've spent time together on family holidays, but not much time exploring who we are to each other, so I'm keen for us to find that.

She's studying nutrition. She's always been very health conscious, always eaten well. She has a dancer's body, one of those bodies that's in annoyingly immaculate shape at all times, even when pregnant. I spend most of my time around her with my stomach sucked in.

The second glass of red wine usually loosens it up a bit though.

Mary's closest friends are a few of the mothers of my niece's schoolmates. They go on a walk around the neighborhood as many mornings as they can, and she always comes home as refreshed from the conversation as she does from walking.

One of them, Susan, has been talking about having the umbilical cord cut between her and a friend that she needed to let go of. I've never heard of anything like it before. Makes sense - if there's a way to release this cord it could be done.

And that makes me think of Gregory.

Yes. I still feel a strong pull to him that I know is unhealthy. I thought I'd released it all, but walking the labyrinth in Aiken showed me how open this all still is with me. He's moved on with someone else, and I've just moved away.

A Sharman in town, Molly, the cord severer, did it for Susan, why not for me.

"Call her," Mary says, handing me her phone number. Voodoo, surely.

Which is why you're totally sold.

I make an appointment for the next morning.

I'm expecting incense flowing through the room, bells chiming and scattered scarves over low-lit lamps. Instead I find a normal, well-adjusted woman in a quiet room of whites and pale vibrations.

She begins the conversation with me about my life, simply asking questions, as if I've met a new friend and we're getting to know each other. I get to the part about Gregory and I tear up a bit, so I suck that bit down and move on.

Classic.

When I take a breath to transition she carefully pulls me back to the place where "the emotion rose." I didn't even realize it was happening to be honest. It wasn't a checkpoint for me, we were just talking and then, there he was.

A guided mediation takes me to the seashore where for a moment I am the tide, throwing shells, rocks, shipwrecked pieces out of myself, and then withdrawing but taking nothing of that back with me. When I turn back the sea has evaporated into a forest and in front of me there is an uprooted tree and I

233

have to decide how to get through it, because on the other side everything I need is waiting for me. There's no way beyond it other than to go through it.

I weave my body through each one of the roots however I can. Each branch came alive winding its way into my body, or perhaps it was that they wound out of my body.

The tree that appeared to be a separate entity, sprung from you.

It's Gregory and I, how we've wound inside of each other all these years, into a ball of knots. When I turn to face it on the other side, the tree is standing straight up, roots dug down again, where they should be, *outside of anything you are at all.*

For the rest of the day these images are constantly alive in my head – a real and active memory. A tide withdrawing with only what it needs. He has his own foundation, and so do I now.

My parents fly in a day or two after I arrive for my niece's birthday, and our timing is spot on perfect. We are all here before snowmageddon hits.

"We haven't had a snow storm like this for five years!" everyone in the neighborhood is saying, over and over. Everyone knows everyone on my brother's street so when the snow hits, all the wagons, sleighs, surf boards, whatever can skid down a road in the snow, come out and everyone shares.

The street is on a steep incline so it's perfect for risking your life and potential bone fractures on. My mother, who is more forty than seventy, seizes her chance back to childhood. Up she drags her borrowed death sled, climbs on, and dashes down, screaming into the wind.

She digs her hands into the snow for a control that never comes, and crashes into someone's garden.

And she gets up and goes again.

And again.

Dad is manning the camera and eventually he mounts up and heads down too. We're in some kind of wonderful snow globe someone's shaken up. For these few hours before the gangrene threatens to set in, all else drifts away, all ails magically heal and worries fade. I wish you could feel this. The snow cover feels like crème brûlée under your feet – a crunchy cap on a creamy center.

By night the Buddha in the garden sits tall in the melting drift snow, and while I dream, the shinning snowflakes melt away their individuality into a fresh collective waterfall sweeping the magic down into the river at the end of the lane.

As the beauty of the world would have it, Ally, one of the popular girls in my high school class, lives only a few minutes away from my brother. We haven't seen each other since the early years of college.

You always envied her.

She was the first American punk I'd ever seen. She was edgy and everything I dared not be. She was in my Theatre Major Studies class in high school, and only because of the fact that she was in theatre, she, unlike many of your typical popular people - cheerleaders, drill teamers and such like, spoke to me.

She was a year ahead of you and D'Ann in school. She could already drive.

She might even have smoked.

All the cool people did.

You wouldn't have. I was not cool. I was what you might call... *awkward.*

Outfitted in classic Clarks shoes and sensible hemlines. Ally helped to open my eyes to the boundaries I could cross if I could summon up a bit of courage. I had a very traditional long hair cut in those days - she followed her own look.

Right before graduation you did too though. You got that perm.

And cut it to look like Madonna's in "Like a Virgin." It all seemed ironically safe and daring at the same time.

Ally wasn't stuck up like the rest of the popular people were, and she, D'Ann and I all hung out. I couldn't believe my luck at the time, being the new, slightly strange foreign girl with the lofty accent, *and gold shoes -* that someone that cool would allow me in her car, and be seen talking to me.

After graduation we all crossed over a year or two at the University of Texas, but after that Ally moved on to Los Angeles. She became a writer on a soap opera. More coolness.

As adults we met once during her time in LA when I moved out there fifteen years ago. I met her just off the lot and we went to lunch. We seemed at different places in our lives then, though. I remember it as a distracted, unsure meeting. I think we both related more when D'Ann existed in the mix with us. We had a bridge between us that balanced out all the energy that had been us in school. Both Ally and I have a strong relationship with D'Ann - each in its own right, but this day, over mixed greens, I knew we didn't have that with each other yet.

So meeting her in Oregon fifteen years later you're not sure what you'll find.

She only lives about twenty minutes from my brother. I'd say it's odd that out of anywhere in the world she could have chosen to live, she's here, but it isn't, is it?

And you're about to find out why.

We meet at the coffee shop attached to the local grocery store. She enters the same way as she exited – tall, edgy with the hippest haircut and color. Eclectic, cool people like that don't shift, I don't think. They feel who they are so early on in life. Becoming is no longer tied to image because that slid down the birth canal with her.

There's a silliness to us as we sit here sipping tea, finding the place where we cross back over. It's easier than I thought. When things are slightly strange and unexpected it seems to take the pressure off.

We take off to Powell's bookstore where I pitch a tent in the middle of the travel section. I'd come from volunteering at the Children's Book Bank in Portland.

"Did you know the ratio of books to children is 1:300?"

"Well, that's fucked up."

"And here we are in this city of books."

"I want to buy them all and truck them over."

I take the seventeen travel memoir books I can't live without to a wine bar, as you do.

No, as you do.

Ally used to be a wine rep so she knows her vines. I drink what she tells me to and my body is relaxed and mooshy. I love every swallow of our company.

Back at the house, it's the creative energy I love. I tap away in here and Billy taps away in there. It bleeds through the walls. When we're apart, which is most of the time, we stay in touch over the phone. He typically calls me on the way from the grocery, to a restaurant, waiting for a flight or babysitter to arrive. However time is carved, it is carved out, and we take it. It's like we have one of those tin cans with the string in the middle that joins them together; the string is always there, even when the cans are silent. He usually answers the phone with a funny accent that takes us back to childhood, and the conversation steers to what we're most passionate about and it never veers off.

He's a very focused person, you brother; he's got a clever mind.

Which is why he's such an interesting writer. I think that when he looks at his wife and child he can't get over how fortunate he is to have found one, and created the other. He values time, his friendships and his books. He doesn't believe in kindles and it drives him crazy that he uses one.

It should. But we all have flaws.

Ha! You got that right.

He's brave too.

He leapt long before I realized how rational it all is. He stands up for himself and won't allow himself to be taken advantage of, by man or corporation. He makes me want to climb on the train and ride it without knowing the destination.

He worries about you – can't quite get over some of the choices I've made - *laughs with you –* and when something happens to someone he loves, it also happens to him. He encourages me, he'll look at the rosy picture I paint and show me where the flowers will never grow. He's like my shadow hobbling beside me, only we're just connected at the one foot, the other one's broken away to steer by.

He keeps a light on inside of you.

I am thankful every day that he invests in and brings so much to my life.

He looks at you and tells you it's okay to come on through.

Relationship Intuition Number Twenty-Three: **The Other Friendship**. This is the friendship that mirrors your own core and challenges it to come to the forefront of your brain and stay there; the rock, that rocks. He'll float around in the brilliance with you, armed with a hoop full of keys, and he'll try every one of them with you to find the one that fits.

"What ya doing, Sara?" Billy flops down on the bed, the ripples pop Stanley off and under the chair. "I can't work anymore, my brain is fogged up."

"Yeah, well, I'm in the middle of something, so bugger off."

"Oh, no. If I'm not getting any writing done, then you're not allowed to either. No writing can be going on if I'm not writing, sorry."

"I'm almost done, I'm just editing the last page."

"How many do you average a day?"

"I don't know three to five."

"Oh, well that doesn't make me feel so bad... wait, single spaced?"

"Yep."

"Ahhh. Stop, stop now. The dogs need walking. It's going to rain, then they won't get a walk – just sayin' – get your priorities right, Sara."

"Ahhh, you're such a pain."

"Look at poor Stanley, deprived of love and the freedom of a good walk."

"Poor Stanley would rather be under that chair than fighting for space with your two hit men dogs."

"We're leaving in five minutes." It is nice just to be able to take off and walk in all this glorious beautiful landscape, as much fuss as I make about it. I take a picture in my head - stop for a moment and gaze around like a panorama photo and tell my brain to remember.

You first did that in Versailles. You were nine years old. You were lying on the couch; you leaned your head under a lamp and stared into the light.

Yes, I did. I can still see the satin cream and gold tassels and feel the heat on my forehead from the bulb. *Jeu de Vingt Heure* was on the television and all of my family was in the room laughing. Walking in this bitter cold with my brother, laughing, feeling out of breath as hills overtake my airwaves, I'm happy.

Blink so you'll know it all over again.

There is a boy on my list from my college acting class who was a big flirt and had the presence of Othello. Martin and I lost touch completely after graduation but Hermosa Beach Jill had stayed in contact with him. He'd lost his way for a while, I knew that. Now, he's completely turned his life around, and is back into acting. I wonder how guarded he'll be, if he'll open up to me at all – if he'd even meet with me.

He has two tickets to Pinter's, *The Caretaker*, and would I like to go. I ask if Ally is able to go too but he seems uneasy. His memory of her is slight and he'd prefer it if it were just us.

Fair enough. It may feel strange enough to him as it is, that the two of you are meeting up.

I know him immediately, his cheeky grin starts and slips a bit and our hug has an air of hesitancy about it.

Everyone here knows him. Actors, directors, friends all coming up to him, hugging him, thanking him for coming, talking about what other shows he'll be seeing, and when he'll be on stage next.

"It's good to see you," he says. We stand looking at each other for a bit and start to head towards the theatre. "This is weird," he adds, and we sit down. We smile at each other and the talk is fast with a trace of tentativeness about it. The play is dark and brooding and by intermission the tone has swept into our bones with a quiet that doesn't add more to catching up. I decide that instead of going out for a drink as planned after the show, I'll just say how lovely it was to see him and know he's doing well and I'll go on home. I can tell he's uneasy about this, guarded and I need to leave him be. This might be the first encounter that's met with withdrawal, within our core acting class at any rate.

The clearest thing to learn is that it's all about listening - to know when someone's pushing back and accept it.

After the show though, Martin immediately says he has a place in mind to go and have a drink, and since he brings it up, we go. He drives. In the car my mind whirls with lots of different questions.

Wait.

There is silence, and there are soundless moments like this one that blink away in the background, left to exist on their own. So we sit with it. After a few minutes he speaks first.

"I'm not sure how much you know about what happened to me after we graduated. I mean I'm not sure how much maybe Jill may have told you."

Hold back.

"Well not that much. I know you got into some trouble a while back." I don't want to taint the conversation with parts from anywhere else.

Allow him to tell you what it meant for his life.

"It was such a messed up time for me. I got fucked up and it all came down, you know. I was out of control. But I've fixed all that now, no more of that, no more drinking."

"Well, you're obviously in a great place now. You're a big part of this theater community, you know everyone. They respect you a lot that's clear enough."

"Yeah. Thank you. I've worked hard. I bartend, I have my girl and I'm getting back in shape for a show. It's all good. It's all really good." We pull over to a restaurant and have a coffee, and what I thought would be a quick moment of relative catching up turns into a conversation that slices us back open. There's nothing trivial. We are uncovered. He looks over the table at me with the first complete smile I've seen cross his face since we met, and there he is, there's the Martin I know.

It's beautiful.

In the parking lot back at the theatre I hand over his Goldrush mustard, and as I drive away from him I know something very special has happened for us. We both allowed this meeting to happen, regardless of the strangeness, and the hesitancy. We held inside those moments together and allowed it. It's one of those rare times when I can honestly say that I've been completely present with another human being by following their rhythm as delicately as my own. And this we had to see in each other's eyes. Without that, there would have been no weight to it.

I don't know if I'll see Martin again, it's not that either of us wouldn't want to, but more, for right now, that neither of us needs to. I wouldn't have felt like I could call him my friend without this exchange though. I'm not sure how much we can ever truly know or understand about another human being in this short amount of time, but I know I'm closer to it with him.

There's a door ajar for either one of you to step through should the time present itself again.

Part 7 Marrow:

> The fat contained in the osseous tubes and cells of the bones; The essence, the best part;
> Spinal marrow, the spinal cord, or cord of nervous matter; To go down on one's marrow bones, to assume a kneeling position.

- The Library of Universal Knowledge

The Feed of Memoriam

> One of the Immutable Laws of Being Human is that whoever shows up is the right person, or the right people, and boy, were those the right people.
> - Anne Lamott

It's my ex-boyfriend, Gregory's birthday the next morning, February 13ᵗʰ. I grab my phone like a robot to leave the newsfeed birthday buzz along with the rest of the friend sheep. As I scroll through the newsfeed I see a post from one of D'Ann's friends saying how he's going to miss his friend, Lucius, her husband. I pause a second and read it again. He must have gone on some sort of fishing trip. But there's something about it.

Scroll back up, read it again, click into the comments.
This person is saying goodbye. Lucius hasn't gone fishing. This isn't a temporary missing. I pick up the phone immediately and call D'Ann. I don't know if she'll answer. Maybe it's some kind of joke, that they're getting ready for work as usual, and then she answers the phone.

"What's going on? I just..."

"Oh, Sara, it's horrible, it's just like they say it is, it's horrific - you can't believe it. It's just like they say. He thought he was having a heart attack."

"Are your parents there?"

"Yes, they drove in last night. They took me to the hospital when the ambulance left with Lucius. How did you know?"

"Someone posted on Facebook that they were going to miss him, and I wasn't sure what it meant. Well, you know, was sure what it meant but didn't want it to mean what it did."

241

"Oh, yes, his best friend, he must have put something out there."

"Well I'm coming. I'm going to get on a plane." I don't want to ask her anything else. I don't want her to have to speak about it. What's real and understood at this point? "I love you, D'Ann."

"Thank you, Sara." I can hear her dad in the background as the receiver hangs in the air not yet hung up. "I love you, Sara."

Her life's flipped onto a beam.

What do I do? He should be warm, not so cold. Why is this happening to her?

He's the conduit for something bigger for her, like I am to you.

What do you mean like you are to me? What's that supposed to mean?

No, for Lila.

Who you are right now is *my* obstacle. I need to see my own head. Rational world head. I can see him in the house making meat loaf, lifting his daughter Lila into the air - she's not even two years old yet, how do you explain this to her? How is she supposed to process the lack of him?

How did you?

She's two years old.

You can't see the picture.

Fuck the picture. I can't see any picture other than the one in front of me. And it's pretty messed up.

I'm sorry, yes. We are slamming doors.

I have to get out of here. Where can I go? I don't want anyone to hear this.

To the shops. Sit in the car and cry as loudly and for as long as you need.

I buy a razor I don't need and I sit inside the car and scream frustration into the icy air. I'm having difficulty stringing one thought; any words at all.

It was a restless night, Stanley was up and down, up and down with an upset stomach.

Sometimes when we got to the door he would just look at the open space and turn around again.

Pacing around the bedroom and staring at you.

I was irritated at the rustling, so annoyed. And today –

Lucius' wandering.

My friend's heart is broken open. I'm so angry. So angry that this man who turned his life around, who had a new lease on his career, on fatherhood, who embraced it with passion,

242

has been pulled from all that's beautiful to him. He was cut to fit, and now his piece is missing.

The pictures changed.

I'm glad I hugged him - saw him loving his wife and daughter. "You'll come around more often now?" *He asked you that.*

Yes. I told him, yes, I'll come around more often. Such an odd question.

It makes sense today.

I had no idea it was a dying man's wish.

I call Ally. We meet for lunch and talk about our plans to get to D'Ann. It's Thursday and I've made arrangements to leave on Monday and stay for a few weeks. I just want to get there. The only thing I can do is be present in this slow motion migraine of time.

Not a lot's gonna lift the veil.

And the bastard gods have put Valentine's day on the calendar - a day of love while we swim on in search of the marrow sucked away from us.

He's in the invisibility.

Maybe he'll just take pity on us and come back.

It's up to you to grab a hold and rebuild him.

He's dancing in Lila's shadow - *and her smile. His reflection is in the well of her eyes.*

He's the quiet.

He's the yet to be found purpose for someone in the room.

The flight's an early one and I don't know what I'm doing from the word go.

Show up and let go. Whatever she needs.

Fill the gap.

With each connecting flight I'm one step closer to watching this live in someone so important to me. My sorrow is seeing it in her eyes.

There's one thing to remember though - this is not your grief.

The plane lands and I head to William's house. D'Ann has a lot on this late in the day and I want the timing of when it feels right to go to her to just be there. I don't push, I don't invite myself, I just sit with William and we try to take it all in.

"You know I saw him at Home Depot a little while ago. 'Come over to the pool and have a swim with us.' Sure I said, I will. I never did. I didn't go. Why didn't I go, Sara? I didn't go."

"Go now. He invited you. He doesn't have to be there for you to go. Perhaps he invited you for this reason. You're needed there now more than anything. Lila will need you. Now's the time to show up." We talk for hours and hours and drink an absurd amount of vodka & Fresca. We say it's for Lucius, but it's really for us.

D'Ann and her mom pick me up the next morning, early, after they drop Lila off at school. They keep her routine much the same as possible - playing with her friends, laughing and maintaining what an almost two-year-old does. D'Ann has a mug full of hot tea and we're both thankful to be with each other. We talk around Lucius, about the flight, how wonderful it is to spend time with each other and how hot it is even now in early February.

Her mom looks completely shattered.

She's holding it together for all of them. The focus in her eyes is the tight grip on the steering wheel.

Walking in the house I feel Lucius at once - not that he's here, but that he isn't. At all. I walk from the kitchen where he'd apologized for the fried chicken dinner that they don't normally eat, to the garage so full of all that's him still, and to the bedroom where he fell. And it's all eerily silent with a thick nothing pressing into my chest. It's not just his not being here, it's that it seems so ridiculous and stupid that he's not - that I'm here and he isn't.

"Jesus, this makes no sense," whisper vomits out of me. She shakes her head and makes more tea. Her eyes are heavy, but now in company, if she's anything like me, she has motivation to stay in control. D'Ann has always been in tune with everything around her, and if I know one thing it's that she allows a guidance to track her in that.

He's not here anymore.

"I know he's gone. I just feel that. I'd know if he was still here. He isn't..." She gets up. "I just have to move this." She opens the back door and picks a blue blanket off of the chair and brings it inside. "I'll give this to Goodwill or someone. One of the blankets fell off the gurney as they were wheeling him out." She's been staring at it outside the bay kitchen

244

window for four days. She's beginning to clear it all away - starting with the most glaring piece of evidence there is.

When she goes outside to water the plants her mother looks out the window and then shifts her eyes down to her feet.

"How is she really?"

"She's doing okay, I think. It's just so strange, Sara. I still can't believe it. Of course you know something's wrong when the phone rings at 1:00am, but then when the guy said he was the Sheriff I thought something had happened to her. But he said right off the bat that it wasn't - he was calling *for* her, that Lucius had possibly had a heart attack and that we needed to get down here right away. Her dad drove like a bat out of hell. It took less than an hour from San Antonio. By the time we got here the ambulance was ready to leave with him so we went up there. We weren't there but a couple of minutes and they came out and said they'd pronounced him. It's just so weird. Weird that it happened. Weird that it's true."

"You're going to stay here with her for a while?" She nods as D'Ann comes back in for squirrel food. I make more tea. It's so difficult to say anything encouraging in these situations, or know what the boundaries are of what's capable of being shared.

Leave it all alone. Be there when she shares.

"It's Lila, she keeps asking for him. Where he is. And I'm not sure what to do, how to talk that out."

"It's not going to make any sense to her, is it."

"He can't disappear though. He has to stay alive in her."

"She looks just like him. He's alive in her, but I know, I know what you mean." For a beat we sit and drink our tea and then we go into the garage to take the garbage out.

"I'm going to have to clear out some of these things. I mean I can do it now. Lucius wouldn't throw anything away. I know he'll pitch a fit but, now I can do it."

"It might be cathartic in a way. Just don't rush into it all."

"And his clothes. He's such a clotheshorse. He's got way more clothes than me. I just want to save a few things for Lila, like his hat..." We bring a few things inside and I make more tea. "I think I'm going to have a bath before we go and pick up Lila," she says, taking her tea into the bedroom. I take a walk out into the garden. I wander around the pool cursing Lucius for letting go. You shouldn't have done this. You shouldn't have gone. What have you done?

245

When I get back inside D'Ann's knitting. Her eyes are red and her face is blotchy. She'd let go in there by herself. Perhaps that's how it works. You stay in control and you bathe whatever it is that needs to leave you - then you gather yourself up and begin again. I make tea.

"You know what's weird? A few weeks ago Lucius had been with a guy who'd had a heart attack and lost consciousness. They worked on him for a while, but I remember him saying, 'if they don't come back in the first fifteen minutes, they're not coming back.' They worked on Lucius for like an hour and a half before taking him in. I knew then he was really gone, I mean, you know. His words just flashed in and around my head. But they needed to keep trying. One of their own, I guess. And so did I. And the strange thing is I'd already seen this a little while back. I'd seen it, I saw him die in a dream. Not a dream like in sleep, but a dream as in I see this and it will be true. I knew it was coming but I never told him anything about it. I knew he couldn't handle that. In some ways it helps now, you know. Even though it's a shock still and it still makes no sense, there is a small piece of me that was prepared."

Over the next few hours we sit, she knits, we put some reality TV on and she applies for about ten jobs on the internet. When she comes back into the room again she notices that her mom has cleaned up, as mother's do. She's looking for something that has been in the same spot on the coffee table, and it's not there anymore. She disappears for a minute or two and when she came back she's clinging to a small hand drawn picture.

"I needed to find this. Lucius drew it. It's Lila. Easy to throw away but I needed to get it back. I don't want to lose this piece." She puts it back on the coffee table ledge again, where it's always been.

We pick up Lila from school who's having a good giggle with some friends on the playground when we get there. When we walk in though there's an immediate tone shift. The room fills with the "there's that poor woman whose husband died and left this poor little girl fatherless." It comes down like rain. We get in and out of there before Lila feels it. As we drive home Lila looks at me and says my name.

"Sara." There is a pause as she's looking at me remembering where she's seen my face before. She holds on to a sippy cup but isn't drinking. Then she says it.

"My daddy got sick."

"Yes, Lila, Daddy died, didn't he?"

"Yes, my daddy died. He was sick."

"And he's in heaven now."

"In heaven now."

"He lives in our hearts now, doesn't he?"

"Yeah, Daddy lives in our hearts now." There's a long pause. I have to look out the window and concentrate so I don't cry.

"Daddy coming?"

"No Daddy died, but he's in our hearts. Would you like your snack? Mimi packed your snack for you." She keeps her eyes fixed on me as her hand dips into a container of Goldfish. She crunches them with the cutest two front teeth, and she smiles.

The asking for Daddy. For Lila when the phone rings it could be him, that here he is, finally. She's waiting on the edge of it without knowing the impossibility of it all; that no matter how much pixie dust we throw or how many times we say we believe - it will never be him. She cannot grieve.

She's fresh in beginnings. There is no understanding yet of the dust to which we must return.

For now she's accepted he's alive in a new world. Today he lives inside of the machine. In there he talks to her, he's laughing. She stands quietly in the corner tickling him on the iPad screen and smiling with him. She stares into it, right into his eyes, straining so hard to make them real. I see her over there in front of the mirror, dressed only in her diaper and a pink plastic necklace, watching her father love her from a different dimension. A part of me is so grateful for the hours of video she has to keep him present, that she can dive in there with him whenever she wants to. But it's surreal, that in her way, this almost two-year-old has found her own way to cope. It's heartbreaking, and yet I'm thankful that there's something, that the air isn't completely empty around here, not for her.

"Daddy was sick." She tells me as Barney flounces purple happiness on the TV. Daddy was.

D'Ann is strong in the sight of her child and I have never seen anything more beautiful as the light that passes between the two of them. Her daughter sits on her knee watching her daddy inside the phone and they talk as best they can to one another, guiding the other through. They sit eye-to-eye, mother explaining why, as best she can, and child repeating the question from a place of innocent non- understanding, again and again. The answer falls into a fathomless pile of dirty un-washable clothes.

It's the nights that are the hardest. It's when the normal hour of sleeping rises that the baby wonders why he hasn't arrived at all again today. Seeing the look on her face when the doorbell rings, all of that hope on her face - that this time it could be him - you wait as long as you can to erase it away. Her entire body shifts with the ding-dong bell, maybe it always will. Shouldn't we at least give her that, that millisecond where it could be true?

Maybe you need it for yourselves.

The baby won't sleep – much as if she's keeping a night vigil just in case he comes home. She wouldn't want to miss it - she must be there for the first sound of his feet at the door, the sound of his voice in her ear as she is partially drifting off once again. She stays alert and on guard with their dog Spartacus; they are on lookout, the first shift, and they will never give up the fight, never give up the vigil because he will come as he always has and there will be laughter again. It's just a matter of time, it's just a matter of patience and waiting. This fragile questioning is leading her to a different level of knowing all together.

Over the course of the next few days some friends of theirs fly in from around and about. One couple pop by D'Ann's to share their grief. They haven't seen each other for a long time, and used to be very close – going on vacations together as couples. They want to know what happened. They're in shock, in their own state of loss, sitting here wanting to bleed each and every detail out of her. Something about this doesn't feel right. I haven't seen her cry yet. She maintains and retreats when she needs to. In this living room she's being asked to go back, go over each detail.

"We just can't believe it. We're all in shock. Was it a heart attack?"

"Well, they don't really know. He woke up about 1:00am and he was sweating a lot, but that had happened before, you know. But he said he felt like he was having a heart attack. So I picked up the phone to call 911, but he said no, go warm up the car for Lila and just like drive him to the hospital. So I basically went out into the garage and turned the car on and when I got back he'd already fallen back on the bed, unconscious." I want her to stop.

She knows they need more.

"So I called 911 and they told me to pull him off the bed and onto the floor and they walked me through CPR until the

248

paramedics got there which only took a few minutes. They got there really fast. They kept working on him, you know. They were there for an hour and a half just trying again and again, but I knew he was gone. I mean as you, like don't want him to be. I knew he was. I knew." They still look at her, not ready for a commercial break. "They're doing an autopsy – his doctor wanted to have one done because he couldn't believe it could be a heart attack. He'd had all the tests done and a full work over to become a paramedic. They're doing drug tests on him to check that. But they're not going to find anything. They won't. Just insulin." There is a still hovering. "So we don't have the body yet. They can't release it yet." No one is saying anything. They just keep staring at her.

They need more.

"He had a good last day though. He got to go fishing with his best friend, and come home and play with Lila…" She just kept talking from one thought to the next without much breath separating much of it, marching to the end so the little fish heads at the top of the tank can feed at the surface.

For the briefest of moments, she smiles at them and I know what it is she's doing by making this confession – it's not only to comfort them, but in telling the story she's trying to help them to make sense out of something that never will to her. There is the importance to her that every one of her friends is okay in their grief. She honors and respects their loss, as much as she embraces her own. It is extraordinary.

Talk quickly moves to happier times sharing Lucius's past escapades and adventures. This softens her tears. It doesn't stop them, but they're able to flow through smiles, and her legs release themselves a bit from underneath her chin and her body fills the chair again.

The day before the funeral, Ally arrives from Portland and I pick her up at the airport to take her to our friend Kirsty's.

"How is she?"

"She's handling it. I think it's flowing out of her in inches because she has Lila to think about. She has to protect her, to deal with… no that's the wrong word, not deal with, she tends to what Lila needs. They're going through it together. People have been saying that while it's so tragic, that Lucius was fortunate to have almost two years with his child, that he was so thankful for D'Ann giving him this gift of a daughter - something she had given him that made the last few years of his life so happy and fulfilled. I think it's all backwards

249

though. When I looked at the two of them last night, I saw it as exactly the opposite. I think it's all been a gift from him to her. I really don't know how she would survive the minutes without having Lila in her mind. I really don't. But that may be my own weakness."

Lucius's funeral is an outpouring of celebration for his life - every nook and cranny of it. Three endearing, emotional, funny, heartbreaking hours of memory fueled tales of himself. So many people speak that there has to be an intermission. He would have loved that, that a celebration of him had a pre- party, an intermission and an after party. This is his show. The room fills beyond capacity, so much so that the outside doors have to be opened to allow the spill to continue in.
This is someone hundreds of people miss.
People come that have known him for forty-five years, and others that have known him for as little as a few months. He was one of those people that made an impression, made you laugh, found your weakness and exploited you in it, backed you up. Some of us go to a funeral to hear someone's story, others to help in the telling of it.
He made the energy shift. That kind of loss is felt in any room.
At a memorial service, when a room is filled to capacity you know something has gone terribly wrong. You feel it in your bones. Only the young dead get such great attendance.
Of course with any one as eclectic as Lucius, there will be a few kooks coming out of the woodwork and one woman definitely led the parade there. A psychic arrives claiming that Lucius had dictated his eulogy to her. D'Ann is looking forward to this most of all. There's a certain amount of levity brought up when someone who doesn't really know the ins and outs of a person gives the most personal part of the funeral. To our disappointment she's not as whacked out as we thought she'd be, albeit the situation was kooky enough for those who were aware it was going on.
The most poignant moment of the service comes from a young paramedic that gets up to speak. In a room full of actors this man stands up as himself. He's nervous at the podium and he has one of those flowering gift bags in his hand, like you buy at Walgreens. He looks out at D'Ann for a moment before he speaks.
"Lucius was my mentor in school. He got me through so

much of it. But I do know that devil side of him too. He was always playing jokes on us, giving us bear hugs when he shouldn't. I just, well, I didn't know him for a long time, but I'm glad I got to know him as much as I did. He supported me. I don't know who I'm going to call now. I don't know what I'm going to do without him being there. I just don't know." He doesn't say that he promises to stay in touch, because he won't – what he says is that Lucius' memory is alive in him, in the job that he does and in the lives that he will save. The room gets the quietest it's been. He walks inside that silence up to D'Ann and hands her his little paper bag with a gift inside for her. And for the first time tonight she cries. Lucius is all around this moment. She hugs him for a few minutes and they both cry around the quiet expressions of his "I'm so sorry. I'm so, so sorry." She calmly eases his grief, which at that moment, she sees just as deeply as her own.

Lucius is most definitely in the room at the onset of it all to watch it all unfold. He couldn't have been there too long though, because it's a Thursday, and that was always daddy/daughter date night. He's off with his girl, watching her on her play date, away from all this – smiling, dancing and reflecting who he is in the mirror. He instilled such a deep love and warmth in her. Those memories will stay with this newly two-year-old, keep in her sight for the rest of her life, and because of that she will always know him – not remember him, know him.

In his fifty years he achieved more than many do in ninety. When the pistol sounded he took off from the starter blocks and rushed to get all of it in, in perfect timing, unbeknownst to him. The last day of his life came sitting on a boat fishing with his best friend, a peaceful moment in quiet competition, seeing who would catch the only fish of the day.
He did.

After the funeral my body goes into a revolt and my throat closes up along with my nose and my ears. My entire head wants detaching. I think I've eaten one too many cheerios that Lila's been chewing on and feeding to me. I shove airborne, vitamin C, honey and lemon and all other magic potions into my body to keep it afloat because William has gotten us three complimentary tickets to see *The Vibrator Play*. It'll be good for D'Ann to get out of the house and try to laugh a bit.

"I feel like I'm on vacation," she says as we stand in the lobby by a cardboard cut-out of William and take selfies of ourselves with him. "You're here, William's here. I'm drinking a beer... I can drink beer again. It's like a vacation. I'm like, just away from him."

There is distraction in numbers.

I hope that her local friends who keep repeating the same mantra, "we'll have you over for dinner," "we'll have sleep overs," "we'll be here for you," won't renege when their lives get busy again. I can already see it some people's eyes, the ones who won't know how to look at her when they see her at some event down the line and realize they haven't reached out since the day of the funeral.

Try to see what you're capable of, what you will show up for –

Down in myself, yes. Where I will stand. To own up to a responsibility is an instinct. That's what her mother is doing, without question, without doubt, without effort. You could say that's what mother's do, but that's not it – it's what we should all emulate. And you know what, if you say it, live up to it. Show up. Keep your word.

Ally and I leave town back to Oregon together. We drop off Lila at school and say our goodbyes. I will phone. Once I get my car I'll drive back down the mountain.

I watch her walk to her car with her mother, as we, the last of the out of towners, drive away. There is a slight turning down, a slightness to her that I hadn't noticed before. Inside that car is the first moment of the next phase of life for her.

The new normal.

The celebration of life has subsided in public and now retreats inside for the two of them to live inside of for themselves. I wonder at what's going on inside her mind inside that car as it goes into its first day of a new routine.

"I should have stayed," that's what's going on in your mind.

I wish I could have stayed. Why didn't I stay? There's no reason I can't just say, stop. This is the reason for the journey, this is why I embarked on it in the first place, this is the destination, this is where it's been going and where it should pause.

It is where it has paused.

I can't take on my friend's grief, but I will stand by her in every other way.

I wake up the next morning back in Oregon, half of me still in Austin, knowing I only have 48 hours to get myself together before heading up to Seattle to meet my friend Lenore at the AWP conference.

Then on to Tacoma to see Dad.

The flight home has closed my ears completely and my head feels like a balloon floating in lead.

Stanley is relieved to see me and doesn't leave my side. He's been sleeping in our bedroom by himself, and not eating too well while I've been gone. Poor thing.

And here you are unpacking to repack and go off and leave him for another week.

There's guilt on the other side too, I see.

The night before I leave, Visitation Man works his way back into my dreams for the next assault - his enduring patience running out. He comes in the dark hour of night when the murdering kind slip into our homes and steal away with what's most precious to us. He's kept his distance over the last few months. My nights have been blank without any visions at all. I began to crave him in that sick way you wish you'd break your leg so someone will love you more.

He draws my breath back as the dream begins. I'm on the phone inside an old, barren farmhouse looking out into a field that takes up the rest of the world. There's a woman on the other end of the line telling me to trust her. I tell her that I understand.

In a blink the dream shifts and I'm lying face up in bed. The curtains are white and flowing in the wind of an open window. I'm aware of a gnawing and as I turn my head, a green, psychedelic pterodactyl has a hold of my left arm and is biting down hard. His long beaked mouth is griping it sideways like a twelve-inch subway sandwich. Its skin shines watery smooth like a dolphin's and it glows. He has no eyes, nothing to bear down into me this go around, no bargaining this time, nothing to stare into with tears that beg for my release. Not this time.

I don't wonder at what's he's come for. He knows I'm taking you back to your father and he's afraid I won't let you walk in with me. He watched me bury your bones in Wales, but I know the spirit circles with me, and so does he.

He's calling you to the bridge.

My heartbeat sweats through flesh. Liquid pulses through his needle sharp teeth into my blood, damning up DNA - it's neon green like the nuclear fluid they had in that movie with Nicholas Cage on Alcatraz. The pressure jolts my head up and I can see a musical baby mobile hanging over my head. It needs to be wound but the key is screwed into my back. I have to get up, get out and shake him off before he sees it. But I can't wake up. Why can't I wake up? I need to wake up, wake up, wake up, wake up, wake up. He lets go of my arm and begins turning the key around and around with his mouth and it's slowly opening the not so cesarean zip scar sewed into my stomach. Darwin's law is pulsing. I can't watch, but I watch. And the key is turning, it doesn't hurt, and he's behind me with no eyes, and I'm looking, only I can't – I can't see what will come out of there. Not now. Not anymore. Not now not anymore notanymorenotanymore. I cry it out like a mantra until the room is changed, until the room is my room, until I'm back in my room with Stanley's muffled barking under the chair. Awake. But it's not a relief, not a relief to be awake because it's still true and alive in me. My chest is heaving as quietly as it can in case whatever it is in this room now. I've never felt fright like this before.

It has nothing to do with the animal.

My peripheral vision is high and it catches a red floater. I look over at the window and I'm staring into two rows of hollow, outlined red hearts overlapping like the Olympic rings. They float there like heat in a haze. I close my eyes tightly. I open them again. I am awake. I shut my eyes and then open them up again. I want the hearts to go away and at the same time I want them to still be there. They are. Stanley is looking at them too. I blink again and again and they fade slowly as my body rests gradually back down in bed.

Stanley scratches at the door. He's pawing at it like he does to my arm when he wants love. I don't want to get up. I want to stay in the illusion that as quiet and still as I can stay, the safer I am. I wait.

After about a half an hour I move to take Stanley out. I move slowly like you do after an operation. As I open the door going into the garage the light inside one of the cars switches on. Whatever it is has followed us out here now. I'm freaking out a bit. My chest starts heaving in quick breaths trying to stifle the upset from coming on. I can't take my eyes off the light. This is so weird. I don't feel afraid - I just don't know how to follow this. I know that I've entered something I don't understand.

I ease over to the side door and open it. Stanley takes his eyes off the light and goes outside. I keep my eye on it as I watch him in my peripheral. When I close the door again he and I stand at the top of the stairs to see if the light will go out. It doesn't. I wonder if I should turn it off - the car battery might die. But I don't believe it has any attachment at all to the car. Besides, no way I'm going over there.

We stand a few minutes and I open the door with my back to it and retreat. In a weird way I want to stay with it to see what it has to say. I need to know what it has to say. But I turn away instead and don't do the one thing I probably should do – trust it.

The next morning, I ask Mary if the light in her car was on. "No."

"And it started up alright, no problem?"

"Yes, why?" I proceed to tell her what had happened, about her car's possession. I'm so glad this happened to Mary's car and no one else's – she's the kind of person who understands that energy comes at us from all angles in all shapes and forms and that this one was meant for me, which is why it doesn't affect her car this morning.

You're bringing in a lot of outside sources.

My mind is racing in so many different directions, converging. I don't feel myself, but I don't mind.

The AWP conference goes by in a whirl of distraction over what is coming next for me. I drop Lenore off at the airport to go back to Tempe. I hug her longer and completely without giving her a reason why. Only I know where I'm going.

The rain looks like it's coming in for your drive to Tacoma, to Dad's.

It's only a few hours away. We've seen each other once since we said goodbye to all we were in 1994.

The drive down isn't taking as long as I need it to take.

How much longer until we get there?

No struggle with traffic. The alien flows in my blood, along for the ride - that neon green juice flowing through me like some kind of tracking device – right into the heart of my own admission. He knows I'm driving us right into that thing I don't want rehashed again – to the piece of myself that needs its final conclusion; a part that's even outside of you, my love.

255

Why are you driving the speed limit? You hate doing that. We need to try and get ahead of the storm. It's going to slow us down enough as it is.

Fragments of the two of us flash through me. Why did I let him talk me into separating you and I? I need more space between us. The first rain drops.

Great – rain. Ma, come on. We'll be late.

Rain means one thing - traffic slowing, and then perhaps a mudslide – it could happen. This could buy me time up the Via Dolorosa, a welcome carpet handed to me straight from God.

I think that was our exit.

At least he's sympathetic. Red brake lights have already begun tapping ahead of me – a Morse code of relief. It only delays though. It seems like I blink and - *pull up over there. There's a space right out front.* And here we are, pulled up close to the curb in a quiet neighborhood on the outskirts of Tacoma.

It's so grey here.

Yes, that bland shade of grey that no one wants their walls painted - and heavy. You get the feeling that all the old fisherman's wives are still sitting down at the dock waiting for their husbands to wash ashore out of the grey and the wet, stinking of fish and survival.

Aren't we going to go in now?

I'm waiting for the rain to die down.

That's what you tell yourself.

I'm only a few feet away from the first man I ever loved, my first real boyfriend, a man twelve years older than me, the man who at the age of nineteen, I thought I'd spend forever with.

"Thank God I've found him," you thought, "I'm so lucky to have found you."

So very, very lucky. The neon water is raining harder now. It must look like an ocean to the spider clinging on to my driver side mirror. I'm wearing the wrong shoes to get out and battle it with him. I sit in the car for a minute.

Just a minute.

I need a minute. Can he see me through the window, sitting like a mad girl, staring at the steering wheel, wondering why I'm not getting out of the car? Is he watching? Shit, now I have to get out.

Yeah, we should just go in now.

The last day I saw him was when he dropped me off at Sky's. I felt like a box whose label had been misplaced. I can still smell his anxious, sweaty goodbye. Why is he making me get out of my car when I'm not ready?

He's not. He never has.

Yes, he did. That's exactly what he did.

I'm upside down. My palms are sweaty. My hand is on the door handle. I know that once I set out through this water a part of me is going to evaporate backwards and walk in beside me.

I wish I could hold your hand.

In just a minute we'll see where life has taken each one of us without the other. My coat has no hood and I know the watery walk to the door will flatten right down to the scalp the hair it took me an hour and a half to curl. It will fly around in the wind like chewed up, soggy pieces of sodden string that he knows all too well. I'll arrive at the door stripped of any pre-plan, raw.

But that's how it should be.

One night of fucked up timing for Gibson and I – that's what it all goes back to.

Wait, it wasn't fucked up. Please don't say that.

No.

No.

No, not no. That *is* what it felt like. I was alone trying to make a decision. He left me alone - completely alone, and that's the truth. I'm sorry. I needed his support.

All timing is divine.

Yeah well, I wasn't ready.

You're operating from a point of view that you're supposed to be. Are you ready for this moment today?

No.

But you're still here.

Yeah, but... yeah. I see what you mean. But you're missing my point. I needed him to see what I wanted, to recognize it as a possibility, but it never was. His answer was always going to be no, no matter what I said. No matter what I wanted. I loved him. I didn't know what to do with that. I did love your father, very much.

I know you did.

Do you Smell that?

What?

It's as if my head's still buried in his freshly shaved neck. This smell first kissed me on a fresh cut lawn by a lake. He

257

thought I was pretty. He held my hand anywhere we'd go. He was my first everything – first love, first kiss.

Your first loss.

I gave him all of my firsts. He took me further away from myself and into him.

I got pregnant almost the first time out. I guess I'm good at something. Those odds are pretty remarkable, aren't they? There must be some kind of award for that. I wonder if I should have gotten a telegram from the queen - like you do if you live to be a hundred.

I felt happiness about the pregnancy, about you coming into my life. You believe that, don't you?

I felt it.

It never occurred to me that he wouldn't be.

He cried. He cried non-stop about it.

He couldn't be a father, his father had fucked him up and he'd do the same. Was that some BS? I don't know. He couldn't be a father, he said. He just couldn't. Besides, he had plans. Couldn't I just try to understand that? He cried. He cried a lot. He hugged my belly and kissed it. He wants me to send you back like a pair of shoes that don't fit, destroy the family we were in that moment, but he kisses you?

Saying goodbye.

But without the chance at hello. They all said it would be a mistake to keep you. I'd not be able to go to college, so no education. My future would be lost, best to end it now. Best to end it. I wondered if any of these people actually understood how that was supposed to happen. Did they get that this would be happening to us? Did I realize this would be happening to us?

He didn't speak up.

No, he didn't. And do you know what made me most angry? It was his relief that everyone else around us was in agreement with him. Assuming that the decision had been made.

Only you didn't make it.

Not that day.

Or the next.

So he kept on crying.

Until you walked through the door with the black plastic handle.

That's where I let you go.

I went to the light. You didn't. I left you alone with a broken defense.

I broke my own defenses.

To search out your essential something.
There wasn't any poetry in it.
We always were one another's.
I don't know where to begin with that.
You've been in it since I left your body.
   What if I'm just a slightly more wrinkled let down version of who already wasn't good enough walking up to the door to tear the silence up? I'm not sure I can do this.
You just did.

   He says hello, and hugs me like he would anyone else. I held life for him once. Time has stolen all of what we meant to each other. He offers me something to drink. In his space without me our dynamic tries. There is an oddness being around the familiar of our old life: some of the same furniture, pictures on the walls, plates he still eats off of that my mother had given us for Christmas.
   Look, he's using the same shaving dish and brush; the coffee mug you bought in Las Vegas that you packed up and sent back to him.
   It's like waking from a coma. I didn't put that there, but I know at one time it was mine.
   I have a tour. We sit. I talk about my drive and about my family and about the places I've seen. He's taking me to dinner, but a friend of his is with us.
   "Fred. You remember him." Shouldn't we just be sitting down over there talking about what we never talked about?
   "Sure, yes, of course. How is he?" Why am I here?
   "He sells wine, well, it's more than that - he's a sort of partner in a winery. He lives in Walla Walla now." That's great, but you've not mentioned the baby yet. You've not asked how I've been coping. You've not asked how life has been since then, since you left the package that was me at the curb.
   "I invited him down to stay for the weekend. That's ok, isn't it?" How are we supposed to talk about you with him here? Do I sneak you into the conversation now?
   It'll be rushed. It might feel like an ambush.
   Do I really care? He should start the conversation. Shouldn't he start the conversation? Why can't I start the conversation? Why doesn't he man up and ask the question? Ask the fucking question.

He crashes in the spare room. Fred is on the sofa. He gives me his bedroom to sleep in. I almost expect to see the same orange, *furry worn through bed cover.* Yes.

I shut the door and put my hand on it. There's a quiet pulse on the outside. A part of me wishes he would lie down next to me so we can share the truth we already know. Maybe if we could get back there for just a few minutes it would be easier. I feel the same inadequacy about speaking up as I did inside the bathroom at Gregory's parents' house.

Only in here it's time to wash your hands.

I said "yes," when I meant "no "- that's what I want to tell him.

You said yes to something. I need you to hear that.

It's what I need you to understand as well. I meant "no." I do that all the time, say what I think someone wants to hear and then face the consequences. I was the one who did it though. I nodded and walked through the door. I was the one who saw the picture of the sonogram when it fell on the floor that I wasn't supposed to see and somehow managed to do it anyway. Whatever it was in that choice inducing IV that dripped in, it dug its dirty fingernails into my skin and bled me to where I could let go.

Of us.

I saw a baby mobile hanging from the ceiling. It was so real.

It was.

You saw it too?

It was me.

I don't understand why he didn't love me enough. Why isn't he in here listening to this with me?

I'm here. Maybe this is ours.

Yes. Maybe. No, that's some more bullshit. Love should have been enough.

It's a matter of conscience.

Yes, it's a matter of conscience. I should have let my conscience guide me, thank you very much for that. Sure, yes, let's just say that's it, but here's the thing - you can't always see into it so clearly, you see. There is so much that clouds it. It's more than just a question that's not just one person's decision - it's more than that. I had two opposing answers filtering through every single lobe of my brain, searching for who to please, deliberating trust and advice, but at the same time because so much is going on, I'm not aware of any of it because I'm not brave enough to talk about it, not my side to anyone because they can't hear what I'm saying, and it got so fucking noisy. But there was one thing outside of me that slowed all of that chatter down and that was the sound of him crying.

Not me.

No, not you. There was only a promise of you. I could hear him breathing.

Not me.

No, not you. I could see his life turned upside down and I could do something about that.

So you did chose life.

Yes, I did. I chose life. I chose his life.

And if he feels that, do you think it would be easy for him to ask the question?

I don't think I can care so much about whether it does or not. Not anymore. I want to walk to his door and lay my head against it. I want to talk to him.

Why don't you?

I want him to know that I heard the doctor.

Why?

Because I want him to know how hard it was for me.

Why?

Because I want him to feel it too.

Why? So he'll understand the value of what you gave up?

So he'll understand the value of what I gave him. I want him to know that I was aware and that I was awake and that I knew what I was about to do. He didn't have to be in there, he didn't have to do it. I want him to understand that I was aware he was sitting only a few feet away from me in a waiting room reading a novel he'd never finish, that he could have saved us and he chose not to, that I could have saved us but I didn't. That the doctor said that if I didn't stop moving about he'd stop, that he asked me, did I want this, yes or no? That I calmed myself *and you said, no, yes.* I mumbled. He couldn't hear me. I tried to answer. I hope that you believe me. You believe me, don't you?

Of course. I heard you. Your thoughts were mine.

When I woke up to my bleeding new cycle at a table covered in Ritz crackers and orange juice I felt so disgusted with myself because I felt - *relief.* That's why when I walked out of that place that for everyone else was an ending, my new beginning became clear. The years ahead of me would fall down. I wouldn't allow myself to amount to anything. To feel any trace of happiness would mean that this abandonment would be justified, and that was never going to happen. There would never be a liberation. When everything was going well *- you'd stop and pull back. When someone would come up to you and say, "don't stop doing this, you're brilliant, keep going -"* I'd reverse. It wasn't even conscious.

A new instinct had taken over.

Nothing was ever to come of me. I'd prove they got it all backwards.

I'm worried that my thoughts are banging too loudly to the other side of his door when I shouldn't give a shit, but I do.

You want to know why God left you in there all by yourself.

No, I want to know why he did.

He didn't. I was with you.

God's another story. Cat's cradle is one silly little piece of string all tangled up – why didn't he pull on one end of it? How can I walk into his house to ingest him again? Will he save me now or... perhaps he'll make it look like an accident – I'll choke on the wafer after cutting my lower lip on the jagged edge of the chalice swallowing his blood curdling in what's left of my womb. They say that God's nature is to forgive – it's what he gave his son's life to do. I know this. I do. I feel that forgiveness. But I also understand that the trick to my survival is the forgiveness I have to give myself. I didn't give my son's life to feel that. I wanted to talk about that, but your father *left the same night.*

He did. He got into his car and drove to California to start a new life. Do you have any idea what that felt like? Just three hours before that I'd clung to some fucked up notion we would be a family. Why did he help me to do this?

But a few weeks later the phone rang.

How was I? The sound of his voice was back. I loved him. Let's face it, who else was going to love me now? And we shared this bond. This terrible sin connected us, so we would be together always, regardless.

We stayed together for a few years after that. In all the days we were together though, and there were just over 700 more of them, we never talked about you. Ever. The problem was always something else. And the silence of that ate what was left of us alive. I lived the next twenty years or so of my life inside of a mirror not quite fastened to the wall - one of those concave ones where the closer you walk towards it, the further the reflection seems.

All of these repressed emotional actions against myself made me ill – that's the pain of the tumor that visitation man suffocated me into finding that first morning.

You knew where it came from.

Of course I did. That mass on my left ovary appeared and they had to go in and deliver it from me to make sure it wasn't malignant. It wasn't. It should have been. And the ovary was gone.

The one that bore me.

It was as pure as its sibling. That's where all the sadness and the anger, the betrayal, the abandonment and the frustration lived. That surgery cut away my last chance for a child. They left the womb and the other ovary in, but let's face it, with half the chances, my baby window closed. I knew that there was no more time to buy.

Despite your beautiful sister's fight on your behalf with the doctor to avoid the hysterectomy.

It's warm, this scared line where the child never birthed. A crooked scar - uneven, purple – stitched up now much as an empty pocket might be. I want to see it so I go into the bathroom and take off my nightdress and stare at myself naked in front of the mirror.

You've been committing a sort of slow suicide for the last twenty years.

I'd chosen to go missing, and even though I'm finally turning the corner to honor our lives instead of sacrificing them, even though I've sought out an entire team of psychiatrists and alternative therapists to help me fix this, there's something I haven't done.

Come back to him, to face him - returned to as close to the scene of the crime as you can.

His pulse is on the other side of this wall.

The next day Gibson takes me on a tour of the University campus where he works. We visit a museum, and a conservatory. We talk of much of what's happened in our lives since we said goodbye, but nothing of the deep past. My head almost exploded with all the questions in the night and today I've decided to wait for him to speak. But I'm not sure he wants to.

You went through it all last night on the other side of his door - a run through, a final dress. Is it too much for Dad?

But isn't this what I'm doing here in the first place - to sweep it out? I feel so stupid being here and not being able to

263

string more than one thought together of what I want to talk to him about. And about how he finally left me. It was all so quick and...

Are you happy?

That's what he said that Sunday afternoon he broke up with me, *sitting on the patio.*

The end comes over the simplicity of folding laundry.

The CA fires were burning in the hills, the winds carried all the left over ash of someone's burnt memories through the air onto your table.

A weeks' worth of embers surrounded us.

"Yes, are you?" That's what you said.

"I'm not." That's what he said.

We'd stood in the rain of our relationship from the get go, I suppose. There wasn't any hope for what we had, not really, but we didn't know that. When something grows in you like that, you can't let go b*ecause it holds without intent.*

My heart loved what was lost. *Me.* And it required payment from the one who was left beside me.

My dad.

My communication shut down, my need for intimacy closed. Your father, with all his good intentions - he did try. After the laundry was folded up with the question and put away with his withdrawal from the relationship, there were a few days of removed fixing when he looked at me as if he couldn't remember my name. Happiness hadn't disappeared - it had never been allowed in. I boxed up my belongings from our apartment in Pasadena and he drove me to Sky's house down in San Diego. The only thing I owned without an address label on it was me. I didn't need one. I had been delivered.

Before I leave, Gibson and I walk through an art exhibit of Chihuly's glassworks. There's a piece he's built outside in a forest in wintertime: a glass chandelier made to look like it's made of icicles. When I look at that sculpture I see the soul of our lifetime together inside it. We'd built this beautiful thing, but out of ice. We didn't keep it in a safe climate and the sun caught up with us and melted its beauty drop by drop. It can't take away that we built this intricate spiral of feelings, this emotional tunnel, this angled sculpture of anger and suppression, of non-communication, of moss, of understanding, respect, kindness, passion, love and loss.

It still drips in the forest somewhere.

When I look at us in there I can see that your father had the strength to know we needed to come to an end, that we needed saving, and he let me go. He knew we both needed love, and that for me the child was still alive, somewhere circling around in my head, and I'd made my choice long ago, if not physically, then mentally. I couldn't love him when I still blamed him. We did have love; some of the kindest moments of love in my life were with him holding on to me. When my Grandmother died he came home to find me trying to melt my tears away in bath water. He followed me when I ran out into the rain in my favorite pink dress screaming at the un-bearableness of it.

"I knew I loved you then," he said.

I knew I loved him, loved him for just letting me happen in my own space. It wasn't that we were ever without love, that I hope you do understand.

The last night you were together you watched him drift off to sleep.

I lay in his arms and I memorized his face, the shape of his ear, the slight suntan on his neck, the smell of the nape, the blonde receding sunlight in his hair. I blinked my eyes taking a mental photograph of that moment, knowing it was to be the last of so many much the same, nightly disregarded for as many evenings as we'd shared.

The fact that we still don't broach the subject of it *means neither one of you can open it up for the other one again. Not yet. You're still dealing with it in your own way.*

I wish we could have stayed longer.

Why don't you stay? You should stay.

I would like to spend more time with him.

There's no reason you shouldn't. Take your time. I'll be fine. Come back when you're ready.

I love you.

As I drive away from them in the rain I know I'll have to write to Gibson. Perhaps this thing, this one true thing is too huge to embrace face to face again with someone that's like a ghost to me in a way, as I must be to him. It might be too haunting. It might serve no purpose. There was so much that needed to be said years ago, and now the letters of all the words float around us and I can see them all fighting to make sense on our tongues, but they don't. Half of them follow me home, while the other half hold above his head like an umbrella as he walks back to his classroom.

I loved you too.

As is our pattern, we don't allow it to end there. A few weeks later Gibson comes down to my brother's house in Oregon to visit. They had been close and were looking forward to seeing each other. Him being here isn't a cold or distant time for any of us. It isn't testing, or manipulated, or skirting the subjects of years gone by. It's a rejuvenation in a way, a reminiscing, a twenty-year memory recovery of stories that bridge gaps in the love that brought us together. It's reconnecting us all. In an odd way we're getting to feed back into that place of who we might have been this night here at my brother's in the midst of a party, the house filled with couples – and us. There is a familiarity, being around him, that transcends our time apart.

You and Dad are paired up again.

But this dynamic pushes us into a circle where we don't belong.

Sit back and ride with it.

"When's your birthday? June 1·? That's the day before mine. Let me know where you were born and what time and I'll do your chart for you," Mary's friend, April says, snapping me out my intense stare into the kitchen watching Gibson with the other men. My chart for me? Oh, okay. Sure, sure. I wonder what it would tell her about me. Is this like your true fingerprint? Would she know what it means to be me? Should I give her the wrong time?

Maybe you should just trust her, she seems like a nice lady.

And anyway people say they'll do these things and then they never do them, and why am I being so paranoid? "You know we're approaching the age of Aquarius? Some people already believe we're there," she says.

"Yes, yes I'd heard that." That was the truth – seemed logical.

"Where does that leave us?" I ask.

"It's 26 degrees of the zodiac. There is a 26,000 year period of precession." *26.* "Some say it began September, 2012." The Newspaper Soldier died in September of 2012. The bullets came with Aquarius.

Which defines itself in 26's. Well there's your 26 convergence.

266

My glass of red wine spills.

Everyone thinks you're drunk.

And that's so ironic because this is the ultimate sober moment for me.

I hand over my details to her, the real ones.

"Have you been to *The New Renaissance Bookshop* yet?" she asks.

"I'm going tomorrow." I look over at Gibson, sequestered in the kitchen with the boys and the beer. As much as we joke about each other's personality quirks, kid each other in the ways we used to do, I know I'm looking back into another time. It's a forgiving that I haven't bumped into yet. I see it as he turns away from me to answer a question.

He drove away from you.

I asked him to stay, just a few more minutes, but he asked why we should prolong the inevitable.

Have you considered that it might have been his way of grieving? That he needed to drive to an open road where no one could see what he felt. What you have done, he has done.

No. I hadn't thought of it that way.

If you step back – and take my ego out of it for a minute to see the truth of it for him, yes. I can understand that need to be alone, to walk away. As much as it hurt me, he had to deal with his own loss.

In his own way. Of course he cared about you. Of course he wanted to stay, but he lost something too that day.

On his last day we walk in the park, we do all of those things that we might have done, that we could have done, that we never really did when we were together. And there is still a silence, there is a heart murmur of absence and the air is thick with waiting. With each step forward I don't know how to start speaking. It doesn't surprise me when we stop at this monument in the park. It has William E. Stafford's poem, *The Well Rising* carved into it. We both read it silently to ourselves. I look over at him and watch him read the last stanza. A moment later he looks back and smiles at me. And we know.

What neither of you can say is here. "The well rising without sound … hunting for the final curve… I place my feet with care in such a world."

When we get home he collects his bags and we say goodbye. I watch him walk to his car just as I had twenty years before. He turns around, waving as he had then.

He didn't wave that day. He just turned back to look at you.

I watch him sitting in his car, setting the route home, carefully placing his hat on the passenger seat. He sits there for quite a while without turning on the ignition. I keep watch as he sits. It's so quiet for both of us. Then, before he turns the key, unexpectedly, I turn away.

Standing in the kitchen pouring moon water into a glass I hear the car start. This time I don't watch him drive away. Not like I did. When he pulled away from Sky's house all those years ago my heart felt ripped out, like I'd lost my family. I felt unwanted, discarded. I knew what alone felt like.

I go back into the living room to look out the window at the space where his car was. Tears fall down my face in the same way and with the same ache that he has driven away from me again.

The love of your life?

No. The love of my life would have embraced you; he would have embraced me; he would have made sure I was cared for, that I'd never feel hurt or sad, and he would honor my needs and your needs as equally as his own. No. He is not the love of my life. But he was an impactful one.

I go up to his room and I tear the dirty sheets off the mattress and shake the pillows free from the cases where his head slept without me. I curl the sheets and the smell of what's left of him into my body and lie down in the cleansed absence of him. I have this feeling that this will go on, that this is our penance for having loved one another. There is a piece of my heart that is his, is yours, is for the three of us. It's closed, real estate sold, but that's ok. I know that even so, my heart is still whole in the piece that is left to love again.

"Why are you sleeping in here where your friend was?" My niece is climbing over the foot of the bed.

"I came up to change the sheets, and I seem to have flopped down for a rest," I say as she bounces up and down beside me, pillows flying everywhere. She's laughing and her long black hair flies wild around her face. She flops down next to me breathing heavily, pushing sweaty hair out of her eyes, and she lays her head on my chest. I put my arm around her.

"Do you want to read a book?"

"No," she says, "I want to stay like this."

Obviously I am in need of metaphysical help. Before taking off for the Midwest I drive downtown to *The New*

268

Renaissance Bookshop. I barely make it past the front door. I want to eat it all -Tarot cards, Angel cards, Chakra clearings, Animal Totems, Alternative Health Healings... The doorbell keeps ringing on and off as if a rush of customers is storming into the shop when it's just me activating that invisible button underneath the carpet by the door – a musical soundtrack of my own.

I am gently directed away from it by a clerk with crystal earrings. I step my foot back on to it one more time on purpose when I put a copy of, *The Angel Detox*, back on the shelf. It won't go all the way back so I try to cram it, but it won't stay. A pink slip of paper with crumpled up edges is stuck back there between a slim paperback on Paramahansa Yogananda and a misplaced box of Nag Champa. It's a small leaflet that says, *Past Life Exploration and Regression*. A secret note from beyond. I'm still trying to put this Newspaper Soldier puzzle together. I need confirmation from someone outside of myself who is still in physical form. I need to tell them about the first recognition, about finding the statue in New Orleans. I need an affirmation. Perhaps this is the open door I need to find out who he was, who we are.

For just fifty bucks you'll be allowed into the light of all these new answers.

Yeah, yeah. Who knows, maybe it'll all prove to be a lot of hooey. The class is being taught by a couple named, Earl and Linda – they sound like a 1960s folk singing couple. This reassures me. I trust people named Earl and Linda. I take my crumpled pink slip up to the cashier and sign up to attend when I get back from the Midwest.

Wearing Absence

You can't possibly understand my life,
the subject would tell the biographer, because you didn't live it.
And the biographer would retort:
You can't possibly understand it, because you did.

- Joan Wickersham, *The Suicide Index*

I'm leaving Stanley alone again and it hurts my heart, but it's time to hunt around the Midwest for a couple of weeks. My plane descends into the windy city that is Chicago, shifting from side to side like a marionette being messed about with. If I didn't know better, I'd think my Southwest pilot is racing another plane to see who can land the fastest. We rush over the trees rapidly approaching earth at such velocity that we skid up and down on the wheels. Alive, I genuflect.

My first stop in Chicago is straight downtown to see Gabriel who I met two years ago doing a performance art piece in Austin, which Marie, the choreographer had put together in preparation for her Romeo & Juliet ballet in Puerto Rico.

The one where Marie danced with you, impromptu. Beautiful.

Gabriel's like me, she won't shake your hand when you meet her, no matter who you are. She pulls you into a long embrace. "Are you a hugger?" were her very first words to me. "I'm a hugger. I need to feel your energy," she said. Only in her mid-twenties, she is tuned into what she wants in her life, and she follows it with a controlled wildness. She's a super hyped up Buddha. I wish I'd had as clear a vision of what I wanted at her age - that I'd been into Kundalini and meditation, and all that guided trust jazz.

You always seemed to find yourself running off with the bulls.

The first morning I wake up to the sound of a juicer cranking up. She pours out these green, red and orange liquids full of the earth. It actually tastes pretty good, although when she says it's
"cleansing," my bottom tightens. But yeah, feeling good.

She's never been to The Poetry Museum that's in Chicago. How you can live here and not have been there? I don't understand. She knows I love poetry, so this is the place she

270

most wants to take me on our day together. She doesn't know much about poets, so at least here I feel useful, that I can contribute. You can't know all there is about life without consulting the poets. That's my kind of Buddha learning.

I'm preparedish for Chicago and the gusts of the windy city. It may be April, but it's freezing, bitter, so I've left my stylish coat in Portland. Today I sport an extremely large, white puffy Jacket best used for scaling the Swiss Alps.

Fashion isn't its purpose. It looks like more of a shield from nature.

Don't get me wrong, I love to feel chilly, but I don't like my bones to be cold. So I'm waiting for her in my weatherproof jeans, wooly hat, thick gloves and mountain man jacket, when she comes out of the bathroom ready to go. My heart breaks a little bit. Here is this lovely girl with a dancer's body in her skin tight, black pleather pants and white poet shirt, black buckle boots and stylish mid-riff coat with feathery fur on the cuffs Her blonde hair flows freely as she slings a scarf over her shoulder.

She's so beautiful.

I want to cry. This vacuous feeling takes over the pit of my stomach where my youth used to be. I feel my age more clearly than I ever have. I'm suddenly the grown up in the room.

This doesn't usually happen.

That used to be me. Why isn't that me anymore? Where did I go? Why didn't anyone tell me I'm forty-seven?

It's about to get worse.

When the elevator door closes, it's a full-length mirror. The horror of this I cannot explain. I'm forced to stand face to face, side by side the reflection of us both in some kind of perverted before and after moment. And I'm the before. It's like imagining in your head that you're Audrey Hepburn and finding out you're actually Big Foot. I have to tear my eyes away. I used to be the pretty one. Now I'm the one that looks at the time and bundles up for comfort.

The lovely Gabriel is chatting away as we walk down the streets of Chicago to hoots and hollers, whistles and remarks about her amazing ass, while I blunder on behind her trying to keep bits of leaf caught by the wind out of my contact lenses.

How is she not freezing?

Right? I am out of whack. What's in my head doesn't match up to what I just saw. It's all put into perspective. I see who I am, completely, in an instant. There's no adjustment time. All of a sudden here I am, naked. It's all of me, all at once. It's shocking. I'm no longer a two-piece, I'm a one piece and I've always had a flat ass and no miracle of astronomy is going to make it round. I know the angle to work is to accept this, to accept it even in the face of the roundest, most perfect ass walking five feet in front of me. But, since when do I not believe that it's always time for fashion? If you aren't actually climbing a mountain, choose the cute coat. I know this. I won't be twenty-six again, but I can class up the forty-seven tattooed all over me.

I need to unload all this. At the poetry museum I head straight towards Sylvia Plath.

Later that afternoon Gabriel suggests we take a detox yoga class together at the studio where she teaches. Could the day be more challenging? But, hey, maybe if I sit with the folk that can stay in down dog with their oneness my perspective will reset.

"I think it's an hour and half long. It's a specialty class."

Three hours later.

Yes, that's right, after THREE HOURS we emerge. In this hot, oil filled room though, I have no concept of time. Everyone here is so relaxed, going at their own pace. Typically, in these kind of work out situations I'm looking at the clock. All I look at is the time. I'm obsessed with the time.

In this room there isn't a clock.

Now, I don't know if it's because the room is so violently hot that I have to keep focused on not passing out, or that I have to grip my mat with all the Zen I can muster because sweat is pouring off of me and into my hands at such an alarming rate I think if I give up on the physical strength of myself, I might melt completely. Whatever it is, my mind allows my body to flow with it, instead of against it.

You're also carrying a load of inadequacy in here with you.

In each pose my body pushes through a part of me that has come unfastened. I liked being pretty. At a time when all I had inside was failure, I still had pretty on the outside. I could look in the mirror, satisfied that while all else drowned at my feet, I had a young and beautiful face. I'm not sure why that was so important.

Because you felt you had nothing else.

I don't know the eyes I look into anymore. Even that's been taken from me. And once the beauty on the outside disappears with little on the inside as backup, the thoughts that used to be mine are mine again and the false chatter grabs a hold of my sweating instability to remind me I'm not thin enough, not bright enough, not smart enough, not cute enough, not bouncy enough, hair's too short, it's the wrong color, change it, grow it, grow up, grow down, grow differently, get more friends, get different ones, don't keep saying yes, don't agree, challenge, wait, watch your step, watch your step, turn the light on for God's sake, find another switch, calm down, don't call, call, wear less make-up, get different glasses, wear glasses, don't talk so much, look up interesting things on the internet, you're boring, you have nothing to share, you're too kooky, dress normally, grow an herb garden, get smaller feet, squash them down like the Japanese women with the white faces, but get a tan, you've got your Grandfather's knees, cover them up, cover it all up under an invisibility cloak, best no one sees you then you won't have to hear the "no," the "it's not you," the "I'm choosing not to love you," talk. I'm all these words I hate to hear repeated, and they pour out of me in a crunchy liquid. I'm a hard boiling egg. My hands are slipping but there's no way I'm falling down until I hear some of my own sound, just one note of it's all I need, just one, come ooooonnnnnnnn, one note, a sound that's mine, that I am enough sound, the supercalifragafuckinglistic sound and that just maybe enough to get me back for today.

You said it, you just said, it's all run together, it's one word, you've taken it back. You just spoke it.

I collapse into my sound like Darwin. It's unlike any sound, the anti-sound – it is brief and endless and quiet. Still. I lay flat on the mat and slide into the amniotic.

These are the living consequences to connecting your pieces together.

I walk out of the studio without much feeling in my legs at all. At home I write until an ungodly hour because I'm afraid to go to sleep. I know when the morning comes my body is going to feel like it's been put through a wood chipper and put back together off kilter. Which is actually on kilter, on track, forwards, downstream.

Leaving the next morning, Gabriel walks me downstairs. Thank goodness there's an elevator because my legs don't bend at the knee. My large white coat hangs over my suitcase, and I've got my stylish dress and scarf on. My hair is in a braid with a curl left out on purpose, winding around my neck, inching back over to pretty. Gabriel hugs me until all of my chakras are balanced. I kiss her on the cheek and watch her walk down the street. This gorgeous, ancient youth has shown me a doorway to a fresh equilibrium. I feel more myself than I have in ten years, maybe more. I walk down to the curb shimmying my hips from side to side like Monroe did in *Some Like It Hot*, my flat ass rounded.

I wait for Elizabeth to pick me up outside. She's one of my UT acting class friends. It's a busy city street, cars are whizzing by, and I'm unsure how she'll see me; or stop.
Well, that stylish, 'I'm ok with getting older," furry vest should grab her attention.
Luckily I'm the only person standing on the street that looks like she's waiting for someone. I have my eyes on every car passing by, looking for that woman behind the wheel desperately trying to find someone whose image is over twenty years old.

I catch her eye. She smiles, waves and pulls into a space that opens up without notice. She leaps out of the car and we grab a hold of each other. Another moment I've waited for without knowing.

The word gates open up immediately and a thousand-piece puzzle falls from our mouths in no particular order. It gushes. We're back inside who we'd been to each other all those years ago, and so freakin' cool.

We talk about all the people in our college class. We spent every single day together in this acting unit, but only for three years. In that time we formed obvious intense bonds and are clearly still closely connected. Perhaps our class had been thrown together for a reason beyond what we knew.
Now is the time for the three-year intensive which formed its plan all those years ago to make itself known. Weird, but I think true.

Thirty minutes later in the suburbs we sit in the car in her driveway looking at each other, hiding and stealing away from her family.

"I don't want to go in. I don't want to share you with anyone, but they're waiting for you," she says half-kidding. "My son Willoughby, Wil, is more excited than I am." I laugh out loud. "No, he's really intrigued by you. He loves England, all things English. He's written your name down on his hand, counted down the days, and he's organized his room for you

274

to stay in." Sure enough, as I come up the stairs and into their lovely brownstoneish home, here is a ten-year-old boy running towards me, palm held high with, *Sara* written on it. When I ask him to be president of my fan club his smile radiates like the Hope Diamond.

At dinner that night I tell them about my journey and how in Richmond they go around the table and tell each other their favorite part of the day, and can we do that now because I've got so much to be thankful for. At Wil's turn he says,

"I'm just so happy we have this awesome woman at the table with us." I look over at Elizabeth, quietly trying to suppress a laugh.

"Yes," she says, "that's my favorite thing too." Her husband Steve smiles and shakes his head at his son, the Lothario.

During the week they have a "no device" policy for their children, and no TV for anyone - and life still finds a way. At their children's furlough day at school a teacher remarked that their children were the only two kids she'd seen all day without a device in their hands – they had books. They've made it a foundation that their evenings are for creating, playing the old fashioned way, and because of that the kids are co-writing a book. Mae writes while Wil illustrates it. Great gifts have come from steering their children away from the great time stealer.

As Wil shows me to his room to put my luggage away, there's a familiarity about the space.

It's set up almost like your room. He's got one of those typewriter's you want on his desk.

And the back wall is lined with books. Nice.

"You can touch my books if you want to," he says, "but please be very careful with them and put them back where you found them."

You've been cloned inside a small boy's mind and body.

We have.

Elizabeth and I stay up talking about how sometimes life flows the messy unexpected at us.

"You would have loved our old house. It was everything I wanted. We put a lot of money in savings for some renovations we were planning, and then it all just slipped away. We got blindsided. Steve got laid off..."

"And suddenly you're on the other side of the equation."

275

"Yes."

"X no longer equaling what you believe it should."

"It's not such a long fall. We lived on the savings for a while, but things just kept getting worse, pipes cracked, appliances needed replacing, but we kept hanging on you know. Just wouldn't let go. This was what we'd worked for. And then the worst thing you can imagine - the basement completely flooded and all of our photographs of the kids over the years, all saturated - gone; all their toys. The only thing left of my daughter's was one doll and a few clothes for it. And there's no money to replace it you see. All my books from college, my papers, all gone. It was awful." A tsunami of all they had. "Everything we had went into plugging up holes."

"In a beast that was trying to release you."

"You hit the nail on the head there. That flood was the point we realized that we could actually let go and start to repair ourselves. It felt shameful though, somehow. At least it did for me. I had a hard time not feeling embarrassed by the loss."

"About what we think society says is acceptable."

"Yes. I thought all my friends and my neighbors would think we'd failed. But people came out of the woodwork to support us. A good friend of ours that lived down the road said she wished they had the courage to do what we were doing - to downsize and make life simpler."

"We carry this burden, don't we, of status and what's being thought about us in the house next door. And truth is relevant in its own company. Sounds convoluted, but you know what I mean - behind closed doors life is happening to all of us." *And the only path that's worth walking down is the one that holds the promise of something whole.* "It all depends on how you define success too I suppose. And trust in what's happening. Clearly you were meant to get out of that house!"

"Isn't that the truth? And if we had any doubts about it, on the final walk through of the house after we sold it, something else fell apart."

One last gift from their house.

"It's like an affirmation. This place is no longer your responsibility, you know. Leave this fixing to someone else. Sign the dotted line and move toward a connected one for yourself."

"Yes, exactly. And we love it here. The kids play outside. This street's filled with kids their own age. At the last house they only had two kids to play with. And Steve loves his new job. He comes home and he can leave his work at the office. And I work from home now. I can pick up the kids from school, go to all their functions, and give them my time."

They're thankful for the best of times because they know they're living inside of it. They laugh, they tease, they argue, they smile.

They hold each other - that's what it is. It's so exquisite how they love each other. Like they're the same person exploded in to four pieces.

They glow with happiness.

Early the next morning Elizabeth takes me to her favorite place in Chicago, a thrift store. Thrift stores have always been our inner and outer place of bonding.

She was with you when you found the lime green pantsuit.

Bell bottomed, 1960s, with pink flowers all over it. Any bargain hunter knows that this is the Holy Grail of the thrift hunt. I wasn't sure if I should buy it. "You HAVE to," she insisted on it. Even though I told her I'd have no money to eat for a week. She looked at me as if there was even a question about that.

Get your priorities straight.

"I've thought about that pantsuit so many times over the years, Sara, and wished I'd seen it first."

"Every time I wear it I think of you."

Remember when your car broke down.

"Remember when I broke down on I35 and I had to walk down the highway in it. I got whistles and a marriage proposal. So funny. I had to call for help and you came and picked me up, remember."

"I'd forgotten about that! And it was a miracle I was home. I was never home."

Today, twenty-four years after the great find, we slay the racks of vintage wear and both walk away with a lime green gift. We eye the other's rewards.

Her real treasure is at home though.

It waits for her at the dinner table, frustrates her at bedtime, and delights her at the goodnight kiss. She didn't miss the lime green pantsuit, it found her in the end and she wears it every day, regardless of style, because it is her own. I'm so glad to have found her happy and loved, that this perfect beauty that laughs and enjoys with a full heart, is my friend.

Before leaving for Milwaukee the next morning for a quick day trip to see Bob, our old Acting and Movement professor, I bring out the DVD that Hermosa Jill gave me in CA that has our younger selves knocking at the door.

"I don't know if I'm going to be able to watch this!"

"Oh, I am!" Steve smiles at the prospect of seeing his wife in ye old days. The video begins with our class all over at Elizabeth's house for a graduation party.

"Oh, there's that lime green pant suit you bought."

"I still have her."

"Oh, look at Arina. She's so sexy, isn't she? Just standing off to the side watching, mysterious in black, smoking a cigarette..."

"...there's the hair flip. She looks just the same now."

"What am I doing?"

"I think you're going to put on one of your famous bustiers."

"Please don't tell me..."

"...that the camera follows you in, and yes, oh there we go." Elizabeth was famous for how she could transform your average thrift store bra. She'd cover it with flowers, beads, ribbon and voila, a bustier.

In between the laughter and reliving all the embarrassment of who we were, the video jumps to a performance art piece of monologues we'd written. At the time we thought we were on the cusp of radical art.

Oh, boy.

"We're all dressed in white."

"Can't get more edgy and rebellious than that, can you." Elizabeth is watching through her fingers.

"This is so embarrassing, what were we doing? This is so embarrassing. Oh, my God no. There's me." Her head is buried in the sofa and she's grabbing a hold of me.

"Yours is actually one of the better ones, which of course isn't saying a whole lot, but at least yours was funny."

"I can't, I can't look, Sara. Oh, Steve, don't look. Don't look."

"You're so beautiful. Look at you," he says. I'm trying to pry her fingers open, but she won't do much besides the occasional peak from behind her hands. The whole thing leaves us rolling on the floor while our younger selves brood over in the corner, offended at the lack of appreciation.

We sit in the kitchen after the kids have gone to bed and drink a fancy vodka cucumber drink that goes down far too easily, and frequently. Elizabeth sits on Steve's lap and they snuggle together. They have such a wonderful honest love that's strengthened with what life's throw at them. They don't miss what they had. They can see what they've gained just by looking at each other.

They have a visible tenderness that's so rare.

They met at a musical festival in Austin. He assumed she lived in Austin. Unbeknownst to them they'd both been visiting Austin from Chicago. He was bummed that he wouldn't see her again when a friend of his said he knew she worked in a local coffee shop in Chicago, but didn't know which one. To find her, Steve sat in each coffee shop, all day, one by one, until he found her. Does it get more romantic? Every girl's dream. Beautiful. Of course he did follow it up by proposing to her while he was on the toilet, yelling his epiphany from behind the bathroom door, "Let's do it!" but we can't have all romance all of the time. It's important to have a sense of humor about love.

This man sees all the beauty, style, courage and joy that I met all those years ago, and he holds it protectively, caring for her the way we all wish to be cherished. I hope I find someone that looks at me the way that he looks at her.

You will.

It makes me happy, but at the same time wonder if I'm difficult to love.

I'd say you've had too much magic cucumber liquid. Except I know that a part of you actually believes that.

In the early morning I sit at the kitchen table in the quiet, and watch Elizabeth and Steve allow time in their own moment before taking meticulous care to make breakfast for their children – the strawberries cut up, the yogurt set out in cups with the berries. They know how each child needs their morning to begin and have it all lined up and ready to go before their gentle waking.

My head is splitting from all the healing effects of the mystical cucumber juice I drank. Nothing like a road trip with all that bouncing in your head.

The original plan was for Elizabeth to drive to Milwaukee with me to visit Bob. I was looking forward to it. Wil's parent/teacher day came up today though, so I'm off solo. Instead of renting a car they gave me their second car to drive up there. Sweet. Also I brought the car compass with me so as long as I've got battery power I'll know where to go.

My only benchmark for what Milwaukee is like is *Laverne & Shirley* schlameeling down the faux Milwaukee-esque studio lot, arm in arm. In my mind I see it as an over-crowded town full of pollution and bums wandering aimlessly, high on brewery fumes. I imagined it industrial, full of cheese and beer, and here's all this beauty and crisp air. Milwaukee feels like a comfy old shoe with just enough heel to keep it stylish. Lake Michigan is an ocean.

You should keep your eyes on the road though. You still can't find the restaurant.

I circle the block a few times. I don't really need the name of the place though, on my second circle around I see Bob sitting down outside the restaurant – he looks just as I left him all those years ago, only more pastel. His dark hair, now hued with white, the earing still in place, and that smile. I wave my hand out the window at him and holler his name.

"Don't park. This place is closed on Mondays. Can you believe it? We'll go someplace else." With that he hops in the car with a hug. "It's so good to see you. So good to see you. Ok, you're going to turn right here and go down the end and you'll see it on the right. So what is this? What is this you're doing? It's great to see you!"

Bob was one of the younger teachers that a lot of us looked up to for advice, encouragement and understanding. What I love about seeing him after twenty-four years is being back around all his passion again - for teaching, for acting, and for furthering that in his life in whatever shape it takes. It's magnetic - you want to rummage around every syllable of it. I can sit here for days - especially listening to his new venture. He's taken his training in Shakespeare and moved it to a place of healing. He works with soldiers returning from the war with PTSD, using Shakespeare's language to help them express crippling traumas trapped in their minds. He does these healing workshops with his wife, who was an actress herself, and who is now a psychologist. He describes it this way:

"For a moment let's say I'm on stage with you and part of what my character needs to express to you is shame. I check into my memory banks and access a real sense memory of a time when I actually felt that way. The emotion I'm feeling is true, it's mine and it pours through me and into my voice, but it's expressed through a character telling a different story. My story is being told with someone else's words - and what this does is act like a buffer that shields me from revealing myself, or having to say the words of my own story out loud, but I still work through all of the emotion. The soldier can feel the anger, sadness, loss, manipulation, rage, everything that he felt in battle, and express it fully through Hamlet, Henry IV, V, Lear, Othello, whoever. The emotions, the truth of those characters are as real as everything that they're holding in, and they can express it completely in a place of safety. They're coming to terms with their story in a supported space where their heads can explode, regroup and heal."

"What a beautiful gift."

"I hope so. They're pushing something much too heavy to hold on to. We've seen a tremendous success rate. They keep coming back. Iambic pentameter is written in the same rhythm as our heart beat, so when you speak it, it's already in tempo with your body and fills your lungs perfectly. Before you even connect the words to what is going on in your mind, it's picked up inside the heart unconsciously."

He's taken the heart of his life's work and found the source that people need the most.

Maybe that's how you're inside of me now, living iambically – maybe that's our new heartbeat.

"What you're doing, you'll find that part of you in there somewhere, like I did. It's not that you're looking for it. It surfaces."

Let that sit for a moment.

"You know, you've turned into such a beautiful woman," he says as we walk down by the museum after lunch - the pristine, blue sky, and an ocean of lake around us. Even if it is bullshit, I feel pretty.

Why would it be bullshit? You are beautiful.

Bless your heart. Even if, it's nice to have someone see the outside of me.

"Thank you," I say.

And that's a difficult word for you.

Typically, I'd blush, look at the grass and shake my head. Not today though. At one point in my life he knew so many of my weaknesses and pulled out my strengths. If he thinks I'm beautiful, that's good enough for me. I felt pretty at being remembered.

I drive down to the waterfront and stand at the edge of Wisconsin looking out across the water where life is waving a stillness at me. Out there, flesh clings to a skeleton. Out there, beyond the distance I can see, is my friend, Viola who has entered into a contract with her own mind. Here she might breathe a rhythm of words that match her own heartbeat, one that would free the ghost within.

Something to pass forwards.

The night before I leave Elizabeth's I get on Skype and bring Luke and Cindy Jackie from New York, to Chicago. Elizabeth hasn't seen them since graduation.

The picture comes up and there's that pause of adjustment before the screaming and the laughing, and Elizabeth and I are rolling around on the couch.

It's crazy cool fun to watch this much joy.

"This is so fucking cool! Oh, my God, Elizabeth, you look just the same." Cindy Jackie is staring intently at her, examining the twenty-year flash pause.

"Cindy – I mean, Jackie, you're so dressed up and gorgeous."

"Hey, thanks! I felt this need to dress up and do my hair!"

"Well, I put lipstick on," I add to the beauty battle.

"Elizabeth, what was that show you were in where you dressed up like that mummy kind of thing?"

"Didn't look so hot in that did I!"

"You were that creature. I'm not sure why I just said that. Why I'm remembering that now." Luke is wavering about, not sitting still.

"Oh, that was, *Empire Builders*. Yeah, not so glamorous on that one! Remember I got hit in the head with a 2 by 4 that should have been pre-cut to break over my head?!!" Amongst our laughter, there is a silence on the other end.

"Ah, geez, Elizabeth, I actually have a confession to make about that show." Luke is smiling to himself and kind of squirming at the same time.

"Well it wasn't you that did it, it was…"

"No, no. Well, you may or may not remember that I used to work in the shop back then. And well, you know, nobody told us shit. They said they needed a piece of wood so that's what I gave them."

"You just gave them a piece of wood? You made the weapon that gave me a concussion? You did that to me?"

"Yes, oh, shit. Yes, I did – that was me!"

"Luke???!"

Hahahaha! This is hilarious.

282

"Now in all fairness they didn't tell us what it was for, or who it was for. It wasn't my fault. But I felt so guilty. I've felt guilty all these years. Oh, God. I just had to tell you now."

"Bastard. I was out, Luke - on the floor, you know, like a light. That thing hurt, it left a huge ass bruise on my head!"

"I'm sorry, I'm really, really sorry." Now we're all laughing at Luke's secret, and that he's owning up to it almost 25 years later only because he has to, and out of his own guilt, and she's out of arms reach to slap him.

"Man. Elizabeth, I'm really sorry."

"I can't believe it, I can't believe it was you." She sounds like Al Pacino did when he finds out that Fredo's double-crossed him.

"Hey, you guys, I made Elizabeth watch this video Jill put together of us at school. You know what it has on it? That oh, so experimental, awesome show we did – the one where we're all…"

"…dressed in white. Oh, that was awful. I saw that a while back – how did I see that?" Luke says.

I didn't think it was that bad. There was that lovely poem Luke did - you liked it, remember, "some of you ask for criticism when all you really want is praise."

"I wasn't in that I don't think…" Jackie looks at Luke as he's shaking his head trying to erase the experience.

"Oh, it was awful. Be glad you weren't."

"Elizabeth watched it through her hands. It was too painful…"

"…when I came on. Oh my God, what were we thinking?"

"So embarrassing."

"I was telling Elizabeth, I had to freeze frame it on my face. I didn't recognize myself. The part at the beginning of the tape is our last class with Bob."

"She went to see him yesterday."

"Cool! God, I wish we could just come along to see everyone," Jackie says.

"Well, you just let me know and I'll Skype you in. When I was in Cyprus with Arina, we Skyped with Stephen Gerald."

"Ah man, very cool."

"He's been ill. He says he's on the mend though. We need to get a reunion of our class together. It would be great if we could all get together, you know."

"Yes! Well, you know, you're doing it, so yeah, it's possible. We could do that."

"Isn't this great, you guys, what she's doing? I can't

believe she's here. I keep touching her." And we do, there's this need to keep hugging one another, to make sure we're real, not some computer generated 3-D Skype. We're both here in the same space again. Time has pushed out of the glove compartment.

"Doesn't Elizabeth look good! I took a picture of our shadows and posted it yesterday. She's the skinny one." Elizabeth slaps me upside the head.

"What the hell! I said you were the skinny one." She slaps my arm and pushes me back on the sofa.

"You're skinny too, you know."

"Yeah, it's become a love fest now," Luke says as Wil bursts into the room and stands on the couch behind his mother, staring at Luke and Cindy Jackie. Then he smiles. This kid's not shy at all – he wants to be in on everything.

The next morning is one I don't want to come, the part where the three-day visit, which I wish had been ten, is whisked out of sight. The kids are up early for school so a drowsy goodbye is said as they sit at the kitchen table eating the breakfast their father has so carefully made for them.

My cab arrives and Elizabeth walks me out. We hug at the top of the stairs, we hug at the bottom, and then one more time as the cab driver opens the trunk and lifts my bag in. I want them to adopt me.

You took the words out of my mouth.

Better still I want to create a world around me like Elizabeth has found. What I see in them is what I see in the mirror in the distance, but too far out of reach to ever be real – like a fairytale.

It isn't.

I do see the possibility but I've never had a relationship that's been this mutually respected. I'm so thankful for having seen them.

Because now you know what that feels like, what that looks like, and when the time comes, you won't walk away from it.

Letting go of Elizabeth and her family for Viola and hers is a slow melting dissolve through the streets of Chicago, in to the skies of Minneapolis. On the ground the big snow is softening into tears of trodden on slush.

Viola and I worked together on *A Midsummer Night's Dream*. We were on the road to flashy Waco, Texas in that show - sleeping in each other's pockets, chatting until dawn.

You thought you were the bees knees, as my Great-Grandmother used to say.

All we wanted of the world was ours. Viola is like a flying bullet – a whirlwind of energy. That was an inspiration to me. I loved being on stage with her because she made me play harder. She'd come at you with everything she had, something new, and that's exciting to be around. I've only seen her once since graduation. She moved to Chicago briefly after college and I went up there to audition badly for grad schools.

Excuse me, but you actually got an offer to go to OSLO. No bad audition gets you in there. You just decided to go and live with dad instead.

A bulk of life has gone by now.

For both of you.

She got married, had a son, Joseph and a daughter, Bernadette. The same ideal many of my friends have chosen. For her though it came with a heavy curve ball when her fourteen-year-old son died by suicide seven years ago. I've no idea what to expect. Inside of her there must be a hole in ruins. I don't know if she'll want to talk about it. I don't think I should talk about it, but maybe that's me deep in my own denial hiding behind that tree I carry around. I don't know.

So just listen to her - it's her story to open into. This is an unrecoverable event - something like this doesn't walk away from you. You know that.

How do you take that kind of blank space and put a frame around it? Initially I didn't know what had happened to Joseph. I'd seen Facebook picture posts of her gorgeous boy, but little about what happened. Abducted, I thought, or one of those terrible illnesses children get. Then a few months before I arrived she posted his eulogy, and the pieces came together.

Waiting for my luggage I look up to see a tiny woman almost levitating herself towards me with her arms wide open. Her hands wrap around my arms, and mine cross hers, as if we're making a seat for someone to sit on. They slowly slide away and we're holding hands and smiling and smiling and smiling. Then we hug and we're sort of screeching and laughing and saying the same words at the same time, and I don't care if my luggage has been lost to Dante's fifth ring of Minneapolean hell. It's perfect. So few moments are. Everything else pauses. In these moments life is lived most

285

honestly because we're connected to something else set in motion without expectation or awareness.

There is no small talk along the way. Some conversations just continue on even with a twenty-four-year gap.

"I'm sorry Ray is going to be busy while you're here - he just got laid off and he's pursuing some leads. It's all just happened. We haven't told Bernadette yet, so don't say anything. I just wanted you to be aware of what's going on."

"I'm sorry. You should have told me, I could have come at a different time."

"No, no, I'm glad you're here. It's perfect timing, the best distraction for me right now. No. I'm glad you've come. It's so good to see you. I'm glad. I'm glad you're here now." Timing, yes. Something about this entire journey is the timing of right now.

"So tell me about the play you did with Bernadette. How did that all go?"

"Sara, I'm so happy that I went. I needed to get there and do that. It's the first year I've been since Joseph died." It's been absent from her life for the last six years. She was two weeks away from returning to this theatre in Nebraska where she worked during the summer in rep when Joseph took his life. This past summer, her daughter, Bernadette, Joseph's younger sister was asked to Play Alice in *Alice in Wonderland*. She wanted her mother to be with her, not just in the theatre, but on stage with her, as The Mad Hatter.

"You took back the space in a way, do you think?"

"I couldn't go back initially. I knew that it would remind me too much of what happened. I may not go back again, I'm not sure, but it felt good to be there, to be with Bernadette, and to be on stage again."

"I'm sure Joseph was there cheering you on."

"Yes, I like that idea. Yes, I think he was." Her grip on the steering wheel tightens a little more and the tops of her fingers fill with the color red. How fragile she is. What happened to her six years ago, her body still wears.

Viola and D'Ann had a special bond in school, so she is paramount on Viola's mind. So grief begins there, with D'Ann, with how she is. It begins with Lila. It begins with Lucius. It begins with the thread of grief which these two delicate women have found themselves unexpectedly weaving.

"There's nothing anyone can say to you. Nothing anyone can do. Nothing will make it leave your body - nobody can do that for you. You're never going to be in there with us - that's the thing that's so hard for people to understand. I just wanted to be left alone." We pull up to the house and she turns the car off, "You know it's funny – you asked me what my special place is in relation to where I live – where I like to go, and to take you there. I tried to think of somewhere, I did, but I realize it's my house. I really haven't left it much since Joseph died. I kept going to bible study once a week. They've just been so supportive. They let me talk about him. And that's something I need to do. But, I didn't leave the house. So it's my house." As the car door closes, she adds, almost throwing it away, "I've only just recently cut my hair again." Hair, I suppose is a way of tracking time. As long as it remained uncut, the ends were her connection to a part of her that was when he was. When it lies on the floor in front of you, perhaps there's a slight move towards release.

She helps me with my bags and we walk through the front door into her safe place - across the threshold of a heart wide open. To three bedrooms, a basement, and one bed that is permanently made.

She makes me a cup of tea and we go outside and stand on the balcony, leaning on the rail. Her dog Sadie chases after a ball that Viola throws in an arc into the sky.

"I've been thinking of getting a UT reunion together. Get a group of us to meet down in Austin. See D'Ann, you know. It might be the perfect time for that. Pick a date that's good for all of us?" Her hand grabs my arm, her body agreeing as the words form a pile of thought.

"Yes," she says. Just yes. A snowy air falls over us. A piece of sunlight eases past her. She picks up Sadie's ball and throws it again. It rolls back down to a child's rusting red bike in the dirt where the flooding came. "Sometimes, when I'm the only one in the house…" She's looking far off as if the ball's still in the air. "I stand at the bottom of the stairs and I call out his name, as if he's still up there in his bedroom. For just a millisecond of a millisecond the tiniest part of me expects to hear his footsteps over my head. Is that silly?"

"Of course not." She can almost see him bounding round the stairwell.

The half an inch that took all his breath away will return his feet to the ground.

"I feel happy. It makes me happy."

We take my suitcase upstairs to the 'spare' room - her daughter Bernadette's old bedroom. "She wanted to be in his room.

287

Which is good.

It made me go through his things, you know. Not make it into a shrine, leave everything as it was where he left it. It helped me get through that part of it. Except for that, of course." She points to a backpack - the backpack he zipped up the day he died. "I haven't had the courage to go through that yet." There's a poster of Harry Potter leaning up against the wall - he's holding a wand. It says, "Dark Times Lie Ahead," and it's pointing directly down at Joseph's bag.

Viola has become a proficient Paleo cook and whatever it is that's free of carb and sugar smells unbelievably delicious. She turns to me and hands me my plate.

"Oh, you're sitting at the table." I look at her not knowing what she means. "We don't sit down at the table to eat anymore." Her eyes look off to the right of me, "...it's the empty chair." I hadn't even thought of that. I should have thought of that.

How could you have thought of that?

Why didn't I think of that? Without realizing how this space has changed and what it means to her, I've done something insensitive.

"I'm so sorry, I didn't know. I wasn't thinking." I'm scrambling to get up and a part of my skirt is caught under one of the legs so when I get up it catches, and I slam back down in the seat. Pulling it away the leg scrapes against the tiled floor.

"Of course you didn't... no, it's fine. Ah... you know what let's just, umm," she stares at the table for a minute, "we'll sit there. We'll sit there and have dinner. We'll eat at the table. Why not, there are four of us. We should sit at the table for dinner." Ray gets up from his chair and Bernadette sits by me. And so we sit, we four, at the christening table.

A false step leading into a fresh direction.

And we talk about Bernadette's prom and about the dances she has to learn for the musical she's in. We talk about Joseph's Harry Potter birthday party and how he'd wanted to get a real lightning bolt tattoo, how he'd helped other kids in school not doing so well, how much he'd loved his old school. And all the while I wonder which one of us is sitting in the empty chair. I suppose we all are, which is why he's not missing. He sits in all of them now.

That night we continue down memory lane when I pull out The Video. Viola has an easier time watching because she's not in it. It's much easier to watch your classmates make a fool of themselves.

"The big TV is downstairs – we'll have our own movie night."

I haven't been down to the basement yet. I wonder how often they come down here. Doesn't this space still hold, well, after six years...

That's your analysis of it, not hers. You're projecting. Don't get inside of her head – it's not possible anyway. See what you feel.

"We completely re-did it down here. Ray got me this popcorn machine. It's odd, you'll be down here and for no reason the T.V will come on. Bernadette says it's Joseph goofing around with us."

And there it is, a replacement of memory.

What he came down here to do is gone, and what they come down here to do is changed, and he's invited back in. I feel a weight to the air, but that's because there's someone down here that's new to me.

With talk of a reunion, Viola searches out some old photos.

"The boxes are in here somewhere. There are so many," she says and I follow her to a back room kind of like the attic in the basement where all the Christmas decorations and such are piled high. The walls are barren. I stay over by the door. I don't go in. It's cold in there. Viola's only gone a few feet in, and she's leaning across one box to get to another one when she could just as easily have crossed over and lifted it. I wonder if this is the room where it happened, if that's why it's untouched, piled high with boxes covering away the space. One memory came alive down here by dying, so it's packed away with all the others. I don't ask her.

It's not for you to know.

"Found it!"

She's smiling.

She brings it over to the sofa and we go through them one by one. It's so odd to see myself in pictures I've no memory of being taken. I've absolutely no memory of where we all were either.

You're at Michelle's. You came down for this party. You weren't at UT yet.

Yeah? I mean there I am, clear as a bell, posing. All I have is a flash of one solitary second of it. At least I was having fun. We all were. And it's good to watch Viola now, smiling with her entire body - talking about parties we went to and

289

characters she used to play. Remembering it together, acting it all out again. We stay down here for hours, watching ourselves how we used to be, laughing, melting into the sofa with a ghost.

This first night, sleeping amongst Joseph's things, has a spell all its own. I walk around the silence of it and sit cross-legged in front of Harry and his prize possession. I have the same backpack – it's exactly the same, the same color, the same brand. I know each flap inside - where the pencils are kept, where the computer goes, where the notebooks are. I look into Harry's eyes. I pray for wings of time, for an angel's elbow to rub away at anything that needs smoothing over. If there is a child's silly ramblings marking fault into my friend, I want all of it gone by the time courage day arrives and she opens this up. You're a twenty-year-old man now, you can see inside this zipper. Choose to lift it away.
Rain is coming. I wish that away too.

The next morning Viola takes me to The Millennium Garden. She hasn't been in a while and it's nice to share something outside of her routine that was a part of her life before all this. Off to one side there's a Labyrinth carved out of paving stones lined with tall thin evergreen trees. It's hidden so that you only notice you're walking it when your feet are already quietly tracing it. I love the accidentalness of this, of not having to make the decision to walk it. Whatever it is that needs to be spoken puts you there. What needs to be seen is by invitation only.
My intention is hers. I can't find you in here. I am invisible. I follow Viola, side stepping my own empty mind, watching, catching her face as she rounds the circled corners. Her eyes have completely turned inside.

The next day after Palm Sunday services she takes me to Joseph's burial place.
"When he first passed I'd come here a lot. I read Harry Potter to him. He was mad about those books and he didn't get to finish them. I wanted him to know how Harry's story ended. I'd sit right here and read them to him." There is the quiet of a mother's care trying to bridge a gap that she can see but can't cross. She comes here to love him, to feel the missing body. To look for him. To look for why, perhaps. His ashes are interred outside, among the trees - simplicity in brown, pink

marble. The why of his death holds ambiguity at its heart. He made a choice to breathe no longer.

All of her remaining breaths try to come to terms with that.

No matter how rational it is that the body is gone – buried six feet under, or crushed to ash and bone - as human beings we have a need for the physical, to feel someone else's company. If I can't touch you, if I can't reach across the table and caress your forearm or kiss you on the cheek, I am somewhere I can't wrap my mind around. The pain of missing the physical is what I focus on because it's the only thing living inside the hole of the missing for me. I believe in the power of the soul, of the energy that is released that's living all around me, but where I live is with the body, with presence, and I don't know how to fully transition away from what I can't touch. If I can't touch you anymore, I don't know what to do. I must have physical presence, and it's the only part to never have again. It's living matter Viola helped bring into life and it will always exist as a part of her. She can float home on the soul. She's seen the blood spilled already.

A psychic she's familiar with is giving a talk. It's a bit of a road trip, but she'd like to go and listen to her. Of course we'll go.

Of course.

The event passes, and it brings her a small amount of connection. There is something a bit lighter that carries on inside her, but only for a while. Driving home the car fills up with a warm dry ice that can only be Joseph. I can see the whites of Viola's knuckles on the steering wheel again, ghost shapes on her hands. The happening is back again as if it were a minute passed. The risk you have in seeking an answer is that in asking the question you go further down into your own story again - an initiation back into one moment as forceful as a dam splitting your head wide open. She controls its release through her hands. I want to tell her that the voice will come to her, and when it does it will be through the part of her son that is alive inside.

But you don't know that's true, no matter how much you want it to be.

I want it to be true. I want none of it to be true for her. I want to help but I can't.

We pull up into the driveway and she turns off the car. I push away the cold silver lock of the seatbelt knowing I'm only doing it to be able to reach across to her, not to exit the car. We sit here a little while. I want to speak, but I don't know what to say. And all the while the light's disappearing to the left of the earth, and Viola's slight shadow moves a part from mine and is quite still. She is so still. I'm swaying.

You're both looking back.

Over her shoulder I can see the shape of a man's face in the dark and I'm thinking how odd it is that I could see brick a few moments ago and now all I see are these shapes of negative space because that's the world we've stepped into.

And silence.

But this silence is explosive, not mute. If twilight has music, this is the frequency. Every ounce of it is filled, and it bounces around in a vibration that won't back down. It's a red carpet. And inside all of that she has no choice but to be open.

"The plan always was, when we got married, that I would quit my job and be a stay at home mom. And that's what I did. I stayed home with the kids. I was a mom. And I couldn't even get that right. I fucked that up."

No.

"I left him. We weren't even supposed to go out that day, but we did. But he was acting up, and he said he was sorry and that he didn't mean it and asked if he could still come with us and we were just so frustrated you know. And I turned my back on him. I turned my back on my son, Sara. We got in the car. I should have gone back inside to talk to him." I hold her hands tightly. "When we got home I called out and he didn't answer. He wasn't in his room. The basement door was open. And there is my son in his newly ironed shirt he was going to wear for our family pictures hanging in front of me. We tried to hold him back up to life and his little sister is at the top of the stairs saying, 'I don't want to be an only child, this means I'm an only child now,' and the paramedics are shaking their heads. There is nothing. It's the perfect storm - if only we'd installed PVC pipe instead of copper it would have given way, if only he'd used a proper slipknot, if only he'd used rope, and not TV wire - if only one of these things had been different it would have blown up in his face. And at some point I see my reflection in the TV and my head is a post-it-note, so I walk towards the words he wrote. 'I can't take it anymore. I'm sorry. I love you,' and I knew he meant to do it, but he wanted to come with us, so it makes no sense."

"This is not your fault, it isn't. He made a mistake, he made a terrible mistake, and he can't take it back, as much as

I'm sure he wishes he could. He acted impulsively, he was acting out and he took it too far. You know your son; you know he'd take it back. None of this is your fault. He made a choice – he made a bad choice. Like you said he didn't believe it would come to any kind of different reality for him. But it did. *He* did that. He made a terrible mistake. He stood there and he changed his life. You didn't do that. You cannot blame yourself anymore. You can't continue to take this on. You are a beautiful person. You are a wonderful mother, kind, and loving - you can see that in Bernadette." She's holding on to her coat in a knot with one hand, and me with the other, nodding her head.

I feel an emotion that has no word yet. It's sawn off anger and helpless sorrow tornadoing in a blender without enough water. This is my friend.

And this is her son.

And I threw mine away. I want there to be some magic beanstalk growing in the garden so I can climb up to the top of it and bring him back down, and you, or bring down the why and cut this umbilical cord that's grown back for her.

But you can't.

This is hers and the only thing I can do is allow her to feel the truth of what it still is to her. I'm shaking my head that this beautiful soul not only blamed herself, but still blames herself, and there's only a black tide coming at her.

Late that night I'm lying in Joseph's bed, on my side, under the blue-beige and white comforter that's the same as the one I have at home on my bed. The light's falling into the room in a way that isn't right. The angles are off, so I get out of bed and sit cross-legged in front of the backpack with Harry. It's the most sacred part of the room because it's the only untouched part of Joseph. I hold my left hand over the zipper. There's a breath on the other side of this. I can feel the pulse of it, the pressured breath of waiting.

That butterfly, the one that shifts the icebergs into melting, is flapping its wings.

The light shines through the shutters onto the carpet in a silhouette of piano keys waiting to play out a signal in coded song. I look out of the window and my eyes stare back at me through one of the slats. My lips part through the space below it - younger lips; my reflection is nonsensical. I'm in front of my parent's bathroom mirror looking at myself from the other side of it. Joseph touches each hair on my arm and they stand straight up one by one like a wave at a baseball game. I'm sixteen again, and what those eyes are deciding to do I haven't seen for thirty-two years. But you know. You both do.

This you've never told a living soul.

That's how I know that it's you here. There's no point in hiding from me because I'm not like other people - fourteen-year-old ghosts don't scare me. How could I have forgotten this? I've never said it out loud before. There's a price to pay when you sit with the dead. This I haven't ever admitted to myself. That what you have done, I have done. There was a point when these sixteen-year-old eyes looked into that ½ an inch of space as you did. If there's a space that is 26, I'm sitting in it. How can I not have remembered this?

You'd just moved here. It was the night before your first day at school, to walking in to that pressure of making friends again.

Not knowing what people would be like, how they would react to me. My mind was going crazy fast knowing that they'd make fun of me, ignore me, snigger, make fun of my accent. American high school scared the shit out of me…

I can't tell this.

Yes, you can. You'd seen that movie Fame. That was your image of school, remember. Abby's too - bullies and street sing-alongs. I hope it's not going to be like that, Sara, she said.

Yes, yes, I know it seems silly. But there was something so aggressive about it.

No, it was open, unrestricted.

Everything I knew about this country was from movies. It unsettled me.

I know. What would they make of you?

I wore gold shoes. I'm different. I'm a bully's gift card.

Your parents were out that night with the neighbors across the street…

…with my brother and sister, but their daughter came over to tell me about the school. I guess they thought it would be good for us to get to know each other, so I'd already have a friend.

It was a good idea.

As soon as she got there all she did was go on and on about the drug problems - how everyone was on drugs at school. It was back at the beginning of the "just say, no" campaign. I didn't know what that was – or about drugs. Aspirin is as close as I came to drugs. And she kept going on and on about how I was to just turn away from it and say no, to just say no, because people were going to be coming at me from all sides. She frightened the crap out of me. She didn't stay long, just enough time to let the fear seep into my breathing. She left me in such a state. Panicked. I didn't know how to handle it. I was nervous enough. I knew that I couldn't go to school the next day, and that I had no choice because I had to go.

I wish I could figure out how to open this window.

You sat in your bedroom staring at the reflection of the Casablanca poster in the window, crying and wishing we hadn't had to move to this place. I got so angry at everyone. My hormones and all those pent up, unexposed frustrations I'd been feeling for years were working me into a frame of mind where I lost complete control, and my body was being dragged around a still slightly unpacked house alone, room to room. I'm opening all the bathroom cabinet drawers, digging in boxes, trying to find I don't know what, something so I wouldn't have to face these drug people. Is that where you were, in a place of being so fucking mad at everyone for taking you to a place where you don't know what to do, that you just hate everyone for leaving you alone to deal with it? I don't know how I got to that edge, being pushed over to the point where that was the only logical answer that I went looking for. But I saw myself. I caught sight of all that messed up franticness in the mirror. I saw myself… and it stopped me. It was like the volume went from a hundred down to zero in a split second. What I saw looking back at me shut that silent noise off. I didn't know who that was and so I don't do it. There was always a whisper at the back of my throat knowing I wouldn't. I can't imagine any part of me wanting to do anything like that. But I know what that edge feels like and how easily it passes over into nonsense. I didn't do it. I screamed instead.

It was a pretty messy silence that came out.
Right through the mirror.
Life noises.
All the chaos in noise sent me into whatever that missing piece is. I fell that ½ inch without having to jump. What was so much deeper in you that went after death instead of an answer? The momentum must not have let up and it took you the extra step down there. It's a force unlike any other. An out of control that is controlled instability. And you rushed. And when you do that all you know is shut down brain and that animal's only need is to expel everything pent up any way it

can, it has to get out. No brake pedal. It fuels itself. You know what you're going to do, and you know how you're going to do it and you know what you need and where you're going to do it and you go down there and you snatch up the wire from the TV, that's as good as anything else, and go to the back room where all the boxes and shit no one really needs but they keep anyway is kept, there's a sturdy pipe and an old chair and you can jump from there, it's only a few feet, you've seen it all in the movies. Did you just need to feel the wire around your neck, make a mark, let them know you're serious? Then you'll walk away and no one will know, but you'll know, you'll know that one day you went down to the basement and put the wire that used to feed you video games around your throat and let it almost destroy you. Knowing it wouldn't work, not really believing in death because you're fourteen - it won't really come for you, so you step forward inside so much anger that you land into another world entirely and that broke your mother's heart, sweetheart, it broke her. She told me you were doing well, you had new friends, you were settling in. She showed me this badge you got, the one that says "Courage" on it. You spent time with the kids that were "at risk." You counseled them - sat with them and talked through their problems. Did you do it because you thought you'd find an answer by giving them one? Why didn't you just talk to your mom, because now she's blaming herself. There's this haystack as tall as the sky in front of her and she's going through every little piece of it looking for a clue that may not even exist. And that lets the devil inside. I know how easy that is. Can't you scribble the answer on the wall? It has to be made sense of, you have to see that. Why hasn't your mom opened that backpack up – is that where the answers are? It's the only place left to look.

So maybe that's why.

What if the answer isn't in there - then there is no answer. Knowing the possibility that one still exits, she lets it rest in there.

Silence isn't golden - it's a vacuous free fall.

Light is on the floor inside the shadow blinds the next morning. I'm under the comforter I have at home that is Joseph's. The backpack is still and breathing. Something always needs feeding. Not so ironic then that today Viola and I are going to Second Harvest Heartland, a hunger relief organization, for a day of volunteering. I'm still caught up in

296

the night before. I haven't told Viola about remembering my own thoughts of suicide. I'm still getting used to it myself, I suppose.

Your parents don't even know.

How could it have stayed so hidden away that I wouldn't remember? Why did my switch go off and his didn't? I chose life, which is unlike me. How much sense does it make for me to be here, and him not.

Don't fill up that box. Allow it to reveal itself.

I'm distracted by a pile of black hairnets. Viola smiles at me as she does a model walk in hers. I put mine on slanted to the side for a French beret look, but it just makes my head look like it has an elphantiasis hump on it. I'm glad I don't have a beard because they have little nets for those as well. One poor guy looks like a self-conscious Amish person.

Our job here is to fill and seal 1lb bags of rice. I hold the bag under the spout and pour the rice in, while Viola's job is to seal the bags up, or try to, all the machines keep on breaking and she has to keep moving from one to the other. Meanwhile one of my bags splits open and spills all over the floor. I fake non-embarrassment and a bad soft shoe, when a lady walks through my curtain call sweeping it all away as if it never happened.

You're good at that too - sweeping stuff under rugs. It may be your super power.

That's me trying. It's a sharp knife. You're right, of course. It's spilling out now though. All these specks of rice are so fragile, easily dismissed, thrown in the trash.

Like your thoughts that day - ignored to an extreme so as not to be remembered.

And then a flash of image, a boy in his basement gives me a seeming dream I forgot to write down. Years of silence in every corner of the room all along find me all these years later.

Collectively we pack 15,145lbs of rice and feed 11,832 people. I am a machine in here emptying each pound at speed out of a need to understand why things don't pour out of me the same way.

They are beginning to. Like they do for Viola.

At home we sit by the back door - me with my tea, Viola with her soda water.

If you start speaking, you'll have to go on.

"I had the strangest night, last night. It's being here, it's facilitated something for me and I want to tell you about it, but

297

I'm not sure. It's something I've never told anybody. Not even myself. I pushed it so far away - it's unbelievable to me that I did that. Denied something like this. It was too off key to admit to, I guess. I can't hide from it here though, not up there... Joseph. It's... a part of my life has slowed down, being here, somehow, and this caught up to me again last night." My body is as still as hers gets. We are a little in slow motion. "I tried to... when I was sixteen, I got to the edge of attempting suicide. I don't know how I split over to a point where that was the answer for me. I wish I could come up with that answer. More for you than for me, actually. The landing was no longer more familiar than the ceiling. I believed it was the answer and I tore around looking for it." I see her looking at me through the haze of water hanging onto my eyelids.

Blinking might make it all real.

It happened.

It happened.

"I saw myself, I caught sight of myself in the mirror, that's what stopped me. It wasn't me. I couldn't find me. That's what made the difference – that second when I kind of split out of my body and this other part of me was in the mirror, because it couldn't possibly be me. I don't think that I would actually have gone through with it, and I don't know if Joseph thought he would land. But, Viola, what part of a child knows, really understands that acting out can play into something so final? We're too young to know anything but impulse. And that has consequences." She puts her hand lightly on top of mine. This story that isn't hers, the one that may not serve her, I couldn't have said out loud to anyone else.

She's helping you.

She's Listening.

Joseph and I are on the same side, aren't we - and you and Viola are on the other. We were the ones whose actions caused absence. What we did pushed the two of you into a different form. The dropped scroll that slipped out of that angel's hand, your names are on it, and we wrote them there.

This story has crossed inside all of us.

"Thank you. That couldn't have been an easy thing to say. I don't know why he left us. I'll never know, and that has to be good enough, and that is the part that's still with me, because it's not good enough. I've tried to understand it in so many different ways."

"When I was sitting on the sofa the other night, I was looking at the guitar that you said Bernadette asked for, for

Christmas – the one she doesn't use. Do you know what my first thought was when I saw it? That is was Joseph's. I thought it was his. Perhaps Bernadette thought he might like it. That's why it sits there untouched because if he was here it would be his and he'd be the one playing it. A way to age him. She's still filling her role as his sister, just like you still mother him."

That's never ending, of course. He will always be. And she's found a way to make it physical.

"Maybe. She plays the piano. She hasn't picked up that guitar, I know that much."

"What's the star on your phone for?"

"That's Joseph's symbol. When they were kids I used to take their handprints. I put them on a piece of white felt that I cut out - next to each other. For ten years I did that. When Joseph died, I kept doing it for Bernadette, and for him I put a star in the place of his hand. It became his sign. A star. I'll show you." And here it is – a beautiful circle of soft white felt cut out in the shape of a burning sun filled with colored hands that trace the growing of two siblings. Their little fingers trace side by side one another - his palm is always in blue, while hers is a rainbow of different colors each year. The paint cracks a child's lifeline open. It breaks in places. It wraps around each line of fate. Until one heart line…

stops.

The abruptness is visceral. Woeful. While one hand continues on around the arc, the other one stops breathing. It has burnt out into a blue star - a supernova, a part of them all. This star has five fingers, and they are alive, and they continue rotating the circle, like Lazarus at Jesus' side.

Her son stepped into the space between them. He took the girl who would love him, and the children that would challenge him. He took graduation day and the smile he would have had on his face as his sister walked down the aisle towards true love. That moment in the basement should have been something he looked back on, when he thanked God that he couldn't get the rope to hold - to be grateful that at that time, that no, he couldn't even get that right. It would be a memory that he would hold at the back of his mind, that his family would never know, that he would tell to his wife in confidence one night by the fire, for no other reason than to unburden himself. But that's not the decision that he made. That's not the story he chose to tell. The story he chose to leave was his mother's and she spends time shifting in and out of

299

that now standing beside an empty chair at a table set for three. This is a space you cannot fill with anything bought or borrowed. This hole can only fill up with the gradual acceptance of her own understanding, by her own hand. How or when it will mend is open to God's breath moving into her heart.

It's not up to you to tell her to hurry her grief along because you want a happy ending for her, because you want her to plaster that Kellogg cereal box smile again. This is hers to own for as long as she needs it.

I can be with her.

But this is hers.

Her life grows out of the drowning.

Looking those moments in the face. She'll come out of the tunnel in her own time, stronger and more aware of herself and how her son circles around her - which is all he really needs: to be soaked up and released back to the light that took him in, that understood him at his most vulnerable.

One day goes into the next and into the next and the sun never bleeds out in the same point in the sky - time moves forwards inch by inch without label or description. And so have you, my friend. Please don't lose sight of that. I admire how you walk through your experience with all that it is - and you have walked so far - you are never back to one on the road to peace and understanding.

Relationship Intuition Number Twenty-Four: **The Halo Friendship**. *This is a friendship that never rested, not even in its seeming absent evolution. No matter what direction, dark or light, you are by its side and ready to wrestle, joy in, support and alleviate in whatever form you are able. In this friendship no matter how much time elapses, you regroup, rediscover each other and lend your experiences to ease the pain. It is a friendship that finds itself at the same point of questioning and exploration of faith and spirit; it knows no bounds. What has past is what leads you back, and where it leads is its soul purpose.*

300

Descending

> If during the next million generations there is but
> one human being in every generation who will not cease
> to inquire into the nature of his fate,
> even while it strips and bludgeons him,
> some day we shall read the riddle of our universe.
> -Rebecca West

On the plane the timing of my visit with Viola has me leaning into the window - my forehead pushed deep into the unreasonable coldness. There are losses you never totally recover from, and so we live in the overcoming of them. One thing I understand about Viola is the healthy indulgence of her grief, and that she won't allow it to end in a Band-aid of pretend healing. It's okay to be where we find ourselves. You take one moment at a time, then a minute, an hour, a day, a week, and go on from there. These are the aging wrinkles of our insides, and they shouldn't be facelifted. Tears purge something that needs acknowledging.

Ultimately, we see ourselves out of our own sorrow.
Love is never in the wrong place at the wrong time. If we treat each other with open concern, if we make the effort to reach out towards each other instead of hiding inside a three letter cop out text of "U O K?" then we begin to have respect for each other despite the onset of technology which has the capacity to pull us further away from each other.

Viola is sane and she is grounded. Even though there is a depth there that few will ever know, it is a viable state for growth. She's finding what she's capable of more so than most people even dare to open up to. She has already survived.

My arrival back in Portland is one preparing to leave for the drive back to Texas. Stanley is eager. He senses I think that he is closer to home now.

The time with your brother and his family though - At first it seemed like so much time, but it's sped on to an end out of nowhere. Gravity is moving at her own speed - too fast. I've been infused here for six weeks.

Hasn't it been great though? Don't you feel as if you slid inside their family? I mean I know it's our family, but it isn't. You know.

301

Yes, I know exactly. It's great to see what Billy's built - everything that it means to him, you know. His work, his family, his friends.

Don't you feel you know a little more of what makes him up?

Yes. I know he's happy.

You're happy.

Only I have nothing.

Ah, can we not get on that train.

Not make it about me, you mean?

You have so many things in other ways.

Non-traditional, yeah, that's me.

It makes no difference. You'll see things more clearly driving back over the mountain.

Sure, yeah, you're right. I'm so proud of him. He's tapped into something he's great at, that he enjoys, and he's made a life out of it. He didn't give up on anything, he kept at it, and look at what he's accomplished.

I'm glad about getting to know Mary better too. That's been pivotal for us. She keeps the door open, lets things waft around her. She doesn't shut anything out. She looks at all the details in front of her and lets her gut guide her to what's right for her and for her family. She allows herself to be completely aware, but inside a protectiveness. I'm thankful for that, and it's comforting to know my brother is surrounded in that.

You allowed her to see what moved you.

Cracked the window to that a little at least.

Yes. You let Dad walk in here.

So naturally you came in.

So I came in, naturally.

The day before I leave I pop down to The New Renaissance Bookshop for my past life regression class. In addition to you on my mind, the Newspaper Soldier drifts about, even though I don't talk about it. It's confusing to me.

That's why you don't talk about it.

I get here early and the room is filling up. I'd expected there to be a lot of brooding, middle aged overweight women wearing inappropriate clothes, too much off centered lipstick, perhaps some piercings and tattoos, and there are some Gothic, black haired tattooed folk with purple hair here, so I feel good about that. I'm not sure why, but predictability calms me down. There's a middle-aged couple, a few slightly plump, concerned looking middle-aged women, some groupies who've brought all their books to be signed, and me.

302

Take a front row seat.

Damn straight. I've paid my money, I'm going to ask my questions.

In the midst of us all are Earl and Linda who look more like a reserved retired couple from the Midwest than a pair of psychic intuits out to swindle me. I was expecting stage smoke, scarves and jangly jewelry but she looks as normal as I do; even the Goth folk look let down.

Linda talks about a fist full of people we are continually incarnated with? That's what she's saying, and I'm thinking of the Newspaper Soldier, and of you, knowing we didn't share the same space, and I want to step into the magic tardis she's obviously hidden in a cupboard somewhere and plug myself in to watch the slide show of who we are to one another. But these people insist on sharing.

Funny thing though, when all the others in the room share what they've encountered, for the first time since seeing the Newspaper Soldier's picture in the paper I feel normal.

And then it comes to you.

My turn to share him.

Trust in what we are for now.

So I tell my story about finding the weeping angel in New Orleans, and how he drove me to her; about the woman I found there, Sara, and that she died in the same month he and Leonard died, and in 1926, that there was my 26.

"Your instinct switch has been turned from off to on." When she said the word, switch, she swiped her index finger through the air just a few inches from my face as if she was turning a page over. "These moments come for each of us, and this is yours. He showed up for you in New Orleans and took you on a ride. Don't dismiss any of it. Just ask yourself what risk there is in being wrong." And I know the moment I drove up to the tomb I had my answer already.

It was real the moment it happened regardless of understanding. What I needed from these people was for someone to nod their head and say, yes, of course – to validate the normalcy of it. I can't think of him as flesh, as a soldier, or a boy. That's immaterial. His wrist is a flash from everywhere we've been.

You have to let go of a physical understanding of who you were.

I don't need to understand it.

You're involved in a present life regression to understand your soul's trajectory now. That's why he knocked on your door.

And that's why I stand six feet above the physical pieces of what's left of him. I'm attached to what he flew out of because I'm human and I want to touch it, but I'm attaching myself to the wrong thing. Just like with you, Cooper - you're already touching me when you lift my head to see a rainbow, to swerve out of the way of traffic, to notice the way my niece is sleeping.

It's time to wrap your mind around not being concerned with how you were physically present with each of us.

Shed the skin of it.

Make a pair of shoes out of it and keep on walking.

That night I fall asleep into a newspaper dream with the soldier. We lie in bed, he and I, and a billowy white sheet hovers over our heads, cotton floating above us, our breath drifting in and out of each other. A light comes in, but it's opaque like the truth is sometimes, and it's inching towards me. I reach for your hand and place each one of my fingers in the empty spaces between yours and they tighten around mine. Yours is a rough, calloused grasp of allowing. Then your eyes are overtaken by the words on the other end of a phone and you're not lying next to me anymore, you're standing by the bed, tears rolling down your cheek in slow motion. In dream logic your body comes back to me and it collapses fetally into mine. I have your head in my hands and I cup the sadness of it into my lifelines and brush them through your hair. As I'm about to breathe thanks for being able to touch you, you stand up outside the bed again. You stand there for a moment looking into me, and with authority and almost a little contempt you say, "I don't need you to take care of me."

I've been waiting for you to visit me in my dreams. Like a breeze I can see off in the distance, there is the anticipation of it eventually touching me. I watch it wash through the leaves, bending them until it's my turn, until it's walking through me, making what was still, the ribbon on my dress perhaps, curl around my waist into an S, making me think of the curve of your body as you slept near mine. And here it is full upon me in the night, the smell, the touch of a man I've only sat six feet above ground from.

I wake up with the annoyance that you don't need me, and the peace that both of us have been together, naked in our unconsciousness.

I wake out of him to leave my brother and his family in the quiet of the early morning. We had a champagne dinner the night before. We've had this time, these months, which might never come again. More than anything we understand how special it's all been; not just in terms of time, but in terms of what we've been able to know and understand about each other -

On a level that you can't reach if you're filtering your relationship via a week in the summer for the holidays and alternate Christmases.

Sitting outside at dinner, among the trees, wine open, as this family went about its business: cooking, putting a record on the old timey record player, Madeleine playing in her secret garden, spiders winding their way around the storm drains, it is an exact mirror of the moment I arrived to and I want to go back.

You've lived each of these moments fully. You've missed nothing.

This morning there is a light rain falling and for a moment I refuse to turn on the windshield wipers. One drop at a time the view of my brother and his sleeping family fades away outside of the car and I reverse into the street. On down the road I go, past the grocery store that was mine for a time, the allotment where my brother's vegetables grow, and the small village I called home. I turn the roundabout and once I find the freeway what was once mine for a time is gone.

Life isn't in the resting, not right now - it's in the moving on.

The drive back down is uneventful from the outside.

The brakes are fixed.

My palms don't sweat with that. Time whizzes passed the snow caped stones into flat open land where so much of me had been hiding *in plain sight,* and Lucius is gone; *and Lucius is.*

I press play on what I think is a voice recording I made on the way up, but I've clicked on a weird file that has a constant repetition of "this is a test of the new recording system" playing over, until it moves on to me, and there I am but I can't even listen to what I'm saying. The sound of my voice is so foreign to me. My sounds are all over the place. I don't know what my voice is. It's everywhere.

You sound English.

And I sound American.

You sound like a transplant.

You have no idea how much that annoys me.

This imperfection allows you to talk around things. It's a shield. It removes you, takes you a step away from yourself, it diverts, it's avoidance. You can't commit to a sound until that sound is only saying who you are. Who you are really.

I am not secure in what I have to say.

You're not secure enough yet to allow who you have become. You're afraid you're not English enough, too American, not American enough – that you have to be one to some, and the other to the rest.

I am speaking two languages, that does preoccupy me, yes.

No, that's not what I meant: you're not speaking your own language.

My own language can't come until I unravel the three moments in my life I had both a want and inclination to take my voice away.

Answer why the switch flipped over to save me, and not to save you. I chose life for myself, stopped short of crossing over the edge, and I chose to let you fall, to snatch that ½ an inch of solid ground away from you.

In the end, of course, you did take your life for a while. You walked in a physical body stripped of anything that could bring happiness, or a sense of meaning and joy because nothing could ever separate us.

I steer in the silent digestion of this, the airbag light on with the sound of you. The blurring landscape of my own past life fractures beneath me along the surface of a Picasso.

Pulling onto Catherine's street in Oakland, I feel heavy. I'm parked in the same uphill parking spot I was in before I left and all that's past seems to be a dream, and I've actually been sitting here all along in a twisted stop of time. I'm so tired.

The dogs re-engage and I go into a Disney telling of the four mud months I've been away. I'm just so tired. Catherine sits and listens, and little by little that part of me that likes to gloss over and make all life beautiful peels away to Joseph's neck, to Viola's eyes, to Lucius' ash and Lila's expectant doorbell ringing, until it's all lying on the floor. I'm so thankful it's Catherine here that I drop back into. In that same way that women with children understand each other, a woman that's putting herself through life alone understands one who is doing the same. She selflessly gives me her undivided attention.

You have someone listening to you without looking sideways at anything else but the sound of your voice.

While I'm here rebounding I've made arrangements to meet two friends that I missed on the way up. The following morning I try to surprise my friend Mickey at Whole Foods in Walnut Creek but it's his day off. Bugger. I drive over to Santa Ana to see Geoff, an acting friend from UT who's now all grown up and a professor at University. He teaches acting I think. He's also still performing from what I can see in the online book of faces.

As he comes out of one of the building I wave and mouth hello.

You said, "Yoohoo." Out loud.

I like yoohoo.

It is one of your words.

How is it some of us look almost exactly the same, and some of us look like our replacement actor on a soap? Geoff looks the same - only his smile has more responsibility behind it.

He knows this campus like the back of his hand because he graduated from the same school. As we walk the halls of faculty offices and theatre buildings lined with photographs of past shows, he's in most of them. It's a second home to him. He teaches acting, he's directing, doing dramaturgy, and still acts.

He tours me around the campus and into the restored mission church that the site of the school is founded on.

Remember your first time inside a Catholic church?

Geoff took me.

"Do you remember when we were doing that play about the catholic country singer? I can't remember what it was called - directed by that lady with long red hair. God, I can't remember her name either. Sorry I'm useless with names, names and doors, anyway, beside the point. It's funny, she told me I wouldn't remember her, and as much as I thought, what a nut, of course I'll remember you, of course, we'll be friends – I don't and we haven't. Ha! Do you remember that play?"

He's smiling at you.
Trying to keep up with my rambling, one supposes.

"Yes, of course. Luther was in that as well, wasn't he?"

"Yes, that's right, yes. Remember I was doing my methody thing and I convinced you to take me to church with you. I'd never been to a Catholic mass before."

"Did I take you?"

"Yes, you did. And you were so funny – you were a bit nervous about it - having some British, Church of England heretic inside your church walls."

"Did I let you come in?"

"You don't remember this? Yes, you did, but you were very specific that when it came time to take communion I should stay in my pew and not participate. But when it came down to it I just couldn't resist it so I got in the line, and all the way up as it got closer and closer to me you kept whispering, put this hand over that one, say this and then that. You were terrified I'd mess up and give you away - as if you'd be excommunicated if anyone found out you were with me."

"That's so funny. I guess I'm a bit more lapsed now. I did that? I don't remember that at all."

"Probably the intense guilt wiped it from your memory in case you were interrogated later." We laugh and continue on through the theatre, the church we've grown up in together. Backstage feels more like his living room.

"Did you live in Paris for a while? Why do I think that? What took you there?"

"Oh, yes, I did. I fell in love. She's my wife now. She found a job in Paris and we lived there for a bit. There wasn't too much for me to do there after a while and I wanted to come home, to teach here. She'll be here eventually. That's what we agreed. But she has a great job that she loves and it means, well, I get to go to Paris. We have a great apartment there and I have summers off so I spend them there. It has its difficulties…"

"Love conquers all, right?" He stops and smiles at me before we walk across the lawn to the cafeteria to have lunch. We talk about our friends, our young lives on stage, about how many of us I've seen.

"I'm not sure I could do it. I mean there are a few people I wouldn't want to see. Not you, I love seeing you again. Some people you just have to leave back there."

"Yes, I know what you mean, there have been two people I've questioned over that, but it's interesting, when I did see them again, even though the surface was rough compared to this, to how this feels sitting here with you, flowing so easily, once we spent some time it peeled away to a part of them I didn't see all those years ago, you know. But this, all this, being able to see your lovely face, and look you in the eye and see how you really are, hug you hello and goodbye, to feel who you are, what I'm finding is that, yes, it's full and rich and makes me feel a kind of wholeness, I think that's the word, a wholeness like a blurry picture coming clear again. Only it's about what it's doing to me, forcing out of me."

"I can see that. I can see how that would be." He's nodding, neither of us touching our lunch much. I don't go deeper than that although with time I could with him. There's a certain movement that is the same for both of us at this point in our lives. I didn't expect that. I knew we'd have a nice chat and a catch up, but there's more to what we have to say that I wish a lunch hour wasn't cutting off.

Out the front gates again he walks me back to my car so I can give him his parting gift of Goldrush Mustard. He hugs me goodbye. We've both felt the value of it, that this time has been important, and we know in all likelihood we'll not see each other again. We've been back in someone's company we hadn't realized we missed. And there it goes, walking away from me again. I'm so exceptionally happy to be doing what I'm doing, even if the pure why of it all is still a bit of a mystery.

Press on down.

Early sunrise at 6:00am in Oakland and I leave with a teary, half-slumbering goodbye to Catherine. We're not awake enough for it to count as a goodbye. I didn't realize that I'd fully left her until I was halfway down the mountain back to the web that is Los Angeles again.

I have a noon lunch to get to with a graduate director I worked with quite a bit at University. Sometimes you find yourself in someone else's mind, looping in their creative process, and they find themselves inside yours. This is what it was like for Oliver and me. I loved to watch him sense the emotional equations, the most sensible and obscure things in the tiniest space in the most nonsensical of plays.

This jaunt down to meet him is all in the timing. The plan is to drop off Stanley at Jill's in Hermosa Beach, then head off to the lunch. I love the thought of being in my tiny perfect house again an inch from the beach. Stanley is self-contained there; he loves the chicken barking at him through the window that he can ignore on his plush bedding. It's all good.

On arrival though, things are in a little bit of disarray - the plumbing is broken. Repairmen are everywhere and we can't go down there yet. But I have this lunch see, with Oliver. Jill says all's well.

"We love Stanley. You can just leave him up here at our house while you're out, it's no problem. He's a great dog, unlike some I know." Yeah, your crazy "I'm so territorial I'll bite your ear off because I don't need me no other dog in my house" dog. I'm not sure about this but she insists it will be alright, and I've got forty minutes to get from Hermosa to downtown Los Angeles, which is pushing it already. So, I abandon my beloved best friend and travel partner to the jaws of Daisy the hound of Hermosa, albeit, she'll be on the other side of the door from him.

Unless she bites through it, of course.

I don't know how I make it to the restaurant before him, but I do. I'm not comfortable driving in downtown areas, they frustrate me with all the one way bits and inevitable construction re-routing when I only know the one way to go. But this is an easy hop off and a valet park only option, which for some reason relaxes me.

Oliver is unchanged. Buff, same haircut, same directness, eager to talk. We drink wine. We catch up. I do the usual, he is here, she is there, can you believe what she's achieved, can you believe how his life changed... We move on to him.

He's fallen in love he says. I love it when people tell me this.

"He's a lot younger than me. He's only nineteen." I cough up a bit of merlot.

"Well, we can't help who we fall for. He's kind to you?"

"Yes, he's such a sweet guy. He's a big guy too."

"Oh, right, well, I'm sure as long as you're supportive."

"No, I mean I love him that way – big. I'm what's known as a chubby chaser. That's what they call us." Wait, what?

"More wine, ma'am?"

"Well, that would be a good idea, yes," I say looking at Oliver trying to take it all in.

The heart wants what the heart wants, as Woody Allen said. At least I think it was him.

And he'd know. It's not the sort of thing that's on my radar though.

310

What love?

No, chubby whatsit. Doesn't sound like a very nice way to say it.

Just listen then. Love is love.

Oliver doesn't pass over it either. He doesn't throw it out there and then change the subject, like I would.

Like the old you would.

It's important to him to tell me exactly what this lifestyle is, with all its prejudices, struggles and judgments.

"You have no idea how many people are out there, Sara, hiding what they feel inside because they're afraid. They live outside of what society is telling them is acceptable, you know? We have what society says is normal, and we've invented labels for everyone that circle around that. Wherever they go there is always a stare from someone who is threatened by something so far outside of their box, of what they think is tolerable for them. A man in high heels, a man in high heels kissing a three-hundred-pound man he's in love with. That's someone's normal, even if it isn't yours. We'll need a few more minutes." The waiter's been hovering around to take our order, Oliver is focused on what he's saying, wanting me to take it all in. He speaks carefully. "I did this event a few months ago. We brought people together so they could hang out without any fear of judgment, or attack. Gay, transgender - they could just be who they are. You should have seen them, Sara. They were coming up to me in tears, so thankful that for one night at least they could relax into who they are. They didn't have to feel ashamed or hide behind their suits and ties, or helmets and stethoscopes."

"Is that how you've felt?"

"Well, my own parents won't talk to me. They don't understand me at all, how I can be attracted to someone that is obese and… well, he's very young. They've pretty much cut me out of their lives. But I love him. We are in love."

From the outside Oliver has stayed in a time capsule, and on the inside is someone I never knew at all. But today he's on the table, heart open. I haven't eaten a bite. He's been so frank. And with me.

What a gift for someone to trust and share themselves so completely and openly.

Yes, that's what it feels like, a gift.

Do you get this now then? Sharing who you are is a giving.

311

Yes. It's brave too. Some words live on your skin so they have no choice but to shed. That's what it's feeling like. Maybe that's what's gradually happening to me. At a slow rate my words are emerging to the surface like a bloated dead body.

So dramatic. How about like a double pearled oyster?

Stanley has survived Daisy and the workman, and our magic cabin is ours again. We're only here for a night or two so Jill and I make the most of it. She's taking me to her book club to meet some friends.

So it's a book club.

Right - all women hanging out together, casual. I throw on a sundress and glaze some lip-gloss on. I arrive just out of the shower with my hair still dripping a little, air drying... this is my first misjudgment. I should have been preparing for this night for months, corrected my skin care regime, invested in some of that magic cream that diminishes wrinkles for my face, makeup'd up and worked out my abs.

These ladies are dressed for battle.

Spike heels, couture pants, hair coiffed, and all with a youthful glow of tautness. I lounge in my loose linen dress and Doc Martens - a steadfast forty something.

"I love that you're so free in how you dress," one woman says to me. She's just being nice, right? I catch myself making that face you make when you're blowing up a balloon to make the lines around my mouth diminish a little. I hold my stomach muscles in and try to fluff up my wet locks. I do all this every three minutes, like contractions.

These women maneuver like beautiful Caribbean fish swimming in an exotic tank. I slouch quietly on the couch in my wrinkled dress leaving a slight wet patch where my hair's rested too long on the back cushion. They pour white wine, while I'm the only slosh drinking red. I feel conspicuous that I might spill some on the almost comfy minimalist furniture. They dip carrots while I eat cake and dip solid cheese into liquid cheese and smother it on wedges of bread.

Well, why bring it and not eat it?

Right? I don't get that. I camp out at the buffet. The red wine is helping.

After about two and a half hours of mingling, conversation turns to the book. It's thought provoking. I hadn't expected that.

'Cause you've been sitting around judging all night.

312

I have nothing to contribute because I haven't read the book. These tipsy, well-dressed beauty seekers may have taken their bodies back in time, but their intellect and education give them away. They wake up in the morning and see the reflection of themselves they want to see. I wake up and see what each day piled on to the next has done. On the inside though, our pile of bones are the same unwavering age.

Only you like covering yours in loose linen and wet hair drying at all angles with boots that steady you. And you don't mind being the only one in the room who does.

I don't know why that makes me feel good, but it does.

I agreed to split my time in LA between Jill's in Hermosa Beach and Penelope's (the one I worked with at a major motion picture studio I won't name because that would be indiscreet... but it rhymes with Pony). She lives in Torrance. We'd only seen each other briefly on the way up so another day will be terrific. It gives her a good excuse to clean out the back bedroom she says.

She's been saying she's going to clean her spare bedroom out since you've known her. That's over five years.

Yep. She'd talk about doing it every day off, or vacation day she took. It continued to pile up. So, if this is the only room in the house for me to stay in, and I plan to show up, then her time has finally run out of excuses not to do it.

Penelope's in love with Stanley so she greets us downstairs and helps us in. She leads us to the cleared out back room, to this room that's been so much a part of the conversation of our friendship, as if it's a living breathing human being. When the door opens I can't imagine how this space could have had more in it - boxes, lamps, baskets, knick-knacks, and shelving. I wonder if I should keep Stanley on his leash in case he goes missing.

You should have had one of those chips inserted into him.

"Now I know that it still looks pretty cluttered in here, but if you could have seen it before. This is so much more organized."

"I can imagine," I say, trying not to let my voice sound judgmental. She'd taken days to do what she'd been threatening to do for years and she's finally done it.

And she's done it for you.

313

In this well-organized hoard, Stanley and I slot into our sculpted out space. He's cool with it because he loves any kind of confined area, so for once it's my turn to conform to his territory. I ritually spread out his blanket in our little bit of consistency from "home," and put his food and water out.

Penelope and I reconnect with our former bosses while I'm here. We'd all survived the studio system together. By that I mean none of us had been legally committed to any kind of asylum, during or after.

Although most of you self-medicated on and off.

Immaterial. Anyway. Having been the subordinates, we're just four women now. At that time we did what had to be done to get the project finished. They had timelines to meet for someone else, we had to meet theirs and so met our own. Obviously four women working together, that much estrogen wasn't always going to be peaceful and pretty. It got messy at times. But we found a way to come out the other side as friends. The dance changed. We've come to the table from a place of heart – the piece we didn't give over or admit to in our working environment.

For my half of the table, sitting across from a woman that had been my direct boss, a woman that had put me through my paces in a small amount of square footage, I find a person who's in transition as much as I am. We all stumbled out of that studio raw, you can't help it. None of us are left there now.

My boss began travelling to exotic, remarkable places in the world like Morocco, immersing herself in other cultures - each time bringing something precious back with her. These aren't vacations she going on, they're a kind of pilgrimage to detox out of the parts of herself she took on in that godforsaken job, that were never truly her. She meditates. She's involved in a clearing, just like I am.

On the other side of the table is Penelope's former boss, a woman who used to delve out legal advice to top executives in corporate America. Behind that control sits a mother who watches, *Cinderella* over and over again with her thirty-year old autistic son. What she held behind the shield for years on end in order to battle the men of office now lies on the table with openness, and a raw melancholic joy.

We've all left the battle behind the corporate wall now. We filter what was, having taken the question of what life would be like if we took all that we learned, all the hard work and experiences, people and negotiation skills, and turned them around, putting all that energy to work for ourselves. We no longer ask anything from each other, but rather for each other.

Relationship Intuition Number Twenty-Five: **The Split Misfit Friendship**. This friendship shapes itself out of a developed long-term acquaintance within the workplace, where status is unequal and the evolution seems unlikely. At one point there has been a respect and understanding within a hierarchy. Once that status change has shifted so that all are on level ground, so this acquaintanceship evolves into friendship. The foundation of it is initially hidden in the structure the encounter was formed in. This friend comes to you later in life, is unexpected, and one with whom a similar path, or spiritual awareness might be immerging. What was once was only half; what evolves is the personal side - a turning of the mirror to the inside.

Sitting down with my former studio boss is a resolution I needed for my own peace of mind because the challenges I faced in that environment pushed me somewhere I never want to go back to.

A time filled with inadequacy and questioning - time you'll never get back.

I don't want it back. There was so much going on for me during that time. It seemed to be the perfect storm of my life. Gregory and I tearing each other apart, then getting engaged, then... well... All of those things converging showed me just how far I could be pushed. It showed me how little self-worth, how little belief I honestly had in my own possibilities.

What it also did by default though is help you recognize with every cell in your body what it takes to pull you back into believing in who you know you can be.

I'm so grateful for that. You never really know what's going on behind someone's eyes in the way they robot around inside the corporate machine. I didn't realize that inside, her dreams were squashing down, just like mine were. We both wanted something more, when I thought her "more" was what she was already living.

Stanley and I make our way back down the mountain to Orange County to see my brother's friend Matt, his best friend from high school. We've known each other for over thirty years and I've seen him during the years. He's been through a lot. He came through a challenging childhood that led him into a drug fueled twenties, two dead marriages and then a third leaving him a single parent to his son.

He's remarried now, and turned his life around. He went back to school and became an RN. It's one of the most remarkable turnaround stories I've ever seen someone live, and I'm anxious to see him all grown up.

We pull into the driveway, to his 26 license plate number continuum. As I get Stanley out, Matt comes out to meet us. They've adopted a new dog, one whose history he doesn't know too well so we're taking precautions. We go all dog whispery and have them meet on neutral territory outside their house.

You might want to walk them a little further down the road.

The dogs are each on a leash and the two of them start sniffing each other. It seems to be going well, and perhaps I get a false sense of security because Matt and I look away for just a second, and all of a sudden, this dog, let's call him, Asshole, goes right for Stanley's ear and takes a big chunk out of it. We hadn't dog whispered far enough away from his territory.

Obviously.

And Stanley, ever the Buddha dog of friendship, got a little too close.

"Shit, he's not hurt is he? Please tell me he's not hurt." Matt sees the blood all over my hand and I'm trying not to panic so he doesn't feel too badly about it. Stanley is scratching at my arm wanting to be picked up and I'm trying to see how fucked up this is.

"There's a lot of blood. It looks like it's his ear, but earlobes bleed, right? It's pretty torn up though." Matt puts Asshole inside and gets his keys and we rush Stanley to the emergency dog ward. He apologizes the entire way there saying, "Whatever it costs, I'm going to pay for it," over and again. The only calm one in the car is Stanley.

Who is in shock.

At the clinic they shave his ear to see where the wound is. A part of his ear has been bitten away and they bandage it over as well as they can and put the cone of shame on him to stop him from trying to unravel and scratch it. He looks like he's being fitted for a mummy costume.

"Well, Matt, when people ask me the last time I saw you, at least it's unforgettable," I say, trying to be funny and calm him down. He laughs nervously. "It's all good, seriously. It'll build a bit of character in him."

From the emergency room, Matt and I grab a quick lunch before I head back down to the not so polyamorous San Diegans. I keep looking over my shoulder at Stanley in the rear view mirror. They say they've given him pain pills so he's dosing a bit in the sun. I've taken the cone off – I can't make him keep that on for a two-hour drive. I'm paranoid that he'll scratch his mummy head off, but he's so loopy I doubt he'll have much strength for it to amount to much. His one good ear flops into his eye, his head hanging over the side of his bed and his little heart is beating twice as fast as normal from all the medication. My little sleeping addict.

My stopover in San Diego with Sky is only a few days. Having spent a bit of time here already I want to get to Tempe so I can spend a weekend with Lenore.

Going to Sky feels like coming home to family. It's that big sister feeling, wondering what dresses I can mooch, what lovely pie or sweets she'll make me, what she'll let me steal away with from her closet. My three days here are easy. We thrift shop, we eat sweets, she shares her painting work with me, we go to the beach and we watch movies. We fall into being ourselves. Easy, flowing.

You loosen up while you're here.

She allows me that freedom, to be more open. I still hesitate with myself though.

It has to come out of something though. It's not organic yet. You can't just push it out there. The door has opened with other people and you've walked through it.

But I know my voice here – we're English together. I'm not sure how to just start talking. I don't trust the voice outside of myself. I look across the table and I can't take that one step closer to talking.

Why don't you trust why and allow for when it does? How people might react to your story, especially those closest to you, pulls you away from that inch of trust to allow any free flow of open communication. That connection with another human being where you're sharing the same notes on what's fallen passed you –

I don't have that. I'm not capable of it yet.

It's all come barreling down and you have to evaluate it for yourself before extending it into someone that means so much to you. Don't try to control it.

317

Is that an excuse? Isn't it better to share thoughts along the way?

That's what the path for this year is helping you to do, even though you didn't start with that intention. Consider that the two of you already have a silent understanding of one another. Not everything has to be spoken out loud to be known.

Well I know that more than I ever have.

You want her close to you but you are going to be leaving again. There is a protection in not releasing all that you are. For you, anyway.

Before I head back out onto the road I meet Gibson's and my friend Richard again for lunch. His wife Lisa is working, so it's just he and I. He's curious about my having seen Gibson again and how it went.

"It was a lovely time actually. It's been – I mean, so much happened back then. So much that we didn't talk about. I don't know how much he spoke to you about our situation." Richard stirs his coffee.

"Gibson's not known for his communication skills." We laugh and he continues stirring. "He did talk to me quite a bit about the abortion though." His saying the word throws me of guard. "He felt a tremendous amount of guilt over it all, you know." I can feel the sweat in between my thighs and the plastic bench. I'm stuck. He told him how he felt about this? He didn't talk to me.

He had to talk to someone. Like you did.

"No, I didn't know. He didn't talk to me, he never told me anything about how he felt. We never talked about it. For my part, I know that I blamed him. It was difficult to allow him into me mentally or physically because I hadn't forgiven him. I wanted to punish him for it… and myself."

"Well, it's nice to hear you owning that." I'm owning it? Oh.

You need to breathe through this a minute.

God, there is so much he doesn't know, and that makes what he just said sort of ok, but it's pissing me off at the same time.

Take your ego out of it. He's protecting his friend.

"Yes, that's my piece of the responsibility in how we fell apart. The fact that he went to you to talk about the abortion instead of me confirms a lot, don't you think? How could I reveal myself to someone pushing me away? Or vice versa.

Clearly I didn't go to him either." There's so much more not to say.

Hide it down with a smile, you're a pro at this. Slide it on a breeze.

So, there is a time for that.

It's his friend.

A dialogue of images scans through my head - his kneeling by my bed, the fading Old Spice, the spec of dandruff on his collar, the smell of day old hair mixed with sweat and anxiousness that needed to leave me behind. I can't bring what someone has done to me into someone else's friendship.

Not at the table. New information to him about Dad is almost thirty years old to you, and new information doesn't travel with the release of time's lifted weight.

I have found that too. I won't go further.

Instead of driving straight back to Sky's, I take a walk towards the edge of the world on the pier in OB. Your father and I walked this pier each Sunday over the years to hear the great Bob Oaks and his jazz sound. Musicians came in from all over.

Always impromptu.

All of us crammed into that little beach house over the cliff.

Like being inside a pumping heart.

And listen to Clint Cary, the Spaceman of Ocean Beach tell his stories of outer worlds.

Do you have your number?

We all got our tickets.

His psychedelic blind paintings on the walls - flaming hands flying out of a cratered sun beaming under black light.

It's quieter now. Today's voyage out, it's just the three of us.

It's strange that with all the years between us, I know him more intimately than I ever have.

He felt what you did all along.

Neither of us had the courage to speak the words aloud to each other. He took himself down the same road I did.

Aren't you grateful to Richard for saying what he did - we know Dad on a deeper level now.

He hadn't been shutting down, he was running away from it just like me.

And after he left you and went to San Diego he found his own story rewritten when he got there, didn't he? His best friend, the one he was set to live with, his girlfriend was pregnant and they'd decided to keep their baby and get married.

319

The about face of what he'd chosen. The home he went to was filled with the constant reminder of his own choice.

What a test to sit in a house and see your best friend make the other. If the last ring of reckoning has a name, it's housed in there somewhere.

As I reverse out of Sky's driveway, she waves back at me before she turns to pick some pecans off the ground. Kai, one of her black cats jumps on top of the gate and then over into the grass. I look behind me to check the road is clear and steer out onto the street. I look back down and she's gone. Her child is at school, her husband at work, the animals scattered in their territory, and the normality of my absence returns in an instant.

The hug with Sky is as you thought, Cooper. One that says, I wish you could stay, and I wish you'd never left. There's so much heart between us. It empties when I leave. I need us to be closer – in that I want to be able to get to her more easily. Jump in the car and arrive for cake.

Don't hold yourself hostage for that.

I'm so glad I had her in all that passed for us here. It was such a relief to know her then. She kept me going. When your father and I broke up and he dropped me off at her house she was the one who held me in her arms and told me everything was going to be alright. I sobbed my eyes out for days, and she was the one there for me, taking care of me, making sure my mind got straight again.

Well, there's your truth for her. That's really all you need to tell her.

I had to step through the rest to see it.

This place has held on to me. The scent of you and I peeled off into the sands of the desert, into the gut of the mountains and bided its time in the tide of its ocean. I walk both feet on wheels away in the scent of us.

It's not only beautiful, it's natural.

I wink at "The Thing" as it passes to my right. I'm in the desert on a Friday afternoon, when in another world I'd have been a Thing clone behind a desk.

I swing back into Tempe temporarily blinded by the dust and circling weeds. A roadrunner screams across the highway in front of me. That's the speed of our arrival. No sooner is Stanley out the car and greeting Honey's bottom, Lenore is whisking me away to Yoga. I'm relieved actually. My body is knotted like an old lady's ball of forgotten wool.

It's Yoga Nidra, she says. That translates as "yogi sleep." I have to tell you, I love the sound of that. It's supposed to get me in the deepest possible state of relaxation while maintaining consciousness - like lucid dreaming.

The meditation retreats us to the candlelit cave of our potential. My cave has a skylight, and through it I see our family. It doesn't exist on the outside, in any kind of reality we can absorb, but the presence of it breathes with the same pulse that I do. We left our cave almost a year ago, you and I.

We went out into the world to happen to each other.
I suppose this is my potential.

Your potential awakened our collective.
So you won't be alone ever again.

I never was. And neither were you. Our naked light is out in the open now.
Eyes softening, I look over at Lenore sitting in silent repose. It's quite beautiful for us both to live, even if it's just for a moment, at the same pace, to have our in and exhale join - and in presence with you. The Lakota have a phrase - Mitakuye Oyasin – all are related.

Our reflections may change, but we are all interconnected.

In that same heartbeat Lenore and her husband drive me inside the Native American landscape infused with spirits 1,200 feet above the backwaters of Apache Lake, to Skeleton Cave. The road twists tightly and I look over the cliff's edge into the faces of men made of rock, into a sunrise of ancestral breathing. We trail through their land. Present in the place I love you.

There is a richness of spirit about my friendship with Lenore, and in the time we spend in each other's company. As writers and friends, there is a vital part of us that's in the same place.

There is a point on the body, at the sacrum, called the Nagila. The Lakota believe that the spark of God lives there and that the hummingbird flies back and forth between there and God to feed you.

There was no randomness of our pairing as roommates, was there?

You don't believe in randomness any more than I do. You are given the gift of need when you remain open in the place that desires it.
We received each other.

You've received all of these people, just as they have you.

Traveling the road between Tempe and San Angelo, more than the direction has twisted. At the beginning of all this, at the first leaving, I felt out of place, isolated.

Initially you didn't have a clear understanding of what this undertaking was going to take, or give to you, did you?

Why I was so irrationally drawn to the doing of this, no. We've been off on a wild re-enactment through my life in a way, haven't we?

More of a rediscovery.

I have wanted – there's been this nagging for so long to invite you in to hear the un-hearable, to see what up to this point I had Oedipusly forced into blindness. You've helped me ease each emotion out of hibernation.

So we could inhale it together.

Do you have more of an understanding of me now, I wonder, Cooper.

We have found the space to love each other, a timeless present, an invisibility full of the clearest picture of who we are to one another.

Where I've allowed myself to love what I destroyed.

To love what you created. Lay down your head for a while though, there's that one last corner to look around.

In San Angelo, sitting in the audience at a play with Marie, a big thunderstorm darkens the town center taking all the power out. The actors drive their cars round to the windowed front of the theatre and turn their headlights on and hand out some flashlight pens to the audience. We light the second act ourselves. The doors are open, the rain's pouring in and we all became a part of the story and the *collective collides again.*

Barreling down the straight dirt highway out of San Angelo, story runs through my bones to each action and reaction, and the consequence of those past years that said, go back. I am because you were.

Because I am. Happy Mother's Day.

What?

Watch for the ducks.

A mother duck and her six ducklings step off the path and cross the road in front of me. Slowly. I park the car by the lake in my neighborhood, almost home, and watch as she hovers by them, nosing each one of them safely down into the water.

Today is Mother's Day.

It's the only one we're going to have, isn't it?

The only one. But it's ours.

It's always been a tricky day for me.

I know. But today we can sit here with each other.

Feed the ducks.

Yeah. Get used to the quiet again.

Will I hear it when you leave?

Love doesn't leave, Sara.

Say my name again.

Sara.

Your silence will walk with me.

I'm in the life that you love. I am the rhythm of your DNA.

Rounding the corner into the street I grew up on, Stanley's homing instinct kicks in. A gentle whine accelerates into a howling as I pull up to the garage. He's beside himself with so much energy jumping from the backseat on to my lap, his claws scratching my legs. I open the door as fast as I can and he leaps onto the grass and runs through the back gate. His nose is to the ground, immediately picking up all the messages left from passing irritating squirrels and squatter rabbits. He moves from tree to plant, to flower, picking up tracks. He scours the perimeter only picking up his nose when something new flies by on the breeze. I sit down on the paved stone next to him. The wind moves through strands of his wounded ear as a mosquito lands on my left foot. I watch it sucking out my DNA, then jitter fly away. We are three happy souls with an itch of something new.

Philip, in Miami, is the first friend I told of my need to journey out to everyone.

He has been supportive and encouraging from the very beginning.

I had hoped he would be the first friend I visited but our schedules never seemed to be able to hook up. It seems fitting that for all but one reunion, he is the last friend I visit with.

When I left college I had confirmation that my home was the stage.

Remember that.

When he left college with his BFA in acting he knew he realized with all that he was that he didn't want to be an actor.

323

He started producing shows. In pursing what he thought he wanted, he found out it wasn't for him and he fessed up to that right away, which is brave and so smart. Opportunities came up and he followed them through. He moved to Miami, took a job as a trainer at a local gym, and after a few years he bought it, turned it around, and sold it. Now he has a life with so many different creative pockets. He lives a beautiful life in a condo off one of the canals at #426.

We're on the phone as the cab pulls outside his building. He's standing there, arms wide, screeching,

"Saaaaraaaa! You know we haven't seen each other in twenty-four years! Saaaraaa!" he shouts to the poor cab driver who's looking around wondering how he'll ever find his way out of the maze of backstreets I've just led him into.

But the two of us are off, as if we'd just spent a weekend away from each other. He's so glad he's at the end so he can hear about everyone, absolutely everyone, without leaving anything out. He whisks me over to a sushi restaurant where the biggest lazy Susan I've ever seen rotates alongside my stories.

"Cyprus. I can't believe you went all the way out there to see Arina."

I know right. She did all this.

"Neither could she, I think. We just stood there staring at each other. And now I can't imagine not having her as a part of my life, she's so present." And on I go as the lazy Susan story keeps passing around and I'm stuffed with Salmon and wine and rice and Wasabi.

"Charlie wants to meet us for lunch tomorrow. Are you up for that?"

"Black? Charlie Black. Where is he?"

"I don't know, the other side of the swamps out here. He couldn't come to the party you're throwing me so, next best thing." He sucks down a last piece of raw crab thingy and smiles at me.

"I'm throwing you a party on a yacht."

Charlie was an MFA directing student at the same time as Phillip and I were pursuing our BFA's in acting. He directed the production of *A Midsummer Night's Dream* that Phillip produced. Everyone I've visited that was a part of this production mentions it. It had a profound effect. It's what connected some of us, and what grounded a connection for others. That's how it was for Viola and I.

324

Helena, she reminded me a little of you, chasing after a man that loved someone else.

I'd fallen in love with my Demetrius so in essence I wasn't playing at anything. I believed every word I was saying. My real Demetrius, Donovan was engaged to another girl, a strong woman I couldn't begin to compete with. But I was going to throw Shakespeare's best at him, and if that didn't win him over, well, at least I'd go down in poetry.

Donovan and I wrote letters to each other. He had to sneak out at night to post them. He promised me rides on his motorcycle and I imagined us whisking ourselves away to some island where strong women lost all of their powers. We never told each other we liked each other - we used Shakespeare as our code. I chased after him as Helena did Demetrius, and he returned to the true love of Hermia. I didn't have access to any fancy fairy potions, you see.

Because we all want to win true love that way.

Yeah, no, you're right. And here a few of us are again, as a trinity in a restaurant in Miami Beach. Our blurry faces slowly come back to each other.

"Has anyone found Donovan?" Charlie asks.

"No, well you know when he married Lynn they meshed their last names together so no one knows what he's called now."

"They meshed Ballentine and Quisenberry?"

"Yep."

"So Quisenball? Ballenberry? I'm at a loss."

"God, I hope it's not Quisenball, but I hope we find him. He'd round out Midsummer for me. The lovers, I mean."

"What about Luther, has anyone heard from him?" Phillip's staring up people, his eyes darting around the room trying to find them.

"He's in New York, but I missed him there. He had a death in the family. He was in Texas when I was in Manhattan," I said. "Wasn't he in that production of *Zoo Story*? You know you stared at me during most of that show, Phillip."

"Did I?"

"You said you liked the way I was involved in listening."

"Clever. Probably a come on. I'm sure I wanted to sleep with you, but you were too classy for me."

"Speaking of women you slept with, Daisy says hello."

"You know we had the biggest blow out during Midsummer."

325

"I know she said she was escorted out of the park."

"It was so intense with her."

"Yes, she said."

"I bet that's not all she said."

"She hopes you are happy, despite yourself, Phillip, so let's say thank you, shall we?" He smiles at me that way he does at girls, and laughs. I love the flash return of all these invading pictures. Stories are rejuvenating friendships dormant only a few hours ago. They keep on talking.

You go quiet in your head slowly seeing how each stone I've walked over has impacted each person in my life.

It's light here with him though. With Phillip I'm having a full on indulgence into his flow and the city that he loves, and it's pure adventure with unexpected thrills around the corner.

During tabletop conversation when we're out to lunch we end up talking about a popular local drag queen. Gloria is hard to miss, they say - six feet four, slender, bright red hair and four-inch heels.

"She was being followed home by this man one night. She starts running away from him, which trust me isn't easy for a guy in high-heeled pumps, and when she turns into her apartment the guy launches himself at her, so she knees him in the groin, rips off one of her shoes and sticks the heel into him like a knife. He probably thought he was going take down this woman pretty easy, but she turned out to be a brute of a stiletto wielding drag queen. A friend of ours asked her if it had been upsetting, and she said, 'Yeah, he didn't even bother to call the next day.'"

I can't even eat my ice cream I'm laughing so hard.

That's hilarious - a mythical drag queen.

"God, I wish she'd walk by."

You might luck out.

After lunch on our way down to the Arts Centre, I feel Phillip nudging me in the ribs. His eyes are stuck on open and his mouth is wide and mouthing something too excited to get out.

"Sara. There she is, there she is - that's Gloria!"

"Where? Where is she?!" I lock in as she passes right by us in a stunningly tacky turquoise mini dress and black heels, the wind whipping through her un-brushed red wig. She looks seven feet tall and she's walking at a fast pace.

Try to get a picture!

She's weaving in and out of the crowd too fast. Phillip suggests stalking her to get a closer look, so we take off. We finally catch up to within a few feet of her and I get a picture.

It's not a good one though.

I know. I want a better one. We mosey on a bit, but end up losing her so I run into a restaurant to use the restroom. As I look back down the stairway I can see Phillip shifting his eyes to the left in his head, like you do when you want someone to notice something you can't let on you notice to the person you are noticing.

It's her – walking directly towards him out of the downstairs toilet! I rush back down the stairs to walk through her perfume and use the loo she used.

You are about to tinkle where Gloria, the famed Miami drag queen has tinkled.

Standing before the throne I notice that for all the lipstick and the hairspray, the high heels and the spandex, she's left the seat up. I guess there's just so much lady you can put in a man after all. I feel transported into another world out here.

You and me both.

Phillip's throwing me something he's calling a Sara-bration.

You have no idea how spectacularly I love this.

One of his friends has a boat moored in the canal that they call "The Dollar Yacht." It had been left for dead in a hurricane and the owner sold it just so someone would tow it away. So Phillip's friend bought a boat for a buck and we're having a party on it.

The sun is on its way down so we've got lots of candles burning. We'd been out earlier shopping for food so there's tons of yummy cheese, dip, carb greatness being devoured. Friend after friend breaks open another bottle of something, children are running on the boat's rooftop and laughing. I sit back and watch Phillip with his condo people and friends. They glide around each other as family. There's all this energy of support and of rejoicing with one another.

For one another.

I smell it going right through my skin with the mosquito spray and the tidal sway. I want to unmoor the boat so we'll float away.

You're high.

But it's still true. Phillip has given me the gift of seeing him through these people's eyes. We hadn't spent a lot of quality time hanging out together in college. We spent three intense years of every day in school with each other, but we weren't confidantes. Here on this yacht he's included me with his dearest friends. For a minute the Patsy Cline drifts off and all I hear is laughter and three conversations merging. It's one of those moments when you sit back and watch a friend in all that he is.

He's so present with who I am - I hadn't expected that. There is a union forming here that is unexpected. He is kind with his listening, his support. He is genuine in his love and encouragement.

And he's the first one along the way to confront you with answering questions honestly.

He does, yes. He asks questions of me that I can't ask myself. Not on the outside. He's the first person who calls me out on the truth of where I am. He sees the rose tinted version of the voice I offer up about my life, and of people that have impacted me.

"When you look deeper inside, be truthful about what you see. Be direct. Don't just say what you think will please other people. Say what you honestly feel," he said. That's a darkness placeholder to me. I shy away. I've slipped out the back door with you often enough. "Your journey seems to be about finding the best in people. Be careful there, that you're not escaping what you see on another level that might not be so perfect. Don't hide behind any of it."

"That's difficult for me. Of course there are things that I don't want to say and that comes from my own insecurity. I want people to like me, even if they're Hitler, and that's a big problem for me."

"You don't want to offend anyone by telling them how you honestly feel, is that it?"

"That's messed up, isn't it?"

"There's no way you can have an honest connection with what people have brought into your life, the good and the shitty, unless you admit to the whole package."

"It's all a gift. I know that. I do. I need to go back over it."

"You need to just allow yourself to ask the question, and then show up and answer it." Face up to it and tell the truth, that's where he lives. Communicate things as they are; bring them to light. Concerns should be brought to the forefront.

Examine the dust molecule, not the shiny surface.

When he says this, it confuses and unsettles me completely.

It should.

But it turns on the shadow light.

Truth lives in revelation. We have lived on a planet called concealment, you and I.

More of a galaxy I'd say. I see what he means, I do. It's not just about honoring the sacred part of who we are to each other - it's about who we are completely, out in the open.

You need to release the fear you've attached to speaking your mind.

It's ok to reveal us without fear of judgment because there's no anxiety between friends.

There may well be, but what if there is? That's all part and parcel of it.

I know this.

Then speak it.

I watch the last four days of my time dance on top of the water like tiny cracked mirrors.

Phillip was a dark horse.

This is not the friendship I had anticipated, not the one I expected to say, "Anything you need you just have to let me know." But he is. Seeing him at the beginning of this journey, as it had been planned originally, wouldn't have had any where near the same impact as visiting with him now, at the end. He's helping balance my unveiling. Trusting in the timing of everyone around us, Cooper - that has been our key. Where they live gave us our direction, and that has been the compass of our unfolding.

Relationship Intuition Number Twenty-Six: **The Bridge Friendship**. This friendship is the face of yourself that you haven't accepted. It is the voice of courage, the one that says they know the journey thus far has been shaky, that the tower will fall, but at the other end there will be a hand to meet you, and guide you to the outer banks. It is the steadying hand. They remind you that whatever crumbles before you, your strength comes from living in the truth of what you know.

If I were to give this kind of friendship a sound, Cooper, it would be the moment right before the first raindrop hits your face. It's quite beautiful. I'll pay attention next time it looks like rain, and you'll understand.

There is a quiet on the plane ride home from Miami. My knuckles, typically white with tension, pay no notice of takeoff. I'm thinking not just about what Phillip said, but of Phillip himself and how moving it is that he's gone so quickly

329

from a person tucked away in the far past, almost discarded, to a vital, supportive and present friend. I wonder how much of this might bleed over to the reunion at the lake in Austin. It'll be my last stop, the official end to all this wandering.

Your forty-eighth birthday.

So, to a lake retreat on June 1ᵗ. We can let balloons go into a drunken sky and eat cake. It's seems odd that this is the last - that all that road is behind me.

As if it would be endless.

Yet here we are. I'm running out of faces.

One hundred and fifty-four.

That many?

Two more to go.

It seems right to end with a mix of revisiting and new faces then. And to be at D'Ann's grandparent's lake house - I love it here. It's peaceful. We can bathe in it or shatter the heck out of it.

Ally's flown in from Portland, Viola from Minneapolis, Patti and Zoe, the two last faces to see, are coming in from San Antonio and Atlanta respectively; William's already in Austin, and Kathy and I drive in from Dallas. The last time we were all together was seventeen years ago at D'Ann's wedding.

We stand around staring at each other in a comical ridiculousness, before sprinting into Margaritas, vodka tonics, dips and chips, kolaches, and Mexican food. William as the only man dubs us his sister wives and assigns us our order of importance according to what we have on offer for him. Patti's number one wife because she cooks and makes a mean margarita. Ally cooks and knows fine wines, so she's wife number two. My talent appears to be indifference, which doesn't go down very well, so I'm at the bottom as number seven. Ha!

Our new hodgepodge of a family sit around the table in the open living area laughing until our sides ache, playing board games, drinking, eating flame red Cheetos and all things bad for us because they're good for us right now. Viola's gone back to school to study Shiatsu so she gives us all massages. By finding the pain others hold inside each pressure point, her own slowly moves into a catharsis. That she's practicing by moving it through all of us is lost on no one. There's a little bit of magic here. We're all soothed and tipsy in it until the last one of us passes into daybreak.

330

The next morning Patti tries to teach us Yoga, so we hang in a hung over version of downward dog before eating the biggest birthday cake I've ever seen.

I LOVE that they all hold up a candle app on their iPphones and sing at you.

Sitting outside eating cake on the patio, mosquitoes feasting on us all like Christmas lunch, citronella burning, deer wandering below us, time has saved itself for us. We're still growing into each other.

And not just here at the lake.

The Facebook birthday dings come in - my own collective hive humming good things for me. Still, there's a shift: for all the times my phone has beeped with words of love, it hasn't actually rung with any kind of human sound on the other end of it.

Voice.

It's the last thing we choose. I read somewhere that children aren't able to discern tone of voice or facial expressions because they don't speak to each other enough. Communication lives in words now. It's easier to reach a lot more people to give birthday wishes to and I have heard from friends who'd never have called me in the first place today, which is incredibly cool. I'm grateful to connect with so many of them virtually, don't get me wrong. It feeds my ego. I just want to make sure that I'm not allowing it to replace my voice completely

Because that sound feeds your soul.

One by one we disappear. We're sad, obviously, and the hugs are long and often, but there's no sense of loss at all – quite the opposite in fact. We're committed to making this a yearly retreat. The Ladies of the Lake – that's what we're calling ourselves. Ally's idea. And most of us are so goal driven that we'll make sure it happens. The beautiful thing is we reached out to see if there was an interest in getting together, and we all said yes. We showed up for each other and what we have at the end of this weekend is an entirely new building. We shared confidences at the table in a way that we might not have done with anyone else. We could have chosen to surface gossip about the past and make a few drunken revelations, but we didn't. It felt safe, warm, without judgment. What is it reminding me of?

There is a timing to each wound we have, and to whom it's opened.

I know what it feels like - it feels like that net that tightrope walkers have underneath them in case they fall. That's what it felt like to open up to them. They were below if it got too much.

I stay on with D'Ann and Lila for another week. It feels good to spend more time with them. It hasn't even been five months since Lucius died and although you're never sure how much help you are by being present, I think I need it as much as they do. There is a comfort to us that flows understanding. I am myself with her, like with no one else. Now she has this gorgeous little girl, Lila, who stands in the corner of the front room by the wall of mirrors looking at videos and laughing at her daddy. Now, these months later when she asks where he is, she's not asking about where he is in the world, but that she needs help finding his picture in the machine. She knows where Daddy is, where he's come to lie. Relationships settle in new places and theirs has settled into its own reality.

At night she likes to go out and say goodnight to the moon.

"My daddy needs help getting to the moon," she says. "Wolf is coming."

"Is he the wolf protecting you from all the world?" I ask her. She's nodding at the moon. The owl is out at night in her too. She's insistent that he is out there, that she can hear him. Sure enough, when you go outside and listen the owl is right there and Lila's eyes light up and she smiles and concentrates with all of her might to hear him again. Then she looks up at the moon, stretching her eyes as far as she can see and waves off her love to her father.

These aren't stories her family have told her, or that she's read in a book, this is her mind translating a story from a time gone by, from whispers in the night.

Time is stealing piece by piece, the treasure of what is held most dear to her – his smell, voice, laugh, the way he used to look at her when she thought he wasn't looking, the feeling of his arms holding her tight. All these things are stolen into time's tornado disappearing off the plain like a bandit in the night. Time is a healing thief. I've never felt so thankful for something, and so completely destroyed by it at the same time. Lila is onto him though, and she's hidden her father somewhere safe away from him - up there in the white light.

Part 8 Bone Spur:

Bone, a firm substance more or less hollow or cellular internally and consisting of earthly matters.
Bone Breccia, a conglomerate of fragments of bones cemented into a rock by a red calcareous concretion.
Spur, from a root meaning to kick; an incitement or stimulus; something that projects; a mountain mass that shoots from another mountain mass and extends for some distance; to urge or encourage to action.

- The Library of Universal Knowledge

A Trail of Song

I need to remember my stories not because I need to find out about myself but because I need to found myself in a story
I can hold to be mine.
- James Hillman

Back in Dallas a week or so later, I take a walk around the lake and sit on a bench by the old swing set we used to hang out on after hours during high school. I'm scrolling through Facebook looking into faces I know pretty well now. I come to a picture on Gregory's page that makes me go back and look at it again. I've only seen him here and there over the last few years. That first year after the end came we didn't speak at all. It was the big "fuck you" that happens when your heart falls on the floor. Then after a year, just as I'd learnt not to expect an email from him, one arrived a year to the day after we broke up.

He apologized.

He wanted to see if there was any sign of life for us.

To remain friends.

We'd known each other eighteen years at this point, and that's a long time to have someone as a part of your life. If it can be healed, it's worth the time. I believe it is anyway.

So does he. Your closeness just needs redefining.

So, with a cup of coffee here, a glass of wine there, we took it an inch at a time trying to find our way back into a friendship. This time the value is on the friendship alone, there's no sex to brush past and end an argument anymore, nothing to hide behind – we have an opportunity to handle the truth of each other, to get passed where all the hurt ran like a nosebleed. And we've eased into it pretty well. We're on good terms and he's been very supportive and encouraging to me. He owns a theatre and dance studio now. He runs it with his fiancée.

So as I'm scrolling through Facebook, looking at pictures of a children's show they're doing, something about this one picture, makes me stop.

That's when I notice it.

Look at it again.

I look at it again. The kids are caught mid smiles and laughter, the lights are bright, and Gregory's face is exuberant. There they are, he and his fiancée. They look happy. And I want him to be happy. A lot of people don't understand that, they look at me as if I'm in denial. Forgiving comes easy to me. I don't know why, but it does. It's my only grown up skill. I don't see any use in not forgiving. God knows I've had a pass or two in my own life.

Look at it again.

This photo - they're standing in the distance, it's a long shot, not close up. They're standing, hand in hand, smiling; a curtain call end to a kid's recital. How cute.

Something's off though.

Something seems slightly off about her. It's the waistline - the waistline on her dress is too high. It looks funny. I zoom in as tightly as I can on an iPhone – zeroing in just on her. Maybe she just got fat. That would be cool. Well, no, I mean, it wouldn't, but you know. She's a dancer though for goodness sake, she's all muscle. But not today. Not in this photo. This isn't muscle.

There is a bump on this road.

I set the phone in the grass, face up but away from me. It stares into my peripheral. I know what I see. I know what it is. I sit for a long time. Still. Nothing moves. But I can feel it all coming back, all the anxiety welling up inside my gut, the sadness gathering in a tornado of bile. I thought I was over this.

You have your three-year chip in scar tissue to prove that.

My old mind is kidnapping me, lighting the fire to everything I thought I'd burned already.

You know what you see.

I thought I was beyond all this falling backwards shit. It isn't fair. I feel out of control again. I'm looking at something that should make me happy for him, but I don't want to see it.

You're processing it. It's a natural reaction.

Failure.

Perspective.

I don't have perspective, that's just it - that's the first thing to fly out the window, despite everything I've tried. I shouldn't be crumbling apart. I've done everything the self-help books told me to do. I should be prepared for this. I tried everything, found every type of therapy there is - traditional psychiatry, Rapid Eye Therapy, Journal Therapy, Church retreats. I've seen every type of therapist you can think of. I'd taken back my mental health. I was cured, wasn't I? They can't all be quacks. I believed it. I put my soul out there, handed it over. I should be okay with all this. I'm a well-adjusted, mildly happy human being. I've been transformed. I've been on a journey of self-discovery, for goodness sake, I should be fucking bionic. I even dug up Eckhart Tolle's *Power of Now* partner to try that new electro therapy. I bet you couldn't believe it when I found him. Like he was *waiting for you* - and he lives around the corner. Even if he lived on the highest mountain in Tibet though, I'd have got on a plane, a boat and a rickshaw to get to him. But no, *he's right here,* because that's the train I'm on - everything I need is where it needs to be.

This situation is the same. It's in front of you now for a reason.

I did try to distract myself, when I get to Tolle's pal's house, remember?

You can't take your eyes off his white socks.

Why doesn't he have shoes on? It annoys me, I mean it really annoys me for some reason, but I let him attach electrodes to my head anyway and re-wire that one still active thought of what I'd done *to me? You think this is just about me?*

It *is* about you.

It's about us. What it cost us.

I needed that moment to go.

But that moment is more than those seconds when I passed through you - it's the twenty-six years of your own life that came afterwards that you swallowed down.

It's all just a memory, so why can't it just be one and move on? I asked him to move it away. God help me, but I did.

I know you did.

335

I let you down. I dismissed you. I tried to annihilate you.

I didn't feel dismissed.

I thought it was the only way to save myself. You have to understand – you were the first thing I saw when I woke up every morning, and my last thought at night, as if you'd just left me. I'd hung on to you as long as I could. I thought this might allow me to let go. It didn't have to be permanent, just for a little while, you know. A mini excommunication.

I knew what you felt was eating you alive.

It wasn't your fault. I didn't want to erase you, just the feelings that it gave me.

I know, Ma. I understand, I do. I'm so sorry. You were never out of my sight.

He promised that it would move that moment from the part of my brain that told me it had just happened to a part that would catalogue it as a memory. And it worked. You stayed behind. Except that you were gone.

But you willed me back to you.

I made myself ill. I didn't care what it took. There would be evidence that we'd been a part of each other because I knew I would never have a voice of my own until the one I stole was given one.

And you have. We have.

But now here she is. Here Gregory is, and he gets to, what? Have what I don't? I have been unloading this bag of bricks, one by one along the road, all year, all across the land, and when I turn to shake it out there's one more photograph inside?

Yes.

No. It could be the light in the photo, perhaps it's distorted. I need someone else to see it.

I say nothing. Repression is nothing if not always there when I need it - hiding in the old hip pocket. A few weeks later I show the photo to William when I zip down to Austin. I meet him at his apartment before we go back down to the lake with D'Ann. I show him the picture. I say to him, look, look at this picture, the girl in the picture. If you had one word to describe her what would it be? And I wait.

For the word you already know.

I've said it in my head a thousand times.

But never out loud.

"Well," he says, "pregnant." Hey, William could be wrong too - a shadow in the light in the photo distorting shape.

You should probably just face it and ask the question. Just ask Gregory the question.

It'll have to wait until I get back to Dallas. I'll just wait a few more days. I mean it's not like I can just call him up and ask him.

Why not just call him up? This is the kind of happy news that friends share, isn't it?

Except maybe with the one person whose childbearing years have disappeared, perhaps not her. No, I can't think about this right now.

I switch the photo to off, and we all get in D'Ann's car back to the voodoo lake where I can swim in denial.

Perhaps it's what you need anyway.

Yes. What the three of us share, D'Ann, William and I, feels like a collective brain regaining all of its parts. We make each other stronger. We stand around the island in the kitchen by the lake for hours. My legs don't ache, or sway, or buckle. We don't sit. We're in a state of meditation, with, perhaps for, one other. Maybe it is magic water down in the lake that's revitalizing us because it feels like we have this communal knowledge we're feeding off. There is blood in any battle, especially the one for ourselves, and in this room we meet to cushion the consequences. It's a place to lay our fears on the table, to speak them out loud and let them follow us home, outside of the jar that we packed them in for the trip. They won't last long out in this atmosphere.

"There's this experiment I was reading about," D'Ann says, "that given the choice people were asked if they would rather have an electric shock, or be alone with their own thoughts. Most people chose the electric shock."

"Are people so afraid of their own thoughts?" William says, answering the question as he finishes his vodka Fresca drink.

Any input, Sara?

"But surely if you had the electric shock you'd be locked inside your own thoughts forever instead of facing them to overcome them. Being alone with your thoughts you'll feel more of yourself than you would with any shock, don't you think?"

Would you rather have an electric shock than go back up to Dallas and ask your question?

I'd rather walk out into the lake in a Virginia Woolf rock moment. I am Lot's wife again.

Edith.

337

Looking back just like Edith, just like she did, despite my Salton sea'd heart.

I get back to Dallas with the idea of facing the photograph head on.

Which is not easy for you.

I'm not a head on kind of person, never have been. So, I know he doesn't know I know.

But you know you know.

I text, "I want to come and see your show tonight." The bubble, bubble of the text reply is working overtime but not giving me any words, until, "We're sold out. Wish I had known." Built in avoidance for me. Perfect.

Only he invites you to lunch.

Ok, so this is it, he's going to tell me. Mexican restaurant, there will be tequila. I order two.

"So, what's up, anything new?" I say. Only it doesn't come. He doesn't say a word about it. We have lunch, get back to our cars and, zip, nothing. Interesting don't you find though, that I don't bring it up either. Why don't I ask him about it?

Why don't you bring it up? You have salt in your veins now. You've already turned.

I should be crumbling about in my own openness.

What does it mean for you even if it's true anyway?

Right? I want him to be happy. He needs something like this, a child. Who am I to deny someone that walk just because it's not mine? I'm so tired of this. Put a period on it already. I'm so angry at all the wasted time in my life, of all the avoidance, the denying, the choices I didn't make, could have made, should have made, must have made, at time for not letting me cut in line. Now I'm so far back it's like one of those twisted Disney lines where the ride seems just around the corner and when you round the bend you see it's been closed for the last hour. Why does life go on moving in so many grown up directions for everyone I know, except for me - for me it doesn't. I keep making these dumb ass choices, like spending almost forty grand traveling the world visiting everyone I've ever known.

What, instead of saving it, or putting a down payment on a house in a city you don't want to live in.

But that's not how I feel, so why am I feeling it? It's like my neck has grown another head and they're chatting away at each other.

338

"Why wasn't it me?"

I don't like that question.

You don't like the answer either.

I push it under the rug that I've just had dry-cleaned. It's only one thing after all, right? Like that first charge you put on your credit card, it's just one thing. It'll be easy to pay off. And hey, maybe it's not true; maybe I'm just seeing things that aren't there. My mind skips back on some kind of rewind, reviewing the files, accessing the ones still in the delete queue.

Those words are archaic.

They spew into my mind anyway. Why are they so easy to believe again?

What is there to believe in any of that?

That there's never going to be someone that looks at me and wants all of me. That who I am is never enough. Why doesn't my hand fit inside anyone else's?

It does. It fit in mine.

No it didn't. I didn't let it. I never let anyone stay long.

You just need to get this out.

What is so completely wrong with me, why can't I be where I need to be? What am I going to do when someone that I really do care about shows up? He'll withdraw, he will.

Only if you do.

There must be something in me so repellant that makes me compatible with no one. Why aren't I enough for someone the first time out?

Well, the right guy, if he likes you –

Sure, yeah, he'll find a way to be with me. But he hasn't. Most women my age have found stability with someone, so if something like this comes in they have a foundation to support them. Not me though. I don't.

It's growing underneath you. You've sensed it. I know you have.

I feel so utterly exposed.

You're spinning inside the circle. You aren't the circle.

I'm drunk in it.

Some things are not destined to be yours.

I've seen them.

You couldn't have. They were never there.

You should go now.

That's not your decision this time. And incidentally, I love you.

A day later Gregory must have realized I'd be seeing his fiancée at some point, so he knows he should tell me.

What you're forgetting inside your own feelings is that it's not going to be an easy thing for him to tell you.

He knows that this moment is going to be difficult for me, yes. That it might shatter a little piece of my heart. What he doesn't know is that this has already happened. I'm already split. When I see him I've prepared for this moment as much as I can. It's not raw to me. Raw is under the rug building up 19.9% interest. I've practiced this face in the mirror.

He begins.

"Something has happened that's changed my life. Well..." he stammers on a little bit. I know what he's going to say, but maybe it's still not true. I'm watching his face discover how exactly he's going to tell me. Maybe I got it all wrong. I see such a panic, a strange kind of sadness and fear mixed in with a joy he's trying to squash back down. I wish he didn't feel like he had to do that. It still may not be true. "Well, you see, I'm going to be a..."

Going to be a what? A teacher? An adventurer? An astronaut? Alive to the sound of music? Going to be a what? I'm not sure I can do this.

Allow him to do what he has to do to you.

"I'm gonna be a dad." Face ready I stand up, hug him. Smiling.

"How wonderful. You've always wanted a daughter, you'll have a girl, of course you will. It's so great." The percentage rate on all this is way too high. "Wow. Wow," I'm saying with a slight bit of throw up in my throat. He plays it down. He knows how it's affecting me - that I'm putting on a brave face, 'cause that's what I do. That's the part of me he knows the best, the part that would rather just get it all over with without facing the real truth inside of any situation. And so, bless his heart he tries to soften the blow by telling me he wishes the baby was mine. And he's talking on and on and I'm in and out, but I look like I'm listening. He's not in a good place right now with the business, what does he have to offer, it's not the right time. I'm countering him with words about how these things happen for a reason, that maybe the timing will lead to some other great bullshit crap I don't know what, I'm talking out my ass, and trying to believe what I'm selling.

You're happy for him. He knows that. He's more concerned about you. He knows that part of you. He knows me. He's the only one that read that bad play you wrote about me. He knows that your heart is broken, and he knows that you see his heart is whole.

I get into my car and drive deeper into the parking lot out of sight. I'm dizzy in the head like my blood sugar is way too low, and I sit a while, and it starts to rain, it starts to rain hard, and I'm crying in such a way that's out of control and has no choice but to turn into hysterical laughter. I don't want to be the only one who's not capable of creating life, that can't carry it and support it. Why am I stuck out here alone with this?

You're not. Oh, please don't disappear.

I've still got most of my insides, a uterus and one fairly well functioning ovary, and it's worked before. There's some magic trick to this. I've been put in a box and sawn in half. Why wasn't it me?

It was you. Once. And you said, no.

I said no.

Meant to say, no.

By saying yes.

So we are met.

Not yet. There's more, isn't there?

Yes. One thing more.

The rain is still coming down. I put the windshield wipers on extreme. The splashing sound is coming down in waves and takes me back to Oregon.

You need to go back there to understand what happened to you. You're sitting with the family planning a trip to England, remember?

We're all tired.

But you have this idea.

I say that when we arrive in London we should take the train straight from Heathrow, and head to the coast while we're tired anyway. No one seems to respond to the idea, *and even though they've gone beyond it, I say it again* – that even though it'll be a long day for the kids, isn't it better than two days of travelling. And my brother, *without any intention of unkindness* says, "you don't have children, Sara, you just don't understand."

You're sitting so quietly. It makes me nervous.

It's that Virgin Bone Woman rattling the last few bones hastily into place.

You wait until she moves you.

I'm up amid the chatter. It's hard, holding on to my breath until I'm a safe distance away. I'm not sure what kind of noise I'm going to make. I'm thankful the beach is a short walk ahead. My feet hit sand. The water is another minute or two in

341

front of me, further away than I thought. It trickles into my feet. A ripple, no real waves to wreck my skeleton ship. I wade further out into the waters of Lethe for what seems like miles until the water reaches just below my knees.

I'm being induced.

The sand swallows each one of my toes all at once. Hungry. Bone not strong enough to take a stand. The old lady's behind on her work. I'm melted almost ankle deep. I meet the pressure of the tide pushing back towards the shoreline. It's coming in.

Is it allowing you relief?

Yes.

Do you feel what that's like?

I remember what that's like. I don't have happy memories.

There is no resentment in this pressure. Do you feel what that's like?

I don't allow it in.

You do. You sit down in it.

I sat down, yes, with the water breaking around me.

And you held on to Mnemosyne.

I'm so tired.

Just let go of whatever it is you think it is and forget about me.

It's yellow.

Your favorite color.

It's feels like being drunk, sober. It's never broken. It's a fresh change of clothes. It's the smell of absolute absence. It weighs the same as my voice.

Forgiveness smells the same to me too. It's simple.

I'm holding on to it. I see it now.

You should recognize it - you've allowed others to smell it often enough.

I did. That's the one thing I got right. I embraced forgiveness.

Liar. Look at yourself out here. You gave it away? You can't give something you don't believe in yourself, can you? If you do, it means nothing. You never gave it to yourself. You couldn't when you kept blaming myself. That you can't shift from one part of your brain to the other, no matter how many electrodes you attach to your head. It's why I've come for you.

I jumped into forgiveness because it was the right thing to do.

You want everyone else to be okay. But you did that without landing myself in it. I wanted to move to the happy ending.

No, you wanted everyone else to move on to the happy ending while you stayed quietly behind taking it inside.

And I felt that, I did. I didn't know how to label it, or couldn't say it. Then I rushed through to fix it.

To control it. To still keep control of it. That way you could still breathe a tiny piece of it.

I took a cab when I should have walked. I skipped ahead. I went from one extreme to the other. All you, to no you - all *to know me. Letting go of the wrong thing. Dressing one thing up like the other. It wasn't me, you...* It wasn't you I had to let go of. *It was the thought you attached to me that you couldn't bear, that you've never been able to label.* Blame. *That's what you can't let go of. And now* Gregory's child, the child that meant so much.

The promise of me coming again.

She's arriving for only one of us.

The only place I could be with you was *to sacrifice yourself.* Yes, a sacrifice to equal *mine.* I made a conscious decision that success or love would never be mine. When I realized I needed to honor you instead, *you went to the other extreme.* From waking each morning with you and what your face might look like as the first picture in my mind, to moving you into a memory. When I did, *you skipped the walking of the bridge, and the bridge has to be crossed by all of us.* I want you to understand the reason I put those electrodes on my head was that I wanted to wake up for once in my life without the guilt of you in my tea. *But shifting me to memory isn't healing,* it's a different kind of denial. I geared up a busted backup generator. I hid more of who I am and filtered it into something else.

You put on a show. What I thought everyone wanted to see, *so they would accept you.* By not *listening to your own voice.* Again. And that's left me so incredibly lost. *So here we are* – a broken compass *trying.* Fixing back towards *north.*

True.

And then I saw the Newspaper Soldier.

And then you saw the Newspaper Soldier, a man you recognized in an impossible way.

So strange to stare into his eyes. The needle on my compass twitched in the not knowing unknowing of him.

Putting you in touch with an unfamiliar part of yourself.

343

My life changed completely the very moment that I saw him. It's implausible.

He is an improbable hero.

The algebra equation I can never solve.

And yet you believe in him anyway.

And then the 26s came.

Then the 26s came.

My grandmother died 26 years ago on the eve of the day I began this journey.

The Newspaper Soldier died on September 1ˢᵗ.

The first day of my own incubation in my mother's womb before the nine months it took to birth me.

It was him. He opened the door.

A Newspaper Soldier to keep me safe on the road, *to trust the way that you were going even though it felt counter to who you'd been.* He's what led me over the bridge to you. *For me to convince you to believe in all you should be. You mourned me without mourning for yourself.*

That's what I've been trying to do all along this road.

That's what you have been doing all along this road.

I have to mourn that. And what isn't mine, what will not be mine - that I hadn't chosen you, that you hadn't chosen me. And here it is in the face of the irreplaceable replaceable me in her high waisted dress, the family that could have been, but isn't.

I am the family you have – my invisible bones.

The bone spur in my heart.

The last breath that Visitation Man came for that first night is what truly separates us though.

You haven't spoken those four words alone yet.

I didn't tell you why I wanted us to be separate, the out of memory exorcism, because the whole point of the sacrifice was that we weren't. It's my fine print. All I need to do is give him what he won't give up on. But to lighten the blue-black icing is to spell out my complete exposure – big, my secret, manicured with dirty nails. Word salad.

Say it in the right order before I jump through the mirror to bite you.

It's the truth of "I." *The* I. "I" holds my voice hostage.

I made the decision.

You did.

I walked through that door of my own free will and choice. I listened to the lady tell me about regret and nodded yes anyway. I walked into that room and undressed from the waist down. I laid down on that table and even though the doctor said he'd stop because he knew I didn't want this, I calmed myself and said, no, go ahead. I allowed them to pass you through me without breath. That was me. All me. Whatever forgiveness I need to feel, or blame to place, there is none outside of my own mind or my own body. I released you to a bucket burial - no one else did that. That was me.

When I fell asleep the night I knew you were inside me, it was up against the wall that's right behind me, right behind me at my back as I'm writing this, and I want to step through a time continuum and understand because I don't understand myself, I don't. And to say I'm so sorry, not to you because you have forgiven, you have flown into who I am. The sorry isn't for you at all.

No, it's for you.

I'm sorry that I didn't give myself the gift of knowing what motherhood is, of knowing what the unconditional love of a child would be. That this is all I have - traveling in a car with a phantom of a child tucked inside recurring twenty six's and red light flashes of an airbag sign that only feels the weight of what could have been. And of knowing love, true love, of denying myself the strength to feel that in the name of you. *You won't show strength, you thought* - strength is appealing and it's a lie.

You know in the deepest bone taken that you've been denying the one thing I have craved since the abandonment of January 8th Ad 19 hundred and nameless – and that is allowing anyone to love me. I knew no one could possibly love me because of what I did to us - that I'd do whatever I could to push whoever got close to me away, to prove them wrong and find a weakness: too little attention for you? Not enough? Whichever one - *I'll give you the other.*

If I could go back thirty years and abandon all of you, all of you that love me, to make a different decision - I would. I wouldn't hesitate. I'd abandon you all because I've set myself up, haven't I? There is a man out there that I'm going to love with all of my heart and soul, as God loves you, and he will take such care of me, he will recognize me and we'll be attached at the heart because that's the way I was to you. Except he won't love me.

He will love you.

He won't love all of me. And that will be God's revenge.

God doesn't take revenge. And, yes, he will love all of you. A love all its own. You won't see it at first. But I can't do anything about that now. You've already asked. You with your one thing to control. But it will turn the corner. You're still breathing.

I couldn't speak up for you but I need your help to speak up for myself. I don't have to be forgotten.

You have to find your own voice outside of me. I have always had my own voice.

That voice is the only thing *that will restore you.* I just need to figure out how to speak the speech without you.

Think about that Japanese guy that did those experiments on the water molecules. He segregated each one. He treated some with hatred and they shriveled up and darkened. Some he treated with joy and beauty, *and they shone with lightness.* If a tiny molecule of water can react like that, then the over sixty percent of water that is inside of me has reacted the same way to all the negative talk and physical interactions that have come at me.

They revolted, and you have the zip line scar to prove it. It changed them.

But I am changing. I've told you the truth.

You've also told yourself the truth. Sitting with that the water can calm now.

Flying the Ashes

Prepare to drink the wine of the antagonist.
- Splendor Solis, The Inner Quest

Being home a short while I'm trying to wrap my mind around the stillness. In the garage I go through some things I packed away over the years. Trying to lift some things down, a spade falls onto the floor knocking one of the boxes off the top of the pile. The tape on it is so old that it crumbles through my fingers, and what's inside spills out at my feet. Amongst the old birthday cards, textbooks and paintings from my childhood, there is a notebook with a turquoise and red Japanese cover. To find it intentionally would have been like searching for a needle in a haystack.

I know this book.

I open the journal slowly, knowing the words have been waiting for me.

> December 22- I'm late. Maybe he won't leave.
> I don't know quite what I'll do when he
> leaves. If he loved me it would be different –
> but he doesn't.

> January 12 - I can't get used to my new space
> alone. If it all ends with him too, it will have
> all been for nothing. I'm having trouble living
> with myself as it is.

> April 21 - It is incredibly hard to have any
> kind of motivation – it is absent beyond the
> doing of a simple task. I feel as if I have
> abandoned my child. I can't seem to let go
> and get on with my life. It is beyond me that
> one day I will be capable of it. My heart is
> melting wax.

I haven't read this since the day it was written.

This is our conception. The part where I was alive inside of me. We're caged in these pages. The

347

moment I swallowed our dialogue is right here.

Until a year ago when we set foot outside this door and drove away.

No, the night of my dream when you crushed my body into giving you my last breath; sitting there in the doctor's office tossing my heart up and down against the wall like a baseball.

It's the only way I had to breathe – you understand that.

All I wanted was one breath together.

No, you wanted a lifetime of it, but I can only give you this one.

The last year has been the exhale I needed to let you leave, to cut the umbilical cord I wrapped around my neck.

It's the inhale I needed to give you yourself back.

Every breath strengthens my voice. I'm beginning to hear what that sounds like because of you.

And you know what it has to say.

You would have been 26 years old at the inception of this journey, Cooper. The presence of 26, is you. *Always me.* It's pushed me back to this space, to this bedroom in my parent's house where we *were alive together. I'm working my way back from the pile of memory lists at the back of your brain, to bring you back to the front.*

The next morning I go out into the garden. At the foot of the old Maple tree a small broken baby mockingbird has fallen from its nest. Wings tucked to her side, covered in insects, she is slowly being eaten. I stare at her, watching the pieces slowly disintegrate and carried off into waste memory. I wonder if her heart stopped first, or last. I think of both my grandfathers, one whose heart was so strong that even as the rest of his body shut down a fragment at a time, it held tight. The waiting for his passing was all contingent on his heart accepting that it had to break. And of the other whose heart gave out before everything else. It's his old shovel that fell on the box that spilled the journal of Cooper's first breath. It's still lying on the garage floor where I left it. I take it back into the garden and scoop the bird into a burial plot under my mother's orange marigolds. As I drop earth over the top of her, a small flock of birds, the mother and three other babies, fly out of the nest looping around me and through the branches of the tree singing away in non-Disney lyrics. I am Snow fucking White.

348

Walking back towards the garage my left leg gives way. There's an already swollen looking blistered mosquito bite with two holes in it. Some vampire thing with fangs has bitten me just above the knee. The wound is getting white and puffy and it aches to the point where I'm not able to put a lot of pressure down. I put up the shovel and within a matter of minutes my leg has turned from white and swollen, to purple, black and bruised.

I Google it, as you do – most likely a Brown Recluse. And it is, judging by its evolution so far. 'Vomiting, fever…" I minimize the screen when images of flesh eaten skin scroll around. If I don't see it, it's not happening to me. Should I go to the emergency room? There's a $500 fee for that on my insurance. To heck with that, it may be nothing. Man, though, whatever is happening is happening at an alarming rate so odds are the poison is already in route to my heart, or eating away, or whatever it's doing. I'll wait it out and see what happens. I don't need my left leg to drive anyway. For now I'll put it up and get the blood back to my heart - that's what they do on TV anyway, and those TV shows do a lot of research. I mean they pay people to make that stuff accurate. So I'll just put my leg up, it's probably nothing. A friend of my sister's has given me all sorts of miracle natural oils so I pour a little bit of each one on top of the holes and massage them in. Who knows? I'll just believe it'll work. I have spider venom running through me, why fight it. I'll go along to wherever it's delivering me. I pile up the cushions and watch the blackness take over my leg like a time-lapse nature show and smother it in more essential oil. All there is now is to wait for the mad fever to seize me.

It comes, but not in the shape I had expected it.

In the early morning hours, I'm jarred awake by a fly flapping frantically and buzzing inside my eardrum. It's the loudest of the loud of any word or sound I've ever known. I sit bolt right up screeching, pulling at my ear with such violence I'm almost ripping it off. And this poor fly can no more escape than I can swat it away. We're stuck with each other, locked in the same panic of how to escape each other, so we battle on for seconds until the sound war dies out of my ear and he's finally able to make his escape.

I turn on the bedside table lamp and pull the sheet away from my leg. I almost expect to see thousands of tiny spider eggs spinning in my veins hatching out of my matter like in some horror movie I'd never watch and have now been forced to live out – but there's only the blackness with a hue of purple around it like a kind of royal seal.

Prey in one form or another has been coming for me since day one in my dreams, but this is something different, this isn't a dream, this is real animal noise, and I know what I have woven already is coming for me to realize myself. I'm not scared, I'm not clenched up, or tired out, or annoyed. I have no idea what's ahead, but I know it's right to embrace what's gone behind.

The words in the Japanese journal of 26 years ago were waiting in the box, on the top of a stack, knocked over by a spade that buried the bird, that carried the spider, to attract the fly to wake me. I'm an Aesop fable.

I try to drift back to sleep, but the open window for a visitation inside my nighttime head arrives again. In this dreaming I'm not sleeping, I'm lying in full consciousness, my eyes wide open. I can't see anyone, or anything except in my peripheral vision. I watch my right shoulder being pushed backwards into the pillow. It's not voluntary, and I don't like it. I can feel his invisible hand pressing me down, lightly at first and then with more pressure, but there is no one here. I know what's coming next. I know because I've been waiting for it. Perhaps this new venom throbbing in my blood has invited it in, encouraged it I suppose, giving me a strange comfort in that the waiting is over, no matter the outcome. The invisible presence pulls the covers off me. I stare into my throbbing leg. Veins of red spike out of the purple seal reaching down it, moving the infection through me like a wave. They zigzag down and out of the bottom of my right foot, out onto the bedclothes and up into the walls.

The invisible hand that pushed my shoulder down has cupped itself behind my back now and pushes me up away from the bed. It's not voluntary, and I don't like it. I want to get control back and I want to wake up, but piece-by-piece my body is lifted from the bed. It isn't violent, I'm not jerked about, there's something of the sacrament about it, but it's not voluntary. I'm not doing this, and I can't see who is. I'm floating in mid-air, shifted from horizontal to upright, being pulled to the top left corner of the bedroom. At first I feel a kissing, gentle lips on the purple injury above my knee - the toxin is being sucked out of me. It turns yellow when it finds oxygen. It streams out of me and across my walls. The poison sculpts into letters that linger an inch away from the wall, and there is candlelight, and I am drifted passed them slowly, so

350

slowly, shards of words, and a steady kind rhythm relaxes my body.

My arms expand lifting wide sleeves of cobweb. They shine like they do in my memory, over the hedges in a small village in England on the first frost. My skin is see-through. I look at my hands and even though this is my flesh, these are the bones of another, of the visitation, of my son. They split in through mine to operate me like a puppet. We are draped and hovering. There is no fear and I don't suppose there ever truly should have been. *I always took your heart out of me, but I only took the piece you'd already given to those who came before,* that I'd given my love to completely. *Here is the other 5/8ths of it that still beats just as well. Your whole heart shouldn't be asked of from another. Parts of it have already been given and they belong to the taker. That part is theirs and always will be. You gifted it, it was taken and no one else can ever access it. The rest is full and open and free to love. The remainder is your whole heart now.*

The bedroom walls expand and open into worlds and we are flying. I'm walking you home. The wound above my knee begins to throb and tiny threads of my own antidote seep out the yawning holes – the fever is alive and extracted beyond me.

When we land on the floor you walk out of me towards the window, out onto a ledge high above land - far higher up than it should be. I see you like I would through the bottom of a glass held high to drain the last few drops of wine – the thickness of a world all topsy-turvy at the bottom of it. You're that last bit of burgundy slipping down my throat as I realize it's still daylight and I'm already drinking. The animal that morphed into a man that returned as an alien with no eyes, is now completely transparent. I see you. I see the child.

I see you.

It's okay. Go on.

Do you really think I should?

He holds me in his eyes for a few seconds before he smiles. Then he gazes back around, away from me, curves his body and free falls lightly into a watery slow motion absent from me. He falls. I stare down and watch as the white web floats into a million tiny pieces.

When I turn around there is a long stretch of road ahead of me, dust is flying up and I'm walking into it carrying a venom,

351

the one that is real and flowing and fighting its way through my blood stream.

I drift back awake slowly. I don't shudder, I don't gasp. I simply wake up. The covers are at the foot of the bed, the fan is blowing a wind through my nightdress and my leg throbs a yellow hue. I have slept out the fever of it in both worlds.

The Friendship Revolution

We shall not cease from exploration
And the end of all our exploring
Will be to arrive where we started
And know the place for the first time.
- T.S Eliot

Morning of day last.

The real end is the journey, and so I end at the beginning.

I saw the moving van come the week before. One of those fireman truck moving services that you expect buff, pin up calendar men to jump out of – except it's skinny young kids with their pants hanging around their ass instead. I'd seen the truck being loaded up, but I could still see the umbrella stand through the front window. When an Estate Sale sign eventually did appear with that, everything must go look about it, my first thought was that one or both of them must have died.

Walking passed the house with Stanley I see all these people going in and coming out with coolers, plates, towels, slightly chipped dog statues, purses with one broken zipper – all those pieces of someone's life that made up a family once, are now leaking out in dribbles.

Thirty-three years ago I knew the insides of this house so well because my high school friend, Dana, lived here. Her parents still owned the house. I'd see her mom every once in a while, getting the mail. Dana had moved off to Utah, at least that's what her sister said a few months ago when I'd seen her outside the house.

Moving from a small, rural village in England to the vast, barren fields of Dallas, Texas I felt like one of those worms that crawls out of the grass because of the rain, only to get burnt by the sunshine before it can wriggle back to the lawn to start drowning again. Dana was my first real friend. She was on the drill team - I didn't know what that meant at the time but apparently they're all stuck up and can't be seen talking to people like me in case the cheerleaders find out and shun them. I'd thrown myself into the theatre, which didn't improve my popularity at all, but Dana still spoke to me. We must have met in class – I can't remember exactly - and she lived here, only a few houses down from me, so I was always over at her house. I ate my first corn dog here and gagged on my first iced tea. Ice in tea?

She had the thickest, most beautiful brown hair and was always smiling. She didn't care that I wore gold shoes, had a bad home perm, and didn't know what a sponge hair roller was. She was kind anyway. And she was one of the only people who never made fun of my accent - not like all the other kids did. She always included me with her drill friends and invited me over to hang out and play music and have dinner at her house.

Moving here, to these barren lands where I assumed buffalo were still being skinned and eaten I didn't know what to expect. Would I be forced to dig for oil or heard cattle? I only knew it would be a world away from singing folk hymns at the village hall. Dana made the acceptance that I was here to stay more bearable.

We went our separate ways during 11th grade – drifted away as you do. We still talked in the halls and were always friendly, but we ultimately ended up at different colleges with different dreams.

I wish I could remember more about her. It's at times like these I wish I'd bought that year book I thought was so ridiculous with all its team spirit and popular people poster children slashed across the pages, the ones who belonged to every club I didn't understand the purpose of. All of them smiling alongside the smiling faces of the bullies that threw spitballs of multi-colored paper in my hair so my short curls looked like a burning bush. Fuck no, I'm not buying that piece of shit memory hole. Fuck you. That's what I thought at the time. But right now I'd like to see Dana's face. Here in front of me now I might just have the next closest thing.

So this Sunday I walk into Dana's childhood home - through a front door I haven't knocked on since I was seventeen years old. As I put my hand on the doorknob the door swings wide open as the back end of a small blue love sofa bashes the side of it - like it doesn't want to leave and it's trying to hang on to where it's been. It's been a few years since it'd travelled the other way, new and valuable. Pillows fall to the wayside on the front steps - I pick them up and brush that annoying bronze colored leaf that sticks into everything off of them. I'd sat on that couch, spilt soda on it and not told anyone; lost coins in it. I ask the man helping to carry the couch if he's moving out.

"Oh, no it's not my house. The lady that owns it hired us as a service to handle the estate sale. She's moving in with her daughter." There you have it then. She's moving. Where'd he go?

It's an odd feeling to be somewhere you've been welcomed into thirty-two years ago that now you stand in as just one of the stray people off the street to pick through lives that all connected together at some point.

It's the kitchen table I imagine each time I'd walk passed the house – that's where we spent most of our time, so that's where I head to first. Crossing through the living room, it feels barren. Piles of bits and pieces are scattered on tables. Everything that had been of any true value has already been taken out of the house and sent on to her room at the Inn. All that's left are those things that have that "let go of it" sign around their necks. Will we really read this book again even though Aunt Sally gave it to us? Do you really need any of these table clothes now, even though Grandma embroidered them because I've got plenty you can use. How difficult it must be to go over your entire life and put it into two piles: what you treasure most, and what you treasure and let go of.

It makes me uncomfortable being in so much disarray so I head straight to the kitchen, to the space that had always been my comfort zone; into a cozy corner frozen in time. This area of the house hasn't been touched at all. The small white table with four chairs still waits in the bay window with only one difference – a large, cold white sticker with the word, 'sold,' on it. I stand here for a few minutes picking up a plate and pretending to wonder if it'll fit in with my own fictional willow pattern plates, hoping to mask my real reason for standing there. I don't want to be seen as some freaky woman standing in a corner staring off into reminiscences. I want to sit down at the table one last time and look out of the window and see what I'd seen as a seventeen-year-old. Perhaps it'll act like some kind of time portal and slip me back for a do over. I scoot towards the seat on the right, the one I always sat in, lean on the table and scrunch down a little and look out. Although this is the same street I walk my dog down every day, that I drive up and down at will, this view can only be seen from this chair in this house and I want my almost fifty-

year-old eyes to see it the way my teenage eyes had. So I look.
I put the merkin plate down and just look out of the window.
More leaves are falling from the oak tree. I can see the side
fence where that boy lived across the road that I had a crush
on. I had no memory of him until I looked out this kitchen
window at this angle. What the hell was his name? I don't
know, but here he is, backpack over his shoulder, black
trousers and blonde buzzy haircut. It's nice to catch his eye – I
hadn't been that brave at seventeen. It seems okay to wink
back today.

"That's been sold," the lady in the entrance way
approaches me as if I'll break it by leaning on it.

"Yes, I see that. I was just looking out the window. I
thought I saw someone I used to know."

"Oh, well, it's sold, just so you know." I look back out of
the window.

"He's gone anyway," I say and pick up my plate, staring
into the wistful ladies posing.

As I pass through Dana's room to the adjacent bedroom I
walk through the bathroom I would have used. I catch myself
in the mirror and for just a split second the face that I used to
be stares at the face that is. I wish I had a clearer memory of
myself in this house, in this room, looking in this mirror,
knowing the people that waited for me on the other side of
this door. But I don't. I just know I've walked here and that the
last time I did still moves in this room like I'd left a slight
fragment of myself here.

In Dana's old room I find a copy of *The Library of Universal
Knowledge*, published in 1948. It weighs about five pounds, just
what you'd think all universal knowledge would, and it smells
like every generation that's ever lived. All the dust and
comfort of fading ink on aging paper. It's how time smells. I
soak it up on page 359, "ice," and I press my nose into it. No
one is leaving the house with this book but me. And at $2.50,
the cost of all universal knowledge is a bargain.

I'm still reading the definition of "ice" on my way home
and this story about a woman from Iceland pops into my
head. I read the newspaper article a few months ago. She was
on some sort of a bus tour and had gone into the restaurant
bathroom to get something to eat and to change her clothes
because she was cold after a strenuous hike. She didn't tell
anyone, and no one noticed her slip away. It took her longer
than expected and everyone else was waiting on the bus. The
troop leader panicked when he couldn't find her and thought

356

they'd lost her on the mountain so he alerted the rest of the tour and organized a search party. The woman came out of the restroom finding everyone about to go on this manhunt and joined in on the search. It's only in talking with one of the people she was travelling with that she realized they were looking for her. The headline in the newspaper read *Missing Woman Unwittingly Joins Search For Self*. I can't stop laughing all the way up the street. I collapse in my front garden on the roots of a tree that was planted here at the same time as I was. "Unwittingly joins search for self," that sums me up so perfectly. My life's struggle has been the inability to choose life consciously or unconsciously. In not choosing yours, I gave up my own. You and I formed a search party to go back into my life to see all of my friends and family after so many years' absence. You showed me how each one of my friends, each person that crossed my path, pushed me forward, held me back, pushed me down, pulled me up. They did so at the time, or waited for me to return with the words I needed to hear. By doing that there's only one person I was ever going to end up face to face with - me.

I've found a word for all of that though – **Ubuntu**. It means, I am the best version of myself because of my interactions with you. Getting inside of my car with you and one hundred and fifty-six friendships I was able to choose life for the first time. The gut of Ubuntu, our time together over the course of the last three hundred and sixty-five days, is love. People are not who they are without other people. I'm certainly not who I am without you present in me. We experience the deepest part of our humanity, create harmony in ourselves, through our close interactions with others. It's an umbilical baptism, a unique natural trusting of unity. What is at the heart of me? My friends. Just as you are to yours, they are to you, and I am to them. We are connected across the centuries. Argon comprises 1% of the air that we breathe; what I have breathed, you will breathe.

The Egyptian Book of the Dead says, "at the ends of the universe is a blood-red cord that ties life to death, man to woman, will to destiny." I touched that. It's still wrapped around my waist. Friendship surrounds you in trust, support, empathy, sympathy, honesty, and presence. It allows you the ability to be yourself, express your opinions and feelings without judgment. A friend walks you through mistakes, calls you out on your behavior when it's out of line and celebrates your accomplishments as her own. It's how we put love into action.

At the beginning I was invisible ink. In the rebuilding I listened for the tune that we all play together and I now I hear it whole. By traveling into the hearts of my friends I've found my own, and it's made it a better place to live. I had to trace back. I'd left my own story, our story, unheard. It lived in my heart as a tangled root, but traveling our Songline it returned to flesh. My stool isn't wobbling, Stephen.

We can't wonder at our own story, we should finish the waltz. We are a marble slab, perfect on arrival, and without form. Each person we meet, each provoked thought, hand raised, heart offered, chips away until we begin to take shape. That's how the wounds of my identity told me my story. I unpacked what happened to me. Each of us stands like any tree, in the same forest, across from one another, and underneath, buried down, our roots all reach out, tangling inside of each other's. We may stand above ground individually, but we're powered by the courage of our network as a whole.

What began as a bundle of bones turned into the breath of all. It breathes, so I breathe. We arrive together inside a friendship wholeness called, **Ubuntu: I am because you are.**

There are a few lines that stick with me from *Great Expectations*,

> Pause, you who read this, and think for
> a moment of the long chain of iron or
> gold, of thorns or flowers, that would
> never have bound you, but for the
> formation of the first link on one
> memorable day.

A seemingly simple encounter with one person can lead you to the one who regenerates your life in some way. Potential hovers in the first eye contact, new dynamics, new questions, joys, challenges, and happiness. Perhaps today, standing in a café waiting to meet Van, a friend of a friend, to talk about writing, perhaps that's what I'll find.

As I park the car, the airbag light on for the duration of the journey, blinks off.

I've been standing in line for coffee only a few minutes when I turn and see him by the doorway, his back to me, staring out the window. He's looking for me.

After word

What has happened to our ability to dwell in
unknowing, to live inside a question and coexist
with the tensions of uncertainty? Where is our
willingness to incubate pain and let it birth
something new? What has happened to patient
unfolding, to endurance? ...Yet the seduction is
always security rather than venturing, instant
knowing rather than deliberate waiting.

-Sue Monk Kidd

The depth of my gratitude goes to each and every one of
you for welcoming me across your thresholds and opening up
your inner most person to me. If the hamster wheel is spinning
this journey over and over until my last breath, I'd surely run
it with each of you.
Special thanks to Henry Loughman, Stephanie, Clay & Rowan
Towery, Jack Foltyn, Jenny Nolan, Louise, Bryson & Liv
Bullington, Paul, Mel & Z Lovett, all former AIG co-workers,
Kevin Lusk, Linda Johnston, Beth Burke, Suzanne Criley, Tom
Dikins, Jim Sullivan, Jim Ivey, Martin Burke, Caroline Siemers,
David Sexton, David Elliot, Julie & Mark Nunis, Lorie, Tim &
Mitch Warnock, Sarah Murray-Novak, Janos Novak, Ilona
Murray-Novak, Zoli Novak, Gina Patterson, Eric Midgley,
Jerri Kumery, her mom Toni & Doug Pick, Debra Pyeatt,
Stuart Bbrown, Stephanie Zajchowski, Jeff Bracco, Allison
Wait, Kate Hewitt, Dianne Glover, Michele Pearce, David
Burmedi, Eileen & Alan Cure, Jane, Jay & Katherine Blake,
Rebecca Niziol, Bill Watson, Marina, Varnavas, Alexandros,
Semeli & Maya Kyriazis, Heather, Mick & Mia Cooper, Andy,
Jane, Kai & Jazz Last, Zig & Julie Criscuolo, Zena Khan, Pat &
Ron Izzard, Lucy Quinnell, Alan, Linda & Lindsay Caldwell,
Samantha, Matt, Luke & Joe Holmsey, Bryan Bounds, Emily,
Matthew, Henry & Charlotte Gray, Wendy Welch, Charles
Hobby, Mitzi Doran, Leslie Turner, Irene White, Gill Cude,
Erica Dent, Susan Chapman, Sylvia & Jimmy Simmons, Debi
& Arturo Ruiz-Esparza, Leigh Wyatt-Moore, Christie
Hernandez, Tony Ramirez, Jackie Steiner, Tony Heather,
Robert Fackler, Suzanne Halbert Wohleb, Jon & Fiona
Ecklund, Lex Wootus, Julia Cook, Toni Bravo, Bob Hess, Brad
Taylor, Bradley Campbell, Jimmy Croteau, Carolyn Wickwire,
Cheryl Ammeter, Beverly Nachimson, Christina Coe, Dan

Oliverio, David Leddick, Denece Laborde, Vinny Geraci, Al & Cyla Foltynowicz, Sammy Lewis, Jess Lamb, Francesca Silvestrini, Heather Hollingsworth, Jennifer Carroll, Matt Rose, Michele Imburgia, Minerva Garcia, Pauline Whitaker, John Barrett, Kerry Cole, Kristen Straley, Kristina Delacruz, Stephanie Pearce, Susan Smith Meeke, Tosha Di Iorio, Tom Whitaker, Lee Abraham, Valerie Hauss, Wednesday Tijerina, Laura Poe, Lauri & Rick Bollinger, Matthew & Rebecca Corey, Linda & Gary Swenson, Margaret Lyman, Lyn Sobieski, Eric Maddern, Anne, Steve, Willoughby& Mae Byrne.

Thank you Rory McLean for being on the other side of the email for me, for your writing wisdom and your encouragement. It means a lot to me.

Thank you David Leddick for meeting with me, talking to me and encouraging me.

To my mother and father, the grace of who you both are has allowed me the time to process this gift. For that I am forever grateful.

Much love and exquisite thanks to Stephanie Towery. You read countless versions of this work and were always a guiding hand. Your support and love in our friendship keeps me moving.

Van Quattro - you have brought courage, trust and beauty into my life. No part of this story would be as open, honest and forthright without your constant presence and support. Thank you for reading every version and misplaced word, for finding the hidden parts of me, and helping me to unglue them so this could breathe. There is no part of my mind you haven't walked around inside of. You, my dear, gave me the gift of my child's voice. There isn't a word for what I owe you – only the deepest love, thanks and respect. You know the inside of my heart.

My friends, you supported and welcomed the interaction on this journey, and in writing about you, you often asked how I would write about myself. I hope this book serves well as my letter of reply.

Inspire, in ˈspī(ə)r / *verb*; **breathe in**

To Those I Lost Along the Way

I am part of the whole, all of which is governed by nature… I am
intimately related to all the parts, which are of the same kind as
myself. If I remember those two things, I cannot be disconnected
with anything that arises out of the whole, because I am
connected to the whole.
– Marcus Aurelius

Stephen Dunham
JB
Clay Towery
Stephen Gerald
Viki Atkinson
Jac Alder
Allan Steele
Terry Dobson
Mary Jo Vick
Rachel Hassler
Patrick Blake
Mitch Warnock
Doris Lovett
David Lovett
Rita Cotton
John Cotton
Vera Reynolds
Geoff Reynolds
Cyril Caldwell
Florie Caldwell
Awen Hamilton
Doris Lovett
Orestes
William & Joan Thomson Lovett
George & Vera Caldwell.

Connections

Here are links to the lives some of my friends have created. Each one of them is an expressive inspiration to me. They have all found a strong voice of their own by giving forward what they have learned. I admire each and every one of them.

VOICE creates a unique experience for every performance filled with vulnerability, humor, and passion, leaving the audience and all involved feeling the experience long after the event. VOICE energizes our art and shares dance's intimacy, power, and ability to spark conversation and change lives. We believe in the power of dance and music to uplift, inspire, provoke, draw tears, and elicit screams from our souls, expressing both infinite beauty and the rawness of life. VOICE serves as a vehicle for the creation of vibrant new dance. Fluid in thought and form, we inspire, enrich, and touch people's lives.
www.ginapatterson.com

Author Van Quattro's new book, *Love Lucky* now available on Amazon.
www.vanquattro.com

Kelly Morris – 'The job of the artist is always to deepen the mystery."
www.kellybmorris.com

Lorie Adair
Spider Woman's Loom is an exquisitely woven tale by debut novelist Lorie Adair.
www.lorieadairauthor.com

Work with Soul is an ever expanding community of support that connects who you are and what you do in soulful ways. Founder, Rebecca Niziol, supports creative women through times of career and life transition, helping them do the work that lights up their soul.
Enter your info for an invitation to our free online Community Group, and we'll give you our Manifestation Meditation to get you started.
www.workwithsoul.com

https://ibrake4bakeries.com
I began baking with my Finnish mother and my German grandmother. Both taught me the magic of how flour, sugar, eggs, and butter can be turned into so many things.
Things like love, contentment, nostalgia, and affection.
I love words almost as much as pastry. So it makes sense to mix them together in my own sort of creative recipe.
Curating the most delicious sweets, treats, food, art, travel, sights, words, ideas.

Dream Out Loud Media is a boutique production company with a mission to bring big production values to small businesses, non-profits & socially conscious organizations.
Contact Fiona Jones and Jon Ecklund.
www.dreamoutloudmedia.com

Kerry Cole's magic mustard, for the treasure-hunter of quality taste.
GoldRush. Mustard. Mastered.
www.goldrushmustard.com

Diverse Space Dance Theatre
A multidisciplinary dance company headed by Toni Bravo
www.diversespacedance.com

Sidekick Jenn – Author Assistant
Saving Authors Everywhere from Admin Work
http://sidekickjenn.com/

Feedmore is a Food Bank, Community Kitchen, and Meals on Wheels. It takes care of its citizens by bringing healthy foods to feed those in need. FeedMore's client is the working poor, those between jobs or on minimum wage trying to make ends meet.
www.feedmore.org

Inspired by New Orleans residents' collective spirit and fierce desire to rebuild their homes and communities, Zack Rosenburg and Liz McCartney launched SBP to help the community achieve its recovery goals. Their model is enhanced by AmeriCorps members overseeing the labor of

363

more than 25,000 volunteers, per location, per year.
www.stbernardproject.org

Danielle Swope decided to find a way to give the stacks of books her children had outgrown. The Children's Book Bank has organized over 6,500 community volunteers to channel over 475,000 books into the hands and homes of over 35,000 children in need in the Portland area.
www.childrensbookbank.org

In Newport, RI a group of surfers met and began an effort for coastal cleanup. It's cultivating friendships in the community while taking care of the environment. Get on a pair of gloves, grab a bag and walk along the beach with a new friend and pick up some trash.
www.cleanoceanaccess.org

Permissions

Grateful acknowledgment is made to the following to reprint from previously published material:

Rachel Naomi Remen, MD, Preface to Poetic Medicine, *The Healing Art of Poem Making*, by John Fox

Clarissa Pinkola Estes, *Women who Run with the Wolves*, Ballantine Books.

William Stafford, *The Way it is*. Graywolf Press.

Vyasa, *Bhagavad-Gita*.

Antoine de St. Exupery, *The Little Prince*. Houghton Mifflin Harcourt Publishing Company.

Sue Monk Kidd, *When the Heart Waits*, HarperCollins Publishers.

Ralph Blum, *The Book of Runes*. St. Martin's Press.

Thomas Merton, *New Seeds of Confirmation*. New Directions Books.

Claude Bristol, The Magic of Believing. Pocket Books, a division of Simon & Schuster.

Ruth Stone, *Simplicity*. Paris Press.

F. Nietzsche. *Human. All Too-Human II*. Maxim 223, transl. O Levy (Edinburgh Foulis.)

Sue Monk Kidd, *The Invention of Wings*. Penguin Random House Companies

Jennifer Lash, *On Pilgrimage*. Bloomsbury Publishing

Anne Lamott, *Small Victories*. Riverhead Books, Published by the Penguin Group

William E. Stafford, "The Well Rising."

Joan Wickersham, *The Suicide Index*. First Mariner Books.

Rebecca West, *Black Lamb and Grey Falcon*. The Penguin Group.

Marcus Aurelius, *The Meditations*

Splendour Solis

T.S Eliot, "The Gidding," *Four Quartets*. Houghton Mifflin Harcourt Publishing Company

Book of the Dead

Charles Dickens, *Great Expectations*.

Sue Monk Kidd, *The Secret Life of Bees*. Penguin Random House Company.

James Hillman, *Healing Fiction*. Spring Publications, Inc.

The Library of Universal Knowledge, edited by Franklin J. Meine, Ph.B., M.A. Consolidated Book Publishers.

Jamie Sams & David Carson, *Medicine Cards*. St. Martin's Press

Bruce Chatwin, *Songlines*. Penguin Books, USA

Masaru Emoto, *The Hidden Messages in Water*. Beyond Words

Publishing.